# PERIOD PIECES

# PERIOD PIECES

## An Account of
## The Grand Rapids Dominicans
## 1853 - 1966

MONA SCHWIND, OP

SISTERS OF ST. DOMINIC
GRAND RAPIDS, MICHIGAN

Cover photograph
"The Recording Angel"
courtesy of Francetta McCann, OP

Copyright © 1991 by the Sisters of the Order of St. Dominic
2025 East Fulton
Grand Rapids, Michigan 49503-3895
USA

ISBN 0-9629233-0-3

Printed by West Michigan Printing
840 Ottawa Avenue, NW
Grand Rapids, Michigan 49501-0328
USA

*When we were young we cast stones into the water and watched the 'dead men's ripples' go out, and asked in childish wonder where these ripples ended. Devoted parents told us that they ended on the most distant shores. Tell me, dear sisters, what far shores will feel the final impulse of your combined efforts...? Only God and the Angels will keep the record of their distances.*

*Mother Eveline Mackey*
*September 3, 1929.*

# CONTENTS

# FOREWORD

*PERIOD PIECES* presents a narrative of one group of American women religious, the Sisters of Saint Dominic of Grand Rapids, Michigan, from 1853 to 1966. It is, in many respects, a shared narrative with story-lines similar to the stories of numerous congregations of religious women who pioneered in the upbuilding of the Church in the United States, a narrative of journeys, missions, schools, hospitals, mortgages, professions, deaths. It is as well a narrative shared with church women of all denominations who educated, nurtured, nursed, healed, counseled--all the verbs of women at work. It is a narrative of Dominican women who share with all "westering women"[1] pioneering in new places.

It is especially a narrative shared with the Roman Catholic Church, primarily in Michigan, New Mexico, California, Saskatchewan, Chimbote in Perú--and in all the places where these women lived out their lives of commitment and service. It is as well local history, a part of the story of all the places where the Sisters of Saint Dominic were the school marms, nurses, madres, or perhaps simply the nuns on Church Street.

The title, *PERIOD PIECES*, suggests a certain antiquarian perspective. The narrative begins with the journey of four Dominican nuns from Germany to the United States and ends with the completion of Mother Victor Flannery's third term of office. There are many indicators that the years following 1966 constitute a new time quite unlike the previous era and not yet finished, another period for another volume. While the central treatment concludes with the fifteenth General Chapter in June 1966, there are references to the ever afters, what became of missions from the time of founding to the present and how the mothers general spent their remaining years.

The narrative has a certain antiquarian style. It is more than a chronicle, less than a definitive work of new history. It is written chiefly from congregational sources and, in keeping with the Dominican propensity for governance, from an institutional perspective. The assumption is strong, especially for a religious congregation, that the institution is more than the sum of its individual members. It has its own spirituality, its own life force which its members work to sustain and yet to transform. This will be for many of the sisters their first reading of the book of foundations, the register of the mothers general, the story of diocesan-congregation relations, and for some their first account of the Mothers.

Constituting and yet transcending this framework are the narratives of the individual sisters, some of whom are named in this work, all of whom are necessary for the congregation's wholeness. For all there have been the common life, shared prayer, ministry, study, and vision. This is a work of collected biographies, a story dependent on the contribution of all who have been Marywood Dominicans.

The sisters are, in the words of Alan Paton, "workers in a kind of apostolic succession" with "some noble predecessors, contemporaries and successors."[2] *PERIOD PIECES* acknowledges with gratitude all the workers in our apostolic succession, those noble predecessors, contemporaries, and successors, sisters, families, friends.

# PERIOD ONE

# Peninsula of Promise
## 1853 - 1919

Mothers
Benedicta Bauer
Hyacinth Scheininger
Aquinata Fiegler
Gonsalva Bankstahl

*T*he first period in the story of the Grand Rapids Dominicans stretches from the journey of four Dominican nuns from Europe to the New World, to journeys of hundreds of sisters to their missions throughout Michigan; from a six-hundred year old cloister in Regensburg, Bavaria, to newly broken ground outside the city limits of Grand Rapids, Michigan.

For the members of the congregation this account names the names, telling where possible the names of the pioneer sisters, our links with past and present, who came to America, who settled in Williamsburg, who began the Second Street convent, and who came to Michigan. It names those who began missions throughout the state, to acknowledge both the grace of new beginnings and the sorrow of departures and hard labor.

It is, in many respects, a fragmentary litany: names without full biographies, stories partly told, stories perhaps unrecorded, stories thought best left untold, or stories whose doing exhausted all of the energies of the doers. It tells where possible the nature of the places: simple, pioneer places, places of the heart. It is a first telling of the story and is, therefore, more narrative than interpretation.

# 1

# RATISBON ROOTS
# MOTHER BENEDICTA BAUER

*O*n October 23, 1877, after a three-day journey by train, coach, boat, and wagon, six soberly clad women arrived in Traverse City, Michigan. Alighting from the steamer at Hannah and Lay docks, they looked about for some welcoming group but saw only a solitary farmer with a horsedrawn wagon. Calling to the travelers, the farmer indicated that he was to take them to their new home. This was a two-story wood house on Union Street, arranged for their use by Father George Ziegler, priest of the Diocese of Detroit and pastor of St. Francis parish. It was to serve as their convent and school from 1877 to 1883.

In this unpretentious way the Dominican nuns of New York extended their ministry to the "peninsula of promise" and the Congregation of Our Lady of the Sacred Heart, Grand Rapids, Michigan, the Marywood Dominicans, began. The early sisters told and retold the story of those first days and years, the hardships and wonders of beginning in a rural setting more than 700 miles from their companions. They incorporated in their story the narrative of earlier departures and separations, of heritage and hard beginnings.

The women were members of a newly founded religious congregation, a convent of cloistered Dominican nuns from New York City. They were among the first fruits of the heroic missionary endeavor of four German nuns who had come to America in 1853 from the centuries-old Convent of Holy Cross, Regensburg.[1]

The nuns brought with them to Traverse City some household goods and, providentially, provisions for an evening meal and the next day's needs, potatoes, salt pork, and bread. Father Ziegler, the pioneers related, lived abstemiously, but promised them, "Dear Sisters, rather than let you die of hunger, God will send birds to you for food."

They brought with them their customary garb, the white habit of St. Dominic, reserving the black dresses and bonnets for travel and

*Ratisbon Family Tree*
*Prepared by Holy Cross Nuns*

Kloster der Dominikanerinen zum hl. Kreuz in Regensburg.

*Mother Benedicta Bauer*
*Prioress, Holy Cross Convent*

outdoor use of lay sisters. They brought with them a way of life, a spirituality, and a connection with the Dominican Order, and specifically, a relationship with their motherhouse, the Congregation of the Most Holy Rosary, then on 137 East Second Street, New York City.[2] For seventeen years the sisters lived and worked in Michigan as missions of the Second Street, New York motherhouse.

The sisters were in the strictest sense nuns, vowed members of the Second Order affiliated to the Order of Preachers founded by Dominic de Guzmán (1170-1221). Before the establishment of the First Order of Friars Preachers, Dominic had laid the foundations for Dominican cloistered life for consecrated women in Prouille, France.

There in 1206 eleven noblewomen were led by St. Dominic to live according to the Rule of St. Augustine and the newly formulated Constitution of the Second Order. Dominic established a similar foundation in his native Spain, in Madrid in a monastery which came to be known as St. Dominic of Silos. In 1220 a convent of women at St. Sixtus in Rome reformed their lives according to the Prouille model and specifically to the Rule and new Dominican Constitution. The St. Sixtus Rule was formative for several groups of women religious.

In 1223 the founding members of Holy Cross convent, Ratisbon, Bavaria, formally accepted the Rule of St. Augustine and the St. Sixtus Constitution. Bishop Siegfried of Ratisbon approved the foundation and confirmed the nuns' reception of a gift of land from the townspeople. In 1237 the convent was generously endowed by Count Henry von Ortenburg and a building program was initiated. The Convent of the Holy Cross was consecrated and final episcopal approval was granted in 1244. The following year Pope Innocent IV gave papal approbation to the foundation and placed the convent under the direction of the Order of Preachers.

The nuns of Holy Cross convent point to two critical periods in their seven centuries of existence.[3] The first, during the sixteenth century, was due to the pressures of the surrounding Lutheran Reformation, when much of Germany became Protestant. The second was a direct challenge from the Napoleonic Revolution.

Following conquest throughout Europe, agents of Napoleon devised a thorough reconstruction of state and society, including the Church. In 1802 an edict for the  secularization of religious houses was issued throughout Germany. The Holy Cross nuns were not exempt. Their annals record the appearance of a commissary of Napoleon within their convent. All were summoned to the refectory and given two choices: either to return to the world with a pension or to remain in the convent subject to a newly appointed ecclesiastical superior, the Prince-Bishop Karl Theodore von Dahlberg. All chose to remain at Holy Cross convent.

Prince-Bishop von Dahlberg held Regensburg both as an ecclesiastical see and as an independent city in the Kingdom of Bavaria. He exacted of the two convents which chose to remain in the place of their profession, the Dominican nuns of Holy Cross and the Franciscan nuns of the Convent of St. Clara, a form of civil service new to them, namely, the provision of elementary public schooling on their premises.

The Holy Cross annals tell of the consternation this demand produced among the group of strictly cloistered contemplative nuns. It was not within their experience nor their understanding of the essential aspects of contemplative life. Raymond Brunner, prior of the Dominicans in Regensburg and confessor to the nuns, counselled them that the rule could not be accommodated in this way and that eventually the burden would ruin their conventual life. The Prince-Bishop, it was said, paid a personal visit to the convent, requiring the prioress to inspect the buildings with him. The nuns finally acceded to the ecclesiastical demand. A grain shed with access from the cloister served as a temporary classroom.

This accommodation both physically and religiously, to the demands of the time, in contrast to its steadfast resistance in Reformation times, seems to have readied the Ratisbon community for subsequent calls from the Church. In 1827 Father Edward Fenwick (1768-1832), a Dominican and Bishop of Cincinnati, Ohio, asked the sisters to send missionaries to help German Catholic immigrants in the American Midwest. It appears that some were ready to meet that request; among them Sister Maria Benedicta Bauer (1803-1865). Preparations began for the mission to the New World but were subsequently and inexplicably dropped.

Again, in 1851, the nuns heard accounts of German Catholic immigrants in America, this time from a native of Bavaria now working in Pennsylvania. Father Boniface Wimmer, a Benedictine priest, had come to Holy Cross to visit his cousin, Sister Elizabeth Kissel. He described to the nuns and their new prioress, Mother

Benedicta Bauer, the needs of the Church in America. In their understanding, he was extending to them an invitation to come to America where he would oversee their settling and act as their protector. He told them what steps to take to get ecclesiastical permission for the mission.

Mother Benedicta Bauer[4] was elected prioress of the Holy Cross community in July 1845. The convent then had sixteen choir nuns and six lay sisters. In 1847 she began a comprehensive program of renewal of the convent, which included a return to the spirit of the primitive Dominican rule: the common life, a renewed emphasis on study, and an extension of their apostolate. It included as well the remodelling and renovation of the convent properties.

The nuns were given a newly translated and critical edition of their Rule in their native language, the work of their chaplain, Doctor Franz Joseph Schiml (1813-1854). The edition clearly presented aspects of their life which were essential or customary, those that were traditional in the Order, and those no longer in use. Above all, the considerable accommodation to the Napoleonic edict was now incorporated into their law and spirit. This Rule and Constitution travelled with the Holy Cross nuns to the New World and to the congregations derived from their mission.

Mother Benedicta's reforms included the centralization of learning materials, the development and cataloguing of a common library, together with courses on manuscript illumination and book binding. The nuns, now "book conscious," continued their scholarship through their preparation as school teachers. A music department was organized, string and wind instruments were repaired and bought, and a new organ was installed in the chapel. These refinements were used not only for worship but as complements to the school program.

During the years in which Mother Benedicta was engaged in the reform of conventual life and fabric, she began an endeavor not attempted in the previous six centuries of the convent's existence: the establishment of daughter foundations. "It was," in the words of her biographer, Sister Hortense Kohler, "her great work, probably greater even than the reform of Holy Cross Convent."[5]

In 1846 she negotiated the acquisition of St. Mary's convent, Niederviehbach. It had been one of the many convents altered by the secularization edict of 1802. Once an Augustinian convent, it was now used as a central convent receiving members from other disbanded houses. Mother Benedicta petitioned King Louis I of Bavaria to transfer the properties to Holy Cross in return for the nuns' keeping a boarding school for girls of the middle class, and, should the parish wish, also a village school for girls. The convent would function, Mother Benedicta hoped, as a branch house of Holy Cross. Both royal and episcopal approval were given and the new foundation was made in 1847. Four choir nuns and two lay sisters began the house and within the year the number increased to ten. The foundation flourished into the twentieth century.

A second foundation was made at Mintraching, Bavaria, in October 1853, the plans laid at the same time as the mission to America was finalized. Four choir nuns and two lay sisters opened the branch house. This mission was discontinued in 1859, the year after Mother Benedicta came to America.

In 1857 Mother Benedicta was elected to a fifth three-year term as prioress. Upon the request of Bishop Ignatius von Senestry she, however, submitted her resignation on June 10, 1858, the cause resting primarily in the allegations of two discontented nuns at Holy Cross. On August 15, 1858, Mother Benedicta and Sisters Maria Thomasina Ginker and Maria Cunigunda Schell were granted a dimissory allowing them to go to America. The three Ratisbon nuns and Crescentia Traubinger, a lay woman, left for America on September 23, 1858. They stayed for a time with earlier pioneers from Regensburg as well as with Dominican sisters of American origins. In 1862 Mother Benedicta and Sister Thomasina established the Congregation of St. Catherine of Siena, in Racine, Wisconsin.

In the midst of conventual reform and expansion at Holy Cross, the American mission was begun. From the volunteers four were chosen: Mother Josepha Witzelhofer, Sister Augustine Neuhierl, choir nuns, and Sisters Francesca Retter and Jacobina Rieder, lay sisters. They began their month-long voyage on July 24, 1853. To ease the departure of these four cloistered nuns on their transatlantic journey, Father Joseph Muller, court chaplain and director of the King Louis Mission Society,[6] accompanied them to the train for Bremen where they were to board *The Germania*. He wrote to Mother Benedicta about his days with the nuns:

*July 27, 1853*

*[Dear Mother Benedicta],*

*It is now 12:30 after noon and I have just returned from the railway station, where I entrusted your good children to the Lord and to their Guardian Angels. About 10 o'clock tomorrow they will be in Bremen and wait for the hour of their departure. You will probably wonder that all has been done so quickly, but I am not the man to loiter on the way when once I have set out for a fixed destination.*

*But listen to an account of our journey. We were hardly an hour's distance from Regensburg when good Josepha turned pale and became sick....That was surely not a happy omen for our journey, but I was not discouraged, being accustomed to travel. At the next station we changed places. She took mine near the open window, for fresh air is the best remedy in such cases. We fared better now, but Francesca and Josepha suffered much from the cold, and besides, they could get no sleep all night. Bad as this was, we were to endure worse things. The Postilions (stage drivers) had slept too late and so lost considerable time. It was only at Neumarkt that the station master was aware of the fact. So we were almost an hour late. Not a minute was to be lost in vain regrets. We arrived five minutes before the departure of the stage at 6:15, whereas we ought to have arrived at 6 o'clock. We made headway, for I spent liberal tips, otherwise the whole journey would have been useless. Poor Josepha had to leave without breakfast and then we went to Hof where we arrived at 6:30 p.m. There we had a good supper, and left about 10 p.m. for Leipzig. We arrived there at 3 a.m. had ourselves carried to the Hotel "Stadt-Breslau" and rested for a few hours. At 6 a.m. I set out to find the Catholic Church, secured permission to say Mass, at once drove back to the hotel to get the sisters and then read Mass for a safe voyage in the beautiful new church. Then we took breakfast and prepared for the journey. I hurriedly wrote several letters of recommendation, turned over to them the remaining 430 fl. (florins or gulden) and at 11 a.m. accompanied them to the railway station, for there was a good deal of baggage. The snorting steeds of Vulcan (train) raced away and I made my way back to the hotel. Many a tear had been shed at the station. The departure would have been even more painful to them, had I not been with them. They commend themselves to you and the community and ask your prayers. I cannot leave here before tomorrow morning, since there is no train to be had today. Hence I shall arrive in Nurenberg tomorrow evening, and in Augsburg Friday morning; there I shall remain till Saturday, and expect to be in Munich in the afternoon of that day. I thank you for the kind reception given me. Please remember me to Prof. Schimmel [sic] and to your sisters.*

*I remain in union of prayer*

*Your humble servant Jos. Fer Mueller*
*Royal Court Chaplain and Director[7]*

His last act was to give the four nuns a letter of introduction to another Father Joseph Mueller, a Redemptorist in New York City.

**2**

# CROSS BEARERS
# DOMINICAN NUNS IN NEW YORK

*T*he *Germania* arrived on August 28, 1853, at the Franklin Street dock in New York City. Two hundred and sixteen passengers disembarked. The four Ratisbon nuns in black dress and bonnet, common Bavarian street dress, waited for luggage and for their host-protector, Father Boniface Wimmer, OSB. No manifest tells us what they carried from Germany in their twenty wooden chests. Later recollections were of chapel furnishings, copies of the Rule and Constitution, the white habits and black veils of the Dominican Order. The nuns had on their persons the equivalent of approximately $3,000, the generous gift of the King Louis Mission Society: a relic of the true cross, the gift from Bishop Reidel; and the note of introduction from Father Mueller.

As the day wore on and Father Wimmer, whom they would have recognized from his visits to Holy Cross, did not appear, the nuns negotiated a ride to Most Holy Redeemer parish, where Father Joseph Mueller, CSsR, was situated. They were welcomed by Father Kleinedem, CSsR, and a lay brother, Nicholas. Lodging was arranged for several nights with Catholic families, the choir nuns, Mother Josepha and Sister Augustine, with the Ziegler family in New York City and the lay sisters, Sisters Francesca and Jacobina, with the Blaggi family in Newark, New Jersey. The names of these earliest American benefactors have passed from the direct recipients of their hospitality to the present. There has long been an affection in the congregation for the Redemptorists who, in truth, saved the four cloistered nuns from their fears of the huge city. It was they, it appears, who contacted the Very Reverend Stephen Raffeiner (1785-1861), pastor of Holy Trinity parish, Williamsburg (Brooklyn), in his capacity as vicar general of the Brooklyn diocese.

The uncertainties of the first days were soon replaced by certainties of hard times at hand.[1] There is no direct account from the nuns themselves but the perspective offered by Father Wimmer tells much of the task they had in resuming their cloistered life and taking up an educational ministry in America. Dom Wimmer wrote to Mother Benedicta shortly after he had seen the nuns:

*September 18, 1853.*

*Latrobe, Westmoreland Co., Pennsylvania,*

*Venerable dear Mother Prioress:*

*That your daughters arrived safely in America, you are already aware. As well as I could, I provided that they should be immediately received by my co-frater, P. Nicolas Balleis, in New York. I could come to see them and to provide for them only on the fifth day after their arrival. Because for the time being I knew of no place for them in the country, I agreed with the Vicar General of New York, Father Raffeiner, that he take the Sisters to his parish church in Williamsburg, a suburb of New York, which numbers over 30,000 inhabitants, nearly 15,000 of whom are German Catholics. The place is excellent in location and as a field of activity. Oh, how the girls and mothers rejoiced as they heard that they had Sisters and especially when they saw them! Also the Rt. Rev. Archbishop gladly received them. Because no convent is there, we were obliged to lodge the Sisters in the rectory which adjoins the old church. Do not be alarmed at this. The pastor, the above-named Vicar General, is an old Father, a holy priest, and has only one curate. The rectory is spacious. I remained four days with him to arrange everything. The four Sisters already after the first week have a complete enclosure as regards the outside - the people; and also interiorly with regard to the priests. Naturally they are in considerably close quarters, but it is satisfactory. They have a kitchen; next to it is a study room; on the other side is a dormitory large enough for four. At the same time I bought four iron, very comfortable bedsteads, so that I might see whether there was sufficient room; we found that there was additional space for a table and a chest or bureau. The pastor who lives on the upper floor has access only to the kitchen. I arranged to make even this part of the enclosure by locking the door to his quarters. I had a partition made near the outside door so that now they receive there only mail and no one had access to their house.*

*Thus I succeeded in making an uninterrupted or strictly private passageway which leads to the church and also to a large room under the church where the Sisters may store away their clothes, or if they wish, they may use it for sleeping quarters. A large garden surrounds the church which gives them space in which to recreate and to work. The school also adjoins the church. Their future convent will either be built on that same spot, if the old pastor so desires, or on the west side of the large new church which would be still better. Here the pastor has three lots or places for buildings; between these, however, in the center, there are two small houses which would have to be purchased. They would cost from $5,000 to $6,000. This amount must not alarm you or frighten you. $6,000 here is a trifle. By means of school activities and an institute, that amount would soon be paid - the real burden for your children is this; that they must cook for both priests; i.e., that these will share the food with them.*

*We have arranged that the Sisters will send the meals upstairs by means of a dumbwaiter as they do in the convent. Nevertheless this, we realize, is somewhat annoying and troublesome. Alas, nothing else could be done. The old priest purposely took the Sisters so that he would not be obliged to have a cook and also to save money. He is rich but is very close. Perhaps in return he will some day will the Sisters his money. If he grants them only the lot for building as he promised, he will be donating the right, i.e., if the old priest does not change his mind, and if he keeps his word. I hope he will because he realizes that he is at an advantage, and he likes his parish and he knows the parishioners are eager for and need the services of the Sisters; and lastly because he depends or relies considerably upon me. I impressed sharply upon the Sisters this fact; viz., that they should not be too seriously concerned if they suffered somewhat financially-but I urged them to get in touch with me if they were in want so that I might personally fight it out with Father. In order that the Sisters will not be obliged to arrange the beds and rooms of the priests, the Father engaged the services of a pious widow and I told the Sisters to pay the salary to her for this service because they too would often be in need of her services; in this way the old priest may more easily be satisfied; he is at the same time their ordinary Confessor. I begged a Capuchin Father from New York to be the extraordinary Confessor. Pray with your children at home that the original spirit of charity, union, resignation and patience may continue to flourish among the Sisters here and that the Lord may direct everything for the best.*

*The two exchangeable notes of 6,000 gulden and 1,000 gulden, 4,000 of which was in my name, I collected. The Reverend old gentleman wonders if the Sisters could not lend him the money until they need it. He would give them five per cent interest. I urged the Sisters to accept the offer. The old Father does not need the money personally but he will re-invest it in a so-called Savings Bank which will give him six per cent interest; thus he will gain one per cent. Thereby the Sisters will be worth more to him materially; at the same time the Sisters will benefit for they do not need the money now. When I left they still have 250 shillings on hand wherewith to buy chests, storage cabinets; etc. This money will soon be used up. The money earned by teaching will support them otherwise. Naturally I am not yet in a position to discuss the building of a new convent. We must see how everything develops--at any rate just now there is no need therefore.*

*But there is something which needs immediate attention; you **must** admit one or two postulants who are well versed in English. You may not object to this because the nature of the case demands such. "One who endeavors to attain the object must of necessity use the means." One who has not from youth been brought up in the use of the English language will never be able to master the English language sufficiently well to teach it. You are at liberty to send us German teachers or postulants but we ourselves must admit and train English postulants here. That is what the other teaching sisters do--so do my Benedictines--so your Dominicans must do likewise. Since you yourself confided your daughters to me, and also the Rt. Rev. Bishop in his testimonials, and Rt. Rev. Archbishop of New York, also his Vicar General, consider me the spiritual director of your Sisters, I have, therefore, assumed a definite responsibility for them. I believe that I have the necessary authority to direct the Sisters in this matter--hence I have ordered*

Mother Josepha to admit **promptly** any worthy English postulant who might apply for admission. I told her that you will trust me for I am better acquainted in America and I know better what must be done here, than you at Holy Cross, in Regensburg. I certainly mean well in your regard and that of your Sisters.

Now something else--had I known it sooner your Sisters would have been assigned to a very fine place in the City of New York affiliated with the Capuchin Church. The pastor, Father Ambrose, scolded me sternly because I did not tell him about the Dominican Nuns because he would have taken them. Well for the present that plan is spoiled, but he would like to know whether you could send him four Sisters. He is about to purchase a house next to his church which may be adapted for a cloistered small convent; he is not certain that he will be able to buy the house. If he does, he would want German Nuns for his girls. If you have four more Sisters (two postulants and two Sisters) to spare, (remember-- good and industrious) you may write to me, so that in the fall, if he is able to use them, he need only write to you for them. This must remain a secret just now. I did tell them the place. They too must not further mention the fact--still less if the enterprise fails.

Whether I have performed my task well or badly, I do not know--I certainly did mean well--of that I am certain. I cannot often travel to Williamsburg because it is 400 miles from here and requires at least sixty florins. But if there is need, I will come in spite of that fact. Furthermore I wish to keep in touch with my adopted children by letter-writing and wish to direct them until they are better acquainted and can direct themselves. Every beginning is hard. Much must be endured. But whoever means well with God and possesses good will, God will be helpful to the end. The Sisters were all very well; they served me well, entertained me as long as they could. Please reprove them because they would not accept anything from me for the chest or trunk which cost 34 florins. At the beginning they were somewhat depressed and anxious but when I left they were full of hope and courage (Sept. 7), and I hope all will be well. Everything was so well ordered that one cannot help feeling that the Will of God is being done. Pray for me and write an answer soon. I greet you all in the Lord and remain with utmost respect,

Yours sincerely,

P. Boniface Wimmer, OSB

P.S. I regret that I have been compelled to write you so frankly concerning the character of the Rev. Fr. Raffeiner. But it was necessary that you should know in order to clarify the situation as far as you, your Sisters and my dealings with the priest were concerned. Nevertheless I must add the same priest has been in America almost 20 years. At the beginning he had to endure many hardships and privations, yet he founded many churches and parishes. Now of course he is well-to-do because he has a large parish with a good income. I doubt not in the least that some day he will use all his money for the good of the church--we dare not judge him in this matter. Please do not reveal the contents of my letter "in extenso." You may allow the Rt. Rev. Bishop and the confessor to read the letter. But both should also read these added lines so that they may not through my fault become prejudiced against this worthy priest. Greet both for me heartily.

*When you write to your Sisters, address: Sister Josepha in Williamsburg, near New York, in care of V. Rev. Fr. Raffeiner. They will then receive the letter. The quickest is through Paris and Liverpool.*[2]

Father Raffeiner, a native of Innsbruck and acquainted with Holy Cross convent, arranged for the nuns to cross the East River and take up residence in his parish of Holy Trinity in Williamsburg. They came on September 2, 1853, and took over the instruction of the girls in the parish. Remembering the Redemptorists' kindness, they named the school after this congregation's patron, St. Alphonsus.

The nuns were not the first religious in the Diocese of Brooklyn; the Sisters of Charity had come in 1836 and the Christian Brothers in 1851. The Ratisbon nuns were the third religious foundation in the diocese and the first German-speaking sisterhood engaged in the education of immigrants on the east coast.

In September 1853 the two choir nuns, Mother Josepha and Sister Augustine, began the instruction of 140 pupils in all grades. They taught in German, as English was a second language both to them and their pupils. The curriculum was full and rigorous, determined primarily by the methods and content they had developed in their schools in Regensburg and Niederviehbach. Although the school had been in existence before the nuns came, it was their responsibility to provide supplies and furnishings from the provident support of their motherhouse and from the King Louis Mission Society.

By the following year, enrollment had increased to 243 and more space was required for both school and convent. The nuns were offered a part of the school, that is, the basement of the old church, for their living area. While there appears to have been some relief with more space, the conditions were life-threatening. All the nuns became ill. Sister Francesca contracted tuberculosis from which she died on May 22, 1858.

In the fall of 1853 the nuns purchased a lot nearby, thus depleting the monies given them for the establishment of the mission. Their only known source of income was 25 cents per week charged each pupil for tuition. If all had paid and if Father Raffeiner had asked no further outlay for the use of their basement rooms, first in the rectory and later in the old church, they might have received $50 per week.[3] They were blessed, however, by the interest and care of the newly appointed ordinary of the Diocese of Brooklyn, Bishop

*FACING PAGE (left to right) The two German "protectors": Boniface Wimmer, OSB, Archabbot, Latrobe, Pennsylvania, and Father Stephen Raffeiner, pastor of Holy Trinity parish, Williamsburg, New York. The first Ratisbon motherhouse in America, Holy Cross convent, Williamsburg, dedicated on November 9, 1857*

*RIGHT Mother Hyacinth Scheininger, OSD, Prioress of the second Ratisbon congregation in America, Congregation of the Holy Rosary, fl. 1877-1896. Chapel of Holy Rosary, Second Street, New York, 1869*

John Loughlin. He lent the nuns $4,000 to purchase a small house next to the lot they had purchased. They moved there in May 1854.

The school continued to grow; there were 300 pupils for the two school sisters. In 1855 Mother Benedicta was able to send three more nuns from Regensburg, Sisters Seraphina Staimer, Emilia Barth, and Michaela Barth (who returned to Regensburg in 1857). They reinforced the school staff as well as bringing with them further support from the King Louis Mission Society. It is estimated that they received approximately $10,000 from the society from 1854 to 1869. With their own savings, the support of the Bavarian Catholics, and a mortgage, they undertook the building of a formal convent structure, the origins of the Williamsburg motherhouse before its transfer to Amityville, New York.

It was expected that the nuns were responsible for their convent, its purchase and upkeep as well as their own livelihood. The Catholic parochial system had not evolved to its full array of parish church, rectory, school, and convent, parish-owned and -operated. The arrangement was also a feature of Second Order European convents, whose very foundation required sufficient endowment for building and living for a specified number of vowed members. In many respects the sisters were evidence of the essentially European character of religious life in the nineteenth century.[4]

On November 9, 1857, the four-story convent of the Holy Cross was dedicated by Bishop Loughlin. In 1858 an adjoining lot was purchased, each nun sharing in the ownership of the property as the group had not yet been legally incorporated as a community.

The growth of the school--400 by 1857--led to petitions for more nuns from Regensburg. On October 2, 1858, Mother Benedicta, lately resigned from the office of prioress arrived in Williamsburg, along with Sister Thomasina Ginker, Sister Cunegunda Schell, and postulant Crescentia Traubinger, the last of the nuns to come from Regensburg. At this juncture the convent, considered a *filiale* or daughter house of Holy Cross, Regensburg, took on a mission or *filiale* of its own. It is likely that this endeavor hastened the canonical separation of the Williamsburg convent from Regensburg. The original letters of dismissal indicated that independence was the likely outcome of the mission in America.

Shortly after the first nuns' arrival in America, Father Ambrose Buchmeier, OFM Cap., had heard of them and expressed regret that

Father Raffeiner had snatched them up. He invited the nuns to come to his parish of St. Nicholas on Second Street in New York City and in the Archdiocese of New York. He had served the nuns in their Williamsburg convent as their extraordinary confessor. In February 1858 he asked Mother Josepha for nuns for the girls school in his parish. He had even then a house ready for them. Over a year later, on September 22, 1859, Sister Augustine Neuhierl, Sister Cunegunda Schell, and a lay sister, Sister Rosa Bosslet, opened the Second Street mission. The delay was spent in part consulting on the canonical implications of such a mission and the authority Mother Josepha had in making this transfer of nuns.

In this way the American mission of Holy Cross convent, Williamsburg, laid the foundation for the first two independent "Ratisbon" congregations.[5] The practical separation of the Williamsburg foundation has been dated in the fall of 1860, although canonical foundation was subsequently fixed at 1857, the date of the formal dedication of Holy Cross convent. The congregation was legally incorporated on May 29, 1868. The Second Street congregation became the Convent of the Most Holy Rosary in 1869. A mutually-agreed upon cash settlement was paid by the nuns in the new foundation for the houses bought by the Williamsburg motherhouse.

In 1860 Mother Benedicta Bauer and Sister Thomasina Ginker went on to visit the Dominican sisters in Somerset, Ohio, one of the congregations of American origins. A few of the nuns in Williamsburg had returned to Regensburg; Sister Francesca had died in 1858. In 1861, there were only three professed nuns in each of the two houses, Williamsburg and Second Street, New York City. Recruitment was imperative. As early as fall 1861 Sister Augustine appeared ready to admit postulants to the convent on Second Street, even though the group was not yet independent and was only a few miles from the motherhouse in Williamsburg. The motherhouse, having responded to other calls for sisters, could not provide them for the Archdiocese.

On April 9, 1864, Mother Josepha, then forty-six and in the twenty-fourth year of religious profession, died at Holy Cross, Williamsburg. She was succeeded as prioress by Sister Seraphine Staimer, then only thirty-four and also from Regensburg. Bishop Loughlin suspended the election requirements set forth in their Constitution and appointed Sister Seraphine as prioress for life.

During the twenty-five years of her administration until her death in 1889 the Convent of Holy Cross flourished both in mission and membership.

Mother Augustine Neuhierl, one of the original four missionaries from Regensburg, had been assigned superior of the mission in St. Nicholas parish at 137 Second Street. She negotiated with Mother Seraphine and Father Michael May, spiritual director and supervisor of Holy Cross convent, for the transfer of personnel and properties which formed the nucleus of the new Congregation of the Rosary. With Mother Augustine were Sisters Hyacinth Scheininger, Aquinata Fiegler, Antonio Schmidt, choir nuns, and a lay sister, originally professed at Holy Cross, Williamsburg. There were in all fourteen nuns and two postulants at the time of the establishment of the congregation in 1869. Although permission to receive candidates was granted in 1861, the first documented evidence of reception dates from 1865.

At the time of Mother Augustine's death, May 24, 1877, there were only two members who had been professed for twelve years, the constitutional requirement for active voice in the election of prioress. They were Sister Hyacinth Scheininger who was forty-two and Sister Aquinata Fiegler who was twenty-nine. Consequently, the ecclesiastical superior of the convent, Monsignor William Quinn appointed Mother Hyacinth as prioress. There were one hundred and twenty in the community at the time.[6] Shortly before her death, Mother Augustine told her sisters that "somewhere in the West, I see a vast field of labor--an inland island--and as a field is dotted white with daisies, so this land will be dotted white with the habit of St. Dominic."[7]

Sister Hieronyma Egbert, an Adrian Dominican Sister who died in 1948, gave this account of the actual call to Michigan. In 1877 Father George Ziegler, priest of the Diocese of Detroit and pastor of St. Francis parish, Traverse City, Michigan, wrote to a priest friend, Father Mendel of St. Paul parish, Greenville, New Jersey, asking his assistance in getting sisters for his school. Father Mendel asked the sister superior of his school to send the letter on to Mother Hyacinth. Sister Hieronyma, then a novice in Greenville, was asked to carry the letter as she was bilingual and accustomed to the city transit systems. She put on the black travelling garb, very likely the original dress of the Regensburg nuns when they had arrived in New York almost twenty-five years before, and set off for Second Street, New York City. She knew, she said, the letter was urgent and by the time of her arrival was fairly certain of its contents. Mother Hyacinth, in turn, sent Sister Hieronyma on to St. Dominic convent, Jersey City, where Mother Aquinata Fiegler was superior to ask her to report to Second Street the following day.

The letter which Sister Hieronyma carried to Mother Hyacinth no longer exists. We know only that it was in the fall of 1877, some five months after Mother Augustine's vision. On October 15, 1877, five choir nuns and one lay sister left Second Street for Traverse City.

The first convent in Michigan located on Union Street in Traverse City — 1877

*ABOVE, LEFT*
*First Dominican residence*
*on Union Street, Traverse City,*
*from a 1927 drawing*

*ABOVE, RIGHT*
*Father George Ziegler*

*LEFT*
*The house on Union Street*
*May 1957*

# 3

# GOD'S ACRES
# THE MISSIONS IN THE WEST

$\mathcal{T}$he women who began the work of the Dominican Order in Michigan were the choir nuns Sisters Aquinata Fiegler, Camilla Madden, Angela Phelan, Boniface Hartleb, Borromeo Ahlmeier, and a lay sister, Sister Martha Mueglich.[1] Mother Aquinata, the appointed superior for the group, was twenty-nine; Sister Borromeo, seventeen; the others, about twenty-three. They arrived in Traverse City on Thursday, October 23, 1877, and opened school for six pupils the following Monday.

The house which was to be their convent and school until 1883 was a wood frame building on the east side of Union Street between Eighth and Ninth Streets. It had been purchased by Father Ziegler for a thousand dollars from his own savings. The young congregation in New York supplied an additional six hundred dollars for furnishings.

Julia Seymour,[2] a member of the first class in the sisters' school and the first Dominican sister from Michigan, described the convent-school she attended. The front entrance of the house opened onto a small hall about eight feet wide.To the right a stairway led to the second floor. To the left of the hallway was a doorway leading to the smaller of two classrooms, the first, Sister Camilla's, where there were perhaps six school benches with desks, and a small table for the teacher.

In the second, Sister Angela's classroom, Mass was said on weekdays, and early Mass and Vespers with Benediction on Sundays and holy days. At the back of this classroom were two rows of long, home-made benches and desks. In the northeast front corner of the room was a closet extending from the floor almost to the ceiling. Part of this closet included shelves for the vestments and articles used for Mass. The lower section was used as an altar table, the upper contained a crucifix with a small skull at the base.

A table was used for the teacher's desk. There was a piano which Sister Borromeo played for the religious services.

At the head of the stairs was a small hall leading into the combined community room and refectory. This room had two windows, one to the south and the other to the east. In it were a table and chairs for the six nuns. There was also a piano. A door at the northeast led into the kitchen which was furnished with a wood stove, a table, a cupboard, and two or three chairs. At the east was an outside vestibule, from which a covered stairway led down to the woodshed where water was drawn. To the north was a yard enclosed by a board fence about six feet high. In the upper vestibule hung the convent bell which Sister Martha rang for the Angelus, morning, noon, and evening, and also for Mass and Vespers.

There was a very small room off the kitchen where Sister Martha slept. The other nuns slept in a dormitory to the left of the front hall. A door at the northwest corner of this dormitory led into the chapel, a room about ten feet wide, furnished with a small altar where the Blessed Sacrament was reserved instead of in the parish church, some five blocks away at the edge of the town.

Mother Aquinata stayed in Traverse City about two months, setting up the household, the order of the school and, with the nuns, the basic pattern of enclosed conventual life combined with growing apostolic responsibilities. Sister Boniface Hartleb[3] became superior of the mission and Mother Aquinata returned to Jersey City to oversee the completion of a large convent-school building. That work completed, she returned to Traverse City in May 1879.

The first public notices of the sisters' presence in Michigan are oblique references in the *Grand Traverse Herald* for Thursday, December 20 and December 27, 1877:

> *The Catholic chapel is being neatly decorated with evergreens and mottoes. Two trees will be used for the gifts. Mass will also be served at 6 o'clock on Christmas morning.... The Catholic school celebrated the day in the usual manner. Mass was served at 6, 9, and 10½ o'clock on Christmas day. A Christmas tree was prepared for afternoon exercises instead of Monday evening, and the gifts were distributed at that time.*

By January 1878 there were fifty pupils attending the sisters' school. There was, however, little income. To help support themselves, Sisters Boniface, Camilla, and Borromeo gave lessons in fancywork in the evenings. Sister Boniface gave lessons in

German and Sister Angela, in English. On October 31, 1878, the *Grand Traverse Herald* announced that "the Sisters will begin on next Monday evening a series of evening lessons in French and German." From time to time the farmers in the area brought them vegetables and meat. On one occasion when the sisters were in need, Sister Boniface asked Father Ziegler for money. He sent a penny; it was all he had.

The winter of 1877-1878 was severe and life in the wood frame building very demanding. Sister Martha Mueglich, the lay sister primarily responsible for the domestic work in the convent, rose at four each morning to light the stoves in the dormitory and kitchen, and later in the school. Oftentimes the wood was wet, and the house cold for sisters and pupils. At times wood was dried in the kitchen oven. On one particularly wintry night, Sister Martha began a lively piece on the piano and the sisters marched about to keep warm. In the morning, bloodstained prints were found on the piano keys. Sister Martha, only forty-five, died in Traverse City on May 17, 1893, at the new Holy Angels Academy.

During the first winter Sister Camilla Madden contracted pneumonia. She was transferred to New York at the end of the school term, to return to Michigan within four years to open the mission at St. Joseph parish, Bay City, Michigan. Sister Borromeo Ahlmeier, born in Jersey City, New Jersey, was scarcely seventeen on her arrival at her first mission. She and Sister Camilla had made their first profession of vows on August 4, 1877. Sister Borromeo's first task when the school opened was to prepare the children to sing a High Mass. After learning the Mass, the children learned to sing Vespers. With her gifts of music and joy, Sister Borromeo was a great favorite of the children. In 1880 she was sent to join other sisters from New York to open St. Philip school in Battle Creek. There she contracted tuberculosis and was recalled to Traverse City, where she died on December 31, 1881. She was buried in Oakwood Cemetery, Traverse City, the first Dominican buried in Michigan.[4] She told the sisters at her deathbed, "Do not toll the bell but ring the chimes."

The parish of St. Francis, Traverse City, was within the Diocese of Detroit which then encompassed the entire lower peninsula of Michigan. For several decades there had been a mission church in the area. In 1870 a small parish church was built on the south side of Tenth Street, then the edge of the village and still an area of open grazing. In the summer of 1877 Father George Ziegler, a French priest working in Cincinnati, became the first resident pastor. He enlarged the church in 1880. Between 1885 and 1889 a new wooden church was built on the corner of Cass and Tenth Streets by Father Theophile Nyssen and the generous Catholics of the village. One of the stained glass windows in the church was given by the Sisters of St. Dominic. In December 1889 Mother Aquinata and the sisters, along with Father Joseph Bauer, third pastor, supervised the alteration of the old church for additional school space.

Traverse City developed from the mid-nineteenth century logging activities of Horace Boardman, Perry Hannah, A. Tracy Lay, and James Morgan. In 1872 Hannah succeeded in bringing a railroad to Traverse City. The Grand Rapids and Indiana Railroad was the pride of the city. The village was incorporated in 1891 and became a city in 1895. In 1880 the population of the settlement was 1,897; by 1894 it had almost doubled to 3,414.[5] At the close of the nineteenth century, the lumber industry was in sharp decline. Fruit-growing and tourism, however, became major sources of income and growth and the city grew to be a substantial center in northwest Michigan.

The hard and courageous beginnings in Traverse City were repeated throughout the state. Pastors continued to send requests to the motherhouse at 137 Second Street, New York City, and Mother Hyacinth endeavored to send sisters to each of them. In the spring of 1879 Mother Aquinata returned to Traverse City where she resumed the leadership of the convent and school. In late summer and fall of that year three more foundations were made in Michigan by the New York Dominicans.

On August 28, 1879, Sisters Boniface Hartleb, Ludovica O'Donnell, Athanasius McCormick, and Alexia Flynn, a lay sister, arrived in Adrian to open a sisters' school in St. Mary parish for Father Peter Wallace. Within a week another group arrived at St. Mary's, Muskegon, to direct the school of almost 400 pupils previously staffed by the Sisters of the Immaculate Heart of Mary from Monroe, Michigan. For this school Father Edward Van Pammel had secured from Mother Hyacinth the services of Sisters Cecilia Horner, Clementina Coyle, Barbara Bittner, and DeSales Desmond, a lay sister.

In the same month Sisters Amelia Kempter, Baptista Phelan, Walburga Hagan, and Gonsalva Bankstahl began their ministry in St. Michael parish, Port Austin. The boat on which they were expected had capsized in Lake Huron and the sisters were assumed among the lost. The sisters, having missed their originally scheduled departure, arrived several days later. Two others, Sister Raymond Hudzinski and a postulant, Mary Dorsey joined them later in the fall. Mary Dorsey as Sister Blanche would later become prioress of the Newburgh congregation. Two additional missions were added in 1880: a second school in Adrian at St. Joseph parish, and one in St. Philip parish, Battle Creek.

In 1881 Mother Aquinata and Sisters Hieronyma Egbert, Ligouri McCarron,[6] Eugenia Glaab, and Lawrence Doyle took over the school of 150 children in St. Boniface parish in Bay City, Michigan. Father Joseph Ebert, CPPS, pastor had arranged for sisters to instruct the children in this predominantly German parish. Another mission was added in Muskegon in 1882 where, at the request of Father Joseph Bennings, sisters began to staff a school in St. Joseph parish. About one hundred pupils appeared for the opening in the fall, some of them having come from the sisters' school in St. Mary parish.

The sisters' presence in Bay City was expanded with the opening of St. Joseph school in September 1882. Mother Aquinata and six others began the work which had resulted from a chance meeting between the pastor, Father J.V. Thibideau, and Mother Hyacinth on her first visit to Michigan. Mother Aquinata taught French to the higher classes and served as principal of the Bay City school until 1884, when Sister Angela Phelan took her place and began the high school. The old church of St. Joseph, Bay City, was the site of the sisters' annual retreats until 1886;[7] the parish was often the summer residence of those sisters who did not return to the East during the long vacation.

While Mother Aquinata was involved in the opening and administration of the convents and schools in Bay City, a considerable building project was under way in Traverse City. Sister Boniface Hartleb, superior in Traverse City, must have been locally in charge of the arrangements as her name is on land transactions and mortgages. There is no record that Mother Aquinata was then supervisor of all the Michigan missions and of

*Sister Martha Mueglich, OSD,*
*(1848-1893), lay sister,*
*on her profession day,*
*March 29, 1875*

*Sister Boniface Hartleb, OSD,*
*(1855-1930), choir nun,*
*on her profession day,*
*October 25, 1873*

*Holy Angels Convent - Academy*
*1883*

*Holy Angels with 1913 addition*

the new congregational house in Traverse City, though subsequent accounts give her this role.

The growing numbers of school children in St. Francis parish, the limited convent space, and the general condition of the building on Union Street prompted the sisters to plan for larger space both for education and for a gathering place for the sisters in Michigan. Mother Hyacinth gave permission for the project and J.W. Hilton of Traverse City was engaged as architect.

Perry Hannah, one of the founding fathers of Traverse City, gave the sisters six lots on Tenth Street. Additional land and money came from Father Ziegler and Bishop Ignatius Mrak. The bishop had retired as bishop of Marquette, Michigan, in 1878 and was living among the Indians in Eagletown, near Traverse City. He was a frequent visitor at the Traverse City convent, to which he brought gifts of encouragement and sometimes of financial help. He gave the sisters ten lots for which he had paid $1,200.

The building was begun in April 1883, and dedicated on September 6, 1883, by Bishop Henry Joseph Richter, ordinary of the newly established Diocese of Grand Rapids. A memorandum, presumably by Mother Boniface, summarizes what we know of the financing. As of July 1, 1883, the writer notes, $1,141.25 had been received toward the erection of the convent in Traverse City, $54 for stones for the foundation and $25 to the architect for plans. It appears that the New York motherhouse was handling the transactions as there is a record of a disbursement from Traverse City: "sent Mother Hyacinth at New York $1,700.00." On June 1, 1883, a sum of $1,250 was sent from New York for the June 1883 building expenses of $1,529.01. At this point, a $3,000 mortgage was arranged with the Hannah and Lay Company. The compiler gives a total of $9,376.40 ($8,676.40 for the building; and $900 for the land) to erect the original wood frame building.

From April through fall 1883, mention was made periodically in *The Grand Traverse Herald* of the sisters' project. On September 6, 1883, readers were informed of its completion.

### The New Catholic School

*The completed catholic school building is certainly a great credit to the town and, as remarked elsewhere in a communication, to the architect, J.W. Hilton. The lot upon which it is located will give ample room for the further improvements contemplated, and which will be completed at no distant day for it is well known and readily admitted by all that the catholics never fail to do all they plan to do.*

*The **Herald** has already, some weeks ago, noticed in full the plan of the building, the details of which, as then given, have been carried out in full. It is a handsome building in itself, but as we have stated before, this is only a part of a much larger and a more imposing structure, the plans for which are all made.*

*The present building has cost about $8,000. It is 40 x 60 feet in size, is of wood, the leading features Swiss, is surmounted by a handsome bell tower, and makes a fine appearance from whatever point viewed. The inside work is all pine, with a hard oil finish. The rooms are light, airy and pleasant. The first, or basement floor contains, in the center, the kitchen, and on either side a pleasant dining room communicating with the kitchen by slide panels. The kitchen is provided with all possible conveniences for work. On this floor are the furnaces, two in number, which supply the entire building with hot air for heating. Here, also are the laundry, play room, cellar, pantry, etc.*

*The heating arrangements, as well as those for ventilation, are as nearly perfect as it is possible to make them. Water is supplied from the city water-works.*

The same issue relates,

*The Sisters of St. Dominic are this week moving into their elegant new quarters just completed by J.W.Hilton, architect, of this city, to his great credit, as every one will readily admit, who have seen the building, and to the delight of the sisters themselves, as also to all lovers of art and tasteful neatness. His lordship, Right Reverend H.J. Richter of Grand Rapids, was here on Wednesday, to bless the new school and convent, thus especially setting it apart for the service of God. He was seconded by a number of priests from the neighborhood, and the ceremonies were truly catholic, that is to say solemn, imposing, full of deep meaning and inspiration.*

*Although the part already erected is to constitute but an inferior fraction of the whole building when completed, the good sisters are already prepared to seat 150 scholars, and also to take in, say 30 boarders, at $8 a month for young ladies under 12, and $10 for those over 12 years. These will then be taught all the ordinary branches taught in common schools to such children, and also plain sewing, fancy work (needle and otherwise). Music, etc., extra.*

Mother Hyacinth came from New York for the second time that year, first in the spring for Bishop Richter's consecration and then for the dedication of her congregation's convent in the West.

In the tradition of Second Order foundations, the convent was separated from the school area, and a grille was installed to regulate visiting. On December 5, 1883, the sisters completed arrangements for the legal incorporation of the Academy. Sisters Aquinata Fiegler, Ferrer Smith, Angela Phelan, Ligouri McCarron, and Isabella Ferris, all of Bay City, were the trustees of the new corporation with a capital stock of $5,000.

The convent-academy at 120 East Tenth Street benefitted from several civic improvements: the claying and graveling of Union Street in 1883, tree planting in 1886, and the installation of electric lights in 1889. Sister Scholastica Burghardt planted the trees which distinguished the stately building for years to come. Not until 1911 was the additional portion added, and that was not according to the original architectural plans. A brick annex was begun in April 1911 to provide a large chapel and additional convent dormitory and refectory space. Payments were completed in May 1913 at a total cost of $23,547.88 exclusive of furnishings.[8]

In 1889 the Academy celebrated its first high school commencement. The graduating class consisted of three young women: Anna Shane, Mary Donley, and Stacia Burden. The names suggest that the sisters who had come from Germany to serve their country's immigrants had now a wider mission field.

A few years earlier, the New York motherhouse agreed to a work hitherto new to the sisters in Michigan. On May 20, 1884, Sisters Rose Kempter, Antonia Reinhardt, Kunigunda Weber, Julia Zahn, Adelaide McCue and Villana Carmody undertook the care and nursing of the aged in a small frame house in Adrian, Michigan. The pastor of St. Joseph parish, Father Casimir Rohowski, CPPS, had asked Mother Hyacinth for sisters to staff a hospital for railroad accident cases. St. Joseph Hospital and Home for the Aged was the third Dominican mission in the city. The hospital was incorporated within the state of Michigan on December 5, 1888, a ceremony which Mother Aquinata, now provincial superior, attended. This house was the origin of the Adrian Dominican motherhouse.

The ordinary support gained from tuition, extra lessons in English, German, or French, fancywork or music was lacking for the sisters assigned to the hospital. The lay sisters, therefore, regularly engaged in "collecting" for food and necessaries. The practice of begging was part of their Dominican tradition as members of a medieval mendicant order. But begging was not customary among European cloistered convents whose very condition of foundation was the requirement of adequate endowment. It had, however, become common in some of the New York missions. In 1894 collecting was discontinued among the sisters in Adrian, but it continued into the twentieth century among the sisters in the Diocese of Grand Rapids, primarily to support their work at St. John's Home.

In 1885 the sisters extended their presence on the east side of the state. Father Richard Sweeney asked for sisters in St. Joseph parish in Saginaw. Sisters Gabriel O'Malley, Justina Daley, James Walsh, Eleanor Heinl, and the lay sisters Alexia Flynn and Marcolina Zengel were the first assigned to this largely Irish settlement. For three years, from 1886 to 1889, the sisters also assisted at Our Lady of Lourdes Grotto, Connor's Creek.

About 1886 Mother Hyacinth received a request for sisters from Father Krebs in Gagetown and in response sent Sister Borgia and several others to staff St. Agatha school. A mission was opened nearby in 1888 at Saints Peter and Paul parish, Ruth. The three schools in the "thumb" area--Port Austin, Gagetown, and Ruth-- came under the supervision of the Adrian province when the division of the dioceses and congregation missions was effected in 1894.

In 1887, at the invitation of Bishop Mrak, Sisters Antoninus Jellig, Paschal Farnen, and Henrietta Gagnier, began work among the Indians at Peshabetown (Eagletown) at Guardian Angels mission near the tip of the Grand Traverse peninsula. A sense of history must have struck the pioneers as their recollections were recorded:

*Having come from Traverse City by boat, they were met by a number of Indians who accompanied them to the residence of the Bishop, where they partook of supper. It was a simple meal composed of bread and butter, oatmeal, molasses, berries, and black tea. What a unique sight to see these three Dominican sisters gathered about the plain table in the house of the holy Bishop Mrak, while not a few of the Indians lingered about through a childish curiosity to see more of these visitors.*

*After supper, the sisters were shown to their residence across the street. It was a small four-room building, with an attic requisitioned for use as a dormitory;*

*here were three wooden beds which Bishop Mrak himself had made from boards of the old church and covered with straw ticks of such generous height as quite to dismay the sisters. The sisters were somewhat disconcerted to find that locks on the doors were considered superfluous in this vicinity, and, rather timid after having seen such a number of Indians about, they piled against the doors all the moveable articles of furniture. It needed but a few days' work there, however, to convince the sisters that they had nothing to fear from the Indians. About a mile from their own house they opened a school where, within a few days, about fifty Indian pupils had enrolled.... They found the Indians receptive of religious teaching, happy in assisting at the Holy Sacrifice and other religious services. They liked particularly to sing hymns and really sang very well, many of them having fine voices. To secure their interest and to increase devotion, Sister Henrietta mastered the difficulties of the Indian tongue, spoke it fluently, and taught the Indians to sing their own hymns.[9]*

The sisters remained there about five years, leaving shortly after Bishop Mrak returned to Marquette.

Another northern mission was added in 1888 at Provement (Lake Leelanau). Benedictine sisters had begun the school for Father Joseph Bauer the previous year. At Bishop Richter's request the Dominican sisters replaced them. Sisters Nicholas Philpott, Francis Brady, and Aloysius Miller began the work in St. Mary's parish, which came to be a missionary center for the surrounding peninsula. The sisters, still canonically members of a cloistered congregation, set out from there to teach religion at Good Harbor, Port Oneida, Gill's Pier, Leland, and Peshabetown.

On August 30, 1889, Sisters Charita Kernan, Cyrilla Hallahan, James Walsh, Adalbert Wagner, and Agnes Senecal opened school for some two hundred pupils at St. John's parish in Essexville, where Father C.J. Roche was pastor.

The sisters' first school in central Michigan was begun in Mount Pleasant in 1889. On August 31 Sisters Ligouri McCarron, Clare Brophy, Ferrer Smith, Marcella Farnan, a lay sister, and Sisters Dominic and Stanislaus, who later returned to New York, arrived in St. Charles parish. The parish, newly rededicated as Sacred Heart parish, was under the direction of Father James A. Crowley, a former Holy Cross brother and a dedicated "school man." The sisters opened Sacred Heart Academy for some two hundred pupils in nine grades. The first class of five graduated from the academy in 1893. As early as 1902 the academy had earned full accreditation from the North Central Association. About that time, the sisters missioned in Mount Pleasant began a decades-long ministry among the Chippewa Indians. Every Saturday and Sunday they went to the government school to give religious instructions and they held a daily class two months before First Communion. Sister Bertrand Lalonde wrote in 1928 of her vivid recollection:

> *Saturday rides through the main street of the little college town, in the school bus drawn by a pair of donkeys which took two stalwart Indian youths to manage. The jolts and the humiliations are forgotten, but the piety and sincerity of those first communicants, ranging in age from twelve to twenty-four, will ever remain as a fragrant memory.*

On September 2, 1889, Sisters Cyprian McCarron, Sabina Cavanaugh, Ignatius Deegan, and Alacoque Wingen held the first day's instruction for the children of St. Alphonsus parish, Grand Rapids. The new parish was under the direction of the Redemptorist fathers of St. Louis, Missouri. The sisters resided at nearby St. John's Home on East Leonard Street until the mid-1940's when they moved to the former Finn family residence, prior to the opening of the parish convent in 1948. Perhaps because the parish was under the care of a religious order, there was a formal agreement between the sisters and the Redemptorist fathers on aspects of school management. Both the Redemptorist fathers and the Dominican sisters continued to serve the parish through its centennial year in 1989.

In the fall of 1888 Bishop Richter asked Mother Aquinata to come to Grand Rapids to confer with him on matters of mutual interest. She and Mother Angela Phelan conversed with him for some time and at the end of the interview the bishop alluded to a major undertaking in the near future. Within a week Mother was informed that the bishop wanted the Dominican sisters to take on the supervision of a home for orphans then under construction in Grand Rapids. A gift of $60,000 from the estate of the late John T. Clancy, a lumberman of considerable wealth, had been used to establish a trust for that purpose. Eight acres at the corner of Lafayette and East Leonard Street were purchased, with two and a half acres subsequently sold to the new St. Alphonsus parish. A large wing of the projected building was completed and furnished for about $27,000.

The first sisters arrived at St. John's Home in May 1889, among them Mother Aquinata, Sisters DeSales Desmond and Mary Agatha McCauley. In July 1889 Sister Adelaide McCue joined them from Adrian, Michigan. She was to spend forty-seven years at the Home. As early as June 1889 the sisters welcomed the first of their charges, Alice, Mary, and Kathleen Merritt, whose mother had recently died. The house population increased daily.

On August 25, 1889, St. John Orphan Asylum was dedicated. It was an event of significance both to the diocese and to western Michigan as it was the first institution of child care on the west side of the state. The event was well covered by the local and state press. Special street cars from the city lines were laid on to bring visitors to the grounds. A parade of carriages brought Bishop Richter, the Catholic clergy, members of the city Common Council and other city officials, the architect W.G. Robinson, and Messrs. John McIntyre and Harvey Hollister, representatives of the benefactor John Clancy, from St. Andrew cathedral. The dedication was held in the open at the north entrance to accommodate the huge numbers of invited guests and interested public.

Father Theodore Lamy, CSsR, pastor of St. Alphonsus parish, gave the address, a poignant description of the children's plight, of the high cost of feeding and clothing children, and of the angels of charity who would devote their lives to teaching and tending the residents. "During this speech," *The Telegram Herald* of August 26, 1889, related, "hats and collection boxes were passed in the crowd and the clinks of the temporal aid for the orphans mingled with the spiritual words which flowed from the lips of the preacher." Bishop Richter blessed the building and then spoke briefly to the crowd. He spoke of prosperity of the city not only in its businesses but in its noble charitable institutions. "God is charity. We show our Christianity in the same degree that we show our charity." After the formal ceremonies, the three Merritt girls conducted the guests through the building.

The dedication of St. John's Home with its attendant publicity was the first introduction of the Sisters of St. Dominic to the city of Grand Rapids. Local newspapers of that year boasted that the "City of Homes" had now reached 100,000 inhabitants. To these were added the ten Dominican sisters who were to care for the children of St. John's Home[10] and to teach at St. Alphonsus school.

The building to which they came and which would serve as the core of their motherhouse was described in *The Telegram Herald:*

*...a handsome and substantial structure standing upon elevated ground and commanding a splendid view of the surrounding country. It is built of white tile brick of home manufacture and is three stories in the clear above the basement, with a high, well-ventilated attic, with a slate roof and surmounted with ornamental cupola and belfry. It contains twenty-eight large, airy, high-ceilinged, finely-lighted rooms. Two of these are dormitories, one for each sex, and one is intended for infirmary purposes. The kitchen arrangements are of the most convenient and improved style and the entire establishment will be heated by steam.*

*The main entrance to the building is at the southeast corner and after passing through the vestibule one enters a hall extending north and south, off of which open several rooms, one for the parents of the children if they are so fortunate as to have any, and another for visitors to the school. The dining room is in the south-east corner, a large and well-lighted room which will be filled with long tables and benches. Back of the dining room is a kitchen, well supplied with conveniences, and still further back a large brick oven, substantially built, in a separate room. A room which will be used as a music room and another designed for a serving room are also located on this floor. The rear of the building is L shaped and has a wide veranda opening into what will be a courtyard when the main building is completed. On the second floor is a chapel where the children will daily assemble to worship and back of that the sacristy, where the holy utensils are kept. The rooms which the sisters will occupy as dormitories are in the rear of these. Two well-lighted school rooms are also on this floor near the main hall and they will be suitably fitted for the purpose.*

*The third floor is the dormitory floor and is differently planned from the others. Two large rooms will be used as dormitories and filled with little iron cots, so that each child may have a separate bed. A small room, where one of the sisters will sleep to look after the little ones, opens off one of the dormitories. Back of them is a large room to be set aside as an infirmary for those unavoidable cases of sickness which will occur in the best regulated institutions. A small room is also set aside for a clothes room and has been fitted with closets on every side. Clothing will be made and kept in stock in this room. There are separate linen closets and compartments for the children's changes of dress. The sisters take great pride in the arrangement of this room which is patterned after similar rooms in use in New York City orphan homes. It was their wish to have a washroom arranged with a separate basin for each child, but this was deemed impracticable. There are, however, two very well arranged institutional washrooms and a large bathroom and each child will have his own towel, brushes and toilet articles, to be kept in separate compartments. The plumbing in the building seems excellent and there is certainly an immense amount of it.*

*The water to be used in the bath and washrooms is supplied by four good-sized tanks on the attic floor which are filled from the roof conductors. The attic is very large and it has been planned to set it aside for use in case any contagion should break out among the children. It could then be used as a quarantine and may be finished off with reference to that contingency. On the north side of the building, upon this floor, is a balcony which the sisters think will be a very pleasant place for convalescents in the summer season. The attic will make a fine wet-weather play-ground, but instead of using it for that purpose a large room in the basement has been set aside for this purpose. When the heating apparatus is in place there will still be plenty of storage room below the stairs.*

For thirty years these rooms of St. John's Home and its surroundings were the center of the congregation, its official motherhouse after 1894, and the residence of the mother general and of sisters engaged in ministry there and throughout the city.

In August 1891 diphtheria swept the city. Forty-nine of the children at St. John's Home fell ill, six of them dying of the disease. Sister Isabella Ryan, a novice who had helped with the nursing of the children, became ill and died on October 16, 1891. Father Terrence Clarke, a Redemptorist priest who served the Home as chaplain until 1912, was at the bedside of each of the dying.

As early as 1896 an addition larger than the original building was begun. It was completed at the cost of $48,000, drawn from the Clancy trust fund. Bishop Richter officiated at the dedication of the new wing on February 22, 1897. The new four-story center section was sixty-two feet long and provided four additional classrooms, dormitories, and sisters' quarters.

The third and last section of the building was begun in 1909. The original benefaction of John Clancy had now been depleted. A donation of $100,000 from his sister, Ann McIntyre, had been successfully contested, so funding from that source was delayed. A fire on January 18, 1911, destroyed the southwest corner of the original wing, a cause for further delay. Finally, in 1913, the new four-story and basement addition of 69' x 140' was completed. The new section contained chapel, sisters' quarters, infirmary, chaplain's quarters, dining rooms, kitchen, and two large playrooms. A tower

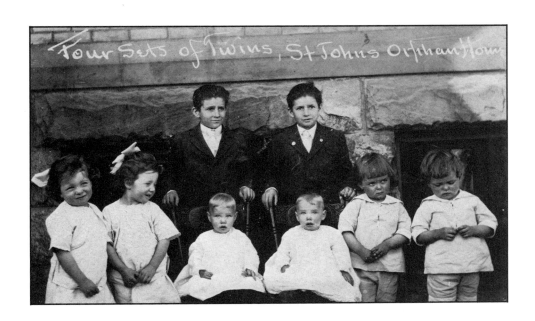

*St. John's Home*
*E. Leonard Street, Grand Rapids,*
*Michigan*

of 106 feet, matching the original tower on the west wing, completed the new east wing.

There was an annual Diocesan Orphans' Collection but it was not enough to meet the financial requirements of the growing institution. The sisters had the major responsibility for providing sustenance, which they often did by "collecting." Sisters Fidelis Reicha, Chrysostoma Schmittner, Paschal Farnen, and Bartholomew Jeunemann were the most frequent of the collectors of farm goods, dry goods from the city stores, and monies from door to door. Sometimes essential supplies came at the hands of anonymous donors who appeared on the final day of novenas to St. Joseph.[11] The sisters themselves took no salary for their work at the Home, and occasionally made a major outlay on behalf of the institution.[12]

The arduous task of collecting brought other benefits. Some sisters traced their religious vocation to the visits of the Dominican sisters who came to their homes, either for goods or the hospitality of a good Catholic home before they made their way to the lumber camps and distant settlements on behalf of the orphans. In 1899 the sisters began to sponsor a benefit supper which they continued until 1917. It was a major fund-raising event, the first supper netting $1,095.26. It was also a welcomed social event scheduled near St. Patrick's Day. As well as a good crowd from the city, supporters from as far as Parnell often came to the supper. In 1917 the Home was affiliated with the Federation of Social Agencies in Grand Rapids and as a result was on a firmer financial basis. The new affiliation was undoubtedly a major factor in causing the sisters to hasten their plans for building their own motherhouse.

Other missions were added in the next decade. It is not clear if Mother Hyacinth as prioress of the New York motherhouse continued to participate in the acceptance of new missions in the Grand Rapids diocese. It is unlikely that parishes were directly staffed without consultation with Bishop Richter; indeed, there is some evidence that Mother Aquinata took on new schools primarily at the bishop's direction.

In 1890 sisters were asked for the newly-established "Holland Parish," St. Joseph's in Grand Rapids, a predominantly Dutch Catholic settlement cared for by Father Henry Frencken, a native of Holland. Sisters Gonsalva Bankstahl, Isabella Ryan, and Lawrence Battle were the first assigned to the parish on Rumsey Street. Father Frencken, born in 1860, was the oldest priest affiliated with the Grand Rapids Diocese. He returned to the Netherlands in 1906 and lived there beyond his ninetieth birthday. In 1928-1929 the sisters on an extensive recruiting visit were his guests in Holland. Thirty years after leaving Grand Rapids Father Frencken told of the sisters' first years:

*...a note from His Lordship about July that same year told me to procure sisters for the school. Mother Aquinata had her headquarters at that time in Traverse City; so I went there, explained my wishes, and she promised me to send 2 sisters for the school and one for the household provided I had a house for them near the school. We rented a little house just behind the church and the parishioners furnished it as well as they could afford. It was just large enough for the 3 sisters but not more. The house was fixed up inside and outside and a few days before school opened the sisters arrived. The Superior was Sister M. Gonsalva, later Mother M. Gonsalva and Sister Isabella, who was only a novice then. Before her profession she was recalled to St. John's Home then the Motherhouse also, where she got, whilst taking care of sick orphans herself diphtheria and died a few days later, but sick as she was, she said the little dead orphans need also a Sister in heaven. She made her profession before she died.*

*...As soon as school was closed, the sisters helped me move to the new home and after my rooms were vacant in the main building, the sisters moved in there.... They liked it very much as they were near the classrooms, and could go to church without going outside.... The next term (September 1891) Sister Gonsalva did not return, but Sister Baptista, later affiliated with Adrian (Detroit) and Sister Philomena, now assistant Mother at Marywood, who had just finished her novitiate, were the teachers for the year 1891-1892.*

*...As there was no water or gas in the street, we had to do with oil lamps and a pump behind the church.... We had started several societies and the meetings were held in the school rooms. However, this did not please our Dutch protestant neighbors for they began to talk about it and thought it was scandalous to have men go in the evening to the building where sisters were living, and consequently I asked the bishop permission to build a meeting hall; to which he consented provided no debt was made....Once finished, little parties etc. were given and soon it was all paid for...I used to keep chickens and when they got old, we used to raffle them. Once I had an old rooster six years old, put him up for raffle 10 cents a chance and Mr. Pipe...was the lucky man, however, he told me it took him considerable time, a whole day to cook him and cost him very much on fuel and still he was tough....*

*...In the course of time the pupils increased and another 3rd room for a third teacher was needed. I decided to build a house for the sisters and transform the sisters' rooms into a class room....Soon the house was finished, hot water put in, also in the Pastor's house, so that a 3rd teacher, and a music teacher Sister Thomas, now at Marywood or at the College on Ransom Street. The exact year in which the sisters moved in their house I do not remember exactly, but I think in 1903 or 1904.*[13]

The last mission established prior to the independence of the congregation was St. Joseph's, Wright, a country parish outside of Grand Rapids. A school had been in existence in the area since 1855, first under the care of Franciscan sisters, then of the Sisters of Mercy. In 1893, due to a shortage of German-speaking Mercy sisters, three Dominican sisters took over the education of some sixty pupils. They lived above the two classrooms in a wood frame building until 1899 when a convent was built.[14]

The New York motherhouse, once the primary source for staffing the growing number of missions, could no longer send sisters. Between 1877 and 1891 there were approximately one hundred Dominican missionaries to Michigan. In 1881 Michigan had given its first candidate to the Dominican Order, Julia Seymour, who joined the sisters in the little frame house on Union Street. In the same year Sister Borromeo Ahlmeier, pioneer from New York, died and was buried in Traverse City.

# 4

# PREPARING
# THE WAY OF THE LORD

*O*n May 19, 1882, the Diocese of Grand Rapids[1] was formally erected by decree of Pope Leo XIII. On April 22, 1883, Henry Joseph Richter was consecrated first bishop of the newly created diocese. The nuns from New York were now in two dioceses in Michigan, Detroit and Grand Rapids. From 1883 to their deaths within a year of each other, Bishop Richter and Mother Aquinata collaborated in ministry throughout the Diocese of Grand Rapids.

At the time of his consecration Bishop Richter[2] was forty-five years old and described as "although not physically a strong man,...in the enjoyment of robust health, and...a man of most genial and refined manners."[3] He was approximately 5'6" tall and slight; shy and retiring in manner, yet receptive and kindly to all he met. He took as his motto the Gospel imperative, "Prepare ye the way of the Lord."

Bishop Richter attended the third Plenary Council of Baltimore in 1886 and was much influenced by its arguments for a parochial school system. He was known as a "school man" and eager to develop a comprehensive and efficient educational network throughout the diocese. He appointed Father Robert Brown, pastor of St. James parish, Grand Rapids, from 1898 to 1921, to conduct the annual examinations. Father Brown used to appear with an ominous black bag with tests for both teachers and students. The bishop himself sometimes conducted the examinations. In Mother Aquinata and the Dominican sisters he found ready and generous administrators and teachers for the developing Catholic school system.

Sister Mary Aquinata, Appolonia Fiegler, was born in Worbis, Germany, on August 16, 1848, to Aloys and Johanna Florentia Iffland Fiegler. A brother, Arnold, had been born in 1846. Their home was situated in Worbis, a town of approximately two thousand inhabitants, in the valley of Eichsfeld, a wooded area between the Thuringer Forest and the Hartz Mountains in the

*Henry Joseph Richter,*
*First Bishop of Grand Rapids*
*(fl. 1883-1916)*

*Sister Aquinata Fiegler, OSD,*
*(1848-1915), choir nun,*
*on her profession day,*
*August 26, 1865*
*INSET Golden Jubilee, 1914*

province of Saxony. Her maternal grandparents lived with them for a time, her grandmother dying relatively young, and the grandfather moving with them during family transitions.

Making a living as a printer became increasingly difficult for her father. In 1858 or 1859 father and son emigrated to America. Mrs. Fiegler joined the household of her widowed sister, Appolonia Hartleb, and her three daughters, among them Wilhelmina who, as Sister Boniface, would join Mother Aquinata in her work in Michigan. The two women worked in the mail service with house and child care left largely to Appolonia; the four girls attended a nearby sisters' school. In 1860 mother and daughter joined the father in New York.

Her brother Arnold, remembered by Sister Boniface as adventurous and unruly, served in the Civil War. He allegedly set out for Brazil and was lost in a shipwreck.[4] The parents returned to Germany in 1867, the father dying there about 1877. In 1889 Mrs. Fiegler returned to America and spent some years in Traverse City, but eventually she returned to Germany where she died in June 1897.

On February 15, 1864, Appolonia, then fifteen years old, was received into Holy Cross convent, Williamsburg. Mother Seraphine, one of the second group from Ratisbon, was prioress. On the feast of St. Dominic in the same year, Appolonia received the habit of St. Dominic and the name Sister Mary Aquinata of the Most Blessed Sacrament. Unlike the custom in European foundations, a large dowry was not required for admission to American convents, a factor which seems to have influenced young women to emigrate to America or to respond to recruiters who went to Germany.

In late October 1864 Sisters Aquinata, Theresia Hoffman, and Magdalena were sent to Holy Rosary convent in St. Nicholas parish, at 137 Second Street in New York City. The convent was comprised of several three- and four-story "New York brownstones," walls having been broken through to create a single residence. Sister Aquinata remained there for eight years, with the exception of a short period before her profession on August 26, 1865. During those years she taught at St. Nicholas school, studied, and gave sewing lessons for additional income for the convent. There she learned the traditions of the Order and developed her spiritual life under the direction of Mother Augustine Neuhierl, one of the Ratisbon pioneers.

In 1869 the two convents, Holy Cross, Williamsburg (Brooklyn) and Holy Rosary, New York City, formally separated. The sisters were free to choose the motherhouse in which they wished to remain; Sister Aquinata remained with the Congregation of the Most Holy Rosary. In 1872 she was assigned to begin a new daughter house of the Second Street convent, St. Dominic's in St. Boniface parish, Jersey City, New Jersey. From there she was called in May 1877 to the deathbed of Mother Augustine. With the other nuns, she heard the prophecy of a "peninsula dotted white with Dominicans." Again, in October 1877, she was summoned from Jersey City to the Second Street motherhouse, to discuss the letter Mother Hyacinth had received from Father Ziegler inviting them to Traverse City, Michigan.

Mother Aquinata[5] then took up the congregation's work of establishing missions in Michigan, with only a year's return to the East when she was engaged in directing the building of the new St. Dominic convent in Jersey City. Sister Mary Philip Roche, a novice at St. Dominic's in 1878-1879 and later a member of the Caldwell, New Jersey, Dominican sisters, had these recollections of Mother Aquinata:

*I lived with Mother Aquinata for eight months, as a novice. She appealed to me more than any other Sister, and therefore, I observed her closely and made every effort to imitate her.*

*Mother was very exact about every point of the Rule, especially the rule of silence which she never violated in the convent. We had strict conventual observance. Not only in letter was she precise but also in the spirit of the rule expressed in the opening clause, 'Above all, beloved Sisters, love God and then your neighbor.' She certainly saw to it that the Sisters exercised a kindly spirit, a sisterly charity towards each other.*

*She was very precise about the processional singing, and if every tone was not in perfect harmony, she would summon all the Sisters to the music room to practice the sacred songs, the Libera, the Salve, the O Lumen. Every morning she would call the Sisters at half-past four and light the gas in their cells. At eight in the evening the bell was rung for night prayers, after which she retired with the community.*

*She never inflicted a penance for breaking any of the kitchen utensils; but for leaving anything out of place, or handling books without having first washed our hands, she certainly was not sparing. When we lived in the little four-room house, it was a model of cleanliness, and Mother radiated a spirit of sweet cheerfulness and love of poverty.*

*Every day found her in the kitchen helping to prepare dinner for the Sisters. It seemed to afford her much pleasure to have something palatable for us when we came home from school. Mother did not teach while I was with her for she had to give her time to constructive planning, gathering funds, building, and so forth. She was generous in giving hospitality to the members of other communities although I cannot vouch for where they slept.[6]*

There is evidence of only three other visits to New York: in the summer of 1883 when Mother Aquinata and Mother Angela Phelan returned to New York and asked for volunteers; in August 1885, when she gathered fourteen sisters for the Michigan missions; and in July 1896 for the funeral of Mother Hyacinth.

In 1885 the missions in Michigan were given the status of a province of the Congregation of the Most Holy Rosary. The convent-academy of Holy Angels in Traverse City served as the provincial house of the Province of St. Joseph. With the creation of the Diocese of Grand Rapids in 1883, the relationship of these Second Order Dominican nuns to the local ordinary had become something of a practical as well as a canonical question. It was Bishop Richter's judgment, and most likely one shared by Mother Aquinata, that separation from the New York motherhouse was dictated both by canonical custom and by the practicalities of the situation. Therefore, Bishop Richter took steps to establish the Dominican sisters within his diocese as a separate, independent congregation, possibly as early as 1883.

Correspondence between Bishop Richter and the Archbishop of New York, Michael A. Corrigan, supports this interpretation.

*July 2nd, 1894*
*Your Grace,*

*The community of Dominicans from 2nd Street New York has increased rapidly in this diocese. Many years ago I proposed a separation from the house in New York. The mother prioress then thought it best to continue the union for some time, and proposed to establish our communities as a province. The community is, I think, according to its intent, diocesan. Hence it seems to me that a complete separation of the Dominican sisters in the diocese of Grand Rapids would be proper. Moreover, the lay sisters are displeased with the black scapular which they were ordered some years ago to wear. I do not wish to make any changes as long as the Sisters are connected with the house in New York. If they were completely under my jurisdiction I would permit or make certain changes which would, in my opinion, make the community more efficient and content in this diocese.*

*As your Grace is the ecclesiastical superior of the community I desire to know your views on the subject, and if the above mentioned separation meets your approval, your assistance in bringing it about.*

*Hoping that your Grace is enjoying good health,*

*I am*
*Very sincerely yours in Xto,*

*s/Henry Joseph Richter*
*Bp. of Gr. R.*

Archbishop Corrigan replied promptly.

*452 Madison Avenue*
*New York*
*July 16, 1894*

*Rt. Rev. Dear Bishop,*

*I understand that the Dominican Sisters of New York will agree to your proposition: and the details can easily be settled by both parties. If I might venture to make a suggestion, I would recommend that the Rule of the 3rd Order of St. Dominic be adopted, as much better suited for our actual wants. It is a rule that can easily be kept by school Sisters, and observed exactly; whereas in the other case there is apt to be constant need of dispensation or modification of the Rule, which impairs discipline.*

*Please excuse this card as I have no suitable writing material at hand.*

*I am, my dear Bishop*
*Very faithfully yours,*

*M. A. Corrigan*

On August 27, 1892, the sisters were legally incorporated as "The Sisters of the Order of St. Dominic of the City of Grand Rapids." Recollections of the pioneer sisters left in the Detroit diocese after 1883 support the interpretation that separation had already begun in the decade prior to the formal announcement.[7] In August 1891 three postulants were brought to Adrian from Traverse City. That fall three candidates entered directly in Adrian, a casual beginning of a second novitiate in Michigan. On May 8, 1892, the first clothing ceremony at Adrian occurred. Bishop Foley of Detroit presided; Mother Aquinata was present. In July 1892 a novice from Traverse City with blood sisters in the Adrian convent was transferred to Adrian. That same month the first "big retreat" was conducted in Adrian where Father J.L. Kearney, OP, preached the retreat for some thirty sisters. Another indication of this separation occurred in early August 1892: all the sisters in the Detroit diocese were called to Adrian and given their assignments for the year. At the same time, their superior, Mother Angela Phelan, announced that she was leaving the Adrian area to direct a new hospital and school in Aberdeen, Washington.

There were now two provinces of St. Joseph in Michigan, a fact known by Mother Hyacinth Scheininger, the New York prioress, the two provincials, Mother Aquinata Fiegler in Grand Rapids and Mother Camilla Madden in Adrian, and Bishops Foley and Richter, but not necessarily known by the sisters in the three groups. Mother Aquinata kept a small notebook in which she recorded spiritual reflections and significant historical items. About this stage, she wrote simply, "In August 1891 the Sisters in the Diocese of Detroit ceased to belong to the jurisdiction of Grand Rapids."

In 1893 Bishop Richter made the required *ad limina* visit to Rome. In his conversation with Pope Leo XIII, the bishop apparently included the status of the Dominican sisters in his diocese. Upon his return, he corresponded with Archbishop Corrigan, and possibly with Mother Hyacinth in New York. On August 30, 1894, at the close of the annual retreat, Bishop Richter announced that henceforth the Dominican sisters in his diocese would be an independent congregation. Mother Aquinata was to be prioress general of the group to be known as the Congregation of Our Lady of the Sacred Heart.

On the same day, the feast of St. Rose of Lima, Mother Camilla Madden told the sisters in Adrian of the separation of the Grand Rapids' sisters from the mother congregation. Sister Mary Philip Ryan records the pioneers' recollections of that announcement. It was for them an overwhelmingly sad day. There were accusations: "Mother Aquinata had looked too well to the ways of her house"; as provincial, Mother Aquinata had carefully staffed her missions prior to the separation with the more experienced and mature nuns; "the sisters had built the nest, the Bishop now took it."[8]

The decision was predictable. It was the way among cloistered congregations and their daughter houses. Nevertheless, the manner was arbitrary and without preparation for the majority of the sisters. The manner of separation left both groups with an unclear picture of their shared past.

As a result of the separation from the New York motherhouse, there remained in Michigan one province of St. Joseph centered in Adrian under the care of Mother Camilla Madden, and a new congregation, The Congregation of Our Lady of the Sacred Heart with its novitiate house at Holy Angels convent, Traverse City, and its motherhouse in the diocesan-owned St. John's Home in Grand Rapids.

The new congregation had sixty professed sisters, twelve novices, and the care of fourteen schools.[9] The province in Adrian had approximately thirty-five members, eleven professed sisters who had entered in New York, nine professed sisters and fifteen novices from the Diocese of Detroit; and the care of six rural schools--Gagetown, Ruth, Port Austin, Port Huron, Maybee, and Marblehead--and a school and a home for the aged in Adrian. St. Mary's, New Salem, was added to their care that fall.

The sisters from the East assigned to Michigan were free to remain in Michigan, either in the Grand Rapids congregation or in the Adrian province, or to return to New York. Some stayed in each of the Michigan areas, others returned. Some were allowed to stay on a loan basis. Mother Clementina Coyle was one who chose first to assist at Adrian, and later transferred to Grand Rapids. On June 21, 1896, Sister Cyprian McCarron and several others who had helped in the transition period returned to the East, a "tearful departure," wrote Sister Gonzaga Udell, then a child at St. John's Home.

By the close of 1894 the formal transition from Second to Third Order status was accomplished. The sisters were asked by the Master General of the Order to observe the Constitution approved for the Dominican sisters of Sinsinawa, Wisconsin, to recite the Little Office of the Blessed Virgin Mary, and to incorporate the lay sisters into the rank of the choir sisters. They were assured that these changes did not alter the essentially Dominican character of the congregation.[10]

There was a final episode in the story of the relationship to the Second Street motherhouse.[11] On July 17, 1896, Mother Hyacinth Scheininger died. Telegrams were sent to Michigan and both Mother Camilla Madden, provincial in Adrian, and Mother Aquinata Fiegler, prioress of the new congregation in Grand Rapids, attended the funeral. The funeral Mass was celebrated by Archbishop Corrigan on Monday, July 20, in St. Nicholas church, Second Street. The following Wednesday, July 22, the nuns meeting the constitutional requirements gathered in Chapter to elect a successor to Mother Hyacinth. Mother Aquinata Fiegler was elected.

Did the sisters in New York not know of the changes in the Michigan missions? Did they think perhaps that dual membership was possible? Did they think Mother Aquinata's ineligibility could be waived for the greater good of the New York congregation?

What understanding did Mother Aquinata herself have of her relationship to New York, to Grand Rapids?

Not only the formal announcement of 1894, the communication with Rome for Third Order status, but also a public event which occurred in 1890, had established formal obligations to the Michigan community. On August 26, 1890, a public Pontifical High Mass was celebrated to honor Mother Aquinata's Silver Jubilee. At the conclusion, Mother knelt before Bishop Richter and "bound herself forever to the work of the diocese." This appears to have transcended a ceremonial renewal of vows.

The New York capitulars seemed to know of the complexities of the issue, for on the very day of election Mother Angela Phelan wrote to Bishop Richter:

*Right Reverend and dear Bishop, I beg leave to present to your Lordship the following petition in the name of our Community here in New York.*

*...Our very dear Prioress, Mother M. Hyacinth was called from this world to her eternal reward on...July 17, and consequently we invited Mother Aquinata, she being the oldest professed sister of this Community, to come and act in her stead until an election should take place. Accordingly, His Grace the Archbishop of New York presided at our election this morning and Mother M. Aquinata was chosen and elected by a vast majority as Prioress of our Community. Therefore, we humbly beg your Lordship not to refuse your consent to her remaining here and accepting the office for which she is chosen and so well qualified. Indeed, dear Bishop, I am thoroughly convinced that by granting your consent thereto you will be instrumental in promoting and continuing here in the East the good and wise regulations, which by your wisdom and good counsel, Mother Aquinata has commenced in the Diocese of Grand Rapids and you may rely on her to send you another competent and good Sister to take her place in Grand Rapids and carry on the work she so humbly began there for the glory of God in 1877.*

*However, if your Lordship would desire Mother Aquinata still to continue to have the supervision of our Sisters in the diocese of Grand Rapids, I am sure she would be very willing to do so even though she be also burdened with the charge here. ...*

There is no record of Bishop Richter's response to this letter. There is, however, a letter from him, dated July 25, 1896, taking up the points with Archbishop Corrigan. It reads:

*Most Rev. Dear Archbishop:*

*There is one reason for which I would like to consent to the withdrawal of Mother Aquinata from her community in Grand Rapids, namely, to please you.*

*I am sure, however, that if you understood the circumstances you would not wish her to separate from her foundation in this diocese. It is much easier to fill the place in New York than to get a substitute for her here. The other day the sisters did not know that she was in New York and it will be best that they do not know what happened.*

*If Mother Aquinata is so well liked by the community in New York, you may well imagine how necessary she is to her children here. There she was the first novice, but here the foundress.*

*Sister M. Angela in a letter to me proposes that she either send a substitute or direct our community from New York. Either solution would not be the proper one.*

*Mother Aquinata herself proposed the absolute separation of the communities. She was aware of the effects of the separation and satisfied. She opposed return of any sisters to 2nd Street, until less than a month ago when she asked my permission for two, who she said were dissatisfied and might cause trouble.*

*Mother Hyacinth, when the separation was agreed upon, made no exception. Before the separation I asked Mother Aquinata whether it might not cripple the community and her opinion was that it would not. When I announced the separation only two or three were dissatisfied but they did not leave. Two sisters asked to have permission to visit their New York friends after two years. I did not promise, and they stayed.*

*I remain,*
*Your Grace's devoted servant in Xto,*
*Henry Joseph Richter,*
*Grand Rapids.*

The letter from Mother Angela was followed up by a delegation from New York--Mother Angela herself, a veteran of fifteen years in Michigan missions, and a Sister Ignatius. The bishop insisted on Mother Aquinata's ineligibility by reason of the separation of 1894.[12] Mother Aquinata then returned to Michigan on August 24, 1896. A second election was held in New York on August 31, 1896, at which Mother Hildegard Suetholz was elected prioress for a three-year term.

After almost two decades in Michigan, substantial changes in the constitutional nature of the group had occurred: the sisters in the Diocese of Grand Rapids constituted a separate congregation. The foundation was of Third Order status, that is, no longer a contemplative cloistered convent, but an apostolic institute. Nevertheless, these changes must be understood in the context of late nineteenth century America and of a missionary, essentially immigrant Church. The mental and material culture of the sisters was derived from their closeness to their Ratisbon roots and to their early Dominican Second Order status, an essentially European and more precisely, German, formation.

These realities were not immediately transformed by the formal canonical transitions. A good deal of that framework and some of its expressions in constitution, custom, and attitude continued in the congregation up to and beyond Vatican Council II.

# 5

# THERE, THE FIRST NOVICE, BUT HERE THE FOUNDRESS.

*O*n July 10 and 11, 1897, the first General Chapter of the congregation was convened at St. John's Home, the events of the previous summer no doubt having some bearing on the need for duly-elected officers. The Chapter, convoked by Bishop Richter twenty-four hours before, had thirty-four members. These were the sisters who on the day of election had been professed at least twelve years (active voice). Those eligible for office (passive voice) had, in addition to the twelve years of profession, to be age forty for office of prioress, thirty-five for councillor. There were nineteen with passive voice and thirty-four with active voice. Of the 34 votes cast, Mother Aquinata received 33. The election was announced and confirmed by Bishop Richter. Her official title was Superior General, though it was customary to speak of her and her successors as Mother General.

The only record of her council is in the corporation minutes.[1] On August 15, 1897, the sixth annual meeting of the trustees took place. Elections were held to replace Sisters Ligouri McCarron, Cyprian McCarron, Bernard Lovell[2] and Adelaide McCue who had resigned. All but Sister Adelaide had indicated a preference to remain with the New York congregation. Sisters Clementina Coyle, Gonsalva Bankstahl, Villana Carmody, and Assissium Finnegan were elected in their places. Mother Aquinata was then elected president, Sister Gonsalva, vice president, and Sister Benedicta O'Rourke, bursar and secretary. Mother Assissium had been mistress of novices since 1894.

In August 1895 the sisters had embarked upon another major project, the building of an academy on the east side of the state, in Essexville, Michigan. Father J.A. Roche, pastor of St. John parish, had donated property for an academy or boarding school for young ladies. The council agreed on the construction of a frame building not to exceed $10,000. The building was ready by fall 1896 and Sisters Gonsalva Bankstahl, Albertina Selhuber, Xavier Connelly, Terencia Finn, and Paschal Farnen opened the school. Bishop Richter dedicated the building as Holy Rosary Academy on August 12, 1896. Four years later, August 15, 1899, Mother Aquinata and her council formalized plans for a third academy with the purchase of "a piece of property 132 feet square with house and barn on same, situated on the corner of Fountain and Ransom Streets, City of Grand Rapids, for the consideration of $11,500, for the purpose of opening a day and Boarding School for young ladies."

In late spring 1899 Sister Benedicta O'Rourke and Sister Genevieve Gauthier were in Charlevoix to write teacher examinations. At the same time Bishop Richter stopped in the village enroute to Beaver Island for confirmation. He insisted the two sisters accompany him on his visit to the island. The following day he offered a High Mass, possibly the first ever on the island, with Sister Benedicta playing the organ and Sister Genevieve as the choir. They were the first sisters to visit the island.

Earlier that year Father Alexander F. Zugelder, recently assigned to Holy Cross parish on the island, asked Mother Aquinata for teaching sisters. He had come from St. Mary's, Provement (Lake Leelanau), where the Dominican sisters staffed the school. Father made the presence of sisters a condition of his going to the island. The first staffing of Beaver Island is one of the few occasions on record when Mother asked for volunteers. Sisters Clementina Coyle and Genevieve Gauthier, then missioned in Provement, volunteered at once. Joined by Sisters Hildegarde Miller and Gabriel O'Malley, they were greeted at the dock by most of the islanders on their arrival on September 6, 1899.

The sisters lived in a parishioner's home until their own house was ready. The church was located about two miles from the harbor but Father Zugelder provided a temporary altar in a small frame building near the harbor and offered daily Mass there. The sisters remarked on the idyllic simplicity of the island. Crime being virtually unknown, the islanders readily transformed a jail-courthouse building into two classrooms for the sisters. They were soon asked to take over the public school about two miles inland. Mother Aquinata visited the island on her circuit of visitations the following spring. In 1908 the school expanded to a high school. Sister Clementina, a native of Ireland and pioneer from New York, remained to become an island legend. Over one hundred sisters served in the island's schools from 1899 to 1991.[3]

In August 1900 the congregational officers met at Holy Rosary Academy in Essexville and agreed to the remodelling and refitting of the Matter estate,[4] the property acquired for a girls' academy in Grand Rapids. It was to be opened in September 1900 and to be called Sacred Heart Academy. The following spring, 1901, an annex was built at the projected cost of $14,000 under the supervision of W.G. Robinson, architect. A loan of $3,000 was arranged from Mr. J. Murray of Grand Rapids. Adjacent land was bought in 1902 with an additional loan of $2,500 from Mr. Murray. Sister Albertina Selhuber was appointed principal; Sisters Benedicta O'Rourke, Adelaide McCue, Sylvester Maus, and Borromeo Donley comprised the first faculty.

Opening day was set for Monday, September 17, 1900. The preceding Saturday was a day of general cleaning throughout the building. Father John A. Schmidt, assistant at the Cathedral, helped the sisters with last minute painting and scrubbing. Bishop Richter stopped by and suggested a delay in opening. But the sisters managed to finish the work by six o'clock and then walked to St. John's Home. On Monday, a rainy day, the sisters came from the Home to welcome thirteen pupils ranging from kindergarten through high school age. Work was assigned and they were dismissed early. Later in the fall two boarders, Gertrude Fleming and Ethel Assay, were admitted.

At first the only lighting was a single kerosene lamp. On September 21 a telephone was installed and directly a call went out to Mother Aquinata to announce the event. She answered on the first ring. The sisters told her of a visit from the Jewish Rabbi and of his invitation to attend service in his synagogue. They were told to decline politely.

The *Michigan Catholic* of September 27, 1900, described the Academy:

> The Sacred Heart Academy was opened Monday, September 17, with a very promising attendance. The institution is beautifully located on the corner of Fountain and Ransom Streets, and all agree in saying that a more suitable site could not have been selected. The choice of this site was very fortunate as the inviting surroundings assist, to a great extent, the intellectual training. The beautifully tinted classrooms are arranged with a view to the greatest comfort and convenience of the students,

*being spacious, well ventilated and light-some, and fitted up
with the latest improvements. The course of instruction
comprises all the requisites of refined and polished education.
The musical department comprises several tastily furnished
rooms, facing Fountain Street, and from all appearances will
soon re-echo with inspiring strains produced by the skillful
hands of the lovers of the art. In one of the coziest corners of
the building is a charming little kindergarten where the tender,
delicate, clinging minds are trained by a gradual and delightful
process.*

Mother Benedicta O'Rourke wrote of those first years at the
Academy where she was assigned to teach the "high room:"

*There were many hardships and inconveniences to be encountered, especially the
first year, as most of the force consisted of sick sisters. Sister Adelaide was
delicate, Sister Sylvester was recuperating from a severe operation, and Sister
Borromeo was by no means robust. However, she and I were the only ones left
to do the weekly washing as Sister Albertina was engaged with the music class.
Often we were busy with household duties till almost time to begin our school
work at nine o'clock. The building was heated by furnace (hot air), and as the
janitor, Fred Smith, resided at St. John's Home often the task of filling the
furnace with coal fell to the lot of Sister Borromeo and myself. Mr. Allen, a
saintly old man who had been retained at St. John's Home for some years was
finally engaged as janitor for the Academy. He was by no means a skilled fireman
but he was agreeable and did the best he could. The furnace had to be cleaned
one day. The water was drawn off and the necessary repairs completed toward
evening. As it was chilly, Mr. Allen was anxious to make us comfortable, forgot
to replenish the water in the boiler, started a roaring big fire. Soon the pipes
began to crackle, and the smell of burning paint filled the house. There was
consternation for an hour or so until the discovery was made. Quickly as it could
be accomplished the fire was extinguished and the boiler filled with water.*

*The first year was filled with just such experiences. One morning a pipe burst and
we took turns in holding a mop over the aperture while waiting for a plumber,
and preventing a flood sufficiently great to float the whole concern down to
Monroe Avenue. After the completion of the Annex more students poured in and
naturally the teaching force was increased.*

*Things looked brighter and moved along more smoothly. I must say that in spite
of all our troubles, all had a redeeming quality, viz., the ability to smile and
even to get a good laugh out of most of the calamities.*

*Sisters Borromeo, Monica and myself were under the tutelage of the Right
Reverend Bishop for Latin, spending on an average of six hours a week in class.
With our regular school work this was quite an additional,--I will not say burden,
but it took a great deal of extra time preparing assignments. Bishop was an ideal
teacher, taking the greatest interest in us, and seldom a lesson went by but a
good hearty laugh resulted at the expense of one or the other member of the
class. So the months were interspersed with joy days, and we jogged along with
a certain amount of success till 1905, when Holy Rosary Academy...was*

Old Sacred Heart Academy where you and I spent many happy days together

1906

Sisters Seraphine, Thomas, Monica, Eveline

Sisters Rose, Borromeo, Bertrand

Mother M. Benedicta
Principal, Sacred Heart Academy

Sister M. Agnes

*opened and Sister Albertina was sent there as Superior, and her place at Sacred Heart Academy as Superior devolved upon me. Along with the duties of full time teaching I can truly say that idle moments were few in number.*[5]

The Academy held its first graduation in June 1901 for Edna McGarry.[6] Commencements were held sometimes at the Academy, sometimes at the Ladies Literary Club on Sheldon Avenue or at nearby St. Cecilia auditorium. In the spring the seniors gave a public recital of music, sometimes of elocution at St. Cecilia's. There were annual dramatic presentations which attracted the civic community and were given full coverage in the city newspapers. Diplomas were presented for three curricula: classical-scientific, classical, and literary-scientific. There were also a commercial[7] and music-art curricula, and domestic science courses. In March 1906 the high school was accredited by the University of Michigan and affiliated with Trinity College, Washington, DC.

That fall the bishop took the first steps in organizing a Catholic high school for the city of Grand Rapids. The Girls Division was temporarily combined with Sacred Heart Academy with the Academy grade school girls going to St. Andrew's. This arrangement continued until 1909 when Girls Catholic Central was opened on the northwest corner of Jefferson and Oakes Street. The Dominican sisters continued as faculty for the relocated girls school, residing either at St. John's Home or Sacred Heart Academy. Boys Catholic Central was under the care of the Sisters of Charity from Cincinnati until 1914. For both divisions, Bishop Richter was listed as "the priest in charge."

In 1912 the congregation purchased property from the Collins' family to expand Sacred Heart Academy. With the move to the new motherhouse on Fulton Street in 1922, the academy was transferred there and by 1925 was called Marywood Academy. The original name was kept for some time in the college division until its evolution to Catholic Junior College. Sacred Heart Academy and the institutions it gave rise to, Marywood Academy and Catholic Junior College, later Aquinas College, came to have a central role in congregational life. The support of these institutions with personnel and material resources was considerable. The institutions were in turn major ways the congregation served the church and were known to the public and to thousands of alumni.

In 1900 another mission was added in the north. Sisters Seraphica Brandstetter, Monica Kress and Appolonia Corneliessens went to St. Michael parish, Suttons Bay, at the request of the pastor, Father Frederick H. Ruessman. During their first winter in Suttons Bay, Bishop Richter visited the sisters and found them living in barest simplicity. They had not a chair to offer the visiting bishop. He personally provided benches and desks for the struggling mission school.

Other schools were added in the next two years in Beal City, Alpine, Maple Grove, and Weare. Miss Mary Miller had been keeping school for the children of St. Philomena parish in Beal City for four months of each year. The pastor, Father John D. Englemann, arranged for three Dominican sisters, Sisters Antoninus Jellig, Rose Callahan, and Bartholomew Juenemann to conduct a full school program beginning in September 1901. In 1924 the sisters took over the direction of the local public school.

Holy Trinity parish, Alpine, also had a school conducted by lay faculty. At the request of Father Francis Beerhorst, Sisters Albina Pirk, Raphael O'Rourke, and Innocence Yaklin took over the school in September 1901. For a time the sisters assigned to Alpine also taught in the area public school. Another rural school was added on the eastern side of the state at Maple Grove (Layton Corners). Sisters Boniface Hartleb, Helena Morio, and Antoinette Knauf were the pioneer sisters there.

In September 1903 Sisters Letitia Smith, Raphael O'Rourke, and Assumpta Ott enrolled the first pupils of St. Joseph's parish, Weare. Father Francis Emmerich, pastor there for forty years, was legendary in his efforts to direct vocations to the congregation. As late as 1987, at the funeral of Sister Francis Clare Alvesteffer, the story was told of Father Emmerich's locking the young woman in church until she had made up her mind to join the Dominicans. Sister Francis Clare entered in 1915 and received a name in honor of her pastor, as did earlier vocations from the area, Sisters Francis Dennert and Emmerica Ziegler.

Throughout the parishes where the sisters were missioned, sisters and pastors influenced vocational choices and the congregation grew. The first quarter century in Michigan, 1877-1902, saw the evolution of Dominican presence from a mission of five nuns in the little frame house on Union Street, Traverse City, to an independent congregation of 104 members and 20 schools throughout the diocese of Grand Rapids.

The next twenty-five years of congregational activity began with the second General Chapter, August 7-9, 1903. Bishop Richter convened the session and presided over the election on August 7. There were now twenty-two sisters with passive voice, thirty-two with active voice. Once again Mother Aquinata was elected almost unanimously, having received 30 of the 32 votes cast. On the following day the Chapter celebrated the prescribed Chapter of Faults and the suffrages for the deceased members of the congregation. They then elected Sisters Clementina Coyle, Gonsalva Bankstahl, Villana Carmody, and Assissium Finnegan as "Mothers of Counsel." Sister Berchmans Deegan was elected by the council as treasurer and Mother Gonsalva as mistress of novices.

Both in 1903 and 1904 the sisters suffered loss through fire. In May 1903 the dwelling on the farm on Alpine Road near Grand Rapids burned. The sisters decided to rebuild, using a $400 insurance payment and an additional $600 from the treasury. There is no record of congregational use of the land, save for its inclusion on a list of possible sites for the future motherhouse.

Near midnight, March 8, 1904, there was an even greater loss. Fire destroyed Holy Rosary Academy in Essexville. The building, not yet ten years old, was a three-story, frame building, housing the sisters and about fifty boarders. Sister Chrysostoma, a pioneer from New York and the house infirmarian, discovered the fire and managed to rouse the household. Sister Alexia Flynn, one of the pioneer lay sisters, had not heard the alarm and was able to leave only by jumping from an upper story window. She broke a leg and her lower jaw and died several days later in Mercy Hospital in Bay City. Sister Gonzaga Udell was the last surviving eyewitness of the fire. She received the habit on January 3, 1904, and was sent at once to Holy Rosary to tutor in grammar and arithmetic. She recorded her memories of the fire and the opening of the new academy:[8]

*... on March 8, 1904, an event occurred that changed the immediate life plans for most of us at the Academy. At midnight, when the quiet of deep slumber hung over the entire house, a wild ring of the doorbell and the terrifying cries of "Fire!" broke the stillness...men returning from their Saturday night gathering at the local bar had caught sight of the flames and given the alarm. I was sleeping on the third floor, as were also the Superior, Mother Villana Carmody, and three little girls. I smelled no smoke but I heard the doorbell ringing and men shouting wildly, so I dressed hurriedly in the habit and veil and rushed to the one and only stairway. Two sisters had already preceded me and behind us came Mother herding the three children. Just as they reached the second floor,*

*the youngest child broke from Mother's hold and scampered back up the stairs and into bed. Clinging to the two children still with her, Mother called to one of the several men now running up the stairs to hold those two till she ran back for the third. Instead, the man himself dashed up the long flight. Before he could locate the child, however, and get her into his arms, the exit across the corridor was cut off by smoke and flames. A tongue of fire extending the entire length of the building was already emerging from the front window, blocking the chance of crossing the hall or even reaching the stairway. The fire department of the little town, however, though handicapped by lack of public waterworks, was by this time in operation, and in a matter of minutes both man and little girl were safe outside rescued by a net held beneath the window. They joined the still dazed group of sisters and girls as they watched their Academy go up in flames.*

*...The only near casualty was an invalid Sister who in climbing through a first-story window had broken her leg. By this time a vast crowd of people on foot and in horse-drawn vehicles had gathered. ...sisters and girls, many clothed only in night clothes, were hurriedly furnished with garments and wraps, put aboard horse-drawn vehicles, and taken into Bay City where convents and homes were hastily opened to receive them. Mother Villana and I were the last to leave the premises, riding in the ambulance with the injured Sister Alexia... to the hospital. There I was assisted into bed for the remaining hours of the night. ...*

*Mother Aquinata was given full details as soon as she could be reached by telephone early Sunday morning.... As soon as she had been assured that all occupants of the house were safe, she advised calm submission to Divine Providence and prayer for wisdom for us all in meeting the emergency. She arrived in Bay City on the first train from Grand Rapids, and in remarkably short time not only were matters pertaining to students and sisters' affairs adjusted, but plans for the rebuilding of a larger academy--this time in Bay City--were well under way. So eager were the people of the region to have a select school for their daughters that the parishes vied with one another in pointing out attractive spots in their vicinity for the most suitable location.*

Mother Aquinata and her council decided to rebuild the academy in Bay City and on a more permanent scale, "a building that would be a credit to the Community--one to be constructed on modern plans and in every way an improvement on the former Academy." The projected cost was $50,000; the school was to open on October 16, 1905. The insurance payment of $12,000 was augmented by $4000 from the treasury. "Collecting" by Sister Paschal Farnen provided additional monies. Property was purchased near St. Boniface church at 506 N. Lincoln Avenue at a cost of $5,334. Contracts amounting to $24,760 were let to area firms and ground was broken on June 20, 1904.

*Holy Rosary Academy*
*Essexville, Michigan*

*Holy Rosary Academy*
*Bay City, Michigan*

*RIGHT*
*Class of 1913*
*Holy Rosary Academy,*
*Bay City, Michigan*
*TOP LEFT Winifred Murray*
*(Sister Jane Marie)*

*BELOW*
*Sisters Berchman Deegan*
*and Reginald Reynolds*
*Carson City, Michigan*

Sister Gonzaga told of the new school's opening:

*...The new building was progressing rapidly...A number of us young sisters not yet assigned to missions were called to Bay City to help with the task of clearing away the sawdust and lumber remnants left by carpenters each day after they discontinued their work on the growing structure.*

*By October 1, the kitchen, girls' dining room, study hall, one dormitory, and several classrooms had been cleared for us. On the evening of October 1 a solemn but somewhat forlorn-looking procession of six sisters, one carrying the only source of light, a kerosene lantern, entered the not quite completed building where they began classes the following morning. It was to the sounds of carpenters' hammers and saws coming through the doorless openings that the scholastic activities of the new Academy began. Of us younger sisters who helped from the beginning of operations, Sister Mildred Hawkins was appointed to the music department and Sister Evangelista Rohrl to the lower grades in St. Boniface school. My appointment was to the Academy to teach history with a bit of English added.*

*Mother Aquinata remained with us several weeks after the school opened. She had appointed Sister Albertina Selhuber as Superior and teacher of music and German, and Sister Beatrice Cottrell as head of all scholastic activities in general...*

The new academy offered a comprehensive education for girls, including a music curriculum, until 1924. By that time the relocated Sacred Heart Academy in Grand Rapids provided a full academic program along with boarding facilities for girls at Marywood. Holy Rosary served as a boarding school for boys until 1971, when it became a coeducational day school. Congregational administration and ownership ceased in 1980 when the building was sold and the school was transferred to lay ownership in another location.

Additional rural missions were founded in these years. In 1906 Sisters DeChantal Burns, Gonzaga Udell, and Alexia Fruchtl began the parish school of Our Lady of Perpetual Help, Chesaning, at the request of Father Alphonsus Studer. In 1907 Sisters Berchmans Deegan, Reginald Reynolds, Terencia Finn, and Marcella Farnen opened school for about thirty pupils in St. Mary parish, Carson City, then under the direction of Father K.J. Whalen. A Dominican sister served there until 1989.

Sisters Adalbert Wagner, Gerard Simmel, and DeSales Rose pioneered in St. Mary's, Hannah. Further north, Sisters Clare Brophy, Carola Jones, and Innocence Yaklin opened St. Mary school in Charlevoix for Father Anastasius Rhodo, OFM. At Sacred Heart parish, Merrill, Pastor Francis Brogger welcomed the first Dominicans, Sisters Celestine McCue, Marcelline Horton, and

Jordan Ruhl. Within two years the sisters offered a high school program, which continued until 1960. Although the grade school program closed in 1971, sisters continue to serve the educational and pastoral needs of the parish.

Several city missions were added in 1906 and 1907. Since 1905 sisters had commuted from Bay City on the inter-urban train to Holy Family parish, Saginaw, for Sunday morning religious instruction. In fall 1906 a school formally opened there with the appointment of Sisters Ignatius Deegan, Ursula Lanciaux, Rose Marie McAllister, Dominic LeRoux, Thomasine St. Laurent, and Caroline Hart. Father Louis M. Prudhomme was pastor of the predominantly French parish. In the following year, 1907, the Sisters of Providence of St. Mary's of the Woods, Indiana, left St. Mary's, Saginaw, where they had served since 1874. Father Michael Dalton arranged with Mother Aquinata for the services of Sisters Eleanore Heinl, Bertrand Lalonde, Veronica Podleski, Gonzaga Udell, Pelagia Douglas, Raphael O'Rourke, Elizabeth Briggs and Annunciata Dwyer.

Sisters Seraphica Brandstetter and Clare Brophy commuted from St. John's Home during 1907 to the new Lithuanian parish of Saints Peter and Paul on the west side of Grand Rapids. The pastor, Father Vincent Matulaitis, arranged for the regular assignment of sisters for the fall of that year. Sisters Lewis Carmody and Alban Fredette were the first appointed there. The same arrangement existed in St. Anthony parish, Grand Rapids. Sisters Seraphine Wendling and Alberta Ryan, stationed at Sacred Heart Academy, had served the parish along with other duties. Sisters Assissium Finnegan and Evangelista Rohrl were the first assigned to the parish as a congregational mission. In 1908 Father Eikelmann moved to Byron Center and sought sisters for St. Sebastian school. Sisters Boniface Hartleb, Loretto Umlor, and Felicitas Gerhardt began the congregational ministry in September 1908. The congregation continued to send sisters there until 1970.

Mother Aquinata completed her second six-year term as mother general in the summer of 1909. The third General Chapter was held August 9-10 at St. John's Home. The previous day Bishop Richter announced the hour of election. There were sixty-five electors with active voice, twenty-eight of these had passive voice. Of the 65 votes cast, Mother Aquinata received 62.

Sisters Villana Carmody, Clementina Coyle, Assissium Finnegan, and Benedicta O'Rourke were elected as Mother Aquinata's third council. Sister Matthia Selhuber was elected as treasurer and Sister Benedicta as secretary general. Sister Gonsalva Bankstahl continued as mistress of novices. It was the custom that sisters serving on the general council were at the same time assigned to full-time responsibilities elsewhere. Thus, during Mother Aquinata's third administration, Sister Benedicta was superior-principal of Girls Catholic Central four of the six years, directress of the Novitiate Normal School, and near the end of the period, novice mistress. Sister Villana had charge of Holy Rosary Academy in Bay City. This practice continued until 1966.

One of the first acts of Mother Aquinata's third administration was the purchase of additional land on Alpine Road, "forty acres of good farm land," the Council Minutes note. This was the third piece of property acquired in the area, the first in 1892 being from Robert Graham for $8000; the second in 1893 from William Platte; and the 1909 acquisition, also from William Platte, for $6,200.

Late summer saw the sisters returning to their missions as well as their opening of several new schools, two in the north and two in central Michigan. On August 11, 1909, Sisters Ignatius Deegan, Winifred McCanney, and Elvara Vanesses began St. Joseph school in East Jordan for Pastor Burchard. The school closed in 1927. The same year Sisters Lewis Carmody, Clarissa Mazurek, Borromeo Clark, and Clotilda Gauthier opened St. Mary school in St. Charles, a mining community near Chesaning. Father Alphonsus Studer had arranged with Mother Aquinata for their services.

In Saginaw another large school was added to the sisters' care. Sisters Eveline Mackey, Leona Malloy, Alexandra Gallagher, Agatha Battle and Norberta Boerraker were sent to replace the Sisters of Providence (St. Mary's of the Woods, Indiana) at Saints Peter and Paul school on the west side. Father Edward LeFevre was pastor. The original parish school was a former public school building, constructed in 1837. In 1910 a new building was opened, and in 1913 the school was affiliated with the University of Michigan. The Dominican sisters first lived in the former Fordney estate on Gratiot Avenue, the later site of the parish high school.

Mother Aquinata also supplied the first faculty of sisters for St. Mary's, Gaylord, at the request of Father Francis Kaczmarek, pastor from 1907 to 1913. Since 1894, lay teachers had conducted a school in the parish. Sisters Raymond Hudzinski, Casimir Zukowski, Edward Sturzmowska, Dolores Winowiecka and Juliana Winowiecka were the first sisters assigned to this predominantly Polish parish in 1910. High school classes were added in 1925.

A new mission area in the northeast of the state was begun in 1911 with the opening of St. Anne school, Alpena. Sisters Cherubina Seymour, Ursula Lanciaux, Ambrose Dupuis, Teresa St. Laurent, Francis Regis Saucier, Stephen Lovay, and Ursuline Pilon were sent to this primarily French parish then under the care of Father Charles DeQuoy. By the end of the decade a high school had been added. In 1950 the parishes in Alpena collaborated in the development of the Catholic Central high school, staffed by Dominican sisters from Adrian, Felician sisters from Livonia, Michigan, and Dominican sisters from Grand Rapids.

Two grade schools were also added in the northwest of the state in 1911, one in St. Paul parish, Onaway, and the other in St. Anthony parish, Mancelona. Sisters Xavier Connelly, Ildephonse Ryan, and Bertha Gutknecht opened St. Paul school, Onaway with about a hundred pupils, for the pastor, Father Oswald T. McGinn. Sisters Reginald Reynolds and Raphael O'Rourke began the school at St. Anthony's mission, then cared for by a Franciscan priest from Petoskey. In the 1920's fires destroyed area forests and lumber mills and the population gradually shifted. Onaway, Mancelona, and East Jordan were forced to close their parish schools in 1926 and 1927. In 1914 another school was begun in the north, St. Augustine's in Boyne Falls, by Sisters Celestine McCue, Hilary Pawlowski, Stanislaus Sowlewski, and Huberta Charron. It was closed in 1920 due to changes in population.

The increasing number of schools throughout the diocese and changing requirements of education caused the sisters to standardize the training for teaching. In August 1910 a Novitiate Normal School was formally established. Sister Benedicta O'Rourke, principal of Girls Catholic Central and member of the general council, was appointed directress. It was to be located at Holy Angels convent, Traverse City, where the novitiate was officially based. At Bishop Richter's request, however, the novitiate was transferred to St John's Home on March 5, 1911.[9] In March 1912 Bishop Richter sent Father Michael Gallagher to St. John's Home as resident chaplain and spiritual director. Father Gallagher immediately began a regular program of Greek, Latin, and philosophy classes for the novices and postulants, continuing even after he became coadjutor bishop on July 5, 1915.

More calls for sisters came from parishes in Saginaw. At Sacred Heart, a "German parish" on the east side, lay faculty had kept a school for over twenty-five years. Finally in 1913 Mother Aquinata was able to send sisters to Father Joseph Reiss. Sisters Rosalie Kropf, Alma Schweikert, and Justina Schwind were sent to staff the school, commuting the first year from St. Mary's, about seven blocks away. The pastor was exceptional in his presence to the sisters and their work. Until his death in 1921 he was a regular member of the school faculty as well as choir director.

Sisters were also sent to two predominantly Polish parishes in Saginaw, St. Josaphat's and St. Casimir's, to open grade schools in 1913. Sisters Theodore Jasinski, Edward Sturmowski and Gelasia Grochowolski began St. Josaphat school and Sisters Clarissa Mazurek and Leonissa Housten, St. Casimir school. Both of the churches were then cared for as missions by Father Francis Kaczmarek, pastor of Holy Rosary parish.

In 1914 Mother accepted requests for missions in Boyne Falls, Fisherville, and Grand Rapids. Sisters Ildephonse Ryan and Natalia Ruczinski were the first assigned to St. Anthony's, Fisherville where they conducted a grade school. A rare financial ledger shows that in September 1914 the three sisters received a "start up" fund of $6 from the motherhouse. To it was added the parish salary of $50, less than $20 per sister per month. Outlays for the month included:

| | |
|---|---|
| *Fare* | *3.90* |
| *Groceries* | *23.10* |
| *Fruit* | *5.66* |
| *Postage* | *1.00* |
| *Butter* | *2.45* |
| *Freight* | *2.12* |
| *Fish* | *2.65* |

The first month at a mission had the unusual expenses of fare and freight and the laying in of staples. By the next month, however, there would be some income from music lessons ($4.00 in the case of Fisherville) but also the expectation of money to be sent to the motherhouse, usually half of the salary and all of the music money. It seems to have been a universal practice among congregations of religious women to support their institutions in this way. The old saw, "Give a music lesson, feed a novice," was not far from the truth.

In 1914 Bishop Richter asked the Dominican sisters to replace the Sisters of Charity in St. Andrew cathedral parish, Grand Rapids. Father P.J. McManus had organized a grade school in 1872 and had secured the services of the Sisters of Mercy. In 1877, the year the Dominicans came to Michigan, the Sisters of Charity of Cincinnati replaced the Sisters of Mercy at St. Andrew's. In 1914 they were to depart, primarily for salary considerations. The earlier assignment of Girls Catholic Central to the Dominicans may have influenced their decision inasmuch as vocations from this source were more likely to be directed to the Dominicans.

The Dominican sisters were now responsible for both boys' and girls' divisions of the Catholic Central as well as St. Andrew grade school. Sisters Philomena Kildee, Xavier Connelly, Henrietta McAllister, Hyacinth Hines, Lawrence Cuddahy, Seraphine Wendling, Alexandra Gallagher, Mildred Hawkins, Maurice Mavelle, Marcella Farnen, Beata LaNore, Eustasia Boundy, Benedict Pashak, Francis Marie LaPorte, Joseph Marie Kuhn, Marguerite Zuker, Jerome Smithers, Richard Kannally, Agatha Battle, and George Little were the first assigned there.

Boys Catholic Central was the last mission Mother Aquinata assumed. It was both an accomplishment and an anxiety, for she realized it would make great demands on personnel as the city and its parishes were growing rapidly. The sisters moved to the mission house on August 4, 1914, the day of celebration of Mother's Golden Jubilee. Sister Philomena, the principal and superior, recorded that Mother visited the convent on the day school opened, anxiously awaiting the sisters' enrollment reports. The diocesan annual report for 1915 indicates there were 648 in the grade school; 158 boys and 140 girls in Catholic Central; and 21 Dominican sisters serving the two schools.[10]

Fifty years had passed since Appolonia Fiegler had received the Dominican habit and the name Sister Mary Aquinata of the Most Blessed Sacrament at Holy Cross convent, Brooklyn. Mother was reluctant to have any public acknowledgement of the event. At Bishop Richter's insistence, the council met in August 1913 to plan for the golden jubilee and to set the date.

The celebration was, in fact, a four-day event with festivities from August 3 to 7, 1914. The occasion had been anticipated with a mid-summer program on June 28 by the "Little Orphans," to whom Mother was a well-loved and kindly member of the St. John's

Golden Jubilee of Ven. Mother Aquinata Gra[...]

*Mother Aquinata Fiegler,*
*Sisters Boniface Hartleb*
*and Cyprian McCarron (NY)*

Aug. 4. 1914

GOLDEN JUBILEE
CONGRATULATIONS
BY THE COMMUNITY
Monday, August 3d, 1914
4 O'CLOCK

❧ ❧ ❧

1 JUBILEE MARCH — — —                                    Eckert
      (4 Pianos, 28 Violins, Viola, Cello, Harp)

2 ADDRESS

3 AVE MARIA            — — —                              Stewart
      (24 Voices)

4 LE DEPART       — — — —                                Dancla
      (16 Violins)

5 "TRIBUTE"

6 "INTERMEZZO AND REVERIE"
      (Harp, Violins, Violas, Cello, Organ, Piano)       Pizzi

7 "JUBILATE"   — — —                                     Scholz
      (Entire Music Corps)

8 CORONATION MARCH                             Meyerbeer
      (Harp, Violins, Violas, Cello, Pianos)

PRESENTATION OF GIFTS
FROM MISSIONS AND SCHOOLS

THE SISTERS

Home household. On Monday, August 3, at four o'clock the sisters extended their special jubilee congratulations with a program of music, an address, and presentation of gifts from missions and schools. The program of the day lists the selections and the number of voices and range of instruments, viz. 4 pianos, 28 violins, viola, cello, and harp for the opening "Jubilee March" by Eckert.

At nine o'clock the following day, the feast of Saint Dominic, Bishop Richter celebrated a Pontifical High Mass, with Bishop Gallagher and Fathers R.Van Rooy, O.Praem., Joseph Bauer, Edward K.Cantwell, CSsR, John G. Wyss, Charles White, and John J. McAllister assisting. The sermon was given by the Provincial of the Dominican fathers from Washington, DC, Father James R. Meagher, OP. The Mass was followed by Papal Benediction and the formal jubilee ceremony of the Dominican Rite. There was an elaborate banquet for the bishops and priests and later in the afternoon a program of music and verse by the alumnae of Sacred Heart Academy. The day concluded with Solemn Benediction of the Blessed Sacrament and a reception.

Solemn High Mass began the events of Wednesday, August 5. Father Casimir Skory was celebrant, assisted by Fathers Henry P. Maus, Thomas J. Reid, and Joseph Pietrasik. Bishop Gallagher gave the sermon. In the afternoon, the alumnae of Girls Catholic Central presented a pageant highlighting Mother's attributes. Solemn Benediction was followed by a reception. Thursday morning, August 6, at eight o'clock Solemn High Mass was sung. Father John A. Schmitt of St. Andrew parish was chief celebrant, assisted by Fathers John E. Troy, George Dequoy, and Charles Harrison, CSsR. Father Joseph Vogl preached. Throughout the afternoon there was an informal reception for friends and benefactors. Solemn Benediction closed the day's public events. In the evening, the novices presented their tribute, "The Golden Rosary of Years."

Jubilee was concluded with "Memorial Day" on Friday, August 7. Father Robert W. Brown, pastor of St. James parish, Grand Rapids and a silver jubilarian that year, celebrated the Solemn High Mass. Fathers Jerome Preisser, OMC, and Alphonsus Studer were deacons; Father Joseph Kaminski was master of ceremonies. Father Thomas W. Albin preached the sermon. After Solemn Benediction, the *Te Deum* was sung and the jubilee ceremonies ended. A special commemorative booklet, "The Fiftieth Year," was printed for the jubilee. It is both an acknowledgment of Mother Aquinata's jubilee and a brief history of the congregation.[11]

Less than a year later, in early May 1915, many of those friends who had celebrated Masses, presented programs, and called on Mother during the days of jubilee gathered for her funeral. In December 1914 she became ill and cancer was diagnosed. She was advised to see a specialist in Chicago. Accompanied by Sister Paschal Farnen, she went to Mercy Hospital in January 1915 for surgical treatment. Reports were favorable and it was thought she would recuperate better in a warmer climate. Several senior sisters journeyed to Chicago for a visit prior to Mother's departure for Santa Rosa Hospital in San Antonio, Texas, on February 24. The first days there were pleasant and restorative but on March 8 there was an unprecedented cold spell and snowfall. Mother was forced to three weeks' bedrest with what was thought to be severe rheumatism.

On Good Friday the sisters were informed that Mother would return shortly with little hope of recovery. She arrived by train on April 8 and was taken to St. John's Home for her final days. In order that Mother would be available to the sisters, her bed was placed in the community room. Sisters from the missions came to her bedside for farewells. On days when she felt strong enough, she looked over a Constitution draft, for it had long been her desire that the congregation should have a Constitution of its own.

In late April Mother called the sisters together and spoke her farewell:

> *My dear sisters, do not go into the world; have nothing to do with its gossip, its seeming grandeur nor its styles and fashions, but bring the world to you by your goodness and exhortations; attract it by your example of a truly Christian life, a life in conformity with evangelical counsels, and then by your contact with those children who in later years must needs mingle with the world, you will elevate their tastes and teach them to reduce to practice the Gospel precepts, by which means alone peace is preserved in the family, the basis of society, and thus peace and union may be preserved among nations. Do this, and the work entrusted to your care will continue to be a subject of joy to men and angels.*

*There, the First Novice*

Just after midnight on April 30 Bishop Gallagher brought Holy Communion to her. When it was time for the community Mass, Mother asked the sisters to attend. Later in the morning Father Byrnes, a Redemptorist priest from St. Alphonsus, visited, and Mother asked that she see him alone. At his request she gave a blessing to him and all the sisters. They remained at her beside throughout the day. She died at three o'clock, Saturday, May 1, while the *Salve* was being sung. On Monday, May 3, her body was taken to the chapel, which had been draped in mourning black, for visitation by clergy, religious, and countless friends and associates. Bishop Richter stood by the casket and wept openly, his sobs heard throughout the chapel.

The Solemn Requiem Mass was sung at eight o'clock Tuesday, May 4, by Bishop Richter, assisted by six clerics. More than fifty priests attended with the sisters and friends. At the Gospel, Bishop Richter, sometimes with tears, spoke of the courageous work Mother had undertaken for the Catholic Faith when priests were few, parishes poor, and conditions so very difficult. He told of the evolution of the group from its New York motherhouse to an authorized diocesan community. He wanted the sisters to keep in mind that Mother's last official act was to prepare the title page for the printer's draft of the Constitution. Bishop Richter said that Mother had built so wisely that the community was, by her labors and grace, solid and lasting. In his message of condolence, Bishop Schrembs spoke of Mother as the sisters' "Tower of Strength."

At the conclusion of the Mass Bishop Gallagher, co-adjutor of the diocese and chaplain to the congregation, delivered a formal and moving eulogy. The burial service ended, Mother Aquinata's body was taken from St. John's Home to St. Andrew Cemetery, burial place of the city's Catholic pioneers, in a slow, solemn procession of carriages and automobiles.

The Sunday, May 2, edition of *The Grand Rapids Herald*, the city's morning newspaper, announced Mother's death and summarized the development of the community with over three hundred sisters, forty-two schools, three academies, the orphan asylum, and two Catholic Central high schools. "She was," the article concluded, "regarded as one of the most beloved members of the Catholic sisterhood throughout the entire country."

# 6

# SIMPLE AND GOOD
# MOTHER GONSALVA BANKSTAHL

*I*t fell to Mother Villana Carmody, first mother of counsel, to take over the administration of the congregation until a Chapter of Election was called. Mother Villana was born in County Kerry, Ireland, in 1854. She came to the United States when she was about twenty and entered the Congregation of the Most Holy Rosary, Second Street, New York, in 1879. She was among the pioneers at Port Austin, then at St. Joseph's, Adrian, and in 1891 she was named superior at St. Joseph's, Bay City. The early years were full of hardship, with work far beyond the sisters' strength and too little fuel during cold winters. As a result Sister Villana's health was fragile. She was superior of Holy Rosary Academy, Essexville, at the time of the fire. In 1903 she was first elected to Mother Aquinata's council. She remained in Bay City as superior of the new Holy Rosary Academy during the years she was councilor except for the few months she was acting mother general.[1]

In July 1915 the council with Bishop Richter set the election date for August 11, 1915. By 1915 eighty-seven sisters had active voice, sixty-five of these with passive voice as well. Of the 87 votes cast, Mother Mary Gonsalva Bankstahl received 85. Her four councilors were Sisters Loyola Finn, Seraphica Brandstetter, Adelaide McCue, and Benedicta O'Rourke. Sister Matthia Selhuber was elected treasurer and Sister Benedicta O'Rourke secretary general. Mother and her council chose Sister Albertina Selhuber as novice mistress.[2] All were elected for a three year term.

After the election Mother Villana returned to Bay City as superior of Holy Rosary Academy. She had a strong premonition of her coming death and gave away all but the barest necessities. On October 28, 1916, at the age of 62, she died of heart failure. She was buried in St. Patrick Cemetery, Bay City.

On August 26, 1915, the annual meeting of the trustees of the corporation was held. Board membership was reorganized with

Sister Gonsalva as president, Sister Loyola as vice president, Sister Benedicta as secretary, Sister Seraphica as procurator, and Sister Matthia as bursar. Selecting a suitable site for a motherhouse was discussed, as well as the authorization of $50 to be expended on the house on the Platte Farm.

At the time of her election as successor to Mother Aquinata, Mother Gonsalva Bankstahl was 55, fourth in order of seniority within the congregation. Mary Bankstahl was born in Westphalia, Germany, on December 24, 1860. Her parents, John and Mariann Schroeder Bankstahl, immigrated soon after her birth and settled in Baltimore. Her earliest formal education was with the School Sisters of Notre Dame. Her education and upbringing gave her a deep appreciation for the arts and a gracious manner which remained with her until death. Her spiritual director guided her to the Dominican sisters in New York. She entered Holy Rosary convent, Second Street, on February 23, 1878, and received the habit from Mother Hyacinth Scheininger on May 24, 1878.

She was among the volunteers to the Michigan missions and in fall 1878 was assigned to Port Austin, among those who had narrowly missed drowning in Lake Huron. She returned to New York for novitiate training and was professed there on June 2, 1879. She taught in several New York schools but longed to return to Michigan. In 1883 she was sent to St. Mary's, Muskegon. In 1891 she opened St. Joseph mission in Grand Rapids, and in 1894, Holy Rosary Academy, Essexville. From 1904 to 1910 she was mistress of novices in Traverse City, and from 1910 to 1915 was superior at Holy Angels, Traverse City. She was elected councillor for all three of Mother Aquinata's terms, a total of eighteen years.

During Mother Gonsalva's administration, August 1915 to November 1919, there were significant changes in the nation and in the Church. The country had been drawn into The Great War against Germany. The Catholic Church in the United States had come of age; it was no longer considered mission territory. A Code of Canon Law had been promulgated. The local Church had lost its pioneer guiding spirit.

On Tuesday, December 26, 1916, Bishop Richter died after only a few days of illness. His body lay in state in the crepe-hung cathedral all of Wednesday and Thursday. Vigil was kept day and night until the Pontifical Requiem on Friday morning. Bishop

*Mother Villana Carmody, OSD,*
*(1854-1916), choir nun,*
*on her profession day,*
*August 28, 1880*

*Mother Gonsalva Bankstahl, OSD,*
*Second Mother General*
*(fl. 1915-1919)*

Gallagher, his successor, was celebrant with many priest assistants and pallbearers. Over three hundred sisters of the congregations within the diocese attended the funeral. Many were turned away from the ceremony and stood outside the cathedral as the bell tolled. The body, temporarily placed in a receiving vault at St. Andrew Cemetery, was transferred to Lima, Ohio, in March 1917. In 1933 the body was relocated in Mount Calvary Cemetery in St. Mary parish, Grand Rapids. Bishop Joseph Schrembs[3] eulogized the many ways Bishop Richter had taken to heart his motto, "Prepare ye the way of the Lord"--as master builder, faithful shepherd of souls, and kind friend of the church in Grand Rapids.

Bishop Michael Gallagher, a native of Bay County, was well known to the diocese and in particular to the sisters. Since 1912 he had served the sisters and orphans at St. John's Home as resident chaplain, and at the same time the vicar general of the diocese. On September 8, 1915, he was consecrated as coadjutor-bishop of the diocese. Upon the death of Bishop Richter, he immediately succeeded to the see. He remained in residence at St. John's Home until January 1917 when he moved to the episcopal residence next to St. Andrew cathedral.

One of the new bishop's first projects was the renovation of the cathedral and the episcopal residence built in 1888. Refurbishing was completed for the celebration of his Silver Jubilee on June 20, 1918. For the occasion the Dominican sisters sent a jubilee poem, "Who is Like God," a hand-lettered meditation on the bishop's name, Michael.

Within a year Bishop Gallagher was transferred to the Diocese of Detroit, the see vacant since the death of Bishop Foley in 1918. He remained in Detroit until his death on January 20, 1937. His last official act on behalf of the congregation was to preside at the funeral of Mother Benedicta O'Rourke in November 1935. Just two weeks before his death he visited Marywood. All the sisters gathered in the Brown Parlor to speak with their old friend. Sister Benvenuta Carroll, who had seen to the chaplain's needs at St. John's Home during his years there, simply greeted him, "My Bishop" and he responded, "My Sister." He was remembered by the sisters as their gracious advisor and teacher, "their bishop."

The third bishop of Grand Rapids was the Most Reverend Edward Dionysius Kelly, Auxiliary Bishop of Detroit since 1911. He, too, was a native of Michigan, born in Van Buren County in 1860 and ordained by Bishop Foley in 1885. He was installed as bishop of the diocese on April 9, 1919. A gala civic welcome was given on June 12, 1919. His episcopacy in Grand Rapids was relatively short, death coming on Friday, March 26, 1926, but his accomplishments were many and far-ranging. His funeral eulogy was preached by the Archbishop of Cincinnati, John T. McNicholas, OP, in the midst of the Holy Week observances at St. Andrew cathedral.

*The Catholic Vigil*, the diocesan paper founded by Bishop Kelly, praised him as the "Builder Bishop" and named seventy-seven sites throughout the diocese where buildings were erected or modernized during his administration. It appears that the affiliation of St. John's Home with the Grand Rapids Welfare Union in 1919 was part of the episcopal program of modernizing. With it came even greater need for the sisters to have a permanent motherhouse.

Since the election of 1915 the congregation had taken several steps to secure its own motherhouse. May 31, 1917, the chief topic at a formal board meeting was "whether the Motherhouse of the Community should be built on the property in Alpine Township, or take steps to secure a more desirable site." It was decided that "a new site should be purchased located more remote from the factory district than said Alpine property." On June 12, 1917, Mr. James Malloy, a Grand Rapids realtor, was authorized to purchase the Charles Fox property of approximately seventeen acres on East Fulton Road.[4] A payment of $200 was made on the required $17,500. On July 6, an adjoining seven and half acres were also purchased. The property selected reflected the current ideal of sheltered female education in a sylvan setting and of a motherhouse as quasi-cloister.

During Mother Gonsalva's administration seven missions were added to the congregation's care. In late summer of 1915 Sisters Ignatius Deegan, Winifred McCanney, DeLourdes Griffin, and Louella Blanchard opened the school in St. Joseph parish, Auburn, then under the care of Father John MacDonald. The congregation continued to send sisters there until 1927. The Sisters of Mercy later reopened the mission.

That same fall St. Henry school in Rosebush (Vernon) was opened by Sisters Clementina Coyle, Edwardine Sands, Lorraine Gibson, Catherine Marie Roberts and Annunciata Dwyer. The opening of the school was announced in the *Clare Courier*:

*St. Henry's Handsome New School - Finest Rural Parish in the State...Modern in Every Appointment. Erected under the guiding hand of Rev. John McAllister in Vernon Township, the school's dimensions are 40 by 70 feet, two stories and a well lighted, airy basement. Approached by both front and rear by wide halls of easy access, on either side of which is a large attractive classroom, lighted in the manner approved by the State....In the southeast corner of the second floor is a large roomy chapel, and to the southwest is the high school classroom. The remainder of the second floor contains the music room and the sisters' living quarters and dormitory.[5]*

Tuition and board was set at $10 a month, tuition alone at $1.00 a month. Father McAllister was to teach French, Latin, and literature. Sister Blanche was in charge of the dormitories and dining rooms as well as keeping the children out of mischief. Sister Lorraine was to teach music, and Mother Clementine to "train the young minds in domestic science." There were 117 pupils the first year and 27 boarders the following year. The girls slept on the third floor of the school in small dormitories, the little boys in a room next to the first classroom on the ground floor; the older boys were on the top floor of the rectory. There was a windmill to pump water and an acetylene gas plant to provide lighting. The sisters kept a garden, a cow and chickens to provide dairy goods and vegetables for the boarders and themselves. Children came from Vernon township, Mount Pleasant and Clare, and as far away as Bay City and Saginaw. The academy, all grades and high school, continued until 1927. It reopened in 1929 as a grade school, but the congregation could no longer send sisters.

In 1916 Mother Gonsalva agreed to staff another school on the east side of the state. Sisters Alberta Ryan, Martin Feyan, and Modesta Ejziel began St. Joseph school in East Tawas. The pastor, Father Thomas Albin, was later to serve as chaplain for the congregation at Marywood. Mount Carmel, Saginaw, was also opened in the fall of 1916. Sisters Xavier Connelly, Petronilla Tureck, and Rosaria Franchowiak were the first sisters to serve the predominantly Italian parish where Father Alfred Hyland was pastor.

On August 21, 1917, Sisters Aloysius Miller, Anastasia Hebert, and two novices, Sisters Electa Miller and Paul Schaub, opened St. Joseph school in West Branch with Sister Caroline Hart as the "House Sister." Sister Electa left an account of their beginnings:

*We were on the train on our way to West Branch...Sisters Aloysius, Anastasia and Caroline were sitting down in the coach, but Sister Paul and I were standing because all the seats were taken. After the train had travelled some distance, a man seated near where the other sisters were rose and went to the smoker, leaving his wife and his little girl...Sister Paul took advantage of the situation and sat down next to the little girl. A short while later the man returned, took in the situation...and cried out to his wife, "Why did you let that wicked woman sit by our little girl?" Sister Paul was so taken by surprise that she jumped up quickly and walked fast towards where the sisters were sitting. The five of us were horrified, and shocked at being the object of so much attention, for the passengers turned and stared at us with wide-opened eyes. Our friend kept on in his loud voice, expressing his displeasure for us....*

*Suddenly another voice was heard and...a man standing offered Sister Paul his seat...and going up to the other man's seat said, "You've said enough, don't say another word or I'll take care of you." A priest somewhere in the coach rose and walked towards me, offered me his seat and also walked out of the coach. Shortly afterward the conductor came into the coach and nearing the sisters, stopped...and spoke to them, faced the man who had shocked everyone by his speech. "I hear you are going to West Branch, sisters. You are needed there and will do much good."*

The pastor, Father William J. Hasenberg, asked two women of the parish to meet their train. They took the sisters to a house adjacent to the jail, "empty except for a pile of mattresses, a pile of bedsprings, and a third pile of unassembled prison bedsteads." The kitchen had a table on its back, and five chairs throughout the room. Their inspection was interrupted by a neighbor bringing blueberries. The sisters accepted the gift but said they had no dishes. Soon neighbors poured in with dishes, spoons, cream, and later a fine meal. Into the evening, citizens called with household goods and greetings. By midnight the house was completely furnished and things were in place. Only when the sisters moved to rooms in the new school two weeks later did they learn that the house was considered haunted and had been perpetually vacant. This inauspicious beginning unfolded into seventy-five years' presence of Dominican sisters in St. Joseph parish.

In 1918, as a result of transactions between the dioceses of Grand Rapids and Detroit, two rural parish schools near Grand Rapids, were temporarily transferred to the Diocese of Grand Rapids and the territory around Birch Run was transferred to Detroit. St. Mary's, New Salem, had a school since its early years, staffed at one time by Franciscan sisters from Wisconsin. In 1894 they left and the school was given to the care of Dominican sisters from Adrian. During the great influenza epidemic of 1917-1918 two sisters missioned there died and were buried in the parish cemetery. With the boundary change, the congregation was asked to staff the school. Mother Gonsalva appointed Sisters Sienna Wendling, Matilda Henze, and Seraphine Wendling to take over the school at St. Mary's, New Salem, under the direction of Father Charles Bolte. Sister Sienna, who remained there six years, described the country convent-school when the sisters began their work:

*When we arrived at this mission, the convent and school were in one building, the convent on one side, and the school on the other side with a hall in between. On the first floor in the convent we had a kitchen, community room, and a small partition of the kitchen served as the refectory. The second floor had three bedrooms, a small chapel and a bathroom. There were three rooms on the first floor for school use. One class room was taught by me, and I had grades 1, 2, and 3. Sister Matilda had the second classroom...grades 4, 5, 6. Sister Seraphine then had grades 7-8 in the last classroom. Sister Matilda taught piano after school and on Saturdays for we needed some cash to pay for our necessities, and since we received no salary, the music teacher provided this. The people of the parish were very kind...and brought in fruit, vegetables and meat in abundance, so we can say they fed us well.*

The mission was under the care of the sisters from 1918 to 1930 and from 1941 to 1970. The second of the transferred parishes, Visitation, North Dorr, was just two miles away. Father A.O. Bossler, the pastor, arranged for the coming of Sisters Marcelline Horton, Amata Baader, Wilfrida Perrault, and Romaine Willing in August 1918.

St. John's Home became one of the agencies in the Federation of Social Agencies in January 1918. In May 1918 the sisters opened Loretto Home for Infants in property loaned them by Michael Finn. Loretto Home averaged a daily census of 18 infants until its closing in 1922.

Mother Gonsalva authorized further educational work for the sisters in addition to the Novitiate Normal program. In June 1917 the first of many groups of Dominicans began attending the Sisters Summer School of the Catholic University of America in Washington, DC. Sisters Benedicta O'Rourke and Estelle Hackett continued there during the 1917-1918 academic year, receiving Bachelor of Arts degrees in June 1918. Beginning in June 1918 when women were first admitted to the University of Notre Dame, five sisters were assigned there.[6] In August 1919 eleven sisters took the State of Michigan Teacher Examinations in Lansing. Five sisters qualified for the "all subjects" level with State Life Certificates in October 1919. College courses and teacher certification programs were a permanent feature of the sisters' lives during the school year and the "long vacation."

Unremitting hard work began to take its toll on the health of many sisters. In the post-war years the sisters were affected by the nationwide epidemic of the Spanish influenza. The first victim in the congregation was Sister Irmina Latuszek, who received the habit on her deathbed on October 3, 1918. The community of Suttons Bay was so badly stricken that the sisters closed the school and went from home to home to assist the ill. Sister Mechtildis Weigl died in Suttons Bay on December 17, 1918, and was buried there. Sister Julia Chesney died in Lake Leelanau on February 29, 1920. The sisters were not spared from tuberculosis, endemic throughout the nation in the first decades of the century. Many fell ill during these years.

At the time of the transfer of the congregation from Second to Third Order in 1896, Mother Aquinata had corresponded with the office of the Master General of the Order in Rome to receive affirmation of the congregation's status as Dominican. She had been assured that such was forthcoming. On her deathbed she dictated a letter to Father Thomas Esser, OP, Socius to the Master General, asking his assistance in getting the desired diploma. Nothing had arrived and by 1918 doubts were expressed about the community's status. Mother Gonsalva consulted Father Clement Thuente, OP, retreat master and mentor to several Dominican groups, who arranged for the diploma of affiliation, dated November 18, 1918.

In early August 1918 Bishop Gallagher and council fixed the date for the election of mother general for August 11, 1918. Mother Gonsalva was elected for a second term with Sisters Benedicta O'Rourke, Seraphica Brandstetter, Adelaide McCue, and Loyola Finn the members of her council. The council selected Sister Albertina as mistress of novices, Sister Loyola as secretary general, Sister Seraphica as procurator, and Sister Matthia as bursar. The chief work of the administration was to build the much needed motherhouse.

On September 28, 1918, Mother and her council met on the grounds of the new motherhouse site. Joseph Brielmeier, prospective architect from Milwaukee, James Malloy, realtor, and a Mr. Cukerski, landscape gardener, joined them. Sisters James Walsh, Alphonsus O'Rourke, Cyrilla Hallahan, and Eveline Mackey were also invited, along with the chaplain, Father Joseph Vogl, for a preliminary discussion of the style and requirements of the new building. Plans were submitted by early December 1918 and studied by all the sisters. Funding the project became a major concern for the next thirty years.

The following year, on September 8, 1919, Bishop Kelly called the council to a meeting at his residence and urged them to begin construction at once. The renters in the house on the property were paid to terminate their lease. A local firm, John McNabb and Son, was awarded the contract and excavation began on November 15, 1919. A certain urgency was impressed upon the sisters to complete their plans and to leave St. John's Home. This was the expressed reason for Mother Gonsalva's resignation, the announcement of which was in her only extant circular letter, dated November 3, 1919. It read:

*Dear Sisters:*

*When you so generously gave me your allegiance at the election of August, 1918, I did not realize that ere long the building of the new motherhouse would become a necessity.*

*Now that it has been decreed by the Right Reverend Bishop that the plans must be put into execution without further delay, I find that the strenuous labor required for this undertaking is beyond my ability and have therefore asked to be relieved.*

*You are already aware that Mother Benedicta was elected First Mother of Counsel and by virtue of her office will take charge of affairs until August, 1921.*

*I hope you will prove your loyalty and submission to our Holy Rule by your entire submission to her commands.*

*Thanking you for your kindness and patience with me in the past, and placing you all under the patronage of the Blessed Mother, I remain*

*Faithfully yours in St. Dominic,*
*Sister Mary Gonsalva.*

Undoubtedly, ill-health was a factor in the decision. Ordinary administration might somehow have been managed; the tasks of immediate building and fund-raising were too great. Mother Gonsalva remained at St. John's Home and continued her contacts with the sisters. In late January 1920 she acknowledged feastday gifts and messages. She wrote to Sister Cecilia Giles on January 24:

*It was so kind of you to remember Jan. 10th and I appreciate your very acceptable gift. Our feast days are the links that bind our past and present. I always feel a renewal of energy when so many of my friends remember me and help to make the day bright and joyous. But one by one these links are broken ones as we see our dear and cherished ones sink into the grave. Does it not seem sad that we shall not meet dear Sr. Camilla and Rev. Fr. Schmitt here below.*

*But then we are only reminded that our time is approaching very rapidly and we may hope to meet them soon in the great beyond.*

Early in 1921 Mother Gonsalva was confined to her room with a worsening heart condition. On Sunday, February 13, she suffered a stroke, and Father Vogl gave her the last sacraments. She was semi-conscious but unable to speak her remaining ten days on earth. She died on February 23, 1921, in early morning, in her forty-second year of religious profession and her sixty-first year. Her funeral was held at St. John's chapel on Saturday, February 26. Bishop Kelly sang the Pontifical Requiem Mass; Father Vogl preached the sermon, remarking on her prudence, her peace-loving, unselfish and charitable presence to all, "a Mother in every sense of the word."

A poignant eulogy came from Sisters Cyprian and Ligouri McCarron, early companions of Mother Gonsalva in religious life, who had shared the pioneer years in Michigan and who chose to return to New York.

*Dear Mother Benedicta and Sisters:*

*Your telegram reached us about two o'clock and both of us appreciate fully your kindness in sending us the same. You have lost a good woman, but none of us would wish it otherwise. Dear Mother Gonsalva! When I look back over some three decades of years since first I was associated with her in the vocation school-work--these days of hoping, planning, working--for the then growing community, my eyes fill with tears at the backward glance, the happy outlook upon life just budding, the plans we would build... even then in our wildest dreams, we never dared to hope for such a fruition of young hopes. Poor Mother! I can see her pucker up her lips and remember the twinkle in her eye when I would sit by the hour and plan for the future. Such castles as we built! However they were not altogether in vain. The foundations were good. They needed no firmer support than poor Mother Aquinata's prayers and who shall recount them or weigh their efficacy with a God who certainly lent an ear to many of them.*

*Could we have looked into the future, would we have dreamed of more or greater success? A success which you and I must attribute to hard and honest labor, sanctified by holiness. For we were not only simply good, but simple and good. Poor Mother Gonsalva! May God be good to her and give her the light of His blessed countenance! She was certainly gifted beyond most of us, and had her health been good, would no doubt have done great things for God and for her Community. You cannot dissociate her memory from that of dear Mother Aquinata because of their closeness all the latter years of Mother Aquinata's life. The office she resigned was ever distasteful to her. On my last visit to Grand Rapids she said to me: "When my term is up, me for the back woods to prepare my soul for heaven!" We all knew...her reticence, her distaste for publicity, etc.*

*Oh, I am so lonely today in thinking of that long past. My heart was certainly with the dear Nuns of the olden days!...*

*Somehow it seems we never quite leave behind the olden days, they walk beside us like shadows. Then what of the Nuns who shared our sorrows as well as rejoiced in our well-being! They are dear, very dear, to both of us and that is one reason why both of us are saddened to-day - your sorrow and loss is ours... May He guide you, Sister dear, to do and bear for His sake and the sake of the dear ones who rest in "God's Acre" there, the tremendous burden of shaping and guiding the work now firmly established....*

*With deepest love and sympathy, we are, affectionately,*
*Srs. Cyprian and Ligouri*

# PERIOD TWO

# A Sturdy
# and Vigorous Growth
# 1919 - 1936

Mothers
Benedicta O'Rourke
Eveline Mackey

*T*his piece links two mothers general, Benedicta O'Rourke and Eveline Mackey, not primarily by their natures but by their works.

There is remarkable progress within the  congregation during this near-quarter century. A new motherhouse is built and begins to shape the character of the congregation as Marywood Dominicans.

The congregation "Goes West," first tentatively with small missions in Wisconsin and Indiana, then to New Mexico and Canada, where other cultures and climates further shape the congregation.

The intellectual and spiritual life of the sisters is enriched through the congregation's collaboration in the liturgical movement and through its development of a Catholic coeducational college.

Collaboration with other Dominican congregations leads to the formation of the Dominican Mothers General Conference, an influence which links congregational leadership with Dominican leaders and developments throughout the United States. Constitutional and adminstrative developments result in a difficult confrontation between the congregation and diocesan authority and a new congregational identity results.

The leadership and personal influence of Mothers Benedicta and Eveline further the transformation of a once markedly immigrant, pioneering congregation into an American Catholic congregation.

# 7

# JOY DAYS
# MOTHER BENEDICTA O'ROURKE

*M*other Benedicta was the first of the Michigan sisters to serve as mother general. Mary Frances O'Rourke was born on March 17, 1871, in the village of Palms, near Minden City in the thumb area of Michigan. When she was about thirteen, sisters who were collecting called at her home. She traced her awareness of her vocation to that meeting. In March 1887, shortly after her sixteenth birthday, she qualified for the third grade teaching certificate. During the summer she became unsure of whether to take a teaching position or to become a sister.

Her cousins, Sisters Ignatius and Berchmans Deegan, had entered the novitiate at Traverse City in January 1886 and encouraged her to contact Mother Aquinata. Because she was so young Mother invited her to "come and see" for a while. She met Julia Brophy at the depot in Saginaw to take the train to Traverse City. Upon arriving on the evening of October 15, 1887, their first welcome was from Sister Martha Mueglich, one of the original five to come from New York, and then from Mother Aquinata and the novice cousins. Three of her sisters followed her to the congregation, becoming Sisters Alphonsus, Thomas Francis, and Raphael.

On April 26, 1888, Mary Frances received the Dominican habit and the name Sister Mary Benedicta of the Most Blessed Trinity. With her classmates, Sisters Clare Brophy and Marcella Farnen, she remained at Traverse City for a formal novitiate program with Sister Ligouri McCarron, novice mistress since July 1886. She was professed on April 27, 1889, and in August sent to her first mission, St. Mary's, Muskegon, where she remained for three years.

After a year of teaching at St. Francis school, Traverse City, she spent three gladsome years at Sacred Heart parish, Mount Pleasant.

The work was rigorous as she was expected to prepare the graduating class to pass the teachers' examination as well as complete the course work. Teaching teachers became one of her many talents. She regarded her years spent in Mount Pleasant as among the happiest of her religious life.

In the fall of 1896 she began her long years in Grand Rapids, first at St. Alphonsus school taking the place of Sister Cyprian McCarron who had returned to the New York congregation that July. After four years at St. Alphonsus, she was among the sisters who opened Sacred Heart Academy on Ransom and Fountain Streets. She became principal of the Girls Catholic Central when it was moved to Jefferson Avenue in 1909. In 1910 she took on the additional duties of director of the Novitiate Normal School and from 1913 to 1917 was mistress of novices. She spent the summer of 1917 and the following academic year with Sister Estelle Hackett at Sisters College, Catholic University of America in Washington, DC. From September 1918 to March 1919, she served as supervisor of community schools, a role she would take up again after her terms as mother general. From 1897 to 1903 she was secretary and treasurer of the congregation, and again in 1909 was secretary and member of the council until her succession as mother general on November 3, 1919. She served the two remaining years of Mother Gonsalva's term with Sister Eveline Mackey as her first mother of counsel.[1] Sisters Seraphica Brandstetter, Adelaide McCue, and Loyola Finn continued as councilors.

The names of Mother Benedicta and Sister Seraphica Brandstetter are central to the story of how Marywood was built and its special place in congregational life. Sister Seraphica had many ties with the early years of the congregation. She was born in Bavaria in 1863 and came to America in 1883, the result of recruiting by Father Bonaventure, a Benedictine monk missioned in Newark, New Jersey, who was studying art in Munich. Three of his sisters belonged to the Dominican congregation on Second Street. The five candidates arrived in New York on August 24, 1883, and were immediately received by Mother Hyacinth. Among them was Sister Cajetan, a blood-sister of Sister Seraphica.

Sister Seraphica liked to tell about her reception and profession Masses at which "little George Mundelein" served. He was "one of the poor boys whom Mother Hyacinth befriended and assisted to go to college." For his good service in 1884, Mother Hyacinth gave him a five-dollar gold piece, the amount needed for his books for his first year of theological studies. Two days after her profession on August 22, 1885, Sister Seraphica and fourteen other sisters set out with Mother Aquinata for Michigan. She recalled in later years:

*It was the most eventful day of my life, for I was very much afraid of Mother Aquinata, but ere long I began to love her more than my own mother. This separation from the Motherhouse and Novitiate was worse than leaving home and country; still I found myself very happy among the good Dominican nuns in Michigan.*

Sister Seraphica had come to the Michigan missions at the time the province was being formed. She was an authentic founder of the new congregation through her mission work, her service on the general council from 1915 to 1930, and her role in the building of Marywood and later of Nazareth Sanatorium.

In April 1915 she spent many hours with Mother Aquinata. Hers is one of the few eyewitness accounts of Mother's preoccupations those last days. She wrote:

*I was at her bedside the last few days, and she directed me to settle all her affairs. Her last words were, "I feel sad to die, because I did not succeed in getting a motherhouse for the sisters, but the Lord wants you to do what I cannot do now." She pointed toward the direction where she wanted us to go and find the right location.*

*I accepted her last wish as an obedience, and ere long a certain Mr. Molloy came along and asked us to look at this location. So, one Sunday Sister Benedicta and I started out to inspect the location; but we were snowbound and could not reach the place. However, Providence watched it and also Our Lady of Perpetual Help. Reverend Mother's last request was that if we succeeded well, we should give the place a name in honor of the Blessed Virgin,--hence its name, Marywood. Fortune smiled on us and on June 14, 1917, we succeeded in buying this beautiful spot, although someone had offered five hundred dollars more than we did.*

*God's ways are wonderful! I was most anxious now to proceed with the building. The year following I met with an accident--a fall--and injured my stomach, so that I was unable to go to school. Again, I saw God's design. I studied and worked on the plans for our Motherhouse. ... November[15], 1919, the ground was broken and on June 5, 1921, the cornerstone was blessed by Reverend A. M. Fitzpatrick, the chancellor of the diocese, and named Marywood in honor of Our Lady of Perpetual Help. Sister Clementina and I spent the three years while the building was under construction in the little cottage at the entrance, and many were our trials and hardships--but we were happy in the fact that we would at last have a Motherhouse on the most beautiful spot around the city of Grand Rapids.*

Building plans were drawn up by Joseph and Leo A. Brielmeier from E. Brielmeier and Sons of Milwaukee and Chicago, a firm which built numerous church structures in Wisconsin and in the upper peninsula of Michigan.[2] John McNabb and Son, a Grand Rapids firm, was the local general contractor, Pulte and Sons the plumbing contractor. The projected cost was $650,000, though the city newspapers described it as a "million dollar building."[3]

Sister Seraphica noted the progress of the building in a journal. On April 4, 1921, she and Mother Clementina went to the cottage on East Fulton Street, having been picked up at St. John's Home by Mrs. John Quigg. Mr. Bertran followed with two loads of furniture. On April 6, Mr. and Mrs. Quigg came with provisions for several days. They stayed to help the two sisters clean the house and paint floors. Sisters Louise Perron and Hortense Belanger joined them to prepare meals while the others set about pruning the trees on the property.

On June 5, 1921, the cornerstone was laid. Mother Benedicta busied the household at Sacred Heart Academy in selecting appropriate items for the cornerstone. Finally she brought medals, a copy of the Gospel for the Sunday, a history of the Church, sundry papers, and the names of all the sisters. On November 4 of the same year the cross was blessed and masoned to the gable. There was, Sister Seraphica noted, "a furious wind." From late November to March the cottage was closed and relatively little construction done during the winter. On March 23, 1922, she and Sister Edward Sturmowski returned to the work of overseeing the building. That day Sister Seraphica hired a new janitor for the property and bought "our first span of horses at an auction sale for $327." The last entry in Sister Seraphica's building log was for September 10, 1922:

*Sunday the first Mass was said in the chapel. Sisters from various missions in the city were present and about fifteen lay people. We had a downpour of rain all the night previous and the following morning the new road from Fulton Street was washed away.*

The first year of Mother Benedicta's administration, 1920, was marked by widespread activity, primarily with the building and its funding, the establishment of a canonical novitiate, intensive advanced schooling for the sisters, and the founding of new missions and new works both in Michigan and beyond.

*TOP*
*Mother Benedicta O'Rourke,*
*third Mother General,*
*(fl. 1919-1927)*

*MIDDLE*
*Laying of cornerstone,*
*Marywood, June 5, 1921*

*LOWER*
*Summer School Faculty, 1923*
*Sacred Heart College,*
*Marywood. Sister Perpet.*
*Davis, Mother Benedic*
*O'Rourke, Sisters Euchar*
*Doris, Noella Byrne, Honora*
*Evans, Bernarda Murray, Este.*
*Hackett, Felix Brand, Berna*
*Marie Maxwell, Merced.*
*Dargis, David Steele, Rober*
*Nickol, Emeline Hessman, a.*
*Jane Marie Murray*

*OVERLEAF*
*Marywood Academy-Convent*
*Grand Rapids, Michigan*

In 1920 Sisters Louise Peron and Hortense Belanger began a ministry new to the congregation. Both were accomplished seamstresses, and they made vestments and altar linens for sale. The business was conducted at Sacred Heart Academy and after 1922 at Marywood. In 1923 Sister Louise became ill with cancer and the ministry was discontinued. The two sisters designed a new serge collar which, along with a serge mantle, was adopted by the congregation on Christmas Day, 1924, and which came to be used by other Dominican congregations in the United States. Sister Louise was the first sister to die at Marywood.

Towards the end of 1921 the heirs of Thomas and Marie Merrill of Saginaw approached the congregation with an offer to conduct a home for women in their family home. Since the 1870's the Merrill residence, 1209 S. Michigan Avenue, had been one of Michigan's stately homes. The three-story, red brick home with white trim filled city block no. 74 south of Cass Street, near Saints Peter and Paul church. The Ministerial Association of Saginaw had previously managed the residence for its retired members but could no longer maintain the enterprise. The congregation made a formal agreement, dated March 23, 1922, with the Merrill-Ring descendants "to promote the well-being, increase and multiply social comforts, and alleviate the ills of persons within the City of Saginaw and vicinity, whose state of being makes just appeal to the conscience of mankind for guidance and assistance...." In January 1922 Sisters Berchmans Deegan and Caroline Hart opened the house to women, young or old, who needed a "home away from home."

The sisters found the house required many modifications to suit the purpose specified by the behest. Benefactors from Saginaw and Grand Rapids assisted in renovations costing over $7000. The sisters took on many fund-raising activities to help pay the bills, doing laundry for residents, sponsoring card parties, catering weddings, ordinations and special functions to support the house. By 1925 they were able to equip a permanent chapel where Mass was celebrated by priests from Saints Peter and Paul parish. *The Catholic Vigil* described the Home "for women or girls who come to Saginaw unescorted, for women who are in Saginaw and want a quiet, safe, reasonable place to board and lodge...not merely a stopping place, a boarding place, a hotel. It is this and more. It is a home with all the environment, accommodations, and kindly attentions valued by persons who find themselves separated from the parental roof." The Merrill Home became a well-known institution in the valley, and a request for a similar home in Bay City was made in 1925 by the League of Catholic Women. The council declined due to the scarcity of sisters.[4]

With the promulgation of the universal code of Canon Law in 1918 the congregation was obliged to provide a program of formation lasting at least a minimum of a year and a day for its candidates. In 1920 a canonical novitiate was formally initiated. Hitherto many a biography told of swift departures of postulants and novices, sometimes on the day of their clothing, to fill vacancies throughout the state where classes were too large or sisters had become ill. Only very young candidates[5] "stayed in" to complete grade or high school. After 1920, candidates were to have a postulancy of at least six months and the canonical novitiate. Spiritual formation and continued schooling were to be the chief emphases. Sister Albertina Selhuber, a New York pioneer from Germany and a gifted musician, continued as novice mistress along with Sister Loyola Finn who had served as assistant since 1918.

In 1920 there was widespread pressure throughout Michigan for the dissolution of the private school system which had grown up alongside the public system. Not only Catholics but other Christian churches--Reformed, Lutheran, Adventist among them--were challenged by various hostile groups. On April 11, 1920, Bishop Kelly published a pastoral letter warning of the consequences of the passage of Hamilton's School Amendment, a proposal promoted by the Wayne County Civic Association and the Public School Defense League. A constitutional amendment requiring attendance of all Michigan children in public schools appeared on the ballot in 1920 and again in 1924, but it was defeated.

The publicity attending the amendment created demands for immediate certification for teachers in all schools within the State. In 1921 the State passed legislation to that effect. As chief administrator of a teaching community, Mother Benedicta had to develop a plan for almost immediate certification. The summer of 1921 was the first for sisters to join lay students at public institutions. In a reflection written in 1932 she remarked:

*About this time, the parochial school question was of much concern--sisters had to be certified within a certain time or they would not be allowed to teach in the schools of Michigan. This concern, together with the building allowed little time for relaxation the next few years, but the splendid spirit of cooperation and mutual helpfulness of the sisters was so earnest throughout the struggle that we came out victorious. It may be appropriate at this point to say how deeply grateful I have felt towards the sisters for this wonderful support.*

During her term of office fifty-six sisters obtained Baccalaureate degrees and nine sisters, Master of Arts degrees. Two hundred and fifty-five received Life Certificates, the latter primarily from the Central and Western State Normal Schools in Mount Pleasant and Kalamazoo. As far as possible, sisters continued degree work at the University of Notre Dame and the Sisters College of the Catholic University of America, Washington, DC, and other Catholic colleges. In the summer of 1927 Sister Marcelline Horton, an accomplished botanist, taught on the faculty of the University of Notre Dame, an achievement which Mother Benedicta listed among the official acts of her administration. At a time when income was desperately needed for construction, mortgages, and insurance, even greater sacrifices had to be made for higher education.

Under Mother Benedicta's direction the congregation began to develop a set of common goals, standards, and curricula for the schools in which they taught. In 1925 Mother appointed Sister Estelle Hackett to direct these projects. In the summer of 1926 sisters worked in several committees under Sister Estelle's direction to prepare a curriculum for the elementary schools. The work came to the attention of the Macmillan Company who published it in 1929 as *Curricular Studies*. In the final year of Mother Benedicta's administration Sister Estelle undertook the development of a series of readers for elementary grades. First entitled the *Veritas Reader,* the work became the origin of the popular and influential series known as *The Marywood Readers.*

In August 1921 Mother Benedicta completed the term she had taken over from Mother Gonsalva. The sixth General Chapter of the congregation convened at St. John's Home on August 6 and 7, with Bishop Kelly presiding over the elections. One hundred and thirty-four sisters had active voice, with 67 of these also having passive voice. Mother Benedicta received 125 votes.[6] Her councilors were Sisters Loyola Finn, Seraphica Brandstetter, Adelaide McCue, and James Walsh. Sister Matthia Selhuber was designated treasurer and Sister Seraphica secretary general.

The chapter of 1921 was the first to publish General Decrees, a small 3" x 7" fold-over sheet listing sixteen items. Some referred to specific constitutional items requiring confirmation; others reflected current needs of the congregation, in particular, economies to be practiced until the motherhouse was completed and the heavy debt at least partially liquidated; and some dealt with the regulation of the sisters' education.

On December 14, 1920, Mother Benedicta wrote to the pastors on all the missions served by the sisters, notifying them of a change in financial policy:

*Reverend and dear Father:*

*At a recent meeting of the Superiors of both Diocesan teaching Orders, it was decided to put forth a petition for the income obtained from the teaching of music on the missions. Perhaps it is unnecessary to tell you that our Community has labored in the Diocese of Grand Rapids for more than forty years, and during that time not even a thought of providing a home for its members has divided its interests in the upbuilding of parishes. Now, with a few exceptions, these parishes are in a better financial condition, and we, obliged to build our Motherhouse,-- the need of which we have felt for years--and also to meet the cost of University and Extension work in educating our sisters, believe we are justified in making the above request.*

*Our numbers have greatly increased, thank God, but our present quarters are no longer adequate for the accomplishment of the work for which our Order was instituted. Accordingly, we have begun the work of construction of our Motherhouse. Our young sisters must receive better advantages to equip them for the demands of the day; other sisters have grown old in the service of the Master and need comforts in their declining years; the sick and the infirm must also have proper care.*

*We need not mention the tremendous cost of construction in these days,--you know it. To whom shall we have recourse for aid if not to those with whom we have labored when the Diocese was passing through its pioneer stages? In many instances teachers were furnished gratis, and the music instructors earned the salaries for the school teachers. This help has never been regretted, but we feel that you will agree with us that we have assisted in no small way financially to bring the schools to their present state of efficiency. May we not count on your generosity to help us in our present emergency? From January 1, 1921 we shall expect the above revenue to be turned in to the Community.*

*In the future, as in the past, believe us, dear Reverend Father, most willing to assist you in every way that lies in our power.*

This letter,[7] signed Dominican Sisters, admirably sums up the years of service the sisters had given to the "upbuilding of parishes," "with no thought of building a home for its members." With the older priests and Catholic families, the sisters had brought the diocese through its pioneer stages, a "help...never regretted."

Outside of the monthly salary, established at $25 per sister per month, and the income from music lessons, community circular letters tell of numerous money-making projects to meet "the present emergency." In 1921 "brick booklets," twelve pages of ten "bricks" per page, were to be sold by the sisters for ten cents each. Missions delinquent in sending in at least half of their salary would be visited and a study of their account books made. In 1922, with the help of gifted lay women, 200 dolls were dressed and raffled and a fancy work and novelty booth was set up for an "Easter Festival." Bishop Kelly sent a letter, ghost-written by Mother Benedicta, to all pastors asking for their support of the festival and funds drive.

On Sunday, January 14, 1923, the Joyce Kilmer Players gave a benefit performance of "The Watcher at the Gate" for Sacred Heart College at the Powers Theatre in Grand Rapids. That spring Sisters Bonaventure and Clare, teaching at Boys Catholic Central, were given an automobile to raffle. In November 1923 all the sisters were grouped in clusters of five, each cluster to raise $100 by Christmas. A newly-formed Marywood Guild helped the sisters put on their first Marywood Festival on November 14, 1923, an event which continued to the 1960's. In 1924 a campaign was launched throughout the missions to increase attendance at Marywood Academy through reduced board and tuition offers. A Building Fund Committee of twenty sisters was established in February 1924 to meet a mortgage payment of $30,000 due by March of that year. The congregation was divided into several units, each unit to bring in $1500. In 1924 each sister was asked to raise $75 and, in 1925, a further $60.

Some of these enterprises were "somewhat of a secret," wrote Mother Benedicta, and the sisters were asked to give them all the support and encouragement they could, "without interfering with the pastor's work and plans." The results of each project were reported to the sisters and thanks heartily given. On December 30, 1923, Mother Benedicta wrote to the sisters:

*Our $20 drive worked out very nicely. Thus far the returns amount to nearly $3,000, more coming soon. I like to think the sisters had some pleasure from their efforts to secure the $20. Some have very funny experiences to relate. May God bless the Nuns!*

At the same time mortgages and loans were negotiated, the last of which was not paid until 1945 during the administration of Mother Euphrasia Sullivan (1936-1948). Wherever possible, community land was sold. In December 1921 the Graham farm in Alpine township was sold back to Mr. Graham for $4,000. In January 1922 the Platte farm was sold to William J. Breen for $24,000. In

August of the same year approximately two acres of land adjoining the parish house in Essexville were sold for $1,200. By such corporate and individual efforts the new motherhouse was financed.

The additional burden of ongoing education was often financed by individual entrepreneurial efforts: the sale of candy, stationery, fancywork; raffles; and family donations. In January 1931, at the first meeting of the General Council of Schools, the sisters reflected on the evolution of their professional training. During Mother Aquinata's time there were annual examinations given at the end of "home summer schools." A small printed certificate, not unlike a business card, identified the sister and her credentials as a teacher for a specified grade in the Diocese of Grand Rapids. Changes in certification policy brought the "summer school era with its unflagging toil, unremitting sacrifice." A sister recalled:

*The ingenuity of these methods of earning deserves great credit. One sister, holding a very responsible position in our community today, one day declared that she felt that her degree ought to be conferred by the Larkin Soap Company, as she had done more work with them than with the university. Indeed many of us **majored** in salesmanship of candy, frost-bites, and red-hots, and **minored** in education. Happy was the sister who left for summer classes with funds sufficient to assure her an easy living. Uneasy was the less fortunate one who must eke out a scanty living by careful selection at the cafeteria or by a bit of home room economics at the expense of the faculty in the way of electric fuel. Sisters, huddled in dormitories, hastily improvised from dismantled classrooms and uncomfortable cots, uneasily slept off the weariness of a hard day in summer classes, without regret that things were as they were. Weary sister housekeepers sacrificed with great cheerfulness their former summers' leisurely duties in the larger convents to giving unremitting service for their sisters in many summer centers of study.[8]*

In many respects the Great Depression was anticipated in the 1920's for economies of every sort were practiced on behalf of the motherhouse and summer schools. The haphazard, albeit necessary, financing of education also had implications for the ideal of common life and for individuals' self esteem.

In early September 1922 Sacred Heart Academy was transferred from its downtown location to the west wing of the new building. On September 10, Bishop Kelly offered the first Mass in Sacred Heart Chapel. Classes began on September 11. That first week Monsignor Anthony Volkert began his twice-weekly lectures in philosophy at the academy. Memories lingered of the first meal the sisters had in their new home:

*The first community banquet in the Motherhouse was held...in the serving room. The silver, china, and crystal were of dubious variety, but the food excellent. Sisters Ernestine, Evangelista, Jane Marie, Mellita and others cooked ham and eggs. Mother Benedicta helped to serve, and they dined like Emperors of old, having attendants who shooed away the flies. The building was without screens. But it was a perfect day--after forty-four years--the Dominican Sisters of Grand Rapids had a home.[9]*

An arrangement was made with "Harry's Taxi Service" to provide transportation from the city for the day students until city bus service was scheduled. A regular column in the social pages of the Grand Rapids papers informed the city of school events. In February 1923 the *Michigan Catholic* announced:

### GIRLS FIND JOY IN KENT SACRED HEART SCHOOL
#### *Everywhere is Found Happiness, Goodfellowship Whether at Work or Play.*

*Grand Rapids, Feb.24.-- Ideas of simplicity, good taste and appropriateness in apparel are inculcated in the young girls, who are students at the Sacred Heart academy and college, by use of a specified uniform.*

*The instructors, adopting this rule a couple of years ago, declare the results highly gratifying. Visitors comment upon the cosmopolitan spirit of the young women, and everywhere about the school, through the sunlit recitation and study rooms, the quiet library and down the long, broad halls there is an atmosphere of study. But this is tempered with laughter of the girls at play upon the large recreation fields about the institution, and occasionally there floats snatches of a well executed opera, played on one of the score of pianos in the music department.*

#### *Fully 150 Girls Enrolled.*

*Hammers still were pounding upon nail heads, the rasp of busy saws was audible and huge piles of shavings were scattered about the large four-story building when the doors of the new home were flung open last September. But these were little worries. Workmen completed their tasks within a few weeks, and, until they left, both teachers and students were so happy to, at last, move into the new building, that the noise of the carpenters failed to make an impression. More than 150 girls are enrolled in the school this year, and when the building is entirely completed, twice that number will be accommodated.*

*Students are enrolled from many northern and western Michigan cities and villages. A bus line makes daily trips to the institution, which has 18 instructors.*

*...It is situated in the eastern suburbs, and because of its proximity to the city, its shady groves, open fields and spacious recreation grounds, where every facility for pleasant outdoor exercise is afforded, it is probably the leading boarding school for girls in the state.*

### Encourages Outdoor Life

*The school, though it does not possess a general reputation for such, is one of the largest of its kind in the state, and is also the most modern and best equipped. The dormitories are splendidly furnished. Large windows make it possible for the students to sleep practically out-of-doors. There are also sleeping porches for use during the summer months and a roof garden, 100 feet square, makes it possible to give entertainments outside.*

*...The students are proud of their chapel. It is on the second floor and has a capacity of 800 persons. The altars are supported by pillars of pure onyx that are a masterpiece of fine workmanship in themselves....*

Fifteen postulants and twenty-one novices and house members[10] moved from St.John's Home into the central wing on October 6. They left behind the sisters who staffed St. John's Home, those serving St. Alphonsus parish, and several infirm sisters. Sister Adelaide McCue, the seasoned pioneer from New York, stood on the back porch and wept as the "Tin Lizzie" left St. John's for the last time. Moving day was spent in hauling household goods throughout the five-story building and setting up bedsteads. About 7 o'clock in the evening Benediction was given. Father Vogl gave a little talk in the hall and then all went to the laundry to complete the day's allotted work. The next day, the first Friday of October, was celebrated with day-long exposition of the Blessed Sacrament.

Veterans of the great move reported days of scrubbing terrazzo floors, painting radiators, transporting furniture throughout the building, and unpacking until dusk. Wiring was completed only in the school wing and the glazing of windows was scarcely done before winter arrived. Crockery and linens had come over from the Home in assorted boxes and barrels. Dr. James W. Shanks, one of several Grand Rapids physicians who gave services to the orphans and sisters at St. John's Home, provided wooden barrels for the move. Some of these remained in the laundry area for several months. "Shanks' Barrels" came to be a common resort for missing items for years after the community had settled into its new home. Cleaning supplies were stored in the elevator shaft until installation of "the works" in 1925, the same year an "automatic icebox" was purchased for the kitchen. Mother Benedicta joined in the labors and laughter of this great adventure. They were, like other beginnings undertaken by Mother Benedicta, "Joy Days."

During the Christmas holidays, on December 29, 1922, all the sisters in the city were invited to spend the day at Marywood. A visit to Marywood during the holidays, provided it was at no expense to the community, came to be customary among the sisters. The following spring, on March 7, 1923, the postulants who had entered at St. John's Home the previous September received the Dominican habit, the first Investiture at Marywood. Bishop Kelly was ill and so Father Vogl presided at the afternoon ceremony.

On Wednesday, June 6, 1923, Sacred Heart College and Academy was formally dedicated. The event began with a Solemn Pontifical High Mass celebrated by Bishop Kelly and many clergy. The sermon was preached by John T. McNicholas, OP, Archbishop of Cincinnati. Hundreds of invited guests came for the Mass and the receptions throughout the day. On Thursday, alumnae of Sacred Heart Academy and religious from the Midwest were invited for Mass, Benediction, and tours of the building. Representatives of the Adrian, Racine, Springfield, and New York Dominican congregations attended. Friday, the feast of the Sacred Heart, was a special congregational celebration. The week of dedication closed with the first commencement ceremony held on the new motherhouse grounds on Sunday, June 10. Bishop Kelly conferred diplomas on ten seniors. By 1926 the academy was fully accredited by the North Central Association.

With the move to Fulton Road the novitiate normal program expanded into a collegiate program that included course work in the traditional disciplines, teacher-training and general enrichment offered during the school year as well as summer. In its first year the college had a faculty of five and a lay student body of three - Marion McGuire, Catherine Schwaller and a part-time student. Sister Estelle Hackett served as dean and instructor of science. Sister Jane Marie Murray taught Latin; Sister David Steele, mathematics; Sister Aquin Gallagher, English and French; Sister Evangelista Rohrl, music. Sister Aquin also supervised the library. All were on the Academy faculty as well.

Sacred Heart College offered, Mother Benedicta wrote, "a uniformly excellent teaching staff, a comprehensive reference library, well equipped laboratories, and a campus of twenty-five acres, far removed from the heat and annoyance of the city." The summer school for 1923, July 2 to August 8, including Saturdays, was open to sisters and lay women with "work of normal grade in addition to high school subjects." The welcome Mother Benedicta sent the sisters reflects her enthusiasm for the coming summer and her gracious relationship with the sisters. On March 26, 1923, she wrote from Sacred Heart convent, Marywood:

*Dear Sisters:*

*I cannot tell you how much I was touched by your devotedness, displayed on my feast day. Let me thank you for your prayers, good wishes, and practical gifts.*

*I can just imagine how invigorating and refreshing it will be to the sisters of the missions when they come to our beautiful Motherhouse to enjoy the fresh country breezes, the home-grown vegetables, the warbling of the numberless birds in our grove nearby, and a comfortable, restful bed, provided for by yourselves. You should have seen the quantity of soft, downy blankets, the sheets and pillow cases that were piled up heavenward on either side of the community room as gifts from the sisters on the missions. I was almost speechless at the hugeness of the pile, but there are not too many. Well, anyway, let me thank you again.*

*I can hardly wait to see you all and witness the enjoyment of your first summer at Marywood. The summer school schedule is planned and enclosed with the letter. It is going to be a summer school second to none in the country.*

*With every good wish, and asking God to bless you all, I am*

*Yours in St. Dominic,*
*Sister M. Benedicta, OSD[11]*

In 1925 a parcel of land adjoining the original Fox property was purchased from Mrs. Doty for $3,600. In 1926 an additional 3¾ acres were acquired from Mr. Grooter at $1,000 per acre, bringing the motherhouse property to approximately 25 acres.[12] As early as 1926 the council considered the feasibility of building an infirmary, and of purchasing property in the Spring Lake area for a "Retreat of Peace."

Marywood became well known to the city through its round of religious, academic, and fundraising events: Rosary Sunday ceremonies in October, the Fall Festival, spring music recitals in Veritas Hall, dramas and operettas at St. Cecilia's, the May Crowning, graduation, the outdoor Corpus Christi ceremony, and Investiture and Profession ceremonies.

In 1944 Blessed Imelda kindergarten, a prefabricated building designed by Harry L. Mead, was built in the grove west of the school wing. Boys were accepted in the kindergarten program while the rest of the school remained a girls school until 1969. In that year the academy closed its boarding facilities and in 1971 became a co-educational day school. A Montessori school was opened in conjunction with the academy program in the "little red school house" and later in a second facility. In 1974 the high school of the academy was closed; the grade school in 1989.

With the move to Marywood, the former Sacred Heart Academy on Ransom and Fountain streets was remodelled to serve as a residence hall for young business women, a ministry similar to that of the Merrill Home in Saginaw. Music education continued to be offered in the studios of the former academy. The new enterprise was named Sant Ilona Hall[13] and was first directed by Sisters Thomas McNamara and James Walsh.

Holy Rosary Academy, Bay City, was also influenced by the completion of Marywood. Bishop Kelly encouraged Mother Benedicta to found a boys school within the diocese. In 1924 it was decided to transfer the girls boarding at Holy Rosary to Marywood Academy and transform Holy Rosary into a boys school. Sisters Cyrilla Hallahan, Apollonia Cornelissens, Coletta Baumeister, Rita Burghart, John Scally, Robert Donaghue, Mellita Tague, and Romaine Willing were assigned to develop the new boarding and day school for boys. Mother Benedicta was one of the boys' first visitors that fall. She wrote to them on November 21, 1924, thanking them for the program they had given her. "You have," she wrote, "made a splendid start and some day, perhaps you will be able to astonish the world." Such courtesies were part of Mother's approach to everyone.

# 8

# UPBUILDING THE CHURCH

*T*here is no written account of the factors which allowed the extension of the congregational ministry beyond the diocesan boundaries. One can speculate on the general influences: the urging of the Holy See to take on foreign missions, the evolution of the congregational identity beyond mother-daughter houses, and the vision and flexibility of the two chief ecclesiastical superiors, Mother Benedicta and Bishop Kelly.[1] Congregational board minutes refer to requests from the dioceses of Detroit and Chicago which were declined and others accepted as places of congregational ministry.

In 1920 the sisters first began to staff a parochial school outside the diocese of Grand Rapids, St. Mary's, Peshtigo, in the Diocese of Green Bay[2] at the extreme northeast of Wisconsin. Father Rutherford H. MacDonald, the pastor since 1915, had been a former Episcopalian priest. He was especially moved by the lack of schooling for the children in the parish and so, along with lay women, instructed the children until he could provide a sisters' school. In August 1920 Sisters Amanda McConnell, Carola Jones, Florence Marie Waters, Mary Jane Flannery, Delphina Pietrusinska, and Robertina McKenna set to work organizing an eight-grade program in a remodelled home which served as school and convent.

A household ledger for the years 1920-1926 shows emphases in the sisters' lives. The first semi-annual report indicates these receipts and expenditures:

| Mother House | 65.00 |
|---|---|
| Salary | 480.00 |
| Music | 317.00 |
| Fare | 57.80 |

| Mother House | 450.00 |
|---|---|
| Living Expenses | 243.40 |
| Clothing & Shoes | 33.07 |
| Christmas Goods | 19.85 |
| Mother's Xmas | 20.00 |
| Piano Tuning | 4.00 |
| Masses | 5.00 |
| Medicine | 14.37 |
| Postage | 3.07 |
| Incidentals | 2.99 |
| School Papers | 2.45 |
| Dentist | 3.00 |

*and a balance of $3.00*

Other years the ledger shows extraordinary outlays for extension courses and summer schools, piano replacements, and in 1922 for the "brick books." A Catholic newspaper was subscribed to and occasionally a spiritual book was purchased. Travel expenses were considerable for this distant mission. "Travel Books" were purchased each January to allow for a clergy reduction on fares.

A high school grade was added each year and soon the sisters moved to another dwelling. In the ensuing years, the sisters suffered with the parishioners the loss by fire first of their church, then of the school, as well as the partial collapse of the convent. For a time, school was held in an empty saloon. The winter of 1928 was a particularly harsh one and the heating system in the convent gave out. Finally, the Holy Name Society assisted with the purchase of a huge potbellied stove from the town's defunct train depot. The burdens of restoration after the fires and the first years of the Depression caused the parish to close its school in 1930. The sisters departed after ten years of service and, in spite of the vicissitudes, with glad memories.

In 1921 St. Mary school in South Bend, Indiana, was staffed by Sisters Anastasia Hebert, Catherine Marie Roberts, and Eustella Bellemore. Within three years the congregation decided they could not meet the needs of the parish, in particular for sisters who could speak the Slovakian language.

Another school in the Diocese of Green Bay was taken on in 1923. Since 1901 the Little Sisters of Mary, a French Canadian congregation, had staffed St. Joseph school in Marinette, Wisconsin. In 1923 they withdrew and the pastor, Father E.H. Vassiere, arranged with Mother Benedicta for Dominicans to come to the small city some nine miles distant from Peshtigo. Sisters Borgia Hawkins, Nicholas Forcht, Agnes Regina Moans, Rosella Poirier, Gerald Grace, Raymunda Boisclair and Angelica St. Onge were assigned the first year. Sister Nicholas left an account of their journey and welcome:

*On August 29, 1923...we went by bus to Muskegon where we were met by Sister Borgia's brother, Pat Hawkins, who loaded all seven of us plus the bags in his car and drove us to the boat dock. We had a night trip across Lake Michigan to Milwaukee, occupying one upper berth, one lower berth, and one stateroom with one large bed in it....We arrived in Milwaukee early the next morning and sought out a place to get some breakfast, then went to the railroad station...for the last leg of our trip to Marinette.*

*On arriving at the Marinette station, we found a delegation waiting with three cars to transport us to the convent where we were served a delicious baked whitefish dinner. After dinner, some of the young people entertained us with a lovely program. I recall particularly that they sang "Out where the West begins," which I thought was very appropriate.*

*During our first year at St.Joseph's we taught grades 1-8 inclusive in an old school with a wood-burning stove and a wood-box in front of each room. Under the stoves the pupils put bottles of coffee to keep them hot for the noon lunch. They sat on their coats. ...*

School was opened for 130 girls and 131 boys. Each year a grade was added, with the first graduation for four in 1927. By 1933 nine teaching sisters were required to meet the numbers and programs in the school. The following year the pastor was forced to close the school due to the ravages of the Depression in that area. Even Mother Eveline's offer of sisters serving for no remuneration was declined. The congregation was invited to return in the fall of 1936 but a misdirected letter caused Father Omer Champagne to engage other sisters. The presence of the Dominican sisters in the Green Bay diocese from 1921 to 1934 was richly rewarded with candidates to the congregation.

Since first coming to Michigan in 1877 the sisters regularly gave catechetical instructions on Saturdays and after the Sunday Masses. In July 1923 they began to direct rural vacation schools in Michigan and Wisconsin. Their first organized summer program was at Fife Lake, Michigan, for sixteen children, ages 6 to 16.

The primary work was to prepare children for receiving the sacraments in areas not having regular church services, but the curriculum often included lessons in health, music, and sometimes language. Each summer more centers were added and these three-to-four week ministries became a regular part of the "long vacation" work.

In Irons, Michigan, a town about twenty-five miles east of Manistee, the sisters conducted the vacation school in an old wooden church, once a public inn. At Maple City, the sisters lived at the County Poor Farm and commuted to the church some two miles away. At Freesoil the sisters gave religious instruction in the morning and Polish lessons in the afternoon. This service continued as a congregational work until the 1960's when new forms of religious education were promoted.[3]

Her term of office coming to a conclusion in the summer of 1924, Mother Benedicta convened the seventh General Chapter of the congregation for June 28 and 29, 1924. Monsignor Edward A. Lefebvre presided in the absence of the bishop. One hundred and sixty-nine sisters had active voice,[4] 102 of these passive voice. Mother Benedicta was re-elected by 104 votes. Sisters Albertina Selhuber, Adelaide McCue, Seraphica Brandstetter, and Alphonsus O'Rourke were elected her council. Sister Alphonsus, a younger sister of Mother Benedicta, was appointed secretary general and Sister Matthia Selhuber was reappointed bursar general. Mother and her council selected Sister Loyola Finn as novice mistress.

While there is no record of further business in the Chapter of 1924, constitutional study was no doubt part of the work. On March 24, 1924, Mother wrote to all superiors asking for suggestions for any changes in the Rule. She wrote:

*The Right Reverend Bishop has been examining our Rule Book and finds there are some things that must be changed in order to conform to the Code. It occurred to him that the sisters themselves living under the Rule as it now stands, would desire other changes. He has accordingly requested me to write to the various houses and ask the professed sisters to discuss the matter among themselves and send in their suggestions....*

*When the necessary corrections have been made, the Bishop will submit the entire document to the Sacred Congregation for Roman approval, and at the same time secure for us the assurance of our affiliation with the First Order of St. Dominic.*

By July Mother was corresponding with Father George M. Sauvage, CSC, member of the Commission of the Sacred Congregation for Religious, who was studying the draft. By

September 1924 constitutional matters became a regular part of the now monthly council meetings. During the school year 1924-1925 Mother met the sisters at mission centers throughout the state to discuss revisions. The work continued throughout Mother's second term.

On October 16 and 17, 1926, the congregation met in an Extraordinary General Chapter for the "Reading of Revised Constitutions."[5] The gathering was authorized by the administrator of the Diocese, as Bishop Pinten was not being installed until October 28 of that year, and attended by superiors of larger houses with a companion, and "superiors of smaller houses and any others who could attend without additional expense to the community." Father Joseph Vogl, Marywood chaplain, presided. Father Sauvage was also present. The draft was read in its entirety, and revisions were made in language and minor points. The draft was approved and, as can be seen from developments in the next administration, it was understood to be enroute to the Sacred Congregation. Mother entered in the official register of mother general, 1919-1927, "1926. Revised Constitutions sent to Rome for Approval." She thought her responsibility in this important area had been fulfilled.

During the pontificate of Pope Pius XI congregations of women religious in the United States were urged to take on foreign missions. There is a tradition among the sisters that a mission to China was seriously contemplated in the early 1920's. Early in 1925 Mother Benedicta and her council were visited by Father Peter Kuppers, a German priest working in the diocese of Santa Fe, New Mexico, who had heard of the congregation from contacts with the University of Notre Dame. In April 1925 Mother Benedicta and Sister Loyola Finn traveled to New Mexico to look more closely at the proposed mission.

Mother Benedicta announced her decision to the sisters on May 25, 1925.

*A Mission in New Mexico, chiefly for the benefit of our delicate sisters who cannot withstand this northern climate, and two schools in Grand Rapids are to be opened this coming September. This will make a considerable drain on the Community, and I foresee great difficulty in satisfying the demands. I crave your patience and your help in every possible way. Pray fervently that the schools will be taken care of to the best advantage.*

Volunteers were sought and dozens applied. They were apprised of differences of climate and culture, of hardships they would

TOP
Sister Seraphine Wendling
with her "bachelors," sixth
grade boys at Peñasco, New
Mexico, 1926

MIDDLE
Mother Benedicta O'Rourke
outside Father Kupper's
house, Peñasco, New
Mexico, 1925

BOTTOM
Father Kuppers and the
Peñasco community with
Sister Seraphica
Brandstetter, ca. 1928

encounter. Sisters Amata Baader, Theodosia Foster, Mechtilde Cordes, and Ernesta Hogan were chosen to begin the "missionary work" in Dixon, a village in Rio Arriba County, New Mexico.

July 22, 1925, the day of their departure from Marywood, was a congregational event. There was a formal missioning ceremony, with ringing of the tower bell and "honor guard" of sisters from the chapel to the property entrance. Sisters Seraphica Brandstetter and Clare Brophy accompanied the pioneers on the train journey. As the train neared Trinidad, Colorado, they found heavy rainstorms had swept away a part of a bridge. The train was rerouted but there was no way of informing Archbishop Daeger and Father Kuppers, who were awaiting the sisters in Sante Fe, of their delay. When they arrived a day late, Father Kuppers took the sisters to St. Vincent Sanatorium, where they first heard Mass in New Mexico. They were then received by the archbishop in his residence. From there, Father Kuppers drove them to Peñasco, some seventy-five miles north of Sante Fe, on partially paved roads made more unsafe by recent flooding of the Peñasco River. The drive took five hours. The parishioners had waited for the sisters since one o'clock. As darkness fell, the car lights were at last seen. The church bell was rung and all gathered first for Benediction, then for a welcome from the community.

Supper was provided in Father Kuppers' adobe home, four sisters seated on the four available chairs, the others on upturned luggage and packing cases. The sisters remained in Peñasco several days, then returned to Dixon to begin their work at St. Joseph school. Sisters Seraphica and Clare stayed with them until late August. Before their departure from Sante Fe they were received by the governor of the state to whom they recounted every detail of their journey and the condition of the roads. They later claimed they had been influential in the completion of the highway which runs from Dixon to Peñasco through Harding Mine and Chamisal.

The sisters left behind set to work expanding the school program which Father Kuppers had begun in 1923 with the help of several generous lay people. At the close of their first year there the sisters had 125 pupils in nine grades. A tenth grade was added in 1926 but the high school level was discontinued in 1928. Instruction was in English, a requirement of State law and a necessity as the sisters could not speak Spanish. On December 23, 1928, a disastrous fire took the church, convent, and school. The news reached Marywood the following day by telegram:

> *MERRY CHRISTMAS. BURNED TO GROUND THIS MORNING. WILL BEGIN TO BUILD SOON. HAPPY NEW YEAR. KUPPERS.*

Father Kuppers arranged for a four-room house for the sisters and a local dance hall and the American Legion Hall served as school and church until 1930. In 1947, a group of Dixon residents filed a civil suit in District Court against the Archdiocese of Santa Fe, opposing the presence of religious in the public schools. The congregation withdrew sisters from Dixon as a result of the litigation.[6]

The people of Peñasco, a village some fifteen miles north of Dixon and one of the thirteen missions in Father Kuppers' large parish, also sought to have sisters for their small school. In 1926 the Taos County School Board agreed to pay teacher salaries but required the village to provide adequate facilities. Archbishop Daeger, Father Kuppers and the people sacrificed to secure a four-room school, with a small adobe house as temporary quarters for Sisters Theodosia Foster, Seraphine Wendling, Sienna Wendling, and Lorraine Gibson. Fall rains and winter snows penetrated the little house; the sisters were often ill. That year the congregation bought land and remodelled a house which, as Sacred Heart priory, was a center for the growing number of Dominican sisters in New Mexico.

St. Anthony school, Peñasco, opened with ninety-three pupils the first day of school. By the end of the year, there were that many in the primary room, 215 in the whole school. Father Kuppers served as school director and was an active and energetic, albeit eccentric, community and parish leader. The school was accredited as a two-year high school in 1928, and in 1930 as a fully accredited high school. In 1931 a new high school building was begun. The methods of the sisters soon came to the attention of county and state educators, who sometimes called upon the sisters to give teaching demonstrations.

In several of the northern New Mexico communities there were schools and clinics sponsored by Presbyterian churches. There was little collaboration between these groups and the leaders of the centuries-old Catholic culture. Accusations of proselytizing and encroachment were common. Unlike their counterparts in Michigan, the sisters in New Mexico were more visibly in the public eye. In their first decades there they were duly contracted teachers within the public school system, though specifically constrained from teaching religion during school hours. The sisters related more closely to their new communities, often visiting homes and being called upon for assistance in health care, at the same time relying upon neighbors for technical and practical help.

The beginnings in New Mexico were similar to those in rural Michigan. The sisters had to set up convent and school largely from their own resources. Just as the Holy Cross nuns had aided the mission in Williamsburg and New York City, and they in their turn had assisted the sisters in Traverse City and other villages throughout Michigan, now the motherhouse and convents throughout Michigan sent household items, school supplies, and gifts of money to New Mexico. Archbishop Albert Daeger of Santa Fe (fl. 1919-1932), a former Franciscan missionary to the Southwest, was a generous and interested patron. The Catholic Ladies of Columbia, a benevolent society in Ohio, sent donations to Father Kuppers until 1935. Nevertheless, the early years were challenging. Over the years the congregation has been enriched by numerous splendid candidates and by the gifts of spirit and culture from the Southwest.

During the remaining years of Mother Benedicta's term and into the early 1930's, Father Kuppers continued to visit Marywood with news of the sisters and pleas for more personnel and material support. In 1927 he brought with him Chief Manuel of the Picaris Indians who entertained the sisters in the formal Brown Parlor with tribal dances. A visit to New Mexico in the fall was part of the mother general's annual visitation schedule and highlights were sent to the sisters in circular letters. The missions in New Mexico were a major focus of the sisters' missionary interests for several decades.

As a result of the division of St. Andrew parish in 1924-1925 two new parishes were formed in the east section of Grand Rapids. St. Stephen parish was located at the corner of Franklin and Rosewood in east Grand Rapids with Father Leo J. Farquharson the first pastor. Sisters Victor Flannery, Wilmetta Murphy, Leonard Lynch, and Vincent De Paul Roberts began the school. For several years they lived in an old farm house on the property.

The second of the new parishes was St. Thomas the Apostle on Wilcox Park Drive. In September 1925 Sisters Monica Kress, Rose Dominic Oakes, and Leonarda Ruff were assigned to the school there. For almost two years they commuted from Marywood until a dormitory above the church and a parish kitchen were fitted out for their use. A cloak room served as another bedroom in the early years. Father Aloysius Fitzpatrick, chancellor of the diocese, was pastor when the parish opened.

In the same year, 1925, Mother Benedicta agreed to the staffing of St. Norbert school, Munger, a rural community in Bay County. She appointed Sisters Ambrose Dupuis, Coletta Baumeister and two postulants to open the mission.

The final mission assumed during Mother Benedicta's administration was in Grand Rapids. In 1926 Mother assigned Sisters Valeria Tomkowiak, Wendell Lennon, and Cyrinus Strauss to Our Lady of Sorrows parish where the pastor, Father Salvatore Cianci, DD, had arranged a convent. Sister Valeria and a companion had been commuting from St. Andrew's to this predominantly Italian parish center on Sheldon and Hall Streets since 1922.

On March 26, 1926, Bishop Kelly died unexpectedly after a brief illness of a week. Once again the Dominican friend of the congregation, Archbishop John T. McNicholas, OP, preached the eulogy. Monsignor Edward A. LeFebvre, pastor of St. James parish in the city, administered the diocese until July 26, 1926, when Bishop Joseph Gabriel Pinten was appointed the diocese's fourth bishop. The new bishop did not arrive until October 28, 1926, the day of his enthronement in St. Andrew cathedral.

The sisters remembered Bishop Kelly for his quiet power of accomplishment, his magnanimity, gentleness, virtue, and scholarship. There appears to have been only the most amicable of relationships between Mother Benedicta and Bishop Kelly. As with the former ecclesiastical superiors, the congregation worked closely with the diocese in the expansion and growth of the schools and in the fostering of Christian life.

In her final year of office Mother continued the ordinary administration of the congregation as well as planning for an appropriate marking of the sisters' golden jubilee of service in Michigan. In 1927, the year of golden jubilee, the congregation numbered 450 professed sisters, sixty having completed their profession unto death. The congregation had by then committed itself to the care of sixty-three parish schools and two academies with nearly 11,000 pupils, an orphans' home, and two residence halls for young women.

From 1927 to 1929 Mother Benedicta served as supervisor of schools, an office she had started upon her return from Catholic University in 1918. In the fall of 1929 she was appointed principal of Marywood Academy, remaining there until her appointment in 1932 as superior of the girls division of Catholic Central, yet another office she had begun. On September 8, 1935, the evening before school opened, Mother suffered a stroke. The following day she returned to Marywood where she recovered somewhat, but on October 22 suffered another stroke. She was unconscious until her death in the evening of Monday, October 28, 1935. She was 64 years old.

During the week of mourning a Solemn Requiem High Mass was celebrated at St. Andrew cathedral for the students of Catholic Central. On Saturday, November 2, the funeral Mass was celebrated at Marywood by Bishop Gallagher of Detroit who was assisted by Monsignor Dennis Malone, rector of St. Andrew's. Representatives of several Dominican congregations and over a hundred priests joined the sisters, friends and former pupils for the Mass. A friend and colleague of Mother's for over forty-five years, Monsignor K.J. Whalen of St. Mary parish, Muskegon, spoke of her life and achievements, remarking that Mother Benedicta:

*...developed the idea of this great edifice of Marywood in which we pay our respects to her today. It was in her mind that the outlines of it were drawn; it was her hand that pencilled the plans which the architect was to develop; it was for it that day and night she sacrificed. This edifice was raised for you, and it will be for her, I hope, a long-time monument.*

*Yet this is only a monument of brick and stone, and I am free to believe that to you who came in contact with her as sister companion, as superior, as novice mistress, as mother general--I am free to believe that in the heart and mind of each one of you there comes today the memory of her many acts of kindness, of virtue, of wisdom, and of religion. She was affable, considerate, and charitable, and she always found time to do for others. The memory of these things, remaining with you, will be a far greater monument to Mother Benedicta than this great edifice of brick and stone.*

It was a custom of the time for the mother general to include in her circular letters details of sisters' illnesses and deaths. Mother Eveline selected this passage from Monsignor Whalen's eulogy, commenting:

*I could just imagine Mother smiling, perhaps, at the thought that she should be the object of such a gathering and such eulogizing, but how true to Mother's character were Monsignor's words! The greatest tribute of all was manifested by the large number of sisters, priests, and friends who came to give testimony of their love and devotion to our dear Mother Benedicta.*

Messages of condolence from throughout the nation echoed that appraisal of Mother's influence. Father Norbert Georges, OP, led the prayers at her grave in St. Andrew Cemetery.

**9**

# TEACHERS' TEACHER
# MOTHER EVELINE MACKEY

*A*s part of the congregation's golden jubilee celebration, *The Catholic Vigil* for September 7, 1927, published a two-page account of the history and works of the sisters. The writer, probably a member of the congregation, remarked:

*As a diocesan community the sisters have enjoyed the special guidance and support of their bishops. The death of Bishop Richter in 1916 took from them one of their most venerated friends and benefactors. His strong unfailing aid in the early days of the community will never be forgotten. No less can the zeal and generosity of Bishop Gallagher, and of Bishop Kelly of blessed memory. In the recent appointment of their new Bishop, Right Reverend Joseph Gabriel Pinten, the sisters recognize another manifestation of the loving guidance of Divine Providence.*

This summary of the episcopal relationship with the congregation from 1877 to 1927 was succinct and appreciative. The expectation for the coming years, expressed in the pious language of the times and within the diocesan newspaper, implied continued collaboration. By hindsight, the concurrence of the administrations of the two chief superiors, Bishop Joseph Pinten, fourth Bishop of the Diocese of Grand Rapids (fl. 1926-1940) and Mother Eveline Mackey, fourth mother general of the Congregation of Our Lady of the Sacred Heart (fl.1927-1936) was a dramatic watershed in the relationship of the two institutions. In retrospect, the appointment of Bishop Pinten was providential but in ways not anticipated in 1927.

On December 3, 1921, Pope Benedict XV appointed Monsignor Pinten[1] Bishop of Superior, Wisconsin. From that see he was called by Pope Pius XI to succeed Bishop Kelly as the fourth Bishop of Grand Rapids. Archbishop John T. McNicholas, OP, as metropolitan of the province of Cincinnati, presided at the ceremony of installation[2] at St. Andrew cathedral Thursday, October 28, 1926. Bishops Gallagher and Schrembs were among the prelates and many clerics in attendance. At the new bishop's request there were no other celebrations to mark his coming to Grand Rapids, a marked contrast to the manner in which Bishop Kelly had been received by the city of Grand Rapids. Bishop Pinten succeeded to the administration of a well-established diocese with approximately 150,000 Catholics and 200 priests.

His seminary training, the Roman education combined with growing up in "God's rugged country," produced a zealous, strong, austere character. Throughout his life he frequently returned to the Upper Peninsula, and especially to its wilderness, to nourish his spirit and energies. At his episcopal consecration, he took as his motto *Spiritus Domini Super Me*--"The Spirit of the Lord is upon me." His manner and emphasis were in sharp contrast to those of Bishop Kelly, who had encouraged growth and development within the diocese. His style was without flair, autocratic, and, in the face of widening depression, frugal and cautious. In retrospect, he was seen to have piloted the diocese through a difficult period in its history with an expertness that allowed it to remain solvent during severe economic crisis.

When Bishop Pinten came to Grand Rapids, Monsignor Anthony Volkert, DD, was rector of St. Joseph Seminary. Monsignor Volkert had been a longtime associate and friend of the congregation. He gave a regular course in religion and philosophy at the academy and was usually on the collegiate summer faculty. Monsignor was given a considerable number of duties in the chancery office and it appears that much congregational business was directed to his attention.[3] In 1933 Bishop Pinten appointed Monsignor Thomas Noa rector of St. Joseph Seminary and on January 21, 1934, named Monsignor Volkert his vicar general.

The first months of Bishop Pinten's episcopacy were at the same time Mother Benedicta's last months in administration. There is no record of a change in the way the two institutions worked during this time. Matters for council meetings in January and February 1927 are consistent with those of the previous years when Bishop Kelly appears to have allowed, perhaps encouraged, a fairly independent internal administration.[4] There are, however, no minutes for meetings from March 1927 to that of August 10, 1927, when the newly elected officers first formally met.

*Bishop Joseph Pinten*
*Fourth Bishop of Grand Rapids*
*(fl. 1926-1940)*

*Mother Eveline Mackey*
*Fourth Mother General*
*(fl. 1927-1936)*

On May 4, 1927, Mother Benedicta announced the convocation of the eighth General Chapter for August 6 and 7, 1927. She informed the sisters that the method of election would be "as directed by the Right Reverend Bishop in his letter of April 19." The bishop had informed Mother that the delegate system would be eliminated and that "each and every sister who on the day of the election has been professed in the community for a period of twelve years shall be an elector and have a right to vote." A delegate system was provided by the Constitution which the sisters had unanimously approved in October 1926. It was, in their understanding, a traditional feature of Dominican government. On the one hand, the bishop's directive implied protection of the rights of "each and every sister" but he followed that insistence with the citation of Canon 506.4 to the effect that "In diocesan congregations the local Ordinary not only presides at the election of the Superior General but has the right to confirm or rescind the election as he in conscience sees fit."

On August 7, 1927, Sister Mary Eveline Mackey was elected as the fourth prioress general of the congregation. She was fifty-two years of age and the fiftieth member of the congregation in order of rank.

Catherine Elizabeth Mackey[5] was born on September 11, 1875, in Marquette in Michigan's Upper Peninsula. Her parents, James Anthony Mackey and Mary Frances McGinnis, were born in the province of Ontario, Canada. They met and were married in Sault Ste. Marie. Catherine's grandparents had come from Ireland. She was taught Christian doctrine by her grandfather, Constantine McGinnis, who accompanied the priests of Marquette as an itinerant catechist to remote areas of the upper peninsula. He taught the children not only religion but also Irish songs and dances. His large family was taken in by James and Mary Mackey when grandmother McGinnis died.

There were eleven Mackey children, Catherine the sixth born. Two daughters died young, nine lived to maturity. When Catherine was about seven, her father left Marquette to run the Antrim Iron Company furnaces in Mancelona, Michigan. Catherine left the Rolling Mill school in Marquette and was placed in St. Peter cathedral school conducted by the Sisters of St. Joseph. It was a difficult few months in school as an inexperienced teacher was substituting. Mother Eveline wrote some fifty years later:

*Coming up the same hill many years later as a Dominican Sister, the same feeling of fear came over me. So as a principal I was anxious that the first grade sister was very kind to the new little ones. I used to say to Sister Norberta: "Even if they learn little out of books, be very kind to the children, and make them love school." Sr. Norberta always did make them love school.*

Catherine spent five years in the public school system in Mancelona where she had good teachers and came to love learning. Her mother prepared the Catholic children of the town for their First Communion so Catherine had many times been prepared but had not yet reached the required age of twelve. In January 1887 she was sent to Holy Angels Academy in Traverse City, the only Catholic school in that part of the state.

The twelve-year old Catherine was deeply impressed by Mother Aquinata, who was both superior of the house and provincial of the Michigan missions. Father Nyssen, pastor of St. Francis parish, began the children's First Communion instructions that spring but left for a visit to Germany. He did not return and so the preparation was continued first by Mother Aquinata, then by Bishop Mrak. The bishop came by boat from Peshabetown for four days each week to say the Sunday Mass and give instructions. On June 13 Catherine received her First Communion from the bishop. That summer, on July 10, 1887, she was confirmed by Bishop Richter in Mancelona.

At the close of each school year it was customary that the students give an exhibition. The *Grand Traverse Herald* for June 14, 1888, announced that the pupils of Holy Angels school would present a Musical and Dramatic Entertainment on the evening of Thursday, June 21, at Library Hall. Katie Mackey was among those who presented "Aunt Jane's Tortures," a dialogue; she was also Sunflower in the Cantata "Who Shall be Queen?"

During her school years Sisters Cyprian, Berchmans, Ignatius, Benedicta, Albertina, Stella, and James were at Holy Angels Academy. Several of her classmates became sisters: Dominicans, School Sisters of Notre Dame, Franciscans. Though only fifteen years old, Catherine was convinced of her own calling to the religious life, though "many times wished my vocation out in the lake--I decided I must follow God's call."

On September 8, 1890, she and her mother travelled once again to Traverse City, this time for Catherine to enter the congregation. Years later Mother remarked it was "incidentally the same day that the Little Flower was professed as a Carmelite in Lisieux in

France." By then Mother Aquinata was in Grand Rapids at St. John's Home and Catherine was received by Mother Angela Phelan, "who sat behind a grate in the parlour." She had entered a Second Order convent in a mid-western province of a congregation located in New York. It was, however, the "time of the great changes."

In retrospect, 1891 was the year there were many signs. The sisters in Adrian had remarked on the sudden appearance of Mother Angela, who had come from Traverse City with a postulant. Mother Eveline wrote almost fifty years later:

*Mother Angela was sent as the first Provincial of Adrian then made a separate province. She asked me if I would like to go with her, and I said I would, but Sister Borromeo Donnelly was sent instead. The postulants and the white novices who belonged to the Detroit Diocese were mostly sent to [the] Adrian novitiate.*

Catherine Mackey spent three months in Traverse City, then in November 1890 went to St. John's Home. Under the direction of pioneer Sisters Adelaide McCue and DeSales Desmond she taught the orphans--"very simple teaching...but my best"--and helped with the housework. "I recall," she said sixty years later, "that there was no electricity and that one of my charges was twenty-six lamps, and to the utter disgust of Sister Adelaide there was always a little corner of some wick that blackened the chimney." Sister Cyprian McCarron, her former teacher, was now superior of the house and principal of the St. Alphonsus school.

In February 1891, she returned to Traverse City in preparation for the reception of the habit. On April 1, 1891, Catherine Elizabeth Mackey received the Dominican habit and the name Sister Evalina [*sic*] of St. Joseph. Within two weeks Mother Aquinata accompanied her by train to Essexville, where she was to teach a class of 84 third- and fourth-graders at St. John school. By the end of June she was back in Traverse City preparing for the Leelanau County teachers' examination. She was assigned to the public school room within the parochial school at Provemont (Lake Leelanau) for the next two years, first with Sister Matthia, then with Sister Seraphica. These and the next few years at St. Alphonsus school, Grand Rapids, were very hard. Huge classes, poor food, cold houses, and church music duties were regular features. On August 4, 1893, she made her first profession of vows, a year before the province was separated from its New York motherhouse.

In 1895-1896, Sister Eveline was missioned to St. Joseph parish, Wright. Mother Boniface was superior and housekeeper, Sisters Scholastica and Eveline were in charge of eight grades in the two-room school. On February 29, 1896, Sister Eveline's father was killed in a furnace explosion in Newberry. The Rule prohibited her going home to attend the funeral or to assist her mother. It was a "terrible winter" eased only by the kindness of Mother Boniface, Sister Scholastica and Father Ege, the pastor.

Prior to the establishment of the novitiate normal program, the sisters took examinations set by the diocese for teacher certification. A priest, sometimes Father Brown and on rare occasions Bishop Richter himself, presided. The sisters were given a formal card of certification by the diocese. In the summer of 1896 Sister Eveline was at St. John's Home to prepare for the three levels of the diocesan examinations.

Duly certified, Sister Eveline was sent to St. Joseph school, Saginaw, where she was assigned the high school commercial program, a course of study she herself had not yet taken. For three of the eight years she was there Mother Assissium was the superior of the house. She left to become mistress of novices. She was, in Mother Eveline's view, "a very fine woman and a religious of the first water" who during her tenure gave them the novitiate they had not had in their first years in the congregation. Sisters Cyrilla Hallahan and Lawrence Cuddahy were with her for eight years and they became lifelong friends. Among her students were young women who later became Dominicans and dear friends: Sisters Richard Kannally, Isabel Foley, and the two Ryan sisters, Ildephonsus and Alberta. On January 12, 1901, while she was at St. Joseph parish, her mother died.

On August 4, 1905, Sister Eveline made her final vows and soon departed for her next mission at Essexville. From 1904 to 1906 she taught in the old school in St. John's parish. Holy Rosary Academy had burned the previous March and the sisters were lodged in a house on Pine Street provided by Father Van Rooy while a new convent was being built. Sister Eveline, who herself loved learning, encouraged the students and found them "lovely, smart, and loyal." Loyalty was an attribute she valued in relationships throughout her teaching and congregational ministries. In 1906, the year of the opening of the Catholic Central high school in Grand Rapids, she was assigned to the Girls Catholic Central. She remained on the faculty during the three years the school was combined with Sacred Heart Academy at 69 Ransom Street.[6]

In 1909 Sister Eveline returned to Saginaw for a six-year stay at Saints Peter and Paul school. Her first year there school was held in a former public school building dating from the mid-nineteenth century. Conditions were perilous for the 130 children enrolled but in 1910 a fine new school was opened and the enrollment grew to about 450. "Mother [Aquinata]," she wrote, "worked hard picking up teachers at every turn for that school. She would hardly have a new teacher in when children seem to roll out of the sand and fill up that classroom. The increase possibly was due to the new school as well as to the hard working sisters that were sent there." Sister Eveline remained in Saginaw until June 1915. Many years later she spoke of the "splendid pupils" from Saginaw who "made their mark."

From 1915 to 1922 she served as principal of Girls Catholic high school in Grand Rapids. The school, with approximately 350 students, was located in the former diocesan seminary on Sheldon Avenue. While Sister Eveline was in this position, Bishop Kelly asked Mother Benedicta to appoint her to fill the vacancy on the general council left by the resignation of Mother Gonsalva, a position she had until August 1921.

In June 1918 Sister Eveline was one of five who attended the first Sisters' Summer School at the University of Notre Dame. She and Sisters Alphonsus O'Rourke, Monica Kress, Henrietta McAllister, and Bertrand LaLonde took the train from Grand Rapids to Muskegon, then a boat from there to Chicago where they boarded the train for South Bend, and finally hired a taxi to the university. Mother remarked that one of the first tasks of their higher education was to learn a more direct route to and from Notre Dame.

From June 1922 to June 1924 Sister Eveline and Sister Henrietta attended the Catholic University in Washington, DC. In June 1923 she received the Bachelor of Arts degree, and in June 1924, the Master of Arts degree.[7] She and Sister Henrietta returned to teach English and Latin in the 1924 summer program at Sacred Heart College. Upon her return she was once again appointed to Catholic Central high school in Grand Rapids. From September 1924 to June 1927 she was principal of Boys Catholic Central and St. Andrew grade school. It was, she wrote:

*the easiest school I ever had because of fine faculties and [the] best type of boys. We had about 200 boys and did they study. In those days we were the Fathers and Mothers. [There was] no priest on the Faculty. Mr. Frank O'Malley, then a plain clothes [police]man and I settled important problems if there was a boy problem but they were few.*

On August 7, 1927, Sister Mary Eveline Mackey was elected to succeed Mother Benedicta O'Rourke as the fourth mother general of the congregation. She was elected on the first balloting, having received 121 votes of the 201 cast.[8] Her council were Sisters Albertina Selhuber, Beatrice Cottrell, Philomena Kildee, and Genevieve Gauthier. This was the first chapter which elected the congregational bursar and secretary. Sister Philomena, a classmate of Mother Eveline's from Holy Angels Academy, was elected secretary general, and Sister Seraphica Brandstetter the bursar general. Mother and her council appointed Sister Jerome Smithers as mistress of novices.

Mother Eveline was to serve as prioress general (a title she preferred for its Dominican character) for two terms, the first for three years, 1927-1930, the second for six years, 1930-1936.[9] There are many areas of continuity between her administration and that of Mother Benedicta: mission expansion in New Mexico, Michigan, and internationally, in Canada; continued evolution of the congregation's institution of higher education; continuance of the fundamental mission of the congregation as a teaching order with a beginning of an external nursing ministry; continuance of the professional growth of the sisters and institutional identity so carefully planned by Mother Benedicta; and the careful management of congregational resources as worldwide depression made its local impact. There were, in Mother Eveline's administration, projects of a far-reaching nature to New Mexico, Europe, and Canada, projects as well of spirit and law.

Hers was "a strict but kindly authority."[10] Especially at the beginning of a school year, Mother's letters to the sisters were a comprehensive policy statement, sometimes running eight or nine typed pages. She sent directives as well as advice on numerous topics under several headings: "Educational Matters," "Music," "Economy and Salary," "Clothes," "Health, Food, etc.," and "Disciplinary Matters." It was required that letters of the prioress general be read in the refectory on the day of receipt, and in the case of longer letters which served as a year-long goals statement, reread on specified occasions. These letters were regarded as in-house communications and were to be seen only by the sisters. As late as the 1970's the expression "When did Mother give that out?" was used occasionally by some older members of the congregation in reference to directives from the prioress.

The health of the sisters was a constant concern of Mother Eveline. In spite of overwhelming debt and the impact of the Depression, throughout her administration she sought to find a suitable summer residence for the sisters. In May 1936 negotiations for a property on White Lake were near closure. George Morrell of Muskegon, acting on behalf of the sisters with the property owners, the Boston Store of Chicago, told them an immediate downpayment of $10,000 would secure the property at $18,000, rather than the market price of $22,000. During the summer of 1936 several vacation weeks at White Lake were arranged for the sisters. As Mother's administration was nearing an end, the matter was left to the 1936 Chapter.[11]

The sisters were urged to get fresh air, to take, in the words of Mother Eveline's directive, a "brisk constitutional" each day. During Mother Benedicta's administration a "teahouse" had been built on the edge of the grove. Sister Seraphica, the bursar, had a keen appreciation for the natural beauty of the property and added extensively to the evergreens. In the spring of 1935 the Fulton Street property was officially designated by the State of Michigan's Conservation Department as a wildlife sanctuary and was posted as such until 1945.[12] The sisters were urged to use these amenities, as well as to "eat everything at table," including brown bread and hot oatmeal. On several occasions Mother visited the Kellogg Spa in Battle Creek and appears to have been influenced by a holistic health philosophy.

In 1927, to mark the fiftieth anniversary in Michigan, the congregation published Sister Philomena Kildee's reflections on the life and work of Mother Aquinata. In urging sales of the book and its use as a vocation aid, Mother Eveline wrote,"That quiet, unworldly Mother, who, when living, could never be brought before the public, is now to have her life revealed to the world by her daughters who loved her so much." Sister Jane Marie Murray also wrote a brief chronicle intended for publication in fall 1928. A funds drive in association with the jubilee was cancelled by Bishop Pinten.[13] Mother followed up that disappointment with a plea to the bishop that inasmuch as he had found it necessary to disappoint them in a material way, he would surely support them in a spiritual drive. Hundreds of sisters signed petitions to him to further approval of their Constitution as a jubilee gift.

Jubilee was formally celebrated in May 1928 at Marywood. On Tuesday, May 15, a Pontifical High Mass was offered at Marywood, followed by a banquet for priests, another for friends of the congregation. The next day there was a Solemn High Mass for the deceased sisters and a reception for the religious communities in the city of Grand Rapids. Ascension Thursday, May 17, was the day for "our own dear sisters." In her 1928 Easter letter to the sisters Mother expressed regrets on the limitations she had to set, "How I wish I could say for you all to come in, but I could not promise to be able to take care of you, and, of course, it would be very expensive. A few of the older sisters may come on May 17, and we shall have a Jubilee day for the rest in the summer time." The times dictated great simplicity.

After her election in August 1927, Mother and her council set to work on the assignments of the sisters. Once school was under way, Mother began her round of house visitations. By late October she was in New Mexico to visit the sisters in Dixon and Peñasco. On November 10 she went to Albuquerque where she met Father Ferdinand Troy, SJ, pastor of the Church of the Nativity in Alameda. Father renewed an offer he had made the previous year to Mother Benedicta of the gift of land on the mesa east of the parish church and nine miles north of downtown Albuquerque. The earlier proposal had with it several provisos which Mother Benedicta thought best to decline. The following day Mother Eveline left for Michigan and, as was her custom, entrusted the issue to the prayers of a saintly sister. She asked Sister Aquino Peterson, her former pupil at Saints Peter and Paul school in Saginaw, to offer her prayer and suffering for the intention. Sister Aquino died of tuberculosis on January 15, 1928, the day on which Archbishop Daeger sent the permission to accept the land. Mother and her council sought the permission of Bishop Pinten to proceed.

As chaplain of St. Joseph Hospital in Albuquerque, Father Troy had met Sister Sienna Wendling. She had been sent to Dixon in 1926 in hopes that the climate of the Southwest would strengthen her. By 1927 the rigors of two hard winters and the labors of pioneering were too severe and she was hospitalized in Albuquerque. She was told she had only a few weeks to live. A campaign of prayer was

## Jubilee Hymn

*For the Fiftieth Anniversary of the Establishment
of the Dominician Sisters in Michigan*

Dear Lord, eternal King, to Thee
We raise our hymn of praise
In joyful hymn of jubilee,
This happy day of days.
We thank Thee, Lord, our Blessed Spouse,
For mercies manifold
All down the years, since first our vows
With loving trust we told.

*Chorus*

Glory to Thee, O Triune God!
Thy gracious mercies still impart
To daughters of Dominic, children true
Of our Lady of the Sacred Heart
Of our Lady of the Sacred Heart.

O Lamb of God, Who from the cross,
Wouldst draw all things to Thee,
Thy love has conquered! Countless souls
Have joyed to follow Thee.
In gladness and in weariness,
In happiness and tears,
Thy love has been our strength divine
All through these fifty years.

The past is pledge of future grace,
Our trust is all in Thee;
We know that Thou wilt never fail
To heed our trusting plea.
Dear Lord, receive this song of praise
From grateful hearts today,
From souls who ardently desire
To love Thee Lord for aye.
　　　　　—Sister Jane Marie, O. P.

*Pioneers gathered for Golden Jubilee, Summer 1928.*

*SEATED
Mother Clementina Coyle, Sisters Albertina Selhuber, Genevieve Gauthier, and Andrew McKernan. STANDING Sisters Philomena Kildee, Seraphica Brandstetter, Mother Eveline Mackey, Cyprian McCarron (NY), James Walsh, and Ligouri McCarron (NY). Sister Andrew, a pioneer to Michigan in 1883, officially transferred to the congregation in 1928.*

*Holy Cross Convent*
*Santa Cruz, New Mexico*

*Nazareth Sanatorium*
*Albuquerque, New Mexico,*
*ca. 1940*

begun both in New Mexico and Michigan. The sisters asked the intercession of Saint Therese of Lisieux and of Sister Reparata Gautier, former member of the congregation who had died in the Dominican cloister in Cincinnati in 1927. Sister Sienna was able to leave the hospital on April 30, 1928, apparently cured of tuberculosis. Dr. William Lovelace, the attending physician, and Sisters of Charity at the hospital spoke of a miraculous cure.[14]

On April 6, 1928, Mother Eveline wrote to Sister Sienna:

*I just received a letter from Fr. Troy, and will write him in a few days. I am so glad that God made you the instrument to bring us to such a prize as that wonderful spot in Alameda... Pray for us all to the dear Little Flower who is taking such good care of you.*

The land offered by the Jesuit fathers was acquired on July 29, 1929, from the Mutual Investment and Agency Company of Arizona. An adjoining parcel of land was also given by Archbishop Daeger, provided the congregation would pay a $900 mortgage on it. The site of approximately 640 acres stood at the foothill of the Sandia Mountains at an elevation of 5300 feet. Ground was broken on December 29, 1929, and building begun in March 1930. A. Rossiter of Albuquerque served as general contractor as well as unofficial architect. Sister Blanche Steves was sent to Albuquerque to oversee the project on Mother Eveline's behalf. She lived with the Sisters of Charity at St. Vincent Academy and sent weekly bulletins to Marywood. Mother Eveline was very much interested in the project. No detail was too small for her attention, for example:

*The dumbwaiter should be 30 x 42...I like the jog in the wall with the built-in bench.... Cover the vault in the office with a wooden door.... Have a small safe set in the wall of the community room....Sister Seraphica says the French doors in the rooms should have slides for ventilation.... High pressure Kewanee boiler and garbage burner; that is what we insist upon having.*

On March 21, 1930, Mother wrote to Sister Sienna with an instruction of another kind:

*I am giving you an obedience to begin at once and work for funds for a Shrine of the Little Flower to be built on Nazareth grounds at Alameda. It can be built of adobe on a cement base, and the statue of the Little Flower placed on an altar on which Mass may be said. In this chapel there should be a statue of the Infant Jesus and a bust of the Holy Face.*

*The shrine might be 15 ft. wide and 30 ft. long. Father Vassiere of Marinette has given us a first class relic of the Little Flower which Mother Agnes, her sister, gave to him for us, and Father has presented us also with a beautiful reliquary. This will be sent to Alameda for the Shrine.*

*You will erect this Chapel in thanksgiving to the Little Flower for her past favors, and to beg her continued help for Nazareth and for those who help in the construction of her Shrine.*[15]

At the request of Father Troy, the site and ministry was called Nazareth.

In September 1930 Sisters Coletta Baumeister, Ernestine Kokx, Blanche Steves, Clarence Hansen,[16] and Marie Therese Harp moved into the partially-completed building. On October 10, 1930, construction was halted because of lack of funds; porches were left without roofs, exterior plastering was unfinished, the two towers were incomplete. Mother Eveline and Sister Seraphica, the congregational treasurer, came in October and were, nevertheless, "more than pleased with Nazareth." After they had visited the missions, Mr. Rossiter arranged an outing for the sisters to Carlsbad Caverns. It was while Mother Eveline was on that trip that Sister Seraphica had a stroke and died on October 28. Mother's telegram arrived at Marywood during the sisters' reception of the Master General of the Order. In her November circular letter Mother related the details of the sad journey home:

*Poor Sister Seraphica, her work was finished! You cannot realize what this meant--we had traveled the ways so often together. The people of Albuquerque were very kind to us, and knowing Sister Seraphica, you will realize how many friends she had made out there. We started home with the remains Thursday, and reached Marywood Saturday evening at sundown. The scene at Marywood was most impressive; the sisters were there in numbers from the near-by missions, and lined the path from the entrance of the grounds to the chapel door. Such a sad but affectionate welcome home for the poor old dear who had the interests of the Congregation ever uppermost in her mind.... Sisters, we will long continue to miss her--she who sacrificed herself in the interests of our Community. The day before she left for New Mexico she supervised the planting of a hundred trees on Marywood grounds. What a tribute of love they will be to her memory!*

The funeral Mass was celebrated on Tuesday, November 4, both for Sister Seraphica and for Mother Boniface Hartleb who had died on November 2. Bishop Gallagher, forty-five priests, Dominican sisters from Adrian, Racine, and Newburgh, and the congregation were present to say "Auf Wiedersehen" to the two stalwart German pioneers. Father Clement Thuente, OP, preached their eulogy.

Work was resumed on the sanatorium in January 1931. Sister Blanche Steves, now congregational bursar, stayed in Albuquerque to watch the construction to its completion on June 15, 1931. Approximately $60,000[17] was spent on the two-story adobe structure with twelve completed rooms on the first floor: six sleeping rooms with adjoining sleeping porches, two bathrooms, a kitchen, temporary dining room and temporary chapel. There remained to be finished on the first floor six additional sleeping rooms and adjoining porches, a lobby, two offices, and a large dining hall. The second story was to have a chapel, chaplain's rooms, a library, sisters' sleeping quarters, a utility room, and ten sleeping rooms for patients, six of these with adjoining porches. In the first five years of the sanatorium's existence, upkeep amounted to over $17,000. The necessary completion, furnishings, ordinary and extraordinary maintenance represented a large and ever present concern to congregational administrations, especially during the years when mortgages and insurance premiums on the motherhouse were due.[18]

On April 20, 1931, the sisters formed a corporation under the laws of the State of New Mexico "to engage in benevolent, educational and religious work in the State of New Mexico; to buy, construct, equip, maintain and operate schools, missions, hospitals, sanatoriums, and other institutions of like nature."[19]

Through the influence of the Superintendent of the Santa Fe County schools, Mrs. Adelina Otero Warren,[20] the sisters were asked to serve in Santa Cruz. The Holy Family fathers of Spain had come to Santa Cruz in 1920 at the request of Archbishop Daeger. The fathers were eager to have sisters in the parish and they built a large two-story convent even before sisters were secured. On August 24, 1928, Sisters Seraphine Wendling, Sienna Wendling, Leonissa Housten and Amata Baader arrived in Santa Cruz. From time to time young girls boarded with the sisters. In October 1928 Mother Eveline and Sisters Seraphica and Jerome, mistress of novices, visited the convent and school. Several candidates for the novitiate and aspirancy were interviewed during the visit. At the time Mother Eveline and Sister Seraphica were studying the feasibility of opening a hospital in New Mexico. Taos was first investigated but at the time the Jesuits renewed their offer of land near Albuquerque which Mother accepted.

The spacious Santa Cruz convent with its sun porches became a popular stopping place for visiting and infirm sisters. Mother Benedicta, having accompanied a sister from Michigan to a sanatorium in Demming, New Mexico, stayed with the sisters throughout December 1928. On July 8, 1929, the first retreat was held there. Father Floribert Blank, OFM, conducted the five-day program for eighteen sisters. Then most moved on to Peñasco for a summer school, an extension of Sacred Heart College, conducted by Sister Kyran Moran.

Sister Seraphine served as principal of the Santa Cruz public school from 1928 to 1949, guiding the school to become a fully accredited four-year high school. As early as 1929 a Dominican sister of Racine, Wisconsin, was on the faculty and lived with the sisters, an early evidence of collaboration with other congregations. As a consequence of the church-state litigation originating in Dixon, the parish opened Holy Cross school, a nine-grade parochial facility in the fall of 1949. Sisters remain in ministry to the parish to the present.

The following year, 1929, Mother Eveline agreed to another responsibility in New Mexico. At the request of Pastor Joseph Pajot, Dominican sisters took up residence at the Indian Reservation of San Juan Pueblo, thirty miles north of Santa Fe. Sisters Loyola Finn, Alacoque Wingen, and Leonissa Housten first opened school in an old residence which the community renovated to provide two classrooms. A third classroom was soon added in the pastor's garage. In mid-November Mother Eveline accompanied the fourth teacher, Sister John Dominic Krausmann, to San Juan Pueblo. Sister Loyola Finn, former member of Mother Benedicta's council and novice mistress, was hospitalized for several months during that hard first year. The school was, like others in the state, a public school with some faculty from religious congregations. Father Pajot, a French priest remembered for his aristocratic origins and gentility, contributed both his labor and his material resources to the building of the convent.

As a consequence of the "Dixon Case," the sisters appeared in the San Juan school for their last day on May 25, 1949. That summer a parochial school was reorganized in an old adobe building. Desks came from St. Francis parish, Santa Fe, and textbooks and supplies from the sisters in Michigan and school began anew on September

6, 1949. In 1968 the elementary school was closed and a religious education center developed to provide a variety of services.

In 1933, St. Mary school, Belen, south of Albuquerque, came under congregational supervision. The Sisters of Mercy had conducted a school in the parish fifty years before and Ursuline sisters reopened it in 1927. When the Ursulines found it necessary to leave, the pastor, Father Boniface Efferam, OSM, sought Mother Eveline's help. In 1930 Mother had met Father Boniface and suggested that after completing Nazareth the sisters might go on to Bethlehem (Belen). On April 17, 1933, Mother wrote to Fathers Efferam and Paul Dywer, Servite fathers:

*These plans take form so slowly that it seems almost impossible to hurry them. The Bishop of Grand Rapids is so deliberate in giving his consent to such affairs that the delay is now in his regard. I know positively he will say yes, and we shall go ahead with the supposition. He never stands in the way of the progress of the community, nor ever embarrasses us in our dealings with others, but I always feel I must get his definite consent before I start to do a thing, in order that the blessing of God may rest on the project.*

*The main difficulty is that teachers being sent to New Mexico from Michigan today must have degrees or a year in New Mexico with six semester hours of college work in the State of New Mexico. We have plenty of sisters with degrees, but we have so many high schools in Michigan demanding degreed teachers that it is not so easy to get degreed teachers for your grade school. I must not start up toppling over some of our Michigan schools and expect Bishop's sympathy with Belen.*

*Now if you wish to get names of sisters to place before your Board, I can give you names, but I am not sure that such names will stand. At present I could say that I have two sisters in New Mexico whose names I can suggest, but it will not be well for you to let our priests of New Mexico know about it until I can get down there and plan with them for a change. They are.... The name of the third sister I cannot tell you, but if you want to call her Sister Mary Smith, you may...*

Bishop Pinten approved the arrangement in July after he was provided information on title ownership of school and convent and the nature and extent of mortgages and indebtedness on properties. Mother Eveline encountered difficulties in assigning sisters due to the Board of Education's interpretation of a state law requiring one year's residence as well as nine term hours credit in New Mexico. She was faced with the possibility of sending sisters as catechists, sacristans, musicians in parishes until residency was fulfilled. She urged the Servites and other pastors to lobby the governor and archbishop for clarification. Difficulties were resolved and a contract between the sisters and the Servite fathers was formalized on August 1, 1933.[21] In subsequent years, salary provisions were points of controversy both with the Servite fathers and the local Board of Education.

In late August 1933 Mother Eveline sent Sisters Mechtilde Cordes, Norberta Boerraker, Marie Therese (Loretta) Tacey, Adorine Grypma, and Ann Perpetua Romero to Belen. Aided by lay teachers James Wayne and Bernice Chavez, the sisters took over the school as a public school. By the end of the school year 334 pupils were enrolled in the eight grades, another 75 unable to attend due to lack of room.

In 1935 St. Francis church, Ranchos de Taos, was given parish status with Father J. C. Balland, an elderly and loved French missionary, as the pastor. Sisters Eugene Marie Forster, Caritas Maturen, and Rose Imelde DeHaus were the first to serve in this historic northern New Mexico community. A temporary school was fashioned out of an old store, with a portable black board and long benches the only equipment. A four-room house, each of the rooms opening to the outside, served as convent. School opened on September 28 for 62 children. At the end of summer, the older children came from the summer pastures and the school numbered about 125. The sisters also tutored several women for high school certificates. Tuition was fifty cents a month; the sisters were paid $15 a month, the rest of the income going to the parish. The following year school opened with 220 pupils, and three lay teachers had joined the sisters. At the end of the school year a new school and convent were planned. Taos County School Board obtained permission for use of the facility as a public school with the sisters continuing as faculty. A larger school was built by the county in 1941. In 1969 the buildings were used as a religious education center and the children transferred to other public facilities. A decade later an elementary school was opened in the building. A member of the Grand Rapids congregation continued to minister in the parish until 1990.

On December 2, 1931, Archbishop Daeger died unexpectedly as the result of a fall. This exceptional representative of Christ was mourned throughout the Southwest. He was kindly, gentle, practical and gracious in his dealings with all. In 1932 Bishop Daniel J. Gerken of Arizona succeeded Archbishop Daeger as ordinary of the Archdiocese of Santa Fe. Mother Eveline resumed negotiations with the new archbishop on matters that affected the congregation in

New Mexico, among them the acceptance of missions, personnel assignments, certain financial and regulatory arrangements, including sisters' attendance at colleges and universities.

It was then the practice that the salaries of sisters teaching within the public school system, approximately $70 per month,[22] were sent to the mother general. She returned a portion to the Archbishop who, in turn, supplied the priests' upkeep. In 1934-1935 the congregation bought land within the Picuris Pueblo for approximately $15,000 to build a high school in Peñasco. At the same time, the public school salaries due the sisters were not paid by Father Kuppers, pastor of the Peñasco-Dixon churches and superintendent of Independent School District No. 30. Archbishop Gerken and Mother Eveline successfully negotiated the difficulty, but until the cash flow was resumed the archbishop personally sent to Dixon "plenty of provisions for the sisters, as a little token from myself so that they will not be in want for at least a few days."

It was the custom that sisters leave their missions at the conclusion of the school year for a full program of study, prayer, and work during the "long vacation." Since 1923 most of the congregation spent July and August at Marywood in the summer school programs. There was also a contingent at various colleges and universities or in rural vacation schools. Due to the distance and the cost of travel, it was understood that the sisters in New Mexico would not return to Michigan until at least six years had passed. By 1929 retreat and summer school were organized for the sisters at Dixon and Peñasco. That year Mother Eveline and Sister Seraphica looked at property near the University of Albuquerque which they considered "invaluable as a center for educational purposes, not so much for the present as the future of the Community." On January 6, 1930, the council approved the purchase of the entire city block adjacent to the northeast corner of the university for $5,250.[23] That spring Sister Blanche arranged for a summer rental for eleven sisters near the University of Albuquerque. In 1935 fourteen sisters attended the University of New Mexico, and six sisters, the Las Vegas Normal College.

There developed a special camaraderie among the sisters in New Mexico. Annals of the sisters' first years in the missions mention visits from house to house and the sharing of school books and household goods. The Summer of '29 came to have an mythical significance among the early missioners: retreat, summer school, excursions, and fiesta. Sister Marie Therese Tacey included in the annals for the opening year at Santa Cruz these memories:

*After Retreat, Sister Loyola, Kyran and I took Margarite to her home in Viocito, a little adobe hamlet about eighty miles southwest of Santa Cruz and isolated in a beautiful mountain valley. We were such a curiosity that all the people of the neighborhood made it their business to get a good look at us. After partaking of a typical Mexican meal of chili, frijoles, Mexican cookies and coffee we returned home [by way of] Ojo Caliente, one of New Mexico's famous curative hot springs.*

*...One of the memorable occasions...was the big fiesta at Santa Clara on August 12. The High Mass was followed by a series of Indian dances in the plaza, after which we were offered the hospitality of the Naranjo home. Meanwhile a sumptuous dinner had been prepared and fearing to displease our Indian host, we accepted his urgent invitation to dinner before returning to Santa Cruz. The long dining table seated about fifty at a time, and the meal that was served would have been a credit to the most exacting American chef, so well prepared were all the foods.*

*Among the guests were Mrs. Naranjo's relatives from Oklahoma, her two sisters and their children, well-fed chiefs, solemn looking Indians and their wives, well representing the wealth of their Oklahoma oil fields by their luxurious limousines, driven by American chauffeurs, and by their costly jewels and rich garments.*

*At the close of the summer school Sister Kyran returned to Grand Rapids. The fruits of her inspiring class work and helpful guidance will long remain with the sisters who attended her classes.*

Santa Cruz convent and the congregationally owned houses, Sacred Heart priory in Peñasco and Nazareth Sanatorium, became retreat and vacation centers for sisters who could benefit from the climate of the Southwest. In May 1930 the fourteen sisters who were professed twelve years gathered for "The First General Chapter in New Mexico." They cast votes for the Prioress General, councilors, bursar and secretary, the results sent to Grand Rapids and combined with the votes cast in the August Chapter of Election.

In 1927 two young women entered the congregation from Peñasco with others coming from various New Mexico communities in following years. The mission to New Mexico, first undertaken in 1925 by Mother Benedicta and courageously expanded during Mother Eveline's terms, continues to enrich the congregation and Church with the generous and gifted sisters who come from that state.

At the same time that the sisters' ministry was expanding in New Mexico, the congregation opened a school in the Diocese of Detroit. It was the first mission there since Bishop Richter's announcement of independence of the congregation in 1894. In fall 1929 Sisters Roberta Nickle, Philippa Schmidt, Edwin Bozek, Rose Gonzaga Sydlowski, Vincent Ferrer Rasch, and Rose Miriam Visner opened the school in St. Mary Magdalene parish in Melvindale, a suburb of Detroit, where Father Edward Saylor was pastor. Sisters continued in the school until 1984, and from 1985 to 1989, supervised a ministry of spiritual direction, retreats, and Christian hospitality in the convent.

In 1930, at Bishop Pinten's request, the congregation replaced the Sisters of Mercy in the food service department of St. Joseph Seminary at 600 Burton Street in Grand Rapids. Sisters Josephine Erbisch, Claudia Bedard, Bertha Gutknecht, Melitta Tague, Ann Therese Ruczynski, Rose Germaine Fedewa, and a postulant were the first assigned there. Father Thomas L. Noa, later Bishop of Marquette, was rector of the 200 students there. He was an accomplished musician and occasionally instructed the novices in Gregorian chant.

The sisters resided in a section of the seminary reserved for them until a convent was built in 1949. The convent served as home to the sisters until 1978, when it was remodelled as the chancery. In addition to those regularly assigned to the seminary, large numbers of sisters assisted in housekeeping tasks during the priests' retreats, clergy conventions, and on special occasions. Two sisters remained in food service ministry at the seminary until June 1981 when the minor seminary program was discontinued. Sister Christopher Steinforth, a registered nurse, served the seminarians as infirmarian from 1936-1970. In her honor, the collegiate seminary residence on Robinson Road was dedicated as "The Christopher House," and upon the sale of that building, the name was transferred to the seminary's new location. It was a ministry which created lasting friendships between the sisters and the priests of the diocese whom the sisters had served as youths.

# 10

# CRUSADES,
# EAST AND NORTH

*I*n early January 1929 Mother Eveline wrote to Sister Ursula Lanciaux in Regina, Saskatchewan:

*Our Christmas at home was a very lovely one. Everything as peaceful and beautiful as usual. After Communion at that midnight Mass my thoughts went off to the dear sisters across the sea, to the sisters on the northern plains of Canada, to the sisters in far New Mexico, and to the dear ones at home; yes, and to those upon whose graves the snows had fallen and the rains had beat; for after all, I knew that they were all now my daughters. A very kinlike feeling comes to me when I think of them and their interests.*

In December 1927 Mother and her council discussed ways and means to obtain recruits to the community. "The work incumbent on the sisters," Mother explained, "is increasing rapidly, and in consequence the sisters are breaking down. Unless every effort is made to increase the number of sisters by getting more good Postulants, the Community will suffer in more ways than one." The European vocation crusade, the Canadian mission, and the aspirancy were undertaken primarily for this reason.

By February 16, 1928, the four sisters chosen for the European project were named and permission for the venture was granted by Bishop Pinten. On March 29, 1928, Sisters Seraphica Brandstetter, Coletta Baumeister, Philomena Kildee, and Edith Welzel[1] departed from New York on the North German Lloyd vessel, the *S.S. Berliner*. Sisters Albertina Selhuber and Geraldine Kenny accompanied them to New York, where they settled in at The Leo House, a new Catholic hospice on West 23rd Street. Bernard Friedrich, the director, had arranged tickets and visas for the sisters. The four departed shortly after midnight, their companions returning to The Leo House until their train left for Michigan.

Council minutes record that Mother Eveline had "mapped out very accurately the work to be done and the places to be visited." A formal resolution of council detailed their mission:

*1. To confer with Fathers Sauvage and Nolan relative to our Constitutions which were then before the Sacred Congregation.*

*2. To obtain recruits for our Community, and to look for a suitable site where a quasi-novitiate house could be established for the purpose of training and testing out the candidates before sending them to the States.²*

In her autobiography, written in 1929, Sister Seraphica noted these purposes and also mentioned that the project was considered a fitting way "to commemorate the fiftieth anniversary of our establishment in Michigan, and the seventy-fifth anniversary of the first four sisters coming from Ratisbon, Bavaria, to plant the Dominican Order in the United States."

A press release, written by Sister Jane Marie Murray, announced that "Dominican Sisters of Grand Rapids, Michigan, open Postulancy in Europe." The names of the pioneers and the general outline of the journey were related, its serious intent underlined:

*Pleasant as this trip should be, the sisters are engaged primarily, of course, with our Father's business. The vital need of many more laborers to carry on effectively the work already undertaken by our community--in view of the ever-increasing demands in the schools and to make it possible for us to extend our services more widely, this need it is which gives the incentive for the present mission of our sisters in Europe. There we hope to establish in some favorable locality a Novitiate House to receive young women, train them in religious life and to prepare them to enlist in the glorious apostolate of Catholic education in America. From Bavaria, from other parts of Germany, from France and Belgium, Ireland and England, and from other European countries they hope to secure postulants and to this end they are laboring zealously. Nor is this problem one which concerns them alone. Rather must it interest deeply all those who see in America vast fields white for the harvest and who earnestly desire to gather in for the Master a glorious harvest of souls.*

In a letter to Father Cornelius Selhuber, OSB, in Savanna, Georgia, native of Bavaria and brother to Sisters Matthia and Albertina, Mother Eveline made clear her understanding of the project in relation to the life and work of the community:

*Of course, Father, I know that this European project is a venture, but in my experience I have found that one has to venture quite a good deal, and I believe I am of the venturesome kind, and yet, Father, I have spent hours and hours, perhaps several hundred hours, interviewing people from all parts, writing them and asking advice. It is true a good many letters have been somewhat discouraging, but I see Communities bringing good subjects over here from time to time, and if there are good subjects there I want to get some. Our sisters are splendid women, but are frail,--excellent teachers, but they have had to work too hard and so I must really almost double their number to save them, and while it is only adding an extra worry to me, still this job seems to be a worrisome kind.*

She prepared a closely typed five-page itinerary with fifteen points and many sub-headings for the travelers. Upon landing at Plymouth, England, Sisters Seraphica and Philomena were to go to the Sisters of Notre Dame on Wyndam Street; Sisters Coletta and Edith were to go on to No. 29, Bergmannstrasse, Munich, Bavaria, as guests of Sister Coletta's relatives, and begin an intensive recruitment program. In one of her first letters to the sisters in Munich, Mother wrote, "Well, how are you? By this time I am sure you are on terra firma, or as the old lady said, on terra cotta."

She continued with inquiries as to the logistics of their arrival, where they spent Easter Sunday, what they felt. She included as well additional addresses and letters of recommendation, further steps in her well-charted crusade. They were to place an ad in Catholic newspapers at once. Their terse entry, in the personals section and in the script of the era, announced:

### Klosterberufe

Gesunde, brave Mädchen im Alter von 14-26 Jahren, welche Klosterberuf haben, nach Amerika, bitten wir auf den Orden des Hl. Dominicus aufmerksam machen zu wollen. Um nähere Auskunft wende man sich an die Dominikanerschwestern München, Bergmanstr. 29.[3]

The next stage for Sisters Seraphica and Philomena was to see Father Bede Jarrett, OP, at St. Dominic priory, Haverstock Hill, London. They were to stay with the Sisters of Providence, all these visits arranged by Mother's letters, sometimes with a $10 or $20 bill included. The sisters were told to:

*Watch for CSC Community Houses. When any priest is very nice, especially good, and helps you out--send me his address at once and I will write him. Advertise in the papers in Ireland....Now Lourdes...my request for Lourdes and for Theresa Neumann are...pray for us that we may be granted: Charity and love of prayer, our Rule and this European project, Canada and New Mexico. For our sisters, and for myself--health for body and soul....*

The sisters took letters of introduction to priests, bishops, and sisters, many of whom Mother Eveline personally wrote prior to their departure. The Redemptorist fathers of St. Louis, Missouri,[4] the Norbertines of St. John's, Essexville, the Dominican fathers of St. Joseph Province, the Holy Cross fathers of Notre Dame, the Holy Spirit fathers of St. Joseph's, Bay City, Benedictines from

Georgia, friends and colleagues of the sisters since their beginnings in Michigan, and superiors of women's groups provided letters of introduction, contacts and advice. Sisters with relatives in Europe sent addresses and messages.

Sister Seraphica kept a small black address book in which she also noted plans, ticket and check numbers, and expense records. On the first page she reminded herself, "In Rome see Frs. Nolan and Horn, Collegio Angelico. Angelus Walz, Card. Fruhwirth on Via San Vitale 15." In another place she noted, "Rome, Msgr. Spellman, Secretariat of State, Vatican...Rev. Fr. Sauvage." A sampling from her expense record, entered in both pounds sterling and United States currency, suggests a bursar's attentiveness and simpler economies:

| | |
|---|---|
| *Tickets on Bremen* | *32.50* |
| *taxi* | *.70* |
| *meal ticket* | *.60* |
| *beer and whiskey* | *.50* |
| *return to Karlsruhe* | *25.00* |
| *laundry and postage* | *1.00* |
| *ticket to London* | *11.90* |
| *telegram to Mother* | *1.00* |
| *chair and blanket* | *3.00* |
| *tips* | *2.00* |
| *trip to Oxford* | *1.80* |
| *Sisters for Board* | *1.50* |
| *stamps* | *.50* |
| *fares from Stone* | *1.25* |
| *lunch at Crewe* | *.25* |
| *Fares through Ireland* | *26.87* |
| *Irish Rosary* | *2.43* |
| *Medicine* | *.75* |
| *Board and baggage, Cobh* | *6.00* |
| *Porter and shoes* | *.25* |

Sisters Seraphica and Philomena reached Ireland in mid-April. Sister Seraphica recollected:

*It being rather early in spring and not being used to the climate, we suffered very much from the cold and inclement weather. Many a tear rolled down upon my cheeks, but all was forgotten when a month later we reached the Eternal City, warmer climate, and hallowed places watered by the blood of so many martyrs.*

Throughout Ireland they presented to the bishops a form letter which read:

*Having obtained the permission of_____ to seek for
Postulants for our Sisterhood in your diocese, I undertake and
promise that any subject whom I may adopt and who may
subsequently, for any reason whatsoever, prove unsuitable, will
be returned to her home at the responsibility and expense of the
Sisterhood.*

*Signed* _____

*Mother General.*

They also presented to the bishops and ecclesiastics a letter from Father Patrick Carroll:

*To my Friends in Ireland:*

*These two Dominican sisters who are in Ireland in the interest of their
Community to seek worthy girls for their order, are deserving of your kindliest
reception and hospitality. They have a beautiful school in Grand Rapids,
Michigan, and are doing great work for Catholic Education all through this great
state. I have two nieces going to school with them and they are making splendid
progress. If they have vocations to the religious life, I hope they will become
members of this Community.*

*If you know of any good Irish girls whom you can recommend, I trust you will
remember these devoted Nuns. Be good to them, they have hearts like our own
people and anyone who comes to them will be in a place that is next door to
Ireland.*

*Very cordially yours,*
*P.J. Carroll, CSC*
*Vice-President, University of Notre Dame*

Having secured permission, the sisters travelled throughout Ireland, visiting schools and convents, leaving vocation material, interviewing girls interested in entering an American sisterhood. Their contacts yielded as well two possible sites for the formation house, one in County Clare, the other in County Cork. "Newhall," a country house, some three miles from Ennis in Clare, with forty acres of land and a "range of out offices" and gate lodge, was offered for £5,000.[5] The entire demesne, house and buildings, and 324 acres was available for £8,000. "Inniscarrra House," a country residence in County Cork, was a twelve-bedroom house situated on fifteen acres of garden and grazing land, with three-quarter mile of salmon fishing on the River Lee. The Cork realtor offered the property, "held in fee simple free of rent for ever," to the sisters for £2,500 and a five percent commission. It was, Sister Seraphica wrote to the sisters on the continent, "a little paradise here on the river Lee."

On April 28, 1928, Sisters Seraphica and Philomena sailed from Cobh, Ireland, on the *Munchen* for France, Holland, Belgium and then to Germany and Italy. During their stay on the continent they remained in contact with the Irish realtors. In Holland, they were guests of Father Henry Frencken (1860-1953), in his youth one of Bishop Richter's recruits to Grand Rapids. He was an assistant at St. Andrew's for several years, then in 1887 began St. Joseph's "Holland Parish" for Dutch Catholics in Grand Rapids. He remained there until his return to the Netherlands in 1908.

The four sisters met in mid-May in Augsburg, Bavaria, where Sister Seraphica met her sister, Sister Generosa, after three decades' separation. The four continued on to Rome, eventually parting on May 31, 1928. Sisters Seraphica and Philomena left for almost a month's stay in Ireland before their June 30 departure to New York on the *Liverpool*. They arrived at the Marywood gates on July 12, 1928, where "all the good nuns gave us a great welcome. They marched in procession to the entrance of the grounds with a tin pan band music. All were eager to listen to our travelogues, etc." By early September Sister Seraphica was enroute to Albuquerque to oversee the building of the new sanatorium. Hearts at home and abroad were still high with the prospects of the European vocation crusade.

Sisters Edith and Coletta remained on the continent to continue the work of recruiting and to find a suitable location for an aspirancy-postulancy. From their base at 29 Bergmanstrasse in Munich, the sisters negotiated with the American consulate for allowance of the candidates on the immigration quotas set for the various countries. One of their first visits was to Regensburg and Holy Cross convent. Their first evening there they joined the sisters for Compline, they in the church, the nuns behind the grille. They could hear the familiar *Salve* but saw "only the light behind the grating." They stayed the night in the convent guest lodgings and spent the next day "face to face" with the sisters engaged in the school.

In June the two sisters visited Theresa Neumann, the stigmatist, in Konnersreuth, Bavaria. Along with a pilgrimage to Rome, the visit was one of Mother Eveline's "obediences" to the sisters. Sister Edith wrote to Mother on June 11, 1928:

*Theresa has not been suffering her usual Friday agony since Easter or I should say Good Friday. It will return again on the Feast of the Sacred Heart so we were just two weeks too soon. The pastor too was absent at the time so we again lost a golden opportunity of learning many things concerning Theresa....Of course you hear wonder upon wonder from the people near by but you know how the story grows and the pastor's evidence would have been genuine.*

*We remained overnight in the house next to Neumann's and the first time we saw the stigmatist she was caring for her flowers in her little garden beside the house with a little white lamb frisking at her side and a group of little children outside the fence watching.... She was dressed in black with the exception of her white head-kerchief. Her hands were covered with black gloves from which the fingers had been cut. She is neither singular or extraordinary in her actions or appearance. A poor humble village girl who talked to the children as she worked or gently pushed aside the little lamb at her flowers....*

*I can see her yet as she came across the street assisted by a younger sister and tho each step caused her an effort she walked remarkably well when one considered her wounded feet. Smilingly she entered the room and sat in our midst so unconcerned and so gentle and unassuming that in two seconds she had completely stolen our hearts.*

*She pushed aside her gloves at the request of one of the priests and showed us her wounded hands. The inner wound is rather oblong and not so large but the outer hand shows a wound about as large as a nickel, over which a thick, healthy looking scab had formed. She says she suffers continually because of the contraction and expansion of the muscles and could at that time work a little with her finger tips as the wounds had not opened for some time or I should have said since her last agony.*

*...She spoke of a little outing the family had at Pentecost and smilingly related that she stood the trip better than anyone. Sister Coletta asked her prayers for our intentions, which had to be given in a general way on account of the number present. She promised them willingly and asked ours in return. God surely works His wonders through His weakest creatures. How impressed we were to witness such a prodigy in the midst of downright poverty. His chosen one was born and raised in an environment as poor and humble as His own. A little white-washed room with bare floors, a bed in one corner, a few chairs and a machine at which her old father who is a tailor, earns his daily bread, and behold the best room in the house of a saint.*

In June they returned to Regensburg to meet Bishop Buchberger and to find housing. He counselled them to purchase property suitable for a preparatory school, not primarily a novitiate.[6] They were aided in their recruiting and housing searches by George Haas, a relative of Sister Evangelista Rohrl, a native of Regensburg, and by an estate agent he had contacted, Herr Kratochwill of a Munich-Regensburg firm. On June 18, they were first offered the estate of the Pustets of publishing renown. There were, the agent told them, other prospective buyers. So on July 1, the sisters went to Munich to see the Pustets and asked them to hold the place without an option until the bishop of Regensburg consulted his council on allowing the sisters to settle there. The house, though lacking steam heating and a bath, was centrally located on spacious grounds. The asking price was 65,000 marks, which along with notary fees, would have amounted to about $22,000 which Mother Eveline considered "a tremendous amount for us."

In early July a second buyer offered more money and without delay. It appears that it was the chaplain of the Dominican nuns of Holy Cross who made the offer. The sisters from Grand Rapids became embroiled in local ecclesiastical politics, though the vicar general of the diocese continued to assist them. Mother wrote them on July 25 telling them of the crusade of prayer at Marywood on behalf of the overseas mission and that she was still conferring with Bishop Pinten who "seems inclined to Holland, as it is near the sea, and neutral...." In a page-long handwritten postscript, she expressed her fear that the sisters had not made clear to the bishop of Regensburg that:

*On board the* **Bremen.**
*LEFT TO RIGHT*
*Sisters Philomena, Seraphi*
*Edith, Coletta, with capt*
*and fellow travelers, July*
*1928*

*You are just getting points and are not sure we can locate there yet...I [am] worried that you were making things too positive about our surely going to settle there. Do nothing further about a house for yourselves until you hear definitely where you are to settle. I have tried to make this clear in each letter, for you must be on very good terms with the bishop of Regensburg and his priests even tho we do not settle there for where will your postulants come from if they get angry. I do not wish to get the Pustet House at all if any priests are against it even tho we got it for a song.*

On July 31, Mother repeated her caution to the sisters and indicated that she had written to Herr Haas declining the Pustet offer. In the meantime, other offers were allegedly made to the realtors for the house and a portion of the gardens. The sisters continued their recruiting efforts throughout Bavaria during the summer. By mid-August the agent of the Bayerische Immobilien und Handels-Gesellschaft involved in the Pustet negotiations threatened legal action for breach of promise. In angry letters to the sisters in Munich and six registered letters to Mother Eveline, Herr Kratochwill demanded payment of $5,000 as redress on his losses while he held the property as well as a bill of 6,000 marks for services. The correspondence held both threat to the congregation and a measure of things to come on the continent. On August 24, 1928, Herr Krachtochwill wrote to Sister Coletta:

*Finally it is no small disgrace for your Order, if at first you leave nothing undone to procure a suitable objective, and having obtained it through great difficulties the whole thing is suddenly overthrown with the excuse that 'the price is much*

Postkarte

15 15
IMMANUEL KANT
Deutsches Reich

NORDDEUTSCHER LLOYD, BREMEN
Bremerhaven
Lloydhalle

Dear Sr. M. Albertina:—
This is what we are looking
forward to now. The
Sisters are leaving me
tonight. We have had
one wonderful trip. Expect
to spend Easter in Hanover
and then for Munich.
Give my love to all
the Sisters.
Lovingly,
Sr. M. Edith

Sister M. Albertina O.P.
Sacred Heart College, Marywood
Fulton St. E.
Grand Rapids, Michigan
U.S. America

*too high and that you do not intend to buy in Germany.' We surely don't trifle
with our business, and won't let ourselves to be led around by the nose for three
months, as has been the case here. If jews act in that manner and treat others
like that, one can account for it; but that catholics, and above all an order of
Religious Women will treat a real estate firm like that is impossible to stress in
words.[7]*

Advice was sought on both sides of the Atlantic. Eventually
sufficient evidence was marshalled to show that the sisters had
signed no contract nor made any formal arrangement with the
company. Mother advised the sisters not to return to Regensburg
but to go on to Holland. She would, she said, clarify the matter
with the bishop of Regensburg.

On October 11, 1928, Sisters Coletta and Edith went to stay with
Father Frencken and his sisters at Vughterdyk 85,
S'Hertogenbosch, Holland. The following day they were once again
involved in a property investigation: a house in Haarlem
recommended by Father Frencken and Monsignor Simon
Pongannis, a pioneer with Father Frencken in Grand Rapids, then
visiting his family in Europe. Earlier Sisters Seraphica and
Philomena had considered a site in the diocese of Roermond[8] near
the village of Venlo. The "Villa Josephine" had a large central
house, an industrial building once used as a tannery, and a brick
caretaker's cottage on a spacious lot. There they envisaged the
postulancy and a supportive ministry, perhaps English language
tuition, fine arts instruction, and the keeping of a school in the
village.

Father Frencken wrote to Mother Eveline:

*The teachers for public or private schools, lay teachers or religious are all paid
by the Government on the same basis, and this is very liberal...As the tendency
in Holland is among the better classes of people, that every young lady should
know English and be able to converse in it, the sisters can give private
conversation lessons, and prepair [sic] teachers to get their diplomas from the
Government in the English language...*

From April to September 1928 Mother Eveline gave serious
consideration to that proposal and asked two sisters to "study
Holland," Sister Clementia Hagen to work on the geography of the
country, Sister Clotilda Gauthier to prepare to give painting
lessons. They were not to tell other sisters lest a rumor reach the
bishop. She also prepared to send Sister Philomena back to Holland
and with her Sister Alexia Fruchtl, a native of Germany who had
entered the congregation in 1905.

The site in Haarlem, a city not far from Amsterdam on the seacoast, was a large house which could readily serve as a house of formation. An infant care apostolate, the "Home of the Little Teresa," on the first and second-story, would support the whole household. The house was offered for $11,500. In a letter to Mother Eveline on October 12, 1928, Father Frencken described the property and apostolate at great length and advised Mother to send the sisters a cable reading, "Go ahead, check follows." On October 16, Mother Eveline cabled Father Frencken:

> *WILL SEE BISHOP PINTEN IN GRAND RAPIDS OCTOBER*
> *29 AND SETTLE MAY GO MYSELF HOLLAND PLEASED*
> *WITH HAARLEM. EVELINE*

By the end of October it was clear to Mother Eveline that Bishop Pinten would not allow any purchase, not in Holland, Germany, or Ireland. On December 6, 1928, she wrote to Father Frencken:

*Words cannot really convey to you how disappointed I am to have to write you the outcome of our final conversation with Bishop Pinten, in regard to the project for which we have paid out money, spent our sisters' strength and time, and spent much time and interest on the part of a few very good friends, but especially your own time, money and attention. If I did not sit down and carefully consider that we are in the hands of God, that we are guided by Divine Providence, and that we cannot go wrong after so many prayers, I would indeed be irritated. I have surely been very much in earnest from the beginning of the enterprise, and have talked hours and hours about it to Bishop Pinten before he consented to let the sisters go; and now, to find that he is withholding the permission to let us go on is very hard to bear.*

*He has now finally decided that it is not well to have a house in Europe at all; but that the sisters should go around, pick up good postulants and bring them home with them. He came to this decision after a meeting with some Bishops about five days ago. If I were as wise a year ago, as I am today, I would not have allowed the sisters to have left home at all; nor to spend themselves as they have.... I am looking for reasons in all directions, but can find none save those I have suggested....I cannot explain it.*

*...I do not wish our sisters in Michigan to know what I have told you. I am afraid they may feel hard toward the Bishop. I shall break the news...little by little before the sisters come home. The poor dear sisters who have worked so hard. I can see them in my dreams, in my waking hours....*

Within a week Mother hastily sent a follow-up letter to Father Frencken telling him neither to accept nor decline the property offers. A rumor was widely circulating in Grand Rapids that Bishop Pinten had resigned. "Do not hold anything, however, for we are clinging to a straw, as it were." It was indeed rumor and straw.

The sisters' stay with the Frenckens in Hertogenbosch had now extended to near three months. They were learning the Dutch language, Sister Coletta with more ease than Sister Edith. They in turn acted as maids and seamstresses for the household. They exchanged small gifts with Father and his sisters on St. Nicholas day, and had a quiet "spiritual Christmas." After New Year's day they returned to Germany for another round of recruiting and contacts with earlier prospects. On January 6, 1929, Sister Philomena, established at Marywood once again as a member of the council and secretary general, wrote them at their Munich address:

*Little did I think when I left you that January would find you in the Old World still without a home. Sr. Seraphica and myself were all enthusiastic on our return and thought that all that was necessary to be done was for you to report something suitable and the Bishop would say the word. We soon found out, however, that things were not to come out as easily and we had only to wait and pray. We prayed (the entire household) as we have never prayed before....We certainly thought the Bishop would allow us some chance to make good after permitting us to go across. Then too, if he had ever told us definitely we would not settle permanently in Europe we could have directed you accordingly, but he simply kept putting us off.*

*...So much for what was and was not. Now for what can be....*

*After you are finished in Germany, etc., Mother wants you to go into Ireland and get us some good girls from there....Everyone knows that it is no easy task to get into Ireland....*

*Now you must both be real **Irish** when you get into Ireland. Everyone will be asking you where you were born. Your parents will have to be connected somehow with Ireland for sure. Make that out if you can...*

Provided with this advice and contacts from the earlier visit to Ireland, Sisters Edith and Coletta prepared to leave the continent to continue recruiting and readying the Irish candidates for their journey to the States. They were instructed by letter from Mother Eveline on February 15, 1929, to go first to Lourdes "in obedience as my delegate to beseech our dear Lady to bless us all." They left Munich by train on April 3 and arrived in Lourdes on April 5 for several days' stay. They bought inexpensive medals for everyone in the congregation and personally touched them to the stone of apparition. A silver medal was sent to P.J. Grace,[9] president of the Grace Bank in New York City, who had given Mother Eveline $500 for the mission.

By April 9, 1929, they arrived in Dublin where they found everything "quite dear." Room and board was finally found for six shillings a day at the Iona Hotel on Upper Gardiner Street across from the Jesuit church. There were other sisters on recruiting missions from the United States, four of whom shared their room their first days in Dublin. The sisters resumed the pattern they had established on the continent for recruiting: calls at chanceries, rectories, and convents, advertisements in the Irish newspapers, visits in schools, and talks to sodalities on Sunday afternoons. Often they were out when the noon meal was served at their lodgings but with "canned heat" they managed to have hot cocoa and cake, presents from Sister Coletta's family. Sister Coletta reported their hardships and improvisations without complaint.

*The day we came it was very nice but now it is very cold and windy, we live in hopes that it won't last long. Our fingers are almost stiff writing it is so cold in the room and we are in a great hurry to make a number of calls today....*

*They don't serve much for supper here, only tea, bread and butter and sometimes some raisin bread with it, but having tea in the landlady's private room we come in for a piece of cake once in a while.*

*Now the laundry work. We brought soap and washing pd. from Munich, wash our clothes the day we take baths, hang them on the line (corset string) that is the large pieces in front of the window for a night or two, the small pieces hang as a decoration on the open umbrella and all works fine. Our mangle or iron cannot be beat and it does the job up fine in fact is serving two and three purposes. Every evening the maid puts a red hot aluminum water bottle in our bed, about the shape of a quartsize fruitjar but again as long and with that we do our pressing and it works fine. We use the water for washing, footbaths...besides heating our beds.*

They repeated the recruiting and housekeeping patterns as they went south and west, making Kilkenny, Waterford, Cork, Limerick, Galway, Sligo, and Roscommon their base for numerous city and country stops. They were back in Dublin by July 26. As time for departure neared, they had to arrange passports, immigration releases, and passage for their recruits as well as themselves. There appeared to be seven "sure ones" though the list changed daily. "If promises were all vocations," wrote Sister Edith, "I think we would have to charter a ship to take all the girls over." There were July appointments with the Consul General, "a Mister Ferris born in Michigan," before the girls were allowed to depart. The sisters did some "collecting" to help defray the costs of the girls' train and steamship fares, and a basic conventual wardrobe. At least on one occasion Sister Coletta arranged with a Dublin employer for work for the father of one of the girls. Discounts were arranged at Clerys Dry Goods Store on O'Connell Street for material for postulants' clothing. Railway and steamship officials were contacted for reduced fares for religious. Thus it was important to have the girls outfitted in some kind of clerical dress. The girls who could not be accompanied or met by sisters in New York were to be cared for by Mr. Friedrich of The Leo House.

Mother Eveline cabled money for passage for six girls on the *Republic* on August 22. Sister Edith was to remain in Ireland to "round up the second group of Irish girls." In mid-September Sister Coletta returned to Germany to expedite the sailing of the German girls. The work of advocacy before the American Consul in Stuttgart was almost as great as the initial recruiting and finally resulted in a year's delay for the German candidates.

As a final directive, Sister Philomena instructed the sisters:

*Here is another injunction from Mother. Do not go near the sisters in New York when you arrive. Go directly to the Leo House. The sisters are too inquisitive. What they don't know will not bother them. Another thing. Do not admit to anyone when you come home that it was on account of the Bishop. Simply say that Real Estate was too high to purchase and to rent at this time would be an expensive proposition also. Be careful what you say of the business part of the trip.*

Mother asked the sisters to return to Holland to pay a short visit to Father Frencken before their departure for America. On October 2 Sister Edith and the second "crowd" of Irish girls left Cobh on the *U.S. George Washington* in tourist third class. Sister Coletta left Bremerhaven on November 1, stopping at Cobh where she and an Irish candidate boarded the *U. S. George Washington* for home. They arrived in New York on November 11 and immediately cabled Mother Eveline, then at St. Joseph Sanitarium in Mt. Clemens for treatment:

> *CONGRATULATIONS JUST ARRIVED LEAVING FOR DETROIT GRAND RAPIDS 4 PM TOMORROW ANY INSTRUCTIONS MICHIGAN CENTRAL. COLETTA*

After more than twenty-one months abroad, the last of the four "crusaders" arrived home. The work had been arduous, filled with disappointments and lessons.

In the summer of 1931 Sister Alexia Fruchtl returned to Germany for a visit to her family after twenty-five years' absence. She was commissioned to continue the crusade. She was able to secure a visa for only one of five young women through the consulate at Stuttgart. Upon Sister Alexia's return, Mother Eveline contacted a

Benedictine house in South Dakota whose motherhouse was in Einsielden, Switzlerland. Within weeks arrangements were made for the four candidates to attend Marienheim, Mary's House, in Einsiedeln. Mother Eveline sent the appropriate affidavits needed for permits from the Swiss consulate and support and travel monies. The candidates stayed with the Benedictines from May until August 30, 1932, when they departed on the *Bremen* for America.

The European vocation trip eventually yielded fifteen fine German and Irish candidates "with hearts like our own."[10] The congregation began its second fifty years with a new infusion of youth and dedication from the homelands of its pioneers.

In January 1928 Mother Eveline and her council deliberated on several matters: the offer of land in Alameda, New Mexico, the European vocation project, renegotiation of congregational loans, a parish's plea for the reduction of the sisters' salary. They also considered an invitation from Archbishop Oliver Matthieu of Regina, Canada, to open a boarding and day school in Rosetown, Saskatchewan. Rosetown was eventually passed by but the archbishop reinforced Mother Eveline's appeal to Bishop Pinten to allow the sisters to take a school in Melville, Saskatchewan.

The Canadian mission grew out of the dream of Sister Ursula Lanciaux. Sister was born in Muskegon, Michigan, to French Canadian parents in 1875. She entered the congregation in 1896 and pioneered in schools with French-Canadian families: Holy Family, Saginaw, and St. Anne's, Alpena. From 1918 to 1926 she taught French at Catholic Central in Grand Rapids. She longed to make a foundation in Canada. Early in her religious life she was given the uncommon privilege of two visits to Canada. Due to a worsening tubercular condition, she was given permission by Mother Benedicta for an extended visit to her brother who lived on a large farm near Herschel in western Saskatchewan. Her companion for the summer months was Sister Mercedes Dargis, also born to French Canadian parents and conversant in French.

There was Mass in the area only one Sunday a month. On other Sundays the sisters were taken to Rosetown some twenty-five miles away. The first Sunday they were in Rosetown the pastor, Father Dubois, turned to the congregation and, to the astonishment of the sisters, introduced them as the community which would be building a convent and boarding school in Rosetown in the near future. Sometime later they met Archbishop Matthieu in Regina. It was these contacts that led to the opening of the mission in Melville, some ninety miles northeast of Regina. A year of negotiation ensued. Mother Eveline wrote Sister Ursula, then in Regina, in the spring of 1928:

*I urged Bishop to be sure and answer the Archbishop's letter soon and I think he will try to do so in the time that he considers soon but you know he doesn't act very hastily. He walks and jumps and hops around hastily, but his official acts have every characteristic of deliberation, provokingly deliberate at times. But what do we care for a few months wait if everything comes out well. I can see the dawn on the northern plains as I used to watch it from the window where I slept, and I still remember the night I woke up at two o'clock and looked out into the moonlight and wondered what the dream all meant,--the dream in which I saw the valley filled with white-robed sisters, and my angel companions, and the white rock. I shall never forget.*

Bishop Pinten's first objection to allowing the sisters to go to Canada was the depletion of the work force in his diocese. The previous year several missions had been closed, due primarily to changed economic conditions in the lumbering communities in the north of the state. He also objected to the costs of travel and of establishing a house. Finally on July 5, 1928, however, Mother Eveline was able to inform Sister Ursula by telegram:

*GOD BE PRAISED BISHOP PINTEN WRITING HIS GRACE THREE DOMINICAN SISTERS AND YOURSELF GO TO MELVILLE IN AUGUST IF ALL SATISFACTORY WHEN YOU VISIT THERE GO AND REPORT IN TEN DAYS I SHALL BE MORE DEFINITE KEEP FROM LAY TEACHERS MOTHER.*

On August 16, 1928, Sisters Mercedes Dargis, Petronilla Tureck, and Evangela Ronning left Marywood for St. Henry Roman Catholic Separate School, Division No. 5 in Melville.[11] They stayed several days in Regina as guests of the archbishop while they arranged the necessary documentation for teaching within the provincial system. Sisters Mercedes and Petronilla set off by train for Melville. They were later joined by Sisters Evangela and Ursula. Sister Ursula, still infirm, served as assistant superior and bursar, trained altar boys, and recruited candidates for the congregation. Except for a brief return to Michigan in 1929, Sister Ursula remained in Canada, sometimes in Melville and then at the Grey Nuns' hospital in Regina, until her death in 1934. She is buried in Melville.

Melville was a railway town with a population of about four thousand. There were about a hundred Catholic families, mostly English and French speaking, in the town, and fifty Catholic families on farms nearby who were of Polish and German background. The school, a separate, that is, Catholic, school within the provincial school system, was housed in a two-story brick building which also served as the church. There had previously been religious congregations at the school with a history of some management and disciplinary difficulties. Although the pastor, Father A.J. Schimnowski, OMI, and some members of the school board had invited the Dominicans to the school, the sisters encountered great reserve, if not outright hostility, their first months in Melville. They gradually proved themselves competent in school matters, however, and came to be a respected group within the community and among provincial school officials.

School opened on September 3, 1928, with 169 pupils in the eight grades and 15 in the high school. The school had formerly had lay teachers of whom two, Bertha Pilon and Blanche O'Neill, remained on the teaching staff. The numbers and tasks increased so much that the sisters begged Mother Eveline for assistance. On December 8, 1928, Mother Eveline arrived with Sister Flavian Murphy, who would take on the fifth and sixth grades. The Oblate fathers in charge of the parish proved gracious and generous colleagues over the years.

Throughout 1928-1929 the Oblate fathers, the town council and the sisters negotiated the purchase of land sufficient to build a convent-boarding school

*for girls of the Roman Catholic Faith from the outlying districts, thus making it possible ...to attend a well graded school and of acquiring that culture and refinement so necessary for society. Girls of other denominations may also be received.*

*Besides the usual Twelve Year Course of Studies there will be departments of: Home Economics which will comprise the Study and Preparation of Foods, the Making of Garments and the Interior Decoration of the Home. Drawing and Painting. Music--Instrumental--Piano and violin. Voice Culture, Choral and Orchestral work.*

Bishop Pinten would not allow the sisters to contract any debts in Canada. They first lived as boarders in the Joachim Pilon home, then in an unfurnished rented house. The adjustment to the western plains and an arduous new school system, and the furnishing of the house were challenging. Sister Mercedes, the superior, and a woman not unfamiliar with hard times, wrote of their first days:

*What a place! At least we had a roof and a kitchen stove which was left in the house by the Jewish family, one double bed loaned us by the Pilon family. No curtains, no chairs, no table, linens, towels nor dishes, only what we had in our suitcases.*

*A few days later Sisters Ursula and Evangela went to town, bought a three-quarter size bed, bed linens, towels, tea kettle, double-boiler, a saucepan and a frying pan, also a long kitchen-table. A small can of spar varnish was purchased and Sister Petronilla applied it to the kitchen table top, which then served as a refectory table also.*

*The Pilons loaned us four chairs, a sewing machine, a rocking chair, pillows, spread and gave us a few dishes.... Wherever we went we carried our chairs.*

The ladies of the parish gave the sisters a donation of $100 which enabled them to pay debts and complete the furnishing. Before they left Regina they purchased a Nordeier piano, "the best piano in Canada," and the time-honored economy for sisters once again resumed in Melville. The pastor provided an annual supply of potatoes; the parishioners gave them sufficient coal for the long winters.

On February 28, 1930, the sisters were legally incorporated by a private bill in the Legislative Assembly of Saskatchewan, with Sisters Mercedes, Ursula, and Flavian as the officers of the corporation. In November 1940 the sisters paid, from their salaries and music income, $2,700 for the house they had been renting from Mrs. M.M. Moher. The purchase included a nearby smaller house, three lots and a garage as well. The smaller house was used for music studios and for some time a boarding home for girls interested in the congregation. The convent of Mary Immaculate came to have vicariate status among the congregational houses.

Educational standards in Canada were high; the school-year was long. The sisters took extension work throughout the year as well as in summer school. Certification and degree work in the United States had to be verified as well as additional requirements of the Canadian system met. In 1931 they began summer catechetical work. In 1934, at the request of Archbishop James McGuigan, four sisters began an eight-week vacation school in several communities near Weyburn. Four hundred and fifty children were given sacramental preparation and general religious instruction. Sister Athanasius also did home visiting and adult instruction. In Canada, as in New Mexico, the sisters were allowed to interact with the people more freely for the sake of effective ministry. In response to enthusiastic accounts from Canada, Sister Philomena wrote to Sister Athanasius, the superior of the group in Weyburn:

*Now here is what I want to tell you: Do whatever the Priest wants you to do; go to the evening devotions, and go to the meetings if there are any more. You are in a missionary country doing missionary work, and Mother says you must be ready to do everything for the salvation of souls. You may go out on Sundays the same as any other day. Of course, you must not overdo. You must have time for a little rest. You cannot afford to break down. All work together and God will bless you.*

*...Mother said that whatever the priests or the Archbishop asks you to do, do it graciously. They will not ask you to do anything you should not. You are* **missionaries now.**

The centuries-old principle in the Dominican Constitution of adaptation was readily applied. Nevertheless Mother Eveline exercised the same attention to this faraway mission as she did to those nearby. She occasionally modified the horaries sent in, "improving" them on several points, clarifying times of silence, the use of the Saturday evening study hour, "which can be used for other things, perhaps Chapter [of Faults], if you find it convenient." She asked the pastor in Melville to get the sisters a good but not too expensive radio as her Christmas gift "to help them along during the Christmas season and keep the Faculty in good spirits." However, the archbishop was not to be told about the radio lest he think the sisters extravagant.

The first summer in Weyburn brought additional requests for permanent missions there and elsewhere. The sisters spoke of the Melville house as the "Canadian Cradle," an indication of their hopes for that mission field. In 1930 an invitation was extended to take over the administration of a municipal hospital in Kindersley, and another in Melville in 1931. When Mother was in Edmonton, Alberta, other opportunities were offered. As a measure of preparedness she tried in 1932 to place several young sisters in nurses' training programs, first in Edmonton, then Saskatoon, finally in Regina. When these efforts failed, she arranged for enrollment in a program in Kenosha, Wisconsin, and later in Springfield, Illinois. In 1933 she sent Sisters Alice Clare Shine and Marybride Ryan to Canada to take the Normal College work at Moose Jaw. They subsequently were missioned in Melville, Sister Marybride to remain until the closing of that mission seventeen years later.

*Mary Immaculate Vicariate,
Melville, Saschatchewan*

*Melville Pioneers:
SEATED Sisters
Ursula Lanciaux and
Mercedes Dargis
STANDING
Sisters Flavian
Murphy, Evangela
Ronning, and
Petronilla Turek*

*The "Canandian Crowd" with*
*Father Francis Ogle,*
*Summer 1934*

*Asprirant graduates with*
*Father Thomas Albin,*
*Marywood Chaplain,*
*June 1933*

*Postulants boarding train at Regina, Saskatchewan,*
*August 10, 1932 (Sisters Rose William St. Cyr and*
*Agnes Dominic Roberge)*

Both the dearth of sisters and Bishop Pinten's refusal prevented further expansion in Canada. At the same time changes in national and provincial governments created uncertainty as to certification, immigration, and the continuance of the separate schools.

The mission in Canada had come to parallel the European vocation crusade in Mother Eveline's mind. Mother Eveline outlined her plans for the school and house staff in a letter to Sister Ursula on July 23, 1928:

*You must get this postulant movement worked up pretty consistently, for the more postulants you send us the more sympathy the Community is going to have for Canada and the bigger the bond we will have with the great Northwest. God will surely bless us with a number of vocations right at the start, and Bishop's words when he told me to send the four sisters were that he could not withstand the appeal of the Archbishop; he felt that our Sisters going would be accompanied with great blessings to the Community and to the diocese. So I take it we must not let the grass grow under our feet to put the children of the Northwest into our lives.*

Again, on October 6, 1930, Mother wrote to Sister Ursula, then in the hospital in Regina:

*The three girls arrived; they all seem to be lovely children. I just imagine how much trouble you had to get everything arranged especially when you had to depend upon a nurse. If they were all as enthusiastic about getting Postulants and Aspirants as you from your bed in a strange city, I think we would have many.... Get us some nurses if you can; we need them very badly.*

Father Francis J. Ogle, pastor in Kindersley and later in Lampman, served as a resourceful advisor and vocation director. He directed many candidates, including his niece, to the aspirancy and novitiate of the congregation. On February 22, 1932, Mother Eveline wrote a long letter to him treating of several matters relative to missions in Canada:

*The other girls from Canada--there are ten of them in all--are getting on nicely. Someday I know they will go back to visit or work in that land, and you will then not regret we took some lovely children back to Marywood. Three girls came last month. The first young woman from Canada, who by the way, already wears our Habit, is now being trained as a nurse at St. Catherine's Hospital, Kenosha, Wisconsin, and is doing well.*

In the summer of 1932 Father Ogle, enroute to the Eucharistic Congress, visited Marywood and saw at first hand how the "lovely children" fared in Michigan. Driving between Grand Rapids and Kalamazoo, he saw evidences of the Depression--men standing along the roadside carrying signs reading "Give us a ride or we will vote for Hoover."

In 1951, on the occasion of Mother Eveline's 60th anniversary, twenty-two professed sisters from Canada expressed their gratitude to Mother's pursuit of her dream of "the valley filled with white-robed Sisters."

> *You sowed a tiny mustard seed*
> *In far Canadian soil;*
> *With faith and prayer you watched over it*
> *And spared not time nor toil.*
> *It seemed too frail a plant to live,*
> *And yet for all to see,*
> *In God's soul-plot it bears its fruits*
> *And grows a noble tree.*

In the summer of 1929 Mother and her council approved the development of an aspirancy program. It was essentially a preparatory school program open to girls who had completed the eighth grade and who considered entering religious life. It was then thought vocational choices were most likely made in the early teens. On occasion Mother Eveline spoke of the instability of the times and considered the disciplined environment of the convent-school a safeguard to vocations. From her return from Europe in 1929 until April 1937 Sister Edith Welzel was mistress of aspirants. The program was under the supervision of the mistress of novices, Sister Jerome Smithers. The girls attended Marywood Academy and were, theoretically, eligible for entrance into the congregation after they had reached the age of 16.

There were accommodations for twelve, and later for approximately thirty, aspirants. At first the girls, "the lovely children" as Mother Eveline was inclined to call them, were obliged to a rigorous semi-conventual life of silence, restricted contacts, and a year-long program of study, prayer, and supervised activities. As the years passed, the girls were allowed greater freedom including home visits during the summer and on major holidays and freer association with the Academy students.

In the fall of 1929 five girls made up the first aspirancy class, three of them newly arrived from Ireland. The following year girls from Canada as well as Michigan joined the original five. In 1933 an extension of the aspirancy was established in Melville. Four girls from Lampman, encouraged by their zealous pastor, Father Francis

Ogle, joined the sisters in Melville. Supervised by Sister Athanasius Chartier, they lived in the little house next to Immaculate Heart convent and attended St.Henry school. In 1934 three of the girls left for Marywood.[12]

Between 1929 and 1936, twenty-six high school girls entered the aspirancy. At Mother Eveline's Diamond Jubilee in 1951 twenty-three professed sisters claimed to be "Mother Eveline's aspirants." On January 6, 1931, Mother wrote to Father James Schnerch, OMI, in Winnipeg:

*We have a nice class of Aspirants, ranging from thirteen to seventeen, engaged in their high school work. We are going to let them finish their high school before allowing them to become real Postulants, although the Aspirants are connected with the Postulancy, and the Novice Mistresses are very much interested in them. This work of education is a slow process, and I find that after they are Aspirants for sometime they learn little by little, without being thrown into it headlong, to keep silence, to pray and to study, and they become very well instructed in their religion before they really get into the Novitiate. Now if you get us a few little Aspirants from good families, girls who show signs of religious vocation, you will help a great deal with the Canadian missions, and I know you are very zealous, hence...*

The aspirancy proved to be a successful complement to the crusades Mother waged in Europe, Canada, and the United States, and gave the congregation well-prepared candidates. In June 1969, during Sister Aquinas Weber's administration, the program was discontinued because of declining numbers and changing patterns of vocational choices.

On the First Sunday of Advent, 1935, Mother Eveline wrote a lengthy letter to the sisters and all priests of the dioceses where the congregation worked. It was to be the beginning of the "Dominican Sisters Advent Crusade for Vocations," an "Apostolic project, a crusade of prayer and actions for vocations to the priesthood and to the religious life." The summons was deeply influenced by Mother Eveline's immersion in the liturgical and biblical renewal transforming the congregation. She wrote:

*The yearnings of the Chosen People for the Messiah made ready their hearts for whatever would further His Kingdom on earth. Our yearnings for His coming on Christmas will purify us and prepare us and be the source of better Apostolic work. The graces of this Advent season will reawaken our desires to do the great work assigned us in our Community, and, in the particular work we are asked to undertake during Advent, we will find greater scope for all our zeal.*

Mother urged the sisters to "talk to your boys and girls, high school and grades, on several occasions," to meet young women of parishes where there are not Catholic schools, even though it be on Sundays. She outlined themes and pedagogy, and gave encouragement to all to undertake the work:

*More will be done by humble efforts to inform the minds of these young people as to what religious life means to those who live it rightly than can be done by the proud brilliancy of learned talk. At the best, brilliancy but startles and astounds and makes no lasting appeal. So, no matter how simple your talk may be, God may allow it to be the means through which His Grace comes to souls.*

Thirty-four sets of sisters were listed to go out "two by two" on the preaching band to thirty-four parishes within the Grand Rapids diocese. Mother had arranged, as well, promises of assistance from twenty-seven priests with other congregations serving in their parishes. The sisters were to keep on file copies of their talks for Mother's perusal on visitation and to send in to her the names of prospective candidates.

In some instances the sisters spoke in parish churches and in the context of the Sunday Mass, or immediately thereafter. Sisters Rosalina Gregoraitis and Francis Xavier Schmitt reported on their visit to Durand, Michigan:

*After Holy Mass had begun Father [Carolan] made his announcements for the week and wound up by telling his congregation that the good holy sisters were here to speak to them this morning and that no one dare leave the Church until we had finished talking to them. He gave a lovely tribute to the sisters in general; told of the noble work they do and he even said they do more work for the Catholic Church than do most priests. He said that the priests actually cannot get along without the sisters. He said their work would be almost fruitless..."You know priests are human!" as if we are not. I suppose some of the people that never saw a sister here...thought we dropped from the sky after the welcome he gave us. But the surprise, Mother, to have to talk to the entire congregation from the front of the church was something I never expected.*

*When the time came for my debut...there was perfect silence. The stillness almost thrilled me to a dizzy waltz down the center aisle with all eyes upon us. I believe that my temperature dropped to a freezing point until I got my balance. I knelt before the tabernacle for a minute and told our Lord in a very short breath that He called me here and must give me the gift of speech. I had prepared a talk to the ladies, and not to old men, and young boys, bachelors and old maids, babies babbling away in their innocent prattle, mothers hanging on to their infants, fathers eyeing me with their curious eyes and a few young girls eagerly hanging on to their sweethearts arms...*

*It seems somehow or other, Mother, that our Lord has something different for me everytime something unusual happens in my life. He gives me such sudden calls and such strange experiences that things seem almost impossible for a moment, when all of a sudden the situation is mastered....I quickly took advantage of the situation and lived up to my title "ORDER OF PREACHERS"....*

*When I saw that sea of faces before me, I felt like a real Dominican at the time of St. Dominic. I thought of what you wrote in your last circular when you said that even if we do not get candidates, our little talks will leave some impression on some poor girl so that she will maybe lead a better life....*

The congregational register includes names of some of the young women contacted through the Advent vocation crusade. Less tangible are the impressions on the congregations who heard Dominican women preaching in churches throughout the diocese.

Before 1927 recruiting was done primarily through the example of the sisters busy at their assigned works. The mother general and the novice mistress were contacted and they arranged for admission. During Mother Eveline's nine years of administration there was planned recruiting executed on a wide scale. Mother Benedicta's longed-for goal of "fifty in the novitiate on the fiftieth year" had been reached and surpassed.[13]

The first great aim of the European vocation crusade, furthering Rome's acceptance of the Constitution, was not mentioned in the correspondence, perhaps by direction of Mother Eveline. In 1929, in response to Mother Eveline's directive that all sisters write autobiographies, Sister Seraphica wrote of the European trip:

*Our Cardinal Fruehwurth received us twice in private audience, and listened most keenly to the history of our Community, and that of the Dominican Orders in the United States in general. We were also received in semi-private audience by the Holy Father.*

The issue of constitutional approval and the congregation's relation to the Holy See would become yet another crusade for Mother Eveline.

# 11

# CRUSADES OF THE SPIRIT

*O*n September 3, 1929, Mother Eveline began her monthly circular to the sisters with a directive, strong even for herself, in her most imperative voice. She wrote:

*My dear Sisters:*

*In the Name of the Divine Victim of the Holy Sacrifice of the Mass I beg you to take up the teaching of the Liturgy at once. Use as a text our new Laboratory Manuals in Religion called "With Mother Church." Encourage each of your pupils to have his own book.*

*I have promised our dear Lord that we will do this work:*

> *To further His own glory.*
> *For the general good of the Church and this Congregation.*
> *That He may bless our Priests and Bishops, and give them a great spirit of zeal.*
> *That He may grant us good subjects and many of them, ways and means of training them well, and opportunities for carrying out the work of the Church, and the special work of this Order.*
> *That He may give eternal rest to the souls of our sisters gone before us, to the souls of our departed pupils and their relatives, and to the souls of our beloved Priests and Bishops.*

*You will endeavor, through the teaching of the Liturgy, to make the children of the Church love our dear Lord and serve Him better than in the past. You will do this work, my dear spiritual daughters, in obedience, in order to earn greater merit than you would otherwise receive.*

During Holy Week in 1929 Sisters Estelle Hackett and Jane Marie Murray[1] first conferred with Dom Virgil Michel at St. John Abbey, Collegeville, Minnesota, on the liturgical education of children. That interview was the result of Sister Jane Marie's attendance at a meeting of the International Federation of Catholic Alumnae at Marygrove College the previous October. There in the college chapel she heard the voice of God and the people of God in the *missa recitata.* For the first time, as she recalled frequently in later years, she consciously experienced the reality of the liturgy as action. She fell into the company of Sister Jane Donnelly, IHM, who, through her studies at Marquette, had come into contact with Father William Busch, one of the pioneers of the American Liturgical Renewal.[2] Sister Donnelly introduced Sister Jane Marie to the new liturgical journal *Oratre Fratres*, edited by Virgil Michel, OSB, (1890-1938) of St. John's Abbey, Collegeville, Minnesota.

On her return to Marywood Sister Jane Marie found a kindred spirit in Sister Estelle Hackett. The two set about an earnest study of all available issues of *Orate Fratres* and soon turned the entire faculty of the academy-college into disciples. Their enthusiasm spread to the student body and the sisters came to see that liturgy itself was a "school." In response to an invitation in *Orate Fratres* for writers of "little meditations" on the liturgy for children, Sisters Estelle and Jane Marie put the prospect to Mother Eveline. Her response was positive and directive, "Get busy!" She arranged for the two to consult Father Michel in Holy Week, 1929. They wrote to Mother Eveline of their journey and their first hours with Father Virgil and later with Father Basil Stegmann, prior of the house and dean of the summer school. The rigors of the journey and the fears of the undertaking prompted Sister Estelle to write, "But truly the Liturgy is worth all this if only Bishop Pinten doesn't learn of it." Because so many undertakings of the congregation had received his scrutiny and sometimes curtailment, it appears Mother Eveline chose to conceal the enterprise from him. She selected sixteen sisters to attend the 1929 liturgical studies summer school in Collegeville, perhaps by then having secured the bishop's permission.

The consultation and summer program began an extraordinarily formative and productive period for the congregation. The sisters were experienced teachers but not proven writers. At the time Sister Estelle Hackett was still awaiting publication of *The Marywood Readers*.[3] The "Collegeville sisters" were earnest students, however, and proficient teachers. The experience was, according to Sister Jane Marie, "knowledge by infusion," an inpouring of the deepest and most illuminating truths of theology and an outpouring in the "little meditations."

From the beginning Mother Eveline committed the entire congregation to the work of liturgical renewal. The sixteen sisters from Grand Rapids outnumbered the representatives from other congregations. While Sisters Estelle and Jane Marie served as the chief writers, all of the sixteen prepared the preliminary drafts. The first visible fruit of that effort was the publication of *With Mother Church,*[4] five books of approximately 80-90 pages each. These books were intended as laboratory manuals to accompany the then essential *Baltimore Catechism.*

In the mid-summer of 1929 Sisters Jane Marie and Estelle realized that the catechism did not adequately serve as a foundation for the manuals. They foresaw the development of a religion text for all levels of primary and secondary education with the theological and philosophical foundations they were learning at the summer session. Father Michel agreed and insisted they were best suited for the work. It was, he said, a work singularly appropriate for Dominicans. Again, Mother Eveline's response was, "Get busy!" Their work began at once and, under the direction of Father Michel and later of his Benedictine confrere Basil Stegmann, resulted in the eight volume *Christ Life* Series[5] published by the Macmillan Company in 1933-1934. In the following decades Sister Jane Marie completed a high school religion series as well as other scriptural and liturgical works.[6]

In addition to liturgical instruction and the writing and editing, the sisters participated in liturgies enriched by Gregorian chant. That experience paralleled Sister Jane Marie's transformation through the *missa recitata* the previous October. Mother Eveline planned for the enrollment of two sisters at the Pius X School of Liturgical Music at Manhattanville College of the Sacred Heart in New York.[7] There Sisters Evangelista Rohrl and Henry Suso Lerzcak came under the influence of the school's co-founder Mother Georgia Stevens, RSCJ, and of the "Ward Method" of choral instruction. These sisters in turn trained hundreds of sisters and students in Gregorian chant according to the principles of the monks of Solesmes, the French Benedictine monastery responsible for much of the liturgical reform in Europe and America. On April 25, 1933, as part of the North Central Music Supervisors Conference, Sister Evangelista directed over a thousand students from Grand Rapids' parochial schools in singing the *missa de angelis* at St. Andrew cathedral.

The Collegeville experience spread throughout the community. On October 25, 1929, *Contacts,* an in-house newspaper "to promote a Community professional spirit, and to encourage and further the spirit of helpfulness among the sisters," was first published. Each month it featured short theological and liturgical essays, book reviews, lesson plans, meditations, and poetry, and a schedule of monthly area pedagogical sessions. Contributions were, Mother Eveline encouraged, to be "written in a natural, ordinary way, with no attempt to have the articles perfect in style, etc. Tell the thing as you did it or as you think it might be done, and let your contributions be motivated by the great motto of our Order: "To give to others the fruits of contemplation."

From time to time there were reading suggestions and helpful hints for housekeepers, bursars and seamstresses. At the same time a liturgical library was developed at Marywood and circulated to the missions in Michigan, New Mexico, and Canada. Sisters Jane Marie,[8] Estelle, and Aquin Gallagher were sent on the circuit of missions to tell the good news during the 1929-1930 school year.

During the 1929 Christmas vacation at Marywood Father Michel gave conferences on the Christian life. In addition to three conferences daily, he prepared with Sisters Estelle and Jane Marie the main outlines for the projected religion series. The following summer a "crowd" of sisters returned to Collegeville for the second liturgical summer school while those at home had the opportunity of making the annual retreat with a Benedictine priest.[9] On March 2-3, 1932, Alcuin Deutsch, OSB, Abbot of St. John's Abbey, visited Marywood. The first retreat of 1932 was given by Father Patrick Cummins, OSB, of Conception Abbey in Missouri. He was, Mother wrote to the sisters, "a splendid retreat master and one imbued with the spirit of the Sacred Liturgy." As a preparation for the retreat the sisters were asked to join the Benedictine community in their yearly novena in honor of the World Consecration to the Sacred Heart of Jesus.

On May 12, 1930, at the end of the first year of the congregation's involvement in the liturgical movement, Mother Eveline wrote to the sisters:

*The work in Liturgy is so dear to the hearts of Christ's own that it is making strides in all parts of the country, old and new, and is becoming a veritable Crusade of Love. To have been among the first to set forth a way and means to enlighten "the little ones and the ignorant, with, in, and for, Jesus Christ," in our book, **With Mother Church**, is our greatest boast. As the distinctive mark of the Dominican spirit is zeal for souls, we cannot do better than to bring the children under our care to the knowledge and love of the Sacred Heart as manifested in* *the Sacrifice of our Altars....Let us then take as our watchword that of the Doctor of the Holy Eucharist, Saint Thomas of Aquin, viz: "To pray, to teach, to suffer."*

*...As the Crusaders of old, loyally responding to the call of Pope Urban VI, sacrificed all things to regain the sacred places from the hands of the infidels, let us with flaming zeal answer the call of Pope Pius XI to reestablish all things in Christ....*

The Collegeville Summer was a time of intense work, weeks of grace, a tremendous infusion of energy and thought which flowed over to the entire congregation and all those the sisters served for decades to come.[10]

In 1930 Mother Eveline commissioned Mother Benedicta to investigate the possibility of accrediting Marywood College as a junior college. While she was attending the summer session at Notre Dame, Mother Benedicta negotiated with the University of Michigan for the acceptance of credits offered in the college division. She reported to Mother Eveline on July 20, 1930:

*Mr. Effinger has sent the report regarding accrediting Marywood as a Junior College.... It does not appear that we can hold any inducements to prospective college students, at least for the present, as far as recognition of their credits at the University is concerned. I don't think we will receive any encouragement from Ann Arbor until we have an entirely distinctive college faculty and a complete separation of High School and College. With so little encouragement from the Bishop, there is little to hope for just now.*

The accreditation of Marywood College was discussed in the General Chapter that summer and resulted in two official acts:

*The Members of the Chapter pledged themselves to carry out whatever projects are put on foot for the establishment of a good college for the Congregation. The Chapter voted in favor of the sisters endeavoring to earn $100.00 apiece within the next twelve months for the first work on a new College building since the University now demands a separate building before it will recognize Marywood College credits.*

Securing a building seemed absolutely necessary. There was no money to build nor buy so the advantages and disadvantages of converting Sant Ilona Hall were weighed against the feasibility of leasing downtown property. Leasing was recorded as the better course of action.[11]

During the spring of 1931 Mother Eveline and her council arranged with Bishop Pinten for the transformation of Marywood College into The Catholic Junior College to be located at Sant Ilona, 69 Ransom Street.[12] On April 4, 1931, Doctor Burton Confrey, known to the sisters who had attended Catholic University and Notre Dame, was chosen as dean[13] of the faculty. During the summer of 1931, fiction written by Dr. Confrey was serialized in the Grand Rapids papers with a note of his new position in the city. On Saturday, August 15, 1931, *The Grand Rapids Herald* announced in inch-high headlines, "CATHOLIC COLLEGE WILL OPEN HERE." Amidst stories of "Lindy's Breeze Over Icy Water To Fuel Cache," the surrender of "Cuban Revolt Chiefs," affirmations for the reelection of President Hoover, plans for guaranteed industrial employment, a "duel" between Standard and Shell cutting gasoline prices to 9.9 cents a gallon, the new "coeducational institution with broad program of studies" in the former Sacred Heart Academy building was described. The same week the college's opening was publicized in the Catholic community.

Bishop Pinten reminded the clergy of the diocese of the central theme of Pope Pius XI's 1929 encyclical on *The Christian Education of Youth:* "Catholic Education in Catholic Schools for all Catholic Youth." He told pastors to "impress upon their people the law of the Church which demands that Catholic students be educated in Catholic institutions." The educational endeavor was described as "a new diocesan institution...placed under the care and direction of the Dominican Sisters of Marywood...."[14] The primary purpose of "The Catholic Junior College" was, the bishop continued:

*to promote the higher education of our young men and women in accordance with Catholic principles. The training in the secular branches of knowledge will be adequately staffed and equipped to meet state requirements and the calendar and curriculum will be identical with that of the State University. Negotiations are now in progress to accredit the college to the State University and other institutions of learning. The courses to be taught are: Catholic Action, liberal arts and sciences, pre-commerce, pre-legal, and courses leading to journalism and the profession of teaching.*

Registration details and the annual tuition rate of $50 per semester were included in the letter to be read at all Masses on Sunday, August 16, 1931. A prospectus appearing in the city newspapers announced:

*Catholic Junior College is not just another College. It is an institution with a definite purpose, for here the course in Religion, which aims to build good character on which to base solidly supernatural virtue, is the very core of the whole curriculum.*

*It is a dynamic institution, housing an energetic attempt to inculcate in our young men and women Christian principles, which if widely accepted, would save American family life, the basis of our national life and of Christian civilization.*

*The work of Catholic Junior College will prepare students for success in business and professional life. By evoking personality, which is a mirror of God, the College will train young men and women for purposeful life in society in a general way, and for a career in a particular way.*

*…The calendar and curriculum will be identical with that of the State University except that Catholic philosophy will inform all teaching, and that there will be a course in Catholic Action. …*

The first classes began on Monday, September 28, 1931, for 73 students. By the fall of 1936 close to 200 were enrolled.

The announced course on Catholic Action, under the direction of Dr. Confrey and the sisters who were in the first enthusiasm of the Liturgical Renewal, pervaded the atmosphere of the college. Mother Eveline found Dr. Confrey an enlivening and dedicated colleague to whom she confided her dreams for the development of the college and the congregation. In several journals he published the results of the first year's endeavors.[15] At the end of the next academic year the Catholic Action course resulted in a novel commencement program. The Grand Rapids papers announced:

### College Closes Successful Year

*The Catholic Junior College, Grand Rapids, will close its school year with a retreat on Flag Day, June 14. There will be no formal commencement exercises. The graduates will make a vigil similar to the knights of old when preparing for their baccalaureate.*

*The contrast between this procedure and the usual graduation exercises is but one phase of the faculty's determination that its charges will be trained to appreciate the interest that resides in prayer as a preparation for usefulness and the folly of living to pursue pleasure.*

*The student leadership groups of the year were a federation of clubs. The apostolic group directed its zeal toward the providing of Catholic books and periodicals for Marquette prison.*

*The polyphonic choir co-ordinated with the Catholic Action classes, which used a text written by Dr. Burton Confrey in which Catholic Action is based on the liturgy.*

The International Federation of Catholic Alumnae, in which the sisters and alumnae of Sacred Heart College had been active, offered a scholarship to sisters of other congregations for attendance at Catholic Junior College.[16]

From its beginnings Bishop Pinten took an active role in the administrative affairs of the junior college. The appointment of Dr. Confrey required the permission of the bishop. In June 1932, a month which Mother Eveline spent at the Mayo Clinic in Minnesota, Monsignor Anthony Volkert, chancellor of the diocese, arranged college affairs with the bishop. That summer a controversy developed between the congregation and the Sisters of Mercy. For several years nurses in training at nearby St. Mary hospital had academic training at Grand Rapids Junior College. In January 1932 the Sisters of Mercy withdrew their students and provided course work at St. Mary hospital and Mount Mercy Academy. Mother Eveline sent a lengthy and formal petition first to the Apostolic Delegate in Washington and then to Bishop Pinten, to which he responded on August 16, 1932, with a formal pronouncement prohibiting the development of any institution of higher education other than Catholic Junior College within the city.[17]

After Dr. Confrey's three years of leadership of Catholic Junior College, Mother found it necessary to inform him, on February 15, 1934, of the termination of his services at the conclusion of the academic year. Economy seems to have been the primary reason. In 1933 Dr. Confrey had offered to take a $100 reduction in his salary of $2,300, an offer which was reluctantly accepted by Mother Eveline. In April 1934 Bishop Pinten appointed Father Arthur Bukowski (1905-1989), a recently ordained priest of the diocese, as chaplain and dean of the college.

After his ordination on April 30, 1933, Father Bukowski had served as assistant at St. Isidore and St. James parishes in Grand Rapids. He had been educated at the diocesan seminary, at the Catholic University of America, and with the Sulpicians in Washington. Father Bukowski served as dean and, after February 1937, as president of the college as it evolved into Aquinas College, until his retirement in February 1969. By vocation and education, Father was devoted to the social teaching of the Church and he gave impetus to the social action foundation laid by Dean Confrey and the pioneering sister faculty. At the time of his retirement, the early years of Catholic Junior College were recalled:

*In the days of the downtown Ransom Avenue Campus...students gathered under the clock in the main hall; Treasurer Sister Agnes Marie kept her tuition receipts in a cigar box--all of them in one cigar box; a never ending ping pong tournament was constantly in progress in Room 105 next to the Dean's Office; Sister Mark paralyzed freshmen chem students with the prediction that ninety percent would flunk out by the end of the semester; Sister Gonzaga groaned about how unprepared Freshman English students were and sentenced them all to diagramming; Sister Aquin acted all the roles in her Shakespeare class entrancing students with her magic; and the late, beloved and diminutive Sister Noella peered over her rostrum and made ancient history more exciting than the World Series. And Monsignor, in his shiny threads, taught all the theology courses--they called it religion then--but he really made his points about what it means to be a Christian more by his own life than by any class instruction.*[18]

In 1935 Monsignor Anthony Volkert, Vicar General of the Diocese, informed Mother Eveline of the appointment of two Sisters of Mercy to the faculty. The appointment was taken as an undue interference and became another point of difficulty between Mother Eveline and the bishop and his chancellor. The matter was resolved with the withdrawal of the appointments. In a letter to Mother Eveline dated May 25, 1935, Monsignor Volkert, now transacting all of the congregational business formerly handled by the bishop, referred to several points of community business, among them sisters' attendance at summer schools, approved vacation spots, and a college faculty matter. He wrote:

*The three lay teachers now on the staff of Catholic Junior College, a diocesan institution, who have been appointed without the knowledge of the Diocesan Authorities, have been kept there during the present year, without our approval. As to the advisability of keeping some of them for next year, I shall consult the Reverend Dean, and make a decision in an opportune time.*[19]

By its second year of operation, the college was affiliated with the University of Michigan and arrangements were under way for offering University of Detroit extension courses at the college. In the spring of 1936 application to the North Central Association was made. Dr. Smittle was engaged to help the faculty develop a new catalog and reorganize about a new objective, the papal encyclicals.

# 12

# VICTORY!

*T*he fundamental relationship of the congregation to the Church was expressed in the Constitution of the congregation. Since the beginning of the Diocese of Grand Rapids in 1883 the bishop had functioned as the highest superior. As episcopal and congregational leaders changed over the decades, the manner of interaction changed.

Mother Aquinata had used the last of her energies to work on a new Constitution. Her death in 1915 and that of Bishop Richter in 1916 delayed the full implementation of that Constitution, though it was to serve as an interim Constitution for a five-year period. In April 1924 Father Sauvage, CSC, had started his review of a new draft. In the summer of 1926 he spent two weeks at Marywood, working with the sisters from eight to ten hours a day on revisions. The new Dominican Constitution of the Sisters of the Third Order prepared by Father Louis C. Nolan, OP, Father Sauvage's colleague in the Sacred Congregation for Religious, was used in the work. On October 16-17, 1926, the congregation held an Extraordinary Chapter to study the draft which was subsequently sent to Rome to Father Sauvage's attention.

As part of the 1927-1928 Golden Jubilee the sisters had organized a petition to Bishop Pinten to hasten the approval of the new Constitution with its central feature of papal status. The bishop responded that he needed to study the issue but the sisters could be assured he would "further any cause that would make for their benefit." Again the following year a petition was addressed to the bishop as he prepared for his quinquennial visit to Rome. Some four years later Mother Eveline learned that he had in fact instructed Father Sauvage to cease work on the Constitution.

On Sunday, August 10, 1930, the ninth General Chapter opened and continued through August 14, the first Chapter to last more than two days and the last Chapter composed of all the sisters professed twelve years or more. Bishop Pinten was on hand to preside over the elections. In a lengthy preliminary allocution the bishop remarked on the Church, its order and rule by law, his episcopal responsibilities in relation to the congregation, and his judgment that the congregation was not yet ready for the revised Constitution. A particular point he would not allow was the term of office of the mother general. He thereby decreed the term of office for mother general and the members of her council was to be six years. Whether he forewarned the assembled capitulars is not known. Of the 281 votes cast Mother Eveline received 216. Sisters Albertina Selhuber, Beatrice Cottrell, Philomena Kildee, and Genevieve Gauthier were elected as her councilors. Sister Philomena was elected to serve as secretary general, and Sister Seraphica to continue as treasurer.

In retrospect, the ninth General Chapter laid the foundation for Catholic Junior College, embraced the implications of liturgical renewal, and organized the activities and supervision of the educational ministry of the congregation. A General Council of Schools[1] was established to oversee the schools conducted by the congregation, to recommend policy, to assist in pedagogy, and to advise on faculty development.

Decisions on financial matters reveal the close control on the common purse Mother Eveline and her council exercised due to the range of congregational projects, the indebtedness on buildings, the living requirements of nearly six hundred members, and the worsening general economy. The purchase of clothing was to be centralized; a committee on the quality of materials for habits was formed; the purchase of "traveling paraphernalia" was banned for three years; the kinds of gifts permissible for pastors and benefactors were described.

The large issue of the congregational status, diocesan or papal, was not new to the bishop. Both in 1928 and 1929 he had received hundreds of sisters' signatures on petitions. It was his will that the issue be set aside by the Chapter of 1930. In particular ways, episcopal control began to increase. With the mother general and council, the bishop was to formulate the daily horary and the policy for defraying and managing of summer school expenses. Nevertheless, the constitutional issue was heightened by the bishop's role in the Chapter of 1930. In a letter to Sister Ursula in the hospital in Regina on October 6, 1930, Mother Eveline related the feelings of the sisters:

*We are sending you a big envelope with the Decrees of the Chapter and the Mission List, etc., so you will have a few days entertainment with all the things. Let me hear from you when you have read everything over. I often thought of you during the Chapter; you would have been so interested in the discussions. I think that Bishop really expects to give us Pontifical Approbation from what he told me, but you never saw such an enthusiastic Chapter. They certainly went downstairs after him when he wouldn't come up to talk to them on the subject. I think he was really afraid of the whole mob of women, but I know how much they were in earnest in asking for it. I was surprised myself; they were even inclined to think that I hadn't been doing anything to get them the Pontifical Rule for a while, but if I had portrayed for them one two-hour battle over that Rule they would have thrown their hands up. I will tell you all about it when I see you since we had many talks on the subject.*

In 1928 Bishop Pinten intervened in the affairs of the sisters in a signal manner. In her Easter circular letter Mother Eveline wrote:

*Bishop does not think it best for us to go out voting at every election, unless there is some particular thing that we want to carry through. He says, and I believe he is right, that after a while we will make enemies by working for one man and then for another. Do not misinterpret this: you are not being robbed of your right to vote, and if there is a necessity we shall know that ahead of time and consider it. He wishes us to be conservative only. When our property or our interests are at stake, or when the interests of religion demand it, we shall go to the polls. Now be very prudent, and do not say anything about this injunction to anyone outside the community.*

On September 28, 1928, she instructed the sisters:

*The bishop insists that the sisters are not to vote, so you are not to go to the polls in November. Say your prayers for the success of the campaign of Mr. Al Smith. They may go farther. The public need not know why you do not vote.*

That year, 1928, saw also the bishop's vacillation over the acceptance of a Canadian mission and, once that was achieved, the securing of property for the sisters' convent; the reversal of approval for a land purchase and even for rental in Europe as part of the recruitment of candidates. In February 1929 a singularly delicate matter came under consideration. On February 6, 1929, Mother Eveline wrote to the bishop:

*Your Lordship has suggested that we lay before you a complete account of the indebtedness of St. John's Home Estate to the Dominican Sisters from the time it was placed in our charge. We therefore, present the following as a fair estimate of the Dominican Sisters' claim against the St. John's Home Estate.*

There followed an account of service for which until 1918 there had been no recompense and in actuality considerable outlays by the congregation. For the period from 1888 to 1906, Mother reckoned the eleven sisters working at St. John's ought to have received $10 a month, or a total of $23,760. From 1906 to 1918, the fifteen sisters working there should have received $15 a month, or a total of $33,400. From 1918 to the time of her writing, the sisters received $30 a month and their board.

In addition, Sister Seraphica made a formal deposition that Bishop Richter had given $10,000 to the sisters with the proviso that it would be used to build the St. John's chapel wing. When the Home estate was more settled, the money was to be returned to the sisters. She further deposed that the original land purchase had involved a transfer of a portion bought by the sisters for a motherhouse to be built next to St. John's. Spoken agreements were made allowing part of that land to be sold to the Redemptorists with reversion of other parcels to the sisters when they were able to build. In 1929 that land was appraised at $14,875. Donations of furniture to the sisters amounted to an additional $9,000. The large features totaled $91,035 without interest.

Mother further detailed the labors of the sisters in running annual festivals and suppers for twenty-five years, enterprises which earned $47,333.69. She mentioned the sisters taking care, with the aid of some orphan boys, of the furnaces for several years, of laundry work done by hand for thirty years, of bakery work "unaided by machinery of any kind" for at least twenty years, of nursing during seven severe epidemics without assistance, all without compensation. During these years the congregation paid to the diocese $34,977.44 for boarding sisters who lived at the Home but worked elsewhere.

"Knowing," she concluded her letter, "the fine sense of justice that marks all your dealings, we humbly place these claims of the Dominican Sisters before your Lordship, and beseech you to adjust them, and place St. John's Home on a purely diocesan basis." The sisters were implored to pray for a favorable outcome. Mother noted in her address-notebook the acts of thanksgiving she would initiate "if the St. John's money came."

It was perhaps a case of "protesting too much." On February 18, 1929, the bishop acknowledged receipt of Mother's letter, noting the total indebtedness of $91,035 and indicated he would "investigate these various claims alleged by you and in due time...shall issue an official opinion and decision." He then pointed out that the chancery held two notes executed by Mother Benedicta, one in May 1922 for $25,000 at six percent interest, the other in February 1924 for $10,000 at five percent interest. He concluded:

*Whereas these two notes are past due and whereas it moreover appears that some of the bank loans were made to enable Bishop Kelly to make a loan to your sisters, on which we are still paying interest, it is hereby ordered that within ten days you pay to the Diocese of Grand Rapids these two notes both as to principal and to interest accumulated and compounded.*[2]

In 1932 the bishop sought the approval of the major superiors of sisters serving in the diocese for a reduction in the sisters' salaries. In early August 1932 he had announced a salary increase from $25 to $35 per month. Within a month, however, he rescinded the arrangement until the emergency passed and allowed for parishes to do what they could.

*In the event, however, that the parish finances, because of the existing debts or for other grave reasons, will not permit the payment of Twenty-five Dollars ($25.00) monthly for each sister, then and under such conditions, We ask that the sisters, for the year 1932-1933, be satisfied with whatever they may be able to get from the parish. Pastors in charge of rural parishes and districts will receive a special request from Us to supply the sisters with farm products and to that end to have some organization.*

*Our aim is to keep all Our schools functioning and to do so it is imperative that We reduce all operating expenses and otherwise practice rigid economy. We most earnestly solicit your hearty cooperation. When in the Providence of God conditions will again become normal We hope to be able to do something to compensate for the sacrifices which you are being asked to make at this time.*

The bishop wished to be informed when parishes were unable to pay the stipends, which was frequently the case. He urged pastors to ask the people to provide the sisters with fresh produce and meat when possible. From 1933 to 1936 he allowed an Easter collection on the sisters' behalf. In some few instances, the amount collected was equal to the sisters' salary for a single month, but in most cases it was far less. Above all, the irregularity of income added great worries. While sister housekeepers were directed to prepare nutritious meals, Mother herself negotiated with grocers for credit.

In fall 1930 the Very Reverend Martin S. Gillet, Master General of the Order of Preachers, was in America to visit as many Dominicans as possible. On October 29, 1930, he came to Marywood, the twenty-third on his itinerary of thirty-eight motherhouses of Dominican women. He was accompanied by Father James Meagher, provincial of the St. Joseph province, Father Thomas Garde, interpreter on his Roman staff, and Brother

Reginald. While largely ceremonial, the visit added to the growing awareness of the congregation's membership in the larger Dominican Order and to a spirituality[3] and governance which transcended the local church.

Mother Eveline was in New Mexico at the time of the Master General's visit, arranging for the sad task of bringing home Sister Seraphica's body for burial. On November 24, 1930, she went to New York with Sister Estelle to confer with the Macmillan Publishing Company. Her first purpose was, in fact, to see the Master General. She put the case of the congregation's difficult relationship with the bishop and the sisters' high hopes for the approval of a new Constitution which would define the congregation as an apostolic institute of papal right. She remarked later that Father Garde had softened the Master General's observations in his translation from the French. Father Gillet actually threatened that the sisters might not call themselves Dominican nor wear the Dominican habit if a more Dominican Constitution was not secured.

This consultation was a particularly painful event for Mother. It was a grief she communicated only to her council and her private journal. The character of the congregation as Dominican was threatened; episcopal control was becoming more pervasive.

That winter, perhaps as a result of the Chapter of 1930, a formal investigation of the canonical erection of the congregation was initiated. A special meeting of the council on December 28, 1930, was held to examine the evidence[4] and to vote on whether to "institute an action before the Diocesan Court to prove by decree of said Court that the erection as a Diocesan Congregation was legally made." The following day a formal tribunal of the diocese met at Marywood and Monsignor Anthony Volkert, Vicar General, took depositions from Mothers Eveline and Benedicta, Sisters Cyrilla Hallahan, Philomena Kildee and Augustine LaFleur, all professed before the formal separation from the New York motherhouse.[5]

On February 11, 1931, a Decree of Erection signed by Bishop Pinten was presented to the congregation. It read in part:

*We found the aforesaid Congregation of Our Lady of the Sacred Heart ...erected in our diocese; we approve and confirm this Congregation legitimately founded by our predecessor, Henry Joseph Richter, in the month of August, 1894, which we again approve, and we decree and declare this Congregation of diocesan jurisdiction, all things prescribed in Canon law having been observed, which shall always remain subject to the government and correction of us and of our successors, according to Canon 492 and following, and of all the decrees and decisions of the Sacred Congregation of Religious.*

There is no evidence of any great tension surrounding the juridical process into which the diocese and congregation entered at the time. Mother Eveline may have considered it as part of her strategy to achieve papal approbation.[6] While there were much larger issues at stake, the conflict had some personal aspects as well. The paternal relationship of Bishop Pinten and Monsignor Volkert[7] served at times to work to the congregation's advantage. The bishop had promoted the cause of Catholic Junior College. In 1932 he ruled against the Mercy sisters' developing a collegiate program within their nurses' training. There were feast day greetings and mutual concern for health: Monsignor Volkert was ill in April 1931; Mother Eveline spent June 1932 at the Mayo Clinic and other shorter periods at the "baths" in Mount Clemens.

Mother Eveline dated the origin of the misunderstanding as November 11, 1934, the day Father Louis Nolan, OP, visited Marywood and then Bishop Pinten and Monsignor Volkert. Father Nolan, an Irish Dominican on the staff of the Master General and a member of the Sacred Congregation for Religious, came to the United States as official visitor on behalf of the Master General. "He questioned our status," wrote Mother Eveline, "said he believed we were always papal and went back to Rome and proved it." Consciously entering this historical note "To the members of our Community of the Future" she continued:

*This act unleashed a great deal of misunderstanding between the Most Rev. Bishop, Joseph H. Pinten, his Vicar General, Monsignor A. Volkert, and our Community. As this is the usual way things go in the affairs of Communities, one is not surprised that it occurred in our Community. Both the bishop and his Vicar General had been good kind friends of the Community and their kindness must not be forgotten. Let us hope the New Papal Constitutions, borne in such labor, will have a sturdy and vigorous growth. Devotedly, Mother M. Eveline, Prioress General.*

Before he left the United States in February 1935, Father Nolan executed a mission which had lasting effect on American Dominican life and mission. On December 2, 1934, he wrote from San Rafael, California a letter to all the mothers general inviting them and a councillor to attend a Conference of Dominican Mothers General to be held at San Rafael on January 1, 1935. While he was favorably impressed by what he observed and learned, Father Nolan was convinced that "as members of the same religious family, the various Congregations of Dominican Sisters have not all that unanimity of spirit and action that is desirable, and that would, no doubt make for greater strength and efficiency."

Father Nolan outlined five topics which were to be the main considerations of the conference: uniformity of Constitution and ceremonial, as far as possible; uniformity of the religious habit, especially with regard to material and form of guimpe (collar) and headdress; the recitation of the Divine Office, in at least the novitiate houses; measures for the training of the young sisters to meet the educational requirements of the day, conforming to the spirit and mind of the Church; a great convent or hostel in Rome where the sisters might receive at the center of Christendom and of the Order the training and the knowledge "that only Rome can give."[8] These points would provide the chief areas of study for the Dominican Mothers General Conference until its transformation in 1970 to the Dominican Leadership Conference.

A questionnaire on its history, membership, and mission data was distributed to each of the congregations. Two questions suggest another level to the agenda proposed by Father Nolan. The congregations were asked, "Is the Congregation of Pontifical right, or only still Diocesan?" and "If the Congregation is still only Diocesan, have any steps been taken, and what are they, to obtain the Pontifical status?" Sister Philomena Kildee, secretary general, responded:

*Yes. Between 1913 and 1915 our Constitutions were drawn up according to Normae of Sacred Congregation for Religious to be presented to Rome for approbation. The Ordinary objected. In 1926, with the approval of the late Bishop Kelly, our Constitutions were revised according to the schema of the Very Reverend Louis Nolan, OP, and the Very Reverend E.M. Sauvage, CSC, then in Rome, was preparing them to be presented to the Sacred Congregation for approval when the Most Reverend Bishop Pinten asked Father Sauvage to discontinue the work for the present. Attempts have been made since to obtain Bishop Pinten's consent but without success so far.*

Mother Eveline sought permission to attend the conference in an indirect manner. It was her custom to visit the New Mexico missions just before Thanksgiving, returning to Michigan for the Advent and Christmas season and a round of city visitations. That year, however, she spent the latter part of December in New Mexico. On December 28, 1934, she wrote Monsignor Volkert from Nazareth Sanatorium, focusing on a difficulty that had arisen with the misuse of state monies due the sisters in Peñasco. She was asked, she said, by Archbishop Gerken to await his settlement of the matter. During the interim of two or three weeks, she wanted

*FACING PAGE*
*Reverend Martin Gillet, Ma*
*General of the Dominican Or*
*visits Marywood,*
*October 29, 1930*
*LEFT TO RIGHT*
*Fathers James Meagher, Ma*
*Gillet, Thomas Garde, *
*Brother Reginald.*

*First Mothers Gene*
*Conference, January 1935,*
*San Rafael, California.*

*Father Louis Nolan, OP, *
*seated in the center. The Gr*
*Rapids, Michigan, delegates*
*Mother Eveline Mackey (sea*
*second from right) and Sis*
*Philomena Kildee (stand*
*fourth from right).*

to visit three of her brothers in California whom she had not seen for twenty-six years, a permission she had received the previous year but not had not been able to use. While in California, she wished to take advantage of an invitation to attend the conference in San Rafael. Monsignor Volkert responded on January 10, 1935, expressing surprise that she "had taken this absence but I suppose it could not be otherwise. I showed naturally your letter to the bishop and he orders me to tell you that the permission for your planned trip to the west and the meeting is granted. We have been informed about the real purpose of this meeting."

Father Nolan served as the general chairman during the four days of meeting. Twelve of the twenty-eight Dominican congregations were represented. Sister Philomena accompanied Mother Eveline. An executive board was formed to communicate to those not present and to plan for subsequent meetings. Mother Eveline was elected to serve as secretary to the Conference.[9] The members decided to accept Archbishop McNicholas' long-standing offer to give a retreat for the Mothers General and plans were made for a July 1935 convening in Cincinnati. Father Nolan traveled eastward, stopping in Cincinnati for a conference with Archbishop McNicholas and a morning in Washington with the Apostolic Delegate, visits of courtesy and diplomacy which paved the way for the growth of the Mothers General Conference and perhaps in some measure the cases of papal-versus-diocesan jurisdiction which were fast developing.

At Marywood, Mother acquainted the council with the proceedings of the Conference and sought formal approval of the uniformities proposed. The council voted unanimously for uniformity of Constitution, ceremonial, religious habit, and the proposed training of young sisters. One dissenting vote was cast to the adoption of the Divine Office[10] and to the House of Studies in Rome. Mother gave a detailed report to the sisters of Marywood and, in February 1935, to the Superiors Councils of North, East and West, a system of scheduled assemblies of superiors which she had devised at the beginning of her administration. She made discussion of the Conference an important feature of her visitations to all the Michigan houses during the spring.

Mother Eveline continued her promotion of the Conference's development. As secretary she developed the report and worked out with Mother Samuel, mother general of the Sinsinawa congregation and Conference president, a strategy for reporting to the absent mothers general. In June 1935 the bishop broke his silence and directly answered Mother's request to attend the Conference retreat in Cincinnati. He wrote on June 27, 1935:

*Reverend Mother M. Eveline, OSD*
*Mother General of*
*The Dominican Sisters of the*
*Diocese of Grand Rapids.*

*Reverend Mother Eveline:*

*Your letter of June 16, addressed to Our Vicar-General, Monsignor Anthony Volkert, DD, asking for certain permissions has been referred to us. In reply thereto, We write to inform you, that your petition asking permission for yourself, Sr. Albertina, Mother Benedicta to attend the retreat and the conferences to be given during the month of July, in the city of Cincinnati is hereby refused.*

*Your Bishop and Superior,*
*Joseph G. Pinten*
*Bishop of Grand Rapids.*

He carefully laid in assertions of his authority, the episcopal "we," a clear and comprehensive definition of his personal power as her "Bishop and Superior," and the localization of the sisters of the Diocese of Grand Rapids. He did not use the title "OP" authorized by the Master General in 1927. The battle lines were drawn.

From mid-November 1934 to May 1936 the bishop no longer directly communicated with Mother Eveline, or in her absence, with Sister Albertina, her vicaress. The chancery refused all phone calls from the sisters. All business was to be transacted in writing with Monsignor Volkert at the chancery office on Sheldon Avenue. Much greater attention was shown to regulating attendance at summer schools. While the sisters were permitted to attend the normal schools in Michigan, their names, programs, even their reading lists were examined. Monsignor Volkert, apparently on behalf of the bishop, denied permission for a sister completing the Master of Arts in English at the University of Michigan to read some of the required texts, while another was allowed to attend to fulfill the residency requirement though "a similar concession will never be granted in the future."

In July 1935 Monsignor Volkert notified Mother Eveline that "it has been found expedient to add two Sisters of the Mercy of the Cincinnati Province, to the faculty of our diocesan Junior College." He took his annual vacation away from the city and the bishop would receive no calls from the sisters. Finally, Sisters Aquinas Byrne, supervisor of schools, and Kyran Moran, assistant dean of the college, took the train to Petoskey and put their case to Monsignor at the Perry Hotel. In the meantime, several priests of the diocese prevailed upon Bishop Pinten to see the difficulties in the situation. He called the provincial of the Mercy sisters and asked them to withdraw gracefully.

Finally, in August 1935, Mother Eveline wrote to Monsignor Volkert:

*Dear Monsignor,*

*Will you please, in the name of Jesus Christ, permit me to have a talk with you? I feel confident that you, who have always been such a father and friend to our Community, and have generously and kindly, on every occasion, overlooked any mistakes I may inadvertently have made, would understand and pardon all if I could but explain matters to you.*

*You must realize, if anyone does that these have been hard months without your counsel and guidance. You know how much I have always depended upon you; how much you have meant to me and my Community.*

*I am certainly sorry, dear Monsignor, for any offense I may have given you, for you are the last one I would want to grieve. I beg you again to give me a hearing. May the kindly heart of the Divine Saviour guide you in this decision.*

*Your devoted spiritual daughter,*

There was no response. Throughout 1935 Mother Eveline was in contact with Father Nolan, who had returned to Rome. Conference business and pontifical status were the main topics. On April 3, 1935, Father Nolan reported he had discussed the case with the Cardinal Prefect and "the opposition of your good bishop" and detailed the steps Mother Eveline should take. He looked forward, he said, to "a successful issue in the case" but urged prayers "for prayer and diplomacy go well together when the cause is good." On May 15 Mother wrote a long letter to him detailing the difficulties of communication and intervention she was experiencing "so you may know how it goes with a Mother General who is found guilty of wanting a Papal Rule."

On May 15, 1935, Father Nolan wrote telling Mother of his efforts on behalf of the congregation. He had taken the case to the Sacred Congregation of Propagation of the Faith which in the years of the origin of the congregation had jurisdiction over religious in America. It was their ruling that the congregation was of pontifical right, "unless the contrary can be proved." Mother was to do nothing, save "be very calm and tranquil," until that decision had been communicated to the Sacred Congregation of Religious which would in turn officially inform Bishop Pinten and herself. Work on the Constitution should continue. In late May he asked Mother to consider the transfer of certain Dominican sisters from the Kenosha, Wisconsin, congregation.[11] Meanwhile Bishop Pinten was corresponding with legal counsel within the Sacred Congregation for Religious on the pontifical issue.

Delays caused by the long Roman summer, Father Nolan's responsibilities, and changes in the Sacred Congregation's membership were compounded by Bishop Pinten's strategy. In mid-November he responded to the inquiry of the Sacred Congregation of June 1935 as to his position in denying pontifical status. The bishop, reported Father Nolan, said he needed time to study the many documents he had on the case. Until the bishop's reason was stated, the Sacred Congregation could not issue its position. In January 1936 Father Nolan wrote Mother that the bishop had appointed a consistorial advocate "to defend his case here and is ready to go any length rather than be defeated."

Final review of the case by the Sacred Congregation was scheduled between April 2 and April 29. At 4 p.m., April 29, 1936, a postal telegram was received at the Mackay Towers, Grand Rapids. It read:

> ROMA 29. MOTHER GENERALE EVELINE
> DOMINICAN SISTERS GRAND RAPIDS MICHIGAN.
> VICTORY. WRITING. NOLAN

The message was phoned to Marywood at 4:45 p.m. There is no record of the manner of celebration of victory "borne in such labor." Father Nolan's explanation came quickly. On May 3, he wrote the details to Mother Eveline, offering his customary diplomatic appraisal of the conflict. "This whole affair," he wrote, "has been strenuous and interesting, and the result is now worth all the trouble taken to vindicate you, and liberate yourself and your Congregation from a position which was growing intolerable." The bishop had been informed of the decision.[12] But, thought Father Nolan, the matter might not be over. He advised as to the steps to be taken in the event "the good bishop henceforth molest you or unduly shew hostility towards you...." An appeal should be made to the Holy See. There was, however, immediate work to be done on the Constitution to bring the congregation through its coming Chapter.

Throughout May, Father Nolan communicated points of the decision, new tasks, congratulations and blessings. Bishop Pinten had, however, worked out a strategy of his own. By June he had not yet acknowledged receipt of the Roman pronouncement and he proceeded to exercise episcopal control once again. The time for convocation of the General Chapter was nearing. The Constitution originally approved for the congregation, that of the Sinsinawa Dominicans, had a representational system of delegates rather than a Chapter of all those professed twelve years. After the bishop had several times denied her access, Mother wrote in mid-June to the sisters to proceed in the election of delegates.

On Friday, June 19, 1936, during the retreat at Marywood, Bishop Pinten and his chancellor, Father Raymond H. Baker appeared at Marywood. He was, the councillors wrote Father Nolan, "unexpected and unannounced."

*The sisters were just leaving the chapel after the conference when they heard the bishop's voice from one end of the corridor, "Sisters, return to the chapel," and from the sanctuary came the voice of the Chancellor, "The bishop is here for Visitation." Mother was given to understand by the Chancellor at once that it was not opportune for her to meet the bishop yet. However, early in the course of the day, she presented herself. He very definitely said, "I am here as the bishop of Grand Rapids in my official capacity and as the Superior of this Community. I will see you when I am through with the sisters." ...The Novice Mistress [Sister Jerome Smithers], however, succeeded in getting in for Visitation and when she raised the question of our status the bishop's answer was, "I have no communication from Rome."*

In the midst of the agitation caused by the bishop's presence, Mother Eveline received word that her sister Margaret was dying. The bishop allowed her the moment necessary to get the permission to leave for St. Paul, Minnesota. The visitation continued throughout the days of retreat. At its close on Tuesday, June 23, the bishop came but stayed in his room while the chancellor called all the sisters to the chapel. There at the bishop's direction he twice read out the following:

*To the Superiors and Sisters*
*of the Third Order of St. Dominic*
*of the Diocese of Grand Rapids*

*Whereas we have not received any communication from the Holy See relative to the juridical status of the Dominican Sisters of the Diocese of Grand Rapids, and whereas grave matters of importance requiring immediate attention and direction are pending, for the good of the community we consider it to be our duty to issue the following precepts and regulations:*

*1) At the coming election for the Prioress General and the Vicaress General, which will take place in August, there shall be no voting done by delegates and it is hereby ordered that each and every Sister, who has completed twelve years of religious profession and who otherwise is not deprived of active voice, shall have a right to vote in person.*

*2) At the coming election, in accordance with the Sacred Canons, the Prioress General and the Vicaress General and the Consultors shall be elected for a period of three years and no longer.*

*3) Whereas the present Prioress General has served two terms consecutively, she is not eligible for a third term at the present time.*

*4) The precepts hereinabove given are binding in the spirit of holy obedience. Let no one presume to act in contravention thereof by word or deed.*

*5) We direct that fervent prayers to the Holy Ghost be offered publicly and privately for guidance in choosing worthy and capable Superiors and for the general welfare of the community.*

*Your Bishop and Superior*
*Joseph Pinten*
*Bishop of Grand Rapids*

The councillors immediately dispatched a telegram to Father Nolan, then in England, followed by a detailed description of the summary visitation and episcopal decree. He instructed them to make a representation to Cardinal Amleto Cicognani, apostolic delegate, in Washington. On July 15, 1936, Mother Eveline, having returned from the deathbed of her sister, wrote to the bishop citing the April 23, 1936, decision of the Sacred Congregation, along with the instructions she had received on the election of delegates. On July 18, 1936 the chancellor, Father Baker, wrote on behalf of the bishop rescinding the prescriptions announced on June 23. It appears the apostolic delegate had successfully intervened and victory was final.[13]

At the conclusion of her term of office, Mother Eveline went to Beaver Island with Sister Leonora Gallagher. The two spent September and October working on the cottage Sister Leonora's uncle Thomas Gallagher had recently given to the congregation. They officially christened the vacation house "Star of the Sea" though it became familiarly known as "Uncle Tom's Cabin." That December she and Sister Albertina went to California to visit some of the Dominican motherhouses on the Pacific coast. A decade later Mother wrote, with her typical attention to detail and connections, of the private retreat she and Sister Albertina had that winter at the hospital of the Sisters of St. Joseph in San Diego.

*We made retreat on the seventh floor, had rooms by ourselves and tray service three times a day, permission to go to the chapel whenever we wished, and an armful of books from the Carmelite Monastery of San Diego. We walked on the roof garden of the seventh floor, from where we could see the ocean, San Diego*

*Harbor, and the Pacific Fleet, afterwards largely destroyed at Pearl Harbor, lying calmly on the waters of the bay.*

*After our retreat was over Father Drinen took us out to the fleet in the officers' launch and we saw a good deal of the fleet and the Lexington plane carrier afterward destroyed in the Second World War and sunk by our men in the Coral Sea. The landing platform was a wonder to me. It was so huge--225 feet long and 90 feet wide, and yet the boys when circling around in the air to come down with planes used to call it the postage stamp. We spent several hours viewing what was afterwards destroyed by the Japs at Pearl Harbor.*

In mid-March, 1937, the two sisters went on to New Mexico to visit missions, Mother Eveline taking an ill sister's place in Peñasco for several months. She spent the summer at Nazareth, where she instructed the final profession class. She returned to Peñasco that fall to resume as a temporary teacher, later doing the same in Belen. From January through June, 1938, she was enrolled at the University of New Mexico in Albuquerque to take some graduate work in education and to work on the translation of the new Constitution.

After thirty years of teaching throughout the state, advanced academic work, and congregational leadership, Mother Eveline returned to Saints Peter and Paul, Saginaw. From 1939 to 1942 she was superior of the house and supervisor of the schools for the newly created diocese of Saginaw. She continued as supervisor in 1942-1943 while she was superior and principal of St. Mary's, Saginaw. Summers were spent in graduate education and sociology courses at Marquette University. On August 7, 1941, Mother celebrated her Golden Jubilee.

From 1943 to her death in 1958 she resided at Marywood, serving until the early 1950's as directress of schools. The final year of her life she spent in the congregational infirmary. She was alert, studious, reflective until her last days. She died on Sunday, September 21, 1958, at 7:15 a.m. while the community Mass was being celebrated. The funeral Mass was celebrated on Wednesday, September 24, at Marywood. Monsignor William Murphy, former pupil and colleague at Catholic Central, preached the sermon. Her finest eulogy comes from her own hand:

> *When we were young we cast stones into the water and watched the 'dead men's ripples' go out, and asked in childish wonder where these ripples ended. Devoted parents told us that they ended on the most distant shores. Tell me, dear sisters, what far shores will feel the final impulse of your combined efforts...? Only God and the Angels will keep the record of their distances.*[14]

# PERIOD THREE

# A Perfect House
# 1936-1966

Mothers
Euphrasia Sullivan
Victor Flannery

*T*his piece links the old with the new: the supposed diocesan community discovered to be papal, the work of women who left the world to enter religion, and the work of church women in the modern world.

In 1936 it was not clear what newly defined juridical status and renewed bonds with the larger Dominican Order would mean. Nevertheless, the years 1936-1948 were largely inward looking. The Rule, secured for the congregation at such great price, became measure and goal.

Works begun in earlier administrations were maintained, major growth of the college was undertaken, and new forms of catechesis developed. Debt was reduced and foundations were laid for further expansion.

With Mother Euphrasia Sullivan and Bishops Plagens and Haas came reconciliation and renewed collaboration with diocesan leaders. The world, irreversibly altered by total war, competing ideologies, and stratification, was increasingly acknowledged as context for the sisters' mission.

Mother Victor Flannery, prioress general from 1948 to 1966, brought forth from the congregation's past its perduring strengths and at the same time directed it through the first strong winds of change. The true character of a papal congregation was evidenced in the response to Pope Pius XII's directives to major superiors, to the imperatives of Vatican Council II, and to the signs of the times.

**13**

# EVER INTERESTED IN YOU ALL
# MOTHER EUPHRASIA SULLIVAN

*A*fter the dramatic events of the summer of 1936--Bishop Pinten's extraordinary visitation on June 23, his stern letter of instruction, the negotiations with Father Nolan and the apostolic delegate, and finally the bishop's letter of July 18 retracting his formal precepts--Mother Eveline took every opportunity to acquaint the sisters with the general outlines of the controversy. In the Chapter she gave a formal report of her second term of office, "by far the most important part...the history of our Constitution, the development of which seems to be a special manifestation of God's providence over us."

On Saturday, August 8, 1936, the tenth General Chapter convened at Marywood. Bishop Pinten, as ordinary of the diocese, sent Fathers Robert Bogg and Emmeran Quaderer to preside at the elections. There were sixty capitulars, present no longer by years of profession but by office or by election, to represent the 536 professed sisters in the congregation. On the first balloting Sister Euphrasia Sullivan received thirty-five votes and thus became the fifth mother general. Sisters Martin Feyan, Alphonsine Reynolds, Michael Jones, and Estelle Hackett were elected as her councilors. Mother and her council later appointed Sister Fabian MacDonald mistress of novices and Sister Leonora Gallagher mistress of postulants.

At the recommendation of Mother Eveline, the delegates elected sisters not on the council for the positions of secretary general and treasurer. Sister Joachim Visner, again at the recommendation of Mother Eveline, was elected secretary general and Sister Felix Brand as treasurer. It was, in the parlance of the sisters, a "clean sweep" but one recommended by Mother Eveline herself.

*Mother Euphrasia Sullivan,*
*Fifth Mother General*
*(fl. 1936-1948)*
*on St. Patrick's Day, 1946*

*A major task of the mother general was making the annual mission assignments. Here, Mother Euphrasia takes the task to the Marywood grove, July 21, 1939.*

At the time of her election, Sister Euphrasia Sullivan of the Sacred Heart was 48 years old, a member of the 1936 Silver Jubilee class. Mary Elizabeth Sullivan was born in Peterborough, Ontario, on August 1, 1888. Within a month, her parents, Timothy and Margaret O'Grady Sullivan, moved the family to a farm east of Mount Pleasant, Michigan. There followed a brother, Frank, and a sister, Seraphia, known to all as "Sibbie."[1]

Mary was confirmed by Bishop Richter on May 31, 1900. Her schooling was with the Dominican sisters at Sacred Heart Academy, Mount Pleasant. As the author of the "Class History," she named her teachers--Sisters Emmanuel, Genevieve, Reginald, Aquinas, Dominica, Bertrand--until the class passed into the "dreaded High School Room." Sister Alphonsus O'Rourke soon dispelled the dread and launched the class into algebra, rhetoric, physics, and Latin, and all the other coursework in the repertoire of the sole high school teacher. The young author noted the diminishing of the class numbers at stages along the way, the death of their beloved pastor, Father Crowley, and the "gleams and glooms" of Sister Dominica's tutelage. The year with Sister Bertrand was "like the gay unwinding of some golden ribbon, so bright and peaceful." Mary graduated on June 18, 1907, and entered the congregation the following year, September 4, 1908. There is no record of how she spent the intervening year. There may be a hint, however, in an entry on her death certificate. Listed as cause of her death at age 82 is "aortic insufficiency and rheumatic heart disease" and the approximate interval between onset and death "65 years." The illness seems to have begun in her senior year of high school.

Mary spent but two days as a postulant at St. John's Home and then was sent to Holy Rosary Academy in Bay City "where," she wrote in her terse style, "she entered the novitiate, and began her career as teacher on September 8, 1908. She taught continuously from that date until the present time, July 25, 1935, without being absent from school one day on her own account." The boast may reflect her awareness of her delicate health.

Sister Euphrasia taught at Holy Rosary Academy for a single year, 1908-1909, not being absent even on the day of her clothing in the Dominican habit, April 13, 1909. In the 1909-1910 school year she taught at Sacred Heart Academy, Grand Rapids, and "made her novitiate." It was just a year before the establishment of the canonical novitiate and she was among those Bishop Richter instructed in theology, philosophy, and Latin. She professed first vows on April 19, 1911. The next years she spent in "The Valley" --from 1910 to 1914 at St. Joseph school, Saginaw, and at Holy Rosary Academy, Bay City, in 1914-1915, and again at St. Joseph school in Saginaw, from 1915 to 1927. In 1922 she received the Teachers' Life Certificate, and in 1927 the Bachelor of Arts degree from Central State Teacher's College, Mount Pleasant. Additional course work in English was taken at the University of Detroit, studies which were interrupted by her election in 1936.

From 1922 to 1927 Sister Euphrasia was superior and principal of St. Joseph mission in Saginaw. She then taught at St. Mary school, Muskegon, from 1927 to 1933, where her superior was her classmate Sister Michael Jones. Though the duties of high school teacher were usually universal in nature, her chief assignments were as teacher of Latin, English grammar and literature. As superior of St. Mary convent, Saginaw, she was present at the Chapter of Election in 1936.

In 1970, at the time of Mother's death, a sister recollected:

*I remember seeing her before 1936 on one occasion only, about 1926. ...I remember asking Mother Eveline what Sister Euphrasia was like and Mother answered in a few words, "She has been superior in our hardest missions and keeps a perfect house. When she is head of a high school she seems to see nothing, but the children simply do not think of doing anything out of the way."*

This appraisal, so typical of Mother Eveline's assessment of character, describes as well the character of Mother Euphrasia's twelve years as mother general. She kept, in many respects, "a perfect house."

Mother Euphrasia was stately in presence, her demeanor serene and her voice well-modulated. In contrast to Mother Eveline who, short of stature and stocky, emanated energy and command, she was a model of repose and reflection. Her style was terse, but not without humor. In January 1937 Father O'Brien, OMI, paid her a New Year's visit and advised her, "Don't let the mother general worry Sister Euphrasia." She replied, "Father, I'll tell you a secret; this is the first time that the mother general has ever worried Sister Euphrasia."

The sisters had the usual concerns about the transition from one administration to another: expectations of differences in style and emphases. There was now also a concern for the status of the congregation within the context of the local Church and, in particular, the implications of being of papal, rather than of diocesan, right. What would change, what would remain the same?

On early Monday afternoon, August 10, 1936, the day after their election and while the Chapter committees were studying constitutional drafts and preparing reports, Mother Euphrasia and her council "presented themselves...to the Most Reverend Bishop Joseph G. Pinten, who received them very graciously."[2] The relation of the new administration and of the entire congregation to the bishop was an obvious concern to all. The courtesy of the visit was both typical of Mother Euphrasia's temperament and presage of the years to come.

She began her administration with similar courtesy toward her sisters. Her first circular letter read:

*J.M.J.D.*
*Marywood*

*Feast of the Seven Sorrows of the Blessed Virgin*
*1936*

*My dear Sisters,*

*My first letter to you must be one of appreciation--appreciation, not because you have chosen me for so responsible a position as that of Prioress General, but for your great confidence in me in thinking me worthy of such an office.*

*Daily, I feel the awful responsibility which you have confided to me and were it not for your promise of continued prayers for me I would find the burden all too great to bear. The task seems more than poor human nature can endure and I rely upon your prayers that I may not fail you. God alone, through your petitions must help.*

*It was not only edifying but consoling to witness the generosity and the resignation with which you received your appointments. Were it in my power, I would have each one of you just where you would be the happiest, but that I cannot do even for myself, so some of us must bear with disappointment for His sake. Is it not helpful to know that even the heaviest cross lasts at best for only a few years?*

*I have already visited a few of the near missions. How kind the Sisters were; how pleasant they tried to make it for me; and best of all how happy they all seemed! May such a spirit continue! Let us pray for each other that we may continue unto the end, loyal to Him and worthy of His reward.*

*Again pray for me.*
*Ever interested in you all,*

*Sister M. Euphrasia*

In 1938 the Catholic Church in Michigan ended its century-and-a-half relationship with the metropolitan of Cincinnati. On March 11 the Holy See announced the creation of the Archdiocese of Detroit, comprised of the dioceses of Detroit, Grand Rapids, Marquette, Saginaw, and Lansing, under the direction of Archbishop Edward Mooney. On April 17, 1938, William F. Murphy was consecrated the first bishop of the Saginaw diocese; St. Mary parish was named the cathedral parish. As the congregation had long provided sisters for many of the new diocese's parish schools, Mother Euphrasia and her council now collaborated with Bishop Murphy as well as Bishop Pinten in Michigan. Since 1925 the mothers general had worked with the archbishops of Santa Fe, Archbishop Daeger, followed by Archbishop Rudolph Gerken, and after his sudden death on March 2, 1943, with Archbishop Edwin V. Byrne.

There was, since the announcement of the congregation's papal status, no longer the close episcopal involvement in the internal life of the congregation. As ordinaries of their dioceses, bishops appointed chaplains and confessors for the sisters who had, by canonical and constitutional law, a weekly obligation to receive the Sacrament of Penance. Bishops regulated, as they did in all churches and chapels of their diocese, liturgical practices. Thus, Mother Euphrasia announced to the sisters at Marywood that Bishop Pinten was giving them the privilege of a Midnight Mass on Christmas eve, 1938, but that there were to be no guests, nor were the sisters to receive Communion at the Mass. The bishop of Grand Rapids, as ordinary of the diocese in which the motherhouse was located, had the canonical obligations of presiding over the election of the mother general and her council, the examination of candidates for admission to vows, the official witness of the profession of vows, and of their dispensation. Bishops had canonical jurisdiction over the finances of religious women's congregations, particularly the acquisition and alienation of property. They had as well the canonical right of visitation of the convents.

After the pronouncement of the congregation's papal status, Bishop Pinten usually dealt with these matters through his vicar or secretary. He tended to send a delegate for clothing and profession ceremonies. In July 1937 he denied permission for a Franciscan priest, once a retreat master to the sisters in Traverse City, to visit Marywood. That same month he responded to Mother Euphrasia's request for clarification on the manner of dispensing sisters under final vows, "As long as you were a diocesan community the Bishop of Grand Rapids had authority to grant certain dispensations. Since your status has been changed I must refer you to the Holy See for counsel and relief."[3] Permissions to attend summer schools, to consult physicians, or for extended travel were no longer referred to the bishop but to the mother general. Letters to the sisters no longer spoke of "Bishop" but "the bishop"; the personal relationship as immediate superior of the congregation had ceased and there were as well other bishops with whom the sisters collaborated.

On November 1, 1940, the fiftieth anniversary of his ordination, Bishop Pinten resigned. The congregational annals record his last visit to Marywood on Christmas Day, 1940:

*Bishop Pinten paid his farewell visit to Marywood tonight. He looked very feeble and we were saddened by his appearance. May our dear Lord and His Blessed Mother soften for him the loneliness that is before him in these last of his years upon earth. He is going to live in retirement.*

*It seems worthy of note that for the first time in the history of Marywood a choir exercise was carried on without the presence of any of the novices. At 7:30, since the Bishop was still in the novitiate, Mother told the professed sisters not to ring the bell but to go to the chapel as usual for Compline. We were quite proud and happy to have all to ourselves the honor of chanting Compline and singing the* **Salve** *on Christmas night.*

Bishop Joseph H. Albers, Bishop of Lansing since 1937, was named apostolic administrator, pending the naming of a new bishop of the diocese. During the few months of his tenure in Grand Rapids, there were several occasions when he visited Marywood. On February 18, 1941, Joseph Casimir Plagens (1880-1943), Bishop of Marquette since 1935, was named the fifth Bishop of Grand Rapids. In his February 1941 "Folks and Facts," Father John J. McAllister, pastor of St. Francis Xavier parish, Grand Rapids, and brother of Sisters Henrietta and Rose Marie, wrote:

*It was love at first sight, Dear Reader. Love born of faith. It was dreams come true. Yes, it was more. It was high spiritual romance, when lovers met and wed and good Bishop Plagens, the prince charming of the priesthood, in a quasi nuptial scene of regal splendor and exquisite grace, plighted his troth to his newly found spouse, the Catholic Church along the Grand and we on our part fell heir to a shepherd in Christ and a new father in God. ...Old St. Andrew's that has seen its shepherds come and pass was never more happy than on that eventful day and perhaps has never looked down upon scenes of deeper loveliness than when she took to her heart Bishop Plagens as it took, long ago, Richter the ascetic, Gallagher the scholar and genius, Kelly the dreamer and Pinten the Pious to part with him no more till the grim reaper comes....The story of the Catholic episcopacy in Grand Rapids is one very much of contrast. From the rigors of Richter to the mildness of Gallagher--from the sweetness of Kelly to the severity of Pinten, but in all, never for a moment and never for one inch did the clergy or laity deviate from their unswerving allegiance and profound reverence for those placed over them.*

The public welcome was in sharp contrast to both the coming and the departure of Bishop Pinten. Bishop Albers and a group of thirty priests of the diocese went to Benton Harbor and boarded the *Pere Marquette* coach bringing the new bishop and other clerics from Chicago to Grand Rapids. A huge crowd of welcomers, delegates from all the Catholic institutions and schools of the city, including Aquinas College and Marywood Academy, the mayors of the city and of East Grand Rapids, judges, businessmen, scouts, and interested lay persons met Bishop Plagens as he descended from the train on Tuesday, February 17. Following the installation ceremony the next day there was a banquet luncheon at the Pantlind Hotel for hundreds of clerics. That evening at the Civic Auditorium a musical program  was presented by a composite of all the parish choirs of the city and the Grand Rapids WPA Symphony Orchestra. Welcomes were given by Governor Murray D. Van Wagoner, by Mayor George Welsh, and by Father Dennis J. Behan, spokesman for the clergy.

On March 2, the sisters' monthly Retreat Sunday, the new bishop paid a surprise visit to Marywood. He simply appeared at the front door, rang the bell, and greeted the sisters as they came from their afternoon retreat conference. The tower bell called all to the blue parlor where each of the sisters presented herself to the bishop. He then visited the novitiate and postulancy and all of the sisters in the infirmary. Benediction followed, the choir producing the appropriate *Ecce Sacerdos* at the bishop's entrance into the chapel with Father Heintz, CSsR, the retreat master, and Father Joseph Luther, the chaplain. The bishop remained for supper with the two priests; the sisters continued their usual First Sunday rosary procession before their supper. After the prayers before meals, the bishop appeared at the refectory entrance and called in to them," I've been listening in on you, not that I don't trust your good Mother Superior, but to make sure that not my command but my desire be carried out that you have no spiritual reading tonight. "

Sister Joachim wrote of that event:

*It was a dramatic moment, for in the history of our Motherhouse we have never seen aught but black and white in our refectory. However, we are proud of our Dominican refectory and our Dominican heritage of prayers and customs, and we are glad that our good Bishop "listened in." After supper we all waited in the parlor and vestibule to bid adieu to His Excellency. When finally he had blessed us again and promised to come often if we would just "call him up," we all followed him out to his car, Mother remarking with a laugh, that she had lost control of her community.*

On March 11, there was a scheduled visit, this time for the bishop's first Mass at Marywood and visit to the Academy. By then the novitiate and Academy choirs had the *Ecce Sacerdos* well-rehearsed. In his message and manner, the bishop endeared himself to every child and sister at Marywood. He became a regular visitor at Marywood, giving benediction for the alumnae retreats, visiting mothers and children on Mary's Day, conferring diplomas at commencement, presiding at reception and profession ceremonies, and sisters' funerals.

The work of healing was well under way but Bishop Plagens' tenure was short. After suffering several heart attacks since his appointment to Grand Rapids, he died on March 31, 1943. His successor, Bishop Francis J. Haas (1889-1953), proved an equally kind and generous pastor.

A native of Racine, Wisconsin, Francis Joseph Haas, DD, PhD, LLD, was called to Grand Rapids from the position of dean of the School of Social Sciences of the Catholic University of America. As a distinguished economist and sociologist, he had taken an active role in the evolution of the New Deal. He served on the Labor Advisory Board of the National Recovery Act, the National Labor Relations Board, and as a special conciliator with the Department of Labor. At the time of his appointment, he was on the President's Fair Employment Practices Committee. President Roosevelt's congratulatory note and expression of loss was read during the civic welcome given the bishop-elect on November 15. In a dual ceremony of consecration and enthronement at St. Andrew cathedral on Thursday, November 18, 1943, he became the sixth bishop of Grand Rapids. He took as his motto *"In Christo Justitia"*--"Let there be justice in Christ."

In his first public remarks, the bishop said:

> *The great need of our times is to think about others--and to care about them. When we do this out of love of God we are producing the finest fruit of Christian charity--and for that the world is thirsting today.*

On December 10, 1943, the bishop called at Marywood for the first of many formal and informal visits.[4] The congregation had prepared the welcoming banquet for Bishop Haas and visiting prelates and, from 1944 to 1954, two sisters were assigned to domestic service at the episcopal residence at 2006 Lake Drive, SE.

St. Dominic had enjoined upon his followers to "cherish holy poverty," a "legacy" which Mother Aquinata stressed on her deathbed. Poverty was not only an aspect of the sisters' spirituality, it was, since their coming to Michigan, a defining characteristic of their material culture.

Since 1922 the sisters had been well-informed by circular letters of the congregation's debt and required to exercise frugality in countless ways. As a member of Chapters, Sister Euphrasia had become acquainted with the financial details. In August 1936 she was reminded that $280,000 remained to be paid on the mortgages and loans related to the building of the motherhouse. The Lincoln National Life Insurance Company held a $275,000 mortgage at 5½% per annum; another loan of $7,000 required 7% annual interest. The stipend of the teaching sisters, $25 per sister per month for ten months, had not changed since 1920. On January 1, 1937, the amount was raised to $35 a month, the stipend which Bishop Pinten had promised in August 1932 but rescinded the following month.

Mother Euphrasia perceived that the Chapter of 1936 had given her a twofold task: to reduce the debt and to put into the hands of the sisters a printed Constitution. She called a special council meeting for August 16, 1936, to be apprised more fully on aspects of congregational finance: the mortgages, the budget for the 1936-1937 academic year at Catholic Junior College, debts and credit problems of Marywood priory, and the costs to the congregation of scholarships to the college. Economy became a consistent theme in her administration. On January 19, 1937, she wrote to the sisters:

*A word about our financial problems. The Bursar General's accounts show that we have received since July 1: $19,993.19 for salary and $3,239.92 for music. Since then we have paid: $7,809.90 for interest and $13,000 on the principal. However, part of the sum paid on the principal was taken from a balance already on hand previous to July 1, 1936.*

*Since the amount paid for interest alone is exorbitant, you will agree that we must attempt to do something at once to lower the principal; therefore, all music money will be received for that purpose. I was pleased to have some of the*

*Sisters suggest that each mission create a "Good Will Fund" wherein the Sisters would deposit any extra donation, money earned, etc. If this is forwarded to me perhaps once a month--be it ever so small--and reserved for our debt alone it would help greatly. May I have your hearty support for this project? ...*

The first year's "Good Will Fund" yielded $688.76. In addition to the debt, congregational buildings were deteriorating. Holy Angels convent was over fifty years old, Holy Rosary Academy over thirty years. The motherhouse, though only twenty years old, needed much work; the houses on Ransom Street used for Catholic Junior College were old and ill-suited to the expanding program. There were almost weekly letters from the superior at Nazareth Sanatorium for help with maintenance needs: a boiler, a new well, a better car, roof repairs, and the like. In 1942 the council discussed the feasibility of either completing or selling the convent-hospital in Albuquerque. To enable continuance of Nazareth, they sold property in downtown Albuquerque for $5,000, along with ten acres of orchard at the sanatorium for $500. In December 1946 the chapel at Nazareth was completed.

Nazareth Sanatorium was founded to serve tuberculosis patients, lay as well as religious. Changes in treatment procedures and the national decline in tuberculosis gradually altered the patient census at the hospital. A brochure dating from the early 1940's advertised it as "a hospice of rest...suitable and desirable for patients suffering from arthritis, sinus trouble, heart ailments and chronic asthma" while excluding "bedridden patients, as well as highly nervous people and those suffering from mental diseases." From time to time, area physicians sought to admit patients needing psychiatric care. In 1947 the hospital became a closed institution for the treatment of nervous and mild mental disorders under the direction of Dr. W.W. Myers.

From January to September 1937 Mother and her council sought help on ways to reduce the debt. Bishop Pinten proved to be a helpful advisor and he arranged consultations with bankers and financiers. On April 23, the council authorized a loan of $285,000 payable at 4% annually. On September 18, 1937, Sister Joachim entered in the congregational annals the conditions of the refinancing:

*The details of the transaction were brought to a successful conclusion today, papers being signed transferring the mortgage to the Connecticut Mutual Life Insurance Company of Hartford, Connecticut. Interest on this new loan is payable at the rate of 4% to September 18, 1942, and 4½% thereafter until the* *maturity of the loan, September 18, 1952. Mandatory payments on the principal are to be $10,000 a year, with the privilege after the first three years of making additional payments of not to exceed $10,000 a term and after ten years from this date to make additional payments in unlimited sums.*

At the same time Mother and the council dealt with aspects of employment of laymen at the motherhouse. They made decisions on the retention and firing of some employees and a salary scale "that we may conform to the laws of social justice in compliance with the mind of Holy Mother Church as to the payment of a living wage."[5]

An infirmary fund was also established, first as a modest way to refurbish rooms on the fourth floor of the motherhouse used for the sick, later as "seed money" for a building solely for that purpose. The fabric of the motherhouse received a good deal of attention in council meetings: rooms to be painted, a new oven for the bakery, the installation of a pressure pump for the heating plant, pointing of bricks and replacement of porches and steps. From September to November, 1939, the Michigan Colprovia Company, a Grandville firm, worked at paving the dirt road leading from Fulton Street to the formal covered entrance and around the exterior of the building, as well as the "Pine Drive." The "Marywood circle" featured in the architect's drawings of 1922 was at last completed. The project was of such magnitude as to merit coverage in *The Grand Rapids Herald* which informed its readers:

> *Paving entails much more construction detail than simply laying a hard surface, according to Dana M. Burgess, president of Michigan Colprovia Company, 2200 Chicago Drive, SW. This point is amply illustrated in a paving project undertaken by Marywood Academy, operated on East Fulton Street by the Sisters of the Order of Saint Dominic.*
>
> *The project at the well known girls' school consists of adjusting grades, installing drain pipe, storm water sewers, curb and gutters, foundation, asphalt pavement and landscaping of adjoining areas. All the work is done under the direction of Harry L. Mead.*
>
> *Inconvenience had resulted in the past from erosion and roughness of the cinder drive surface and the Sisters were unable to maintain their grounds and buildings. The hard-surface asphalt pavement will permanently fix the drive.*
>
> *But paving necessitates proper drainage and the Marywood project called for installation of nearly a mile of pipe, moving 2,000 yards of dirt, placing nearly 100 cubic yards of ready-mixed concrete, furnishing 1,200 cubic yards of gravel and 600 tons of Colprovia asphalt. The project furnishes employment for 25 men for 40 days.*

Donations and the "Good Will Fund" covered the costs of the project. The traditional reliance of the congregation on the intercession of St. Joseph continued. Each year preceding the feast of St. Joseph a novena was made for the material needs of the congregation. The annals for March 19, 1940, the feast of St. Joseph, record the sale of "the Buick car" for $795 and the gift of two $50 bills from benefactors, and "a thousand thanks to good St. Joseph!"

These receipts, the Good Will Fund, and other monies were used to buy a 24 passenger bus for $1,925 and to remodel the barn into a garage for $215. The "Black Maria," and its successors, became a familiar feature throughout the city and county for the next twenty-five years. Its arrival on April 3, 1940, was a community event recorded in the annals:

*The new bus came today. Mr. Stokes called for it at the garage this morning and at ten o'clock it was blessed by Father Delahanty at St. Andrew's. From there it went to Catholic Junior College and made its initial trip in the service of the Dominican Sisters, the postulants who attend Catholic Junior being its first passengers. It arrived at Marywood at high noon as the Sisters were leaving the chapel to go to the refectory. The entire Community went out to the side porch to inspect it and accorded it a hearty welcome. All were agreeably surprised. It makes a very imposing appearance--approximately twenty feet long, seating capacity twenty-four passengers besides the driver, aisle down the center, with six double seats on either side. It is black with a cream border at the top on which "Marywood" is neatly painted. Immediately after dinner, the Sisters, aspirants, and children gave it a try-out around the grounds, and then it left for its first trip. We feel certain that St. Joseph, under whose patronage we are placing it, will give our bus his special blessing and protection.*

Notwithstanding decades-long labor, constitutional work was not complete. Upon the recommendation of Father Nolan, the Constitution of the Dominican sisters of Everett (Edmonds), Washington was studied and modified during the Chapter of 1936. It was the Constitution most recently approved by Rome, and therefore its modification promised the most expeditious path. A draft was to be made from that text, and its Latin original translated into English, and sent to Rome. In the meantime the Sinsinawa Constitution was to be the proper law of the congregation. To the published decrees of the Chapter Mother Euphrasia added a note:

*During the Tenth General Chapter you were told to follow the Sinsinawa Constitution, but since it is impossible for all to have access to these constitutions and since there is so little difference, I would ask you to follow the Constitution given us in 1916 until such time as our new Constitutions are made and approved. We shall make definite plans for work on our new Constitution very soon.*

On January 25, 1938, Sister Joachim wrote in the congregational annals: "Our Constitution with the official Decree of Approbation was received from Rome today. *Deo Gratias!*[6] Mother Eveline and Sisters Beatrice Cottrell, Loyola Finn, and Henrietta McAllister were assigned to translate the text into English. They consulted a Jesuit priest, Father Goni, on particular points and sent drafts to Father William J. Gauche of Mount St. Mary Seminary, Norwood, Ohio, and to Bishop Albers of Lansing. The English text was sent to Rome in the summer of 1939 and approved within the year. After some delay, Bishop Joseph Plagens gave his imprimatur to its publication.[7]

On September 16, 1941, the printed copies arrived at Marywood. Each sister in the congregation received her copy of the Constitution, familiarly known as "the little black book," on September 27, 1941. Apart from the definition of the congregation as an apostolic institute of papal right and the manner of election for Chapter, the new Constitution described a life not radically different from the kind of life the sisters were actually living. There were as well, Mother Euphrasia pointed out, practices and regulations not contained in the Constitution that they were bound to observe. She encouraged the sisters:

> *Dear Sisters, you have waited a long time for this little book. Many of you have been discouraged over and over again-- thought that it would never come. I hope that now you will study it diligently, use it for meditation, make it a part of yourselves. It should mean a rebirth of fervor for each and every one of us.*

The Constitution, prefaced by the Rule of St. Augustine, became the "little book as in a mirror" to which the sisters were to look for the image of the perfect religious.

# 14

# FOR THE DURATION

*T*he change in congregational status coincided with the departures of Mother Eveline in 1936 and of Bishop Pinten in 1940, with the more inwardly-directed administration of Mother Euphrasia and the brief, healing pastoral years of Bishop Plagens, and the decade of outgoing, social justice leadership of Bishop Haas. The release from the direct supervision of the ordinary of the diocese did not change the daily life of the sisters nor their fundamental orientation. Nevertheless the global waning of the Depression and the advent of war irrevocably brought the congregation into the "world."

On August 3, 1937, Mother Euphrasia included with each sister's "ticket," the 1½" x 3" card revealing her annual assignment and chief "obedience" for the year, this exhortation:

*Dear Sisters,*

*Kindly accept your little ticket of appointment to your mission as coming directly from the Holy Ghost through me to you. You have prayed most fervently during the past six weeks to the Holy Ghost to place you on the mission where He willed you to be for the coming year and where you would accomplish the most good.*

*Some of you have been transferred from the east to the west--others from north to south and vice versa--but remember God willed it so; so do not weep but think of our motto, "To praise, to bless, and to teach." You begin to do that today by accepting your appointment in God's name and praising Him, thanking Him, and pleasing Him by your example as a model religious.*

*God bless you all!*

*Devotedly yours in St. Dominic,*
*Mother M. Euphrasia, OP*

Mother's letter suggests the range of spiritual emphases within the congregation: liturgical, Dominican, "regular," and Teresian.

Since their first acquaintance with the transforming power of the liturgy, Sisters Estelle Hackett and Jane Marie Murray continued to espouse that cause, though in different ways. In 1936 Sister Estelle was elected to Mother Euphrasia's council and continued to serve as supervisor of schools until 1942. She applied her energies to the sisters' formation as teachers, to the advancement of schools staffed by the sisters, and the evolution of Catholic Junior College. In 1938 Sister Jane Marie began the licentiate program at the Pontifical Institute of Mediaeval Studies in Toronto.[1] In this singular way, the theological and philosophical underpinnings of the liturgical movement were begun in the congregation. In the following decades hundreds of the sisters received advanced theological training, pioneered by Sister Jane Marie's work in Toronto. Her scholarship, writing, and advocacy served as leaven in the congregation for the next fifty years.

Early in 1942 Sister Jane Marie finished *The Life Of Our Lord*, a high school text "according to the four gospels, with questions for study, moral applications, problems and activities, and catechism questions." Monsignor Thomas Noa, censor of books for the Diocese of Grand Rapids, readily approved the work. The book, published by the Bruce Company of Milwaukee with the imprimatur of Bishop Plagens, was widely adopted in dioceses where the sisters taught. In her efforts to promote *The Christ Life* series and subsequent works, Sister Jane Marie became a nationally known educator and author.

The sisters continued to experience the developments associated with the liturgical movement. Mother Eveline and Sister Estelle, supervisors of schools in Saginaw and, after 1943, for the congregation, directed the continuing education of the sisters and were, in large part, leaders in the intellectual and spiritual formation of the congregation. *Contacts* was an apt forum for their thoughts on liturgy, education, vocation, and spirituality.[2] On September 4, 1938, they attended the Catholic Rural Life Conference in Vincennes, Indiana, the first congregational representation at the conference meetings. The following January 17, 1939, Monsignor Luigi Ligutti,[3] conference president from Granger, Iowa, lectured to the sisters and students at Marywood on Catholic Rural Life and the Homestead Movement. In 1940, he became the first full-time executive secretary of the National Catholic Rural Life Conference, a position he held until 1960. He returned to Grand Rapids in April 1941 and in the summer of 1944 to present a Rural Life conference as part of Aquinas College's summer session. His homespun philosophy expressed in "Liguttisms" were well known throughout Catholic parishes in rural America. It was a message well received by the sisters whose origins and field of ministry were largely rural. The Rural Life Conference also provided an avenue of international education and advocacy.

At the same time, the sisters continued to be influenced by the Catholic Social Action promoted by Father John A. O'Brien and the Sodality Movement of Father Daniel Lord, SJ. The missal clubs begun in the schools in 1929 continued well into the 1940's. To these were added Catholic Social Action groups, sodalities and Angelic Warfare confraternities.

From the earliest years of the sisters' presence in Grand Rapids, there had been many changes in the motherhouse chaplaincy. It was a position within the appointment of the bishop of Grand Rapids and often given in conjunction with other duties. When the motherhouse was moved to Marywood in 1922, a resident chaplain was sought to care for liturgical and sacramental needs of the sisters and students of the academy. There were a series of gifted and generous diocesan priests who served the congregation as chaplains: Father Joseph Vogl (1925 to 1930), Bishop August F. Schinner, former bishop of Superior, Wisconsin, and later of Spokane, Washington (January to August 1931), Fathers Thomas W. Albin (August 1931 to October 1933), Nicholas Irmen (October 1933 to 1936, and in residence 1937-1939), Monsignor Joseph M. Steffes (October 1937 to his death on April 10, 1940) and Father Joseph A. Luther, a former Jesuit from the University of Detroit (September 1940 to July 1942). There were, however, frequent and sometimes sudden changes of personnel. Replacements came from the ranks of the newly ordained, the sick or elderly, or as an extra duty for busy pastors or school administrators.

On July 18, 1942, Father Luther told Mother Euphrasia that he had been ordered by the chancery office the previous evening to depart by noon of that day. While no explanation was given nor sought, it was believed that he had been overly zealous in expressing his opinions on labor controversies in the city. At the same time Bishop Plagens responded to a suggestion Mother Euphrasia had made some months earlier for a Dominican chaplain. The matter had been raised by Mother Euphrasia at the eleventh General Chapter in early July and had received unanimous support. On July 21, she wrote to T.S. McDermott, OP, Provincial of St. Joseph Province,[4] and by July 25, she had the promise of a Dominican chaplain.

On August 20, 1942, Charles Pius Wilson[5] began a 32-year tenure as chaplain of Marywood. Previous to the decree of papal status, chaplains had sometimes been called to make representations on behalf of bishops. Father Wilson, an extraordinarily generous and gracious pastor to the sisters, academy students and their families, aided in the widening of the congregational outlook and spirituality. After his arrival, bishops occasionally asked the hospitality of Marywood for convalescent priests.

It has been conjectured that Mother Euphrasia had, by securing a Dominican chaplain, "made the community Dominican." There was, however, a long history of Dominican connections: the spirituality and constitutional and customary practices derived from the Ratisbon founders; the affiliation of the new congregation with the Order in 1896; contacts with congregations of Dominican sisters and with the fathers of the Province of St. Joseph; emphases on Dominican reading[6] and awareness of the cycle of feasts and observances of the Order. Dominican retreat masters and preachers had served the sisters in every administration, while Dominican lecturers were welcomed and received attentive audiences.[7]

Nevertheless, with the coming of Father Wilson there was an increased emphasis on Dominican practice, particularly with respect to the liturgy. As with the universal Church, there was liturgical revitalization within the Dominican Order.[8] In December 1937 Margaret Leddy of the Pius X School of Music gave a six-day workshop to almost three hundred sisters of the diocese at St. Joseph Seminary. The sisters at Marywood became eager users of *Graduales* according to the Dominican rite. On November 16, 1942, the first funeral according to the Dominican rite was offered for Sister Immaculata Senecal. In the 1943 Aquinas College summer session Father Vincent C. Donovan, OP, began a series of courses in liturgical chant as well as instructing the congregation in the chanting of the office during the annual retreat in August. On April 27, 1947, the novitiate choir sang the first High Mass according to the Dominican rite.

In April 1939 Mother Euphrasia, with Sister Martin Feyan as her companion, first participated in the Dominican Mothers General Conference held that year in Adrian, Michigan. The meetings, by then scheduled biennially during Easter week, concentrated on the uniformities emphasized by Father Nolan in 1935. Membership in this conference contributed significantly to the emphasis on Dominican custom within the congregation. Mother used the conferences and discussions as basis for her directives on various aspects of conventual life, for example, strict observance of silence in the refectory and dormitory.

On May 4, 1948, the congregation once again welcomed a Master General of the Dominican Order. The Most Reverend Emmanuel Suarez, OP, seventy-ninth successor to St. Dominic, was accompanied by Fathers Paul A. Skehan and Timothy Sparks, members of the central administration of the Order. After a courtesy visit to Bishop Haas, the distinguished guests spent the afternoon with the sisters at a formal program in the chapel followed by a reception in Madonna Lounge. Sister Angela LaLonde gave a welcome in Spanish to Father Suarez, who responded in Spanish and in Latin. Each sister was presented to the Master General by Mother Euphrasia. A stop at Aquinas College was made before the visitors' departure for the train station.

From its beginnings, religious life was governed by rule *(regula)*. The "Holy Rule" was considered a school of sanctity, a framework for daily life. The Rule and Constitution were the standard against which observances and practices were measured. "Regular observance," "keeping the rule," was the way the vows were lived. Each of the mothers general had learned the Rule in her formation as a religious, and each understood her first task as superior of the congregation was to see that the Rule was kept. Mother Euphrasia, in particular, used the Rule as the core of her directives and reflections to the sisters. In her circular letter of November 27, 1940, along with announcements of the resignation of Bishop Pinten and of a worldwide month of prayer and fasting for peace, she prefaced several regulations on silence and recreation:

*It is my personal opinion that silence is the most important part of our holy rule. A religious who observes it at the proper time and in the proper places will have little to account for in regard to uncharitableness in act and word, waste of time, and scandal giving. I believe that in a few of our convents this rule is not observed as strictly as it should be. Remember that we cannot expect God's blessings upon ourselves, our family, or our work if we do not observe our holy rule in its every detail. "The habit does not make the religious" is a very true saying.*

Her letters, both congregational and personal, abound with references to the "model religious." It was an ideal measured against the Rule and customs, and an understanding of the congregation's past.

Shortly after the sisters received the long-awaited *Rule and Constitution*, another congregational book was submitted to Bishop Plagens for his imprimatur. There had long been in use a little book commonly called "Table Book," a collection of refectory prayers and private devotions. In November 1941 the table prayers were combined with the "Night Prayer Book" and approved by the bishop as the official congregational *Book of Prayers*. Chapters and clarifications from the Dominican Order provided other changes, among them the return in November 1947 to the weekly recitation of the Office of the Dead, a practice which had been discontinued in 1930.

In winter 1941 there was an occurrence in Muskegon, Michigan, which the sisters considered miraculous. Sister Mechtilde Cordes, one of the first missionaries to Dixon, New Mexico, and then teaching at St. Mary school, became suddenly ill. Pneumonia was diagnosed; her temperature rose to 107 degrees. The physician reckoned that she could not withstand the high fever more than three hours. Sister was anointed; a habit was readied for her burial; the undertaker stood by as the sisters knelt about the bedside singing the *Salve*. Then the administrator of the parish, Father Thomas Martin, told the sisters of a devotion to the Blessed Mother under the title of "My Mother, My Confidence." During the first World War some soldiers had been safely brought through an area of extreme danger, through invocation of Mary under that title. The little prayer had been a constant aid to Father Martin. The Dominican sisters made a promise to pray that invocation three times daily for the remainder of the school year. Sister Mechtilde recovered in less than three hours. The devotion quickly spread throughout the congregation and remains to the present.[9]

In 1937 Mother Euphrasia reported to the sisters that a request had come from Rome for information on Sister Reparata Gautier (1892-1927). She appointed Sister Angela LaLonde, a gifted French and

Spanish linguist and companion to Sister Reparata in her early years with the congregation, to gather information from the sisters and prepare the report for the postulator general of the Dominican Order. It was an endeavor that caused the sisters to reflect seriously on Sister Reparata's extraordinary decade with the congregation and which, it may be conjectured, extended her influence.

Marie Gautier, daughter of expatriate French parents, was born in Sao Paolo, Brazil, and lived there for ten years. In 1902 her parents moved to New Orleans and, in 1905, to Grand Rapids. Within three months, both parents died. Monsignor Schrembs, who assisted in the mother's deathbed return to the faith, placed Marie and a sister and brother at St. John's Home on September 1, 1906. On January 6, 1907, Marie received her First Communion and the next day was confirmed by Bishop Richter in his private chapel. On January 8, Monsignor Schrembs took the three children to New York where they embarked for France. Marie was sent to a boarding school under the care of the Religious of the Sacred Heart. She declined their invitation to join them, for she longed to enter the Carmel at Lisieux. In 1911 she attended a papal audience with Pope Pius X,  who told her, "One day you will be a Dominican." It is not clear whether it was anticlerical legislation affecting cloisters in France, lack of dowry, or her own confusion as to the nature of the Dominican congregations in America that finally led her back to Michigan. On the advice of Monsignor Schrembs, she returned to Grand Rapids to enter the congregation on September 6, 1913. She was among twenty-one postulants to receive the Dominican habit from Mother Aquinata on April 15, 1914, at St. John's Home.

Her first mission was to Sacred Heart Academy, Grand Rapids, where she taught French and violin. Her health soon gave way, on at least two occasions with an inexplicable paralysis, and finally with tuberculosis, a disease common to the times and to those working in difficult conditions. In January 1915 Mother Aquinata sent her to the Kneipp Sanitarium, Rome City, Indiana, for treatments. There she appeared to have been miraculously cured and was able to return to St. John's Home by April. She began her novitiate in August 1915 and made profession on August 17, 1916. For three years she was missioned at Holy Family school, Saginaw, where she taught French and  violin, sometimes giving as many as

*Sister Reparata Gautier (1892-1927), at Kneipp Sanitarium, Rome City, Indiana, January 1915*

*Charles P. Wilson, OP, Marywood Chaplain from 1942 to 1976*

*FACING PAGE*
*"My Mother, My Confidence" Congregational devotion, 1941 to present*

*Master General Emmauel Suarez, OP, Mother Euphrasia, aspirants and novices, May 4, 1948*

# My Mother, My Confidence

300 days indulgence for the aspiration, "My Mother, My Confidence" granted by His Holiness, Pope Benedict XV.

## OUR LADY OF CONFIDENCE

†

Many remarkable favors have been obtained through veneration of this picture of Our Lady of Confidence which has been honored in Italy for hundreds of years. The most famous copy occupies an honored place in the Major Seminary in the Lateran Palace in Rome, and the Eternal City has twice been miraculously delivered from cholera after the seminarians had implored the intercession of Our Lady of Confidence.

Concerning this picture, Sister Clare Isabella Fornary, a Poor Clare of Tadi, Italy, whose beatification process is now under way, tells us that Our Blessed Mother has made a remarkable promise. Our Lady promised, said Sister Clare, that she would grant a particular tenderness and devotion towards herself to everyone who venerates her image in the picture of Our Lady of Confidence.

This devotion has proved itself particularly efficacious when combined with the aspiration, "My Mother, My Confidence." As recently as 1941, a Dominican Sister in Michigan made a remarkable recovery after the Sisters at her bedside invoked the help of the Blessed Lady with the aspiration, "My Mother, My Confidence." In 1917, Pope Benedict XV granted 300 days indulgence for this aspiration.

M. 278 in the Raccolta gives "My Mother, My Hope" 300 days in 1917 "Mater mea, fiducia mea."

Nihil obstat

John M. A. Fearns, S.T.D.
Censor Librorum

Imprimatur

+ Francis Cardinal Spellman
Archbishop of New York

Name _____ Date_____

CLOTHING:                    BOOKS:                          ____Typewriter
                                                             ____Watch
____aprons (cloth)           ____Bible                       ____
____aprons (plastic)         ____Customary                   ____
____caps                     ____Dictionary                  ____
____cloak (rain)             ____Missal(s)                    Miscellaneous:
____cloak (summer)           ____Meditation Bks.             ____Flashlight
____cloak (winter)           ____Office Bks.(s)              ____Hair brush
____collars (extra)          ____Rule & Const.              ____Hair clipper
____cuffs (prs.)             ____Spiritual Reading Bks.      ____Laundry Bag
____girdle(s)                ____                            ____Mirror
____gloves (prs.)            ____                            ____Pencil pouch
____golashes (prs.)          ____                            ____Pocketbook
____habits                   ____                            ____Sewing kit, etc.
____handkerchiefs                                            ____Stapler
____headshawls (summer)      LUGGAGE:                        ____Toilet kit
____headshawls (winter)      ____Book box                    ____Towels
____kimona(s)                ____Brief case                  ____Washcloths
____nightgowns               ____Suitcase(s)                 ____Fancy Work
____rubbers (prs.)           ____Traveling bag
____scapulars (extra)        ____overnight bag               _____
____scapulars (night)        ____                            _____
____shawl                    ____                            _____
____shoes                    ____                            _____
____shoulderette             OTHERS:                         _____
____stockings                ____Clock                       _____
____sweater                  ____Desk accessories            _____
____underwear (summer)       ____Fountain pen(s)             _____
____underwear (winter)       ____Glasses (reading)
____veils (black)            ____Glasses (sun)
____veils (white)            ____Pencil(s)

*Inventory customarily completed by each sister on New Year's Eve, a congregational retreat day. The inventory was submitted to the local superior and superfluities given to the common stores.*

ten lessons a day. Again, in January 1921, her health failed and she returned to St. John's and eventually to Rome City.

After a year's ministry in Charlevoix, Michigan, she returned to St. John's Home for a three-year period, doing sacristy work and sewing for the altars. She made final profession in August 1923 but was soon, with Mother Benedicta's help, to achieve her heart's desire, entrance to a cloister. She was accepted by the Dominican nuns of Holy Name Monastery, Cincinnati, Ohio, on February 21, 1924. Though she soon became ill, again with infectious tuberculosis, the Dominican nuns unanimously approved her retention at the monastery. There she died on October 10, 1927, a "holy death" entered next to her name in the Grand Rapids' congregational register. In the following year, the Dominican nuns made the first efforts in the process toward her canonization. Mother Eveline sent Sister Mercedes Dargis to Cincinnati to aid them. Sister Mercedes had served as foster mother to Marie when the Gautier children first arrived at St. John's Home in 1906, and again when she entered in 1913.

In 1932 the Dominican nuns in Cincinnati arranged for the publication of *A Grain of Mustard Seed, Memoirs and Utterances of Sister Mary Reparata, OP*. The little paper-bound book, approved by Archbishop McNicholas, was published by Benziger Brothers. Mother Eveline ordered sufficient copies for each sister and for those in years to come. The book described "The Little Way," a spirituality of renunciation and sacrifice, of victimhood, and of devotion to "Tiny Brother." There were traces of "The Little Way" of Therese of Lisieux, canonized in 1925, of late medieval mysticism, and of French piety.

It was a spirituality which did not appeal to all in the congregation. Nevertheless the humble "teachings" found their way into the piety of many of the sisters and, through certain sisters charged with formation, into the congregation's spiritual life. The brief ten years she was a member of the congregation left a deep impression.[10] There was general agreement that Sister Reparata was the recipient of special mystical gifts: visions, revelations, joys, and sufferings of the passion of Christ. It was thought she had intercessory power and she was often invoked to secure one good thing or another. She was, in the opinion of both the Grand Rapids and the Cincinnati congregations, a saint.

These aspects, reflective both of the spirituality of the universal Church and of the particular cultural milieu in which the congregation developed, can be discerned in official and personal correspondence, in the mother general's directives, in Chapter deliberations, in decisions made and decisions deferred, and in the personal lives of the sisters.

On December 8, 1941, Sister Joachim entered in the congregational annals:

> *War was declared by the United States against the Japanese Empire. May our Immaculate Mother, patroness of our country, deign to hear the prayers that have gone up to her during this novena for her Feast. May she beseech the God of all nations to bring good from this terrible evil!*

In a circular letter to the sisters on December 18, 1941, Mother asked that the Litany of the Saints be recited daily in common for peace among nations. In her Christmas letter of that year, Mother noted:

*The Christmas star rises this year upon a saddened nation--upon a hate-filled, war-torn world. As we welcome the Christ Child our hearts are filled with sentiments unknown to us before. Our country, our homes are threatened. The world knows no peace. As on that day when angels sang above Judean hills, **Gloria in excelsis Deo, et in terra pax hominibus bonae voluntates,** so today Christ comes again unto His own and His own receive Him not....*

*If our lives have grown self-centered let us remember now that the world has need of our prayers, of our self-sacrifice. We can do our share to help suffering humanity by leading truly religious lives.*

Throughout the congregation, both at Marywood and in the mission houses, annalists noted the declaration of war and the overwhelming anxiety that beset the nation. Listening to the radio and reading newspapers, once proscribed because of "worldliness," became more common though subject to the careful supervision of the superior. On December 24, 1941, many convents included in their horary President Roosevelt's radio message at 5 p.m.

The sisters in the schools were close to the nation's experience of war. To their concern for safety of family and parishioners was added the anxiety of the sisters who had come from Europe. For some, there was no word from home for close to six years, while others' letters were heavily marked by censors. Aquinas College lay faculty and students enlisted or were "called up" and countless war measures affected the lives of all. The school supervisors office at Marywood sent to every convent a three-page directive on "America's Schools at War," a program sponsored by the War Savings Staff of the Treasury Department and the Office of Education. The sisters were encouraged to organize projects which would instill in their pupils the three great "orders of the day" issued by the president to the civilian population, "Save! Serve! Conserve!" Every effort was to be recorded in a sixteen-page scrapbook provided by the Treasury Department. An "outstanding School at War" would be rewarded with a certificate, and the state a "Liberty Brick"—one of the original bricks from Independence Hall mounted in a lighted case before a bas-relief of Independence Hall.

Complementing this secular war effort, a Christian perspective on sisters during wartime was presented in the January 1942 *Contacts*:

> *For about a month now we have been trying to accustom ourselves to the meaning of our national status. What its significance will be to us ourselves personally, to our pupils, and to our people we have not begun to penetrate. Doubtless many new activities and responsibilities will be placed upon the school. As religious teachers we know that these responsibilities are sacred and grave. Let us begin now by inculcating in our pupils an intense love and practice of prayer, especially of the Rosary; by teaching a true Christian attitude toward the mystery of suffering; by resisting and helping others to resist without compromise any feeling or expression of hatred for our enemies; by exhorting and encouraging our pupils to offer themselves daily if possible as co-priests and co-victims with Christ in the holy Sacrifice of the Mass. It is in this sacred Action alone that we and all we are and have are made pleasing to God and in which God makes it possible for us to live the life of Christ by giving us in Holy Communion our Lord Jesus Christ to live by. Thus fortified and nourished by His divine life and energy we are enabled to go forth courageously, wearing as our armor and singing as our war song,*
>
> > *'Christ before me, Christ behind,*
> > *Christ alone my heart to bind.*
> > *Christ beneath me, Christ above,*
> > *Christ around me with arms of love.*
> > *Christ in all who look at me.*
> > *Christ in every face I see....'*

In the fall of 1942 Father Edward Walzer, CPPS, a native of Germany, served as temporary chaplain at Holy Angels, Traverse City. He had escaped Nazi Germany in April 1939, and was aided in his passage to the United States by Cardinal Mundelein, then in Rome for the conclave which elected Pope Pius XII. Father Walzer was an occasional visitor to Marywood and he apprised the sisters of the ferment in Europe.

The sisters, along with their neighbors, applied for ration books for sugar. In New Salem they were appointed district registrars of applicants for gasoline ration books. As the months passed, travel to the missions in New Mexico and Canada was affected by the war. Mother Euphrasia, enroute to New Mexico in April 1943, remarked:

*I never saw so many soldiers. At every large railroad center there were coaches and coaches of soldiers. Attached to our train there was a large contingent of air service men. They were dropped off some time during the night. You might be interested to know how we fared for food...in the evening the civilians could not be served until the military service was ended which was about nine o'clock....*

Later in the month she wrote,

*We had the rare privilege yesterday of visiting the large air port base here at Albuquerque. No one is permitted to enter the base without a special pass. We were taken all around by Colonel Lewis, whose wife was a patient here at Nazareth for a time. He is not a Catholic but a very fine gentleman--a West Point cadet. He conducted us all through the grounds. No one is permitted to enter the buildings. We did go into the chapel. It is a new building and very neat. Both Catholic and Protestant services are held there. Father Regan is the chaplain. The grounds are spotless and the interior of the buildings must be also. Colonel Lewis called our attention to the two types of planes--the two motor and the large four motor. There are 4,500 men at this base continually. It was interesting to note that the only soldiers we saw were those on guard. We were very happy for this opportunity.*

Congregational business was influenced by the war. The Vatican State was a non-belligerent country surrounded by warring nations. Following the General Chapter in 1942, Mother Euphrasia inquired of the apostolic delegate the manner of corresponding with the Holy See in wartime. There were, among other matters, permissions required to revise the Constitution. The delegate responded that constitutional business should be prepared in triplicate for air mail and sent to the delegate for relay to the Holy See. On September 1, 1943, at the apostolic delegate's instruction, Monsignor Noa, administrator of the diocese of Grand Rapids, directed all clergy and religious to abide by the regulations of United States Postal Censorship Office, the United States currency laws, and the Trading with the Enemy Act. No letters nor monies were to be sent, directly or indirectly, to persons in countries at war with the United States or controlled by Axis powers.

The war also had implications for the sisters' education. Since the sisters had first enrolled at the University of Notre Dame in 1918, the number of the congregation attending there had steadily increased. By 1940 nearly fifty attended each summer session. On February 18, 1942, Father John J. Cavanaugh, CSC, announced that Notre Dame had been selected by the Navy Department as an officer training program for over a thousand men. The doors of the university would, therefore, be closed to sisters "for the duration."

Finally, on August 14, 1945, Sister Joachim noted in the congregational annals:

> *THE WAR IS OVER--Japan surrendered unconditionally at 6:00 p.m. On this eve of the feast of our Blessed Lady, history's most destructive war comes to an end. As the world-stirring news came over the radio our retreat was suspended until time for the evening conference.*

During the war years Bishop Plagens, followed by Bishop Haas, had permitted the sisters to have daily Benediction of the Blessed Sacrament in the Marywood chapel. At the beginning of 1946, Bishop Haas extended the privilege to day-long exposition of the Blessed Sacrament which formally began on Sunday, January 20, 1946.

In the postwar years, the Bishops' Relief Fund became a well-known cause for food drives, fund-raisers, and student projects. In November 1947 the sisters organized their classrooms to participate in the nation-wide "Don't Let Them Starve" campaign. Catholic students sent thousands of CARE packages to Europe for starving and displaced persons.

The new Constitution prescribed that Chapter convene on the first Saturday following the first day of July. Notwithstanding that it fell on the Fourth of July, the Chapter began at 9:30 a.m., July 4, 1942, at St. John's Home in the children's library. There were sixty-seven members, only two of whom had not made their novitiate at St. John's Home.

In her report to the Chapter, Mother noted her compliance with the two large tasks given her by the Chapter of 1936: the debt had been reduced from $296,000 to $160,000 and the sisters now had their own Constitution. The congregation had grown from 536 professed sisters in 1936 to 577 professed sisters in 1942. Twenty-two sisters had died; many were growing elderly and ill.[11] The infirmary numbered ten sisters, with an additional 31 limited in their duties. The congregation was largely at work with 535 sisters assigned to mission duties. Departures from the congregation were unusual. In the period of her first administration only two perpetually professed sisters left the congregation, another had transferred to the cloister.

Bishop Plagens presided over the election. Of the 67 votes cast, Mother Euphrasia received 47 on the first ballot. She formally accepted election to her second term as prioress general on July 5, 1942, at 12:00 Eastern War Time. Sisters Genevieve Gauthier,[12] Jerome Smithers, Victor Flannery, and Aline Needham were elected to serve as her council. It was another "clean sweep" achieved only after several ballots. Sisters Joachim and Felix were re-elected to the positions of secretary general and treasurer which they had held in the previous administration. Sister Frances Ann Tatreau succeeded Sister Fabian MacDonald as mistress of novices, while Sister Leonora Gallagher continued as mistress of postulants.

The considerations of the Chapter were far-ranging. The agenda appears to have come largely from the congregation and was, in many respects, a response to dealing with the requirements of the new Constitution which had been promulgated within the congregation for less than a year. Many points were already seen as no longer current or outside of the customary practice of the Grand Rapids congregation. From some quarters there was a request to return to community-wide participation in the election of the mother general, although that had in fact been limited to those professed twelve years or more. There were objections, too, to the new delegate system which was used only for the second time.[13] The deliberations of the Chapter of 1942 also pointed to change within the ministry of the congregation.

Questions were raised about the manner of payment of lay teachers. Their numbers were relatively few: 6 at the college, 9 in the high schools, 25 in grade schools, a total of 40 among the 463 staffing the schools for which the Grand Rapids Dominicans were responsible. It was, however, a number which had grown from 15 in 1936 and would continue to grow as the number of elderly and infirm sisters increased and at the same time the number of new candidates decreased.[14] The Chapter recommended that parishes, not the sisters, pay the salaries of the lay teachers. It was left to the mother general to negotiate the issue with the bishops.

On November 16, 1942, the chancery office released new financial policies which would affect the sisters' income. While the annual salary was raised from $350 to $400 per sister or $40 a month for ten months service, there were regulations which limited the sisters' total income. In particular, music tuition, which accounted for one-fourth of the congregational income from 1936 to 1942, was restricted. A music teacher was to be paid the regular salary and only one-fourth of the net proceeds for music lessons was to go to the congregation. A principal was to be paid the regular salary of a teaching sister. The regulations also covered absences. If "failure to maintain school" was caused by the parish, the regular salary for ten months was paid by the parish. If failure was due to the religious community, then two dollars per teacher per school day was to be deducted from the monthly salary of the sister. The sisters were to provide their own housekeeping service at no expense to the parishes.

The resolution to the payment of lay teachers was equally unsatisfactory. The norms stated that a just wage should be paid, depending on training and experience. If the services of a lay teacher were due to the lack of housing in the convent, then the salary was the responsibility of the parish. If the services of the lay teacher were due to the lack of teachers in the congregation, then the difference between the salary of a sister and a lay teacher was to be paid by the congregation.

The prospects were grave. The congregation had just committed itself to expansion at the college which would amount to near $100,000. Nevertheless, Mother Euphrasia reacted in her customary way, "Let us put our trust in the Lord; He will care for us in the future as He has in the past." Lay compensation was, nevertheless, a matter which Mother frequently laid before the bishops.

In spite of financial straits, Mother Euphrasia responded with great generosity to Bishop Haas' announcement on October 20, 1944, of a fund drive on behalf of Catholic Central high school. On December 7, a city-wide rally for the Bishop's High School Development Fund was held at the Civic Auditorium.[15] On December 14, 1944, Mother sent the bishop a check for $1,200 asking that it not be published in the paper. On January 1, 1947, the monthly stipend in the Detroit and Grand Rapids dioceses was raised to $50. On March 15, 1946, Sister Felix mailed a check for $46,012.50 to the Connecticut Mutual Life Insurance Company, the final payment of the mortgage on Marywood. On March 27, 1946, Mother wrote:

*My dear Sisters,*

*There are some affairs of intimate community interest of which I would like to have you know before they are published in the newspapers, but I am no match for the Grand Rapids Herald and Press reporters. However, I shall try.*

*We have received North Central accreditation. I need add nothing to this statement, for you know as well as I that this recognition means everything for the growth of Aquinas and the education of our Sisters. It remains for us now to be deeply grateful and strive to be daily a little less unworthy of God's bountiful gifts to us. Let us continue in thanksgiving until the end of the school year, the Memorare to our Blessed Mother that we have been saying daily after Compline for this intention.*

*Something else of which you will be no less happy to learn is that the mortgage indebtedness on our motherhouse is now entirely liquidated. We have no debt on Marywood.*

*...Mother Benedicta must be rejoicing today that the work she began concerning both the building and the college has been brought to such a happy conclusion. In her name and in the name of Mother Eveline and myself, I feel that I should thank you today for having made this possible. To you and your predecessors the credit is due. It is your hard-earned pennies that have paid for Marywood. May God bless you. In thanksgiving for these two blessings--North Central accreditation for Aquinas College and liquidation of the debt on Marywood--I am asking you to sing or recite the* **Te Deum** *in choir after Compline on the evening that you receive this letter. You may also have a day of recreation, including recreation in the refectory for dinner and supper, on any day that is convenient for you.*

# 15

# TO PRAISE, TO BLESS, TO TEACH

*I*n 1936 the Michigan State Department of Education reorganized its certification procedure. Catholic Junior College was listed as an approved two-year teacher-training institution with the privilege of offering sisters and lay students a two-year curriculum leading to a Michigan State Limited Certificate. The expense of sending an increasingly large number of sisters to universities and colleges during the summer for further education was becoming too great a burden.

On October 7, 1936, Sister Estelle Hackett, congregational supervisor of schools, arranged a conference with John R. Emens, Deputy Superintendent of the Department of Education, to enable sisters to complete third-year college work at Catholic Junior College. This development could only be authorized by the North Central Association of Colleges. An allowance was made to accept an additional fifteen semester hours of academic work toward the renewal of certificates, provided that three colleges or universities to which sisters transferred would accept the fifteen credits. Mr. Emens recommended that these be done by extension or correspondence courses with accredited institutions. The University of Detroit, the University of Notre Dame, and Marygrove College subsequently ratified this arrangement. Mr. Emens and Monsignor Noa, rector of St. Joseph Seminary and president of the Diocesan School Board, subsequently met at Junior College with Father Arthur Bukowski, and arrangements were made for the renewal of certificates for 1937.

In 1937, at Mother Euphrasia's wish and as a measure to gain the North Central Association approval, Father Bukowski[1] was named president of the college, a post which he held until 1968. From the beginning of the collegiate program, the mother general of the congregation had served as president. Mother Eveline, followed by

Mother Euphrasia and the council, the treasurer and secretary general, constituted the Board of Trustees. Father Bukowski, as chief official of the college, in many respects created the agenda for the Board meetings. The sisters appointed as the academic dean and the congregational supervisor of schools collaborated with Father Bukowski and state accreditation officials on academic matters. Mother and her council, acting as the Board of Trustees, along with Father Bukowski, determined tuition rates, lay hiring and salary scale, as well as purchases and facility improvements. From 1931 through 1972 items of college business were frequently on the congregational agenda.

In the spring of 1937 Sister Estelle again took up the work of negotiating a third-year for the college, the correspondence-extension course resolution proving impractical. Dr. George E. Carrothers, president of the Michigan Association of North Central Colleges, was consulted and agreed to lobby on the sisters' behalf. In July 1938 Dr. Carrothers and others visited the college, reviewed records and observed classes. The report was both encouraging and directive: expand faculty, offerings, and library.

By 1939 third-year work was approved. Eight official visitors from the University of Michigan attended classes in the 1939 summer session. On July 7, 1939, the three hundred sisters residing at Marywood for the summer kept a 24-hour prayer vigil for a favorable report from the visitors. At the same time, due to a change in personnel, the 1936 arrangement with the State Department of Education ceased. Not only Dominican sisters but sisters of other congregations in the diocese were affected and so the matter was negotiated by Father Emmeran Quaderer, diocesan Superintendent of Schools. In May 1940 the college received the letter of approval from the Michigan Association of North Central Colleges, the result of the visitation the previous summer. A fourth year could be added to the curriculum; a four-year institution was created.

The trustees voted to name the expanded institution Aquinas College, beginning with the summer session of 1940. The name honors the great scholar-saint of the Dominican Order, Thomas Aquinas (1174-1224), and the congregation's founder, Mother Aquinata Fiegler. There was some consideration of the name "Richter College," but the stronger affiliation of the college with the Dominicans and the recent contest with the diocese over the control of the institution may have been influential in the final choice. The celebration of the feast of St. Thomas Aquinas, then on March 7, came to be a central event of the college calendar. In the 1940's, "Academic Day" was celebrated with Mass, usually a concelebrated Mass according to the Dominican rite, and breakfast at Marywood for the college students and honor seniors of Catholic Central, Mt. Mercy, and Marywood Academy, and for the members of the Advisory Board, formed in the spring of 1942 to advise on financial matters. Bishop Haas was frequently a guest speaker at the event.

In the summer of 1940 a doubt arose over the college's right to offer course work due to its lack of incorporation. To meet this emergency, the name of the congregation's corporation, "The Sisters of the Order of St. Dominic of the City of Grand Rapids" was changed to "Aquinas College" and sufficient assets were marshalled to meet the State's requirements. Articles of incorporation were filed at Lansing on January 16, 1941. The remaining assets were assigned to a new corporation known as "Sisters of the Order of St. Dominic of Grand Rapids." The officers of the congregation were officers of both corporations until 1972 when the Board of Trustees of Aquinas College was restructured.[2]

The pressing need to expand the college was considered at length during the 1942 Chapter. Proposals were far-ranging, among them, moving the novitiate and motherhouse administration to Holy Angels convent in Traverse City and the infirmary to Holy Rosary Academy in Bay City, and the building of a chapel wing at Marywood with the college occupying the main wing and the Academy the west wing of the Fulton Street property. All of the proposals, lumped under the title "Exodus," were unanimously defeated. Purchase of the "library flats," the Closterhouse property next to the college, was approved. The Chapter formally conferred priory status upon the college convent.

On September 5, 1942, the congregation purchased lots 10 and 11, block 23, adjoining lot 12 on the south from Leon Closterhouse for $40,000, completing payment on January 5, 1943. A two-story brick duplex and a three-story five-unit apartment building which faced Library Street was acquired for the college.

The apartment building at 129 Library Street was modified to provide a convent for the sister faculty who moved there in March 1943. Their former residence, "the red house" behind the main building at 69 Ransom, was subsequently demolished. A chapel, community room, refectory, and kitchen for the sisters' convent were arranged by removing some partitions and erecting others. Exteriorly there were extensive repairs on the roofs, gutters, and porches. Improvements, initially budgeted at $2,000, soared to an additional $32,000. Improvements above the library provided dormitory space initially for fifteen women students in the fall of 1943. The original four-story building at 69 Ransom was used exclusively for college purposes: science laboratories on the third and fourth floors, assembly hall and classrooms on the second, and offices and two classrooms and Women's League on first floor.

At the beginning of the fall term in 1935 Sister Bertrand LaLonde had become directress of studies, chair of the division of language and literature, and teacher of French and Spanish at Catholic Junior College. Mother Eveline had secured from Bishop Pinten a five-year leave of absence for Sister to study in Europe, first at the Sorbonne, then in Madrid, and finally at the University of Fribourg, where she received the PhD in 1935. Sister Bertrand's work in French diction and particularly her thesis on the life and work of Maurice Barres had drawn the attention of the French government. On May 25, 1938, M. Maxime Raingue, French Consul in Detroit, awarded her the *Prix de langue Française*, the gold medal of the French Academy. The event honored the college as well as Sister Bertrand. The ceremony, held at Marywood, was a public event which attracted the attention of the civic and academic community throughout the Midwest.

On November 1, 1937, Sister Mildred Hawkins arrived in New York after six years study in Europe.[3] The following semester she was assigned to teach Latin and Greek at the college and during the summers served as dean of the summer session, a ministry of teaching and administration which lengthened into an almost thirty-year tenure at the college. From January 1939 to June 1942, the years of transition from a junior to a four-year college, she served as dean of senior college and instructor of early Greek history. In the fall of 1943 Sister Jerome Smithers, former novice mistress and member of Mother Euphrasia's second council, began a six-year tenure as dean of the college, years of curricular and campus development. Sister Mildred returned as dean in 1949 and continued until her retirement in 1963.

The sisters who pioneered during the development of Aquinas College were exceptional academicians and managers. In spite of the cautions of economy and the perils of worldliness enjoined on them by Mother Euphrasia, they participated in regional professional societies and collaborated with Michigan colleges on numerous projects. Continuing professional education became a way of life for them. As religious women-scholars they served as role models for women and contributed to the formation of candidates within the congregation. While the greatest number of sisters in the congregation taught children and youth, the college faculty was necessarily involved in adult education and in the preparation of lay leadership in the Church. Tenure in their college roles provided the college community with a stability which other sisters did not customarily have. As a result, the "college nuns" came to have an acknowledged leadership in policy-making and in the intellectual and spiritual development of the congregation.

Among the first lay employees of Aquinas College were Messrs. John Bellardo (instructor of mathematics and science), Thomas T. Murphy (commerce), James A. Fennell (sociology, English and coaching), John A. Oesterle (philosophy), and Miss Dorothy Kardes (physical education). In September 1941 Dr. Thomas P. Neill from St. Louis University joined the faculty to develop the history and political science majors. In his first year, Dr. Neill was assigned eighteen semester hours teaching, including an extension course in Saginaw. In 1942 he also assumed the role of Dean of Men and army-navy advisor. Mr. E.E. Winters, a retired instructor in the Grand Rapids schools and part-time member of Catholic Junior College faculty, became a regular instructor in the commerce program in 1942. He died on January 15, 1948, while walking on campus from his nearby home. He was held in highest regard, not only for the quality of his work, but for his dedication to the college. His wife, a mathematics instructor at Marywood Academy, completed his course work for the semester. John Bellardo, faculty member since 1936, and Joseph Russell, resident janitor since 1937, continued at Aquinas College until their retirement.

In 1942 the annual full-time lay faculty salary ranged from $1,600 to $2,200. In addition to the regular day program, the college offered late afternoon, evening, and Saturday courses, and an extension program in Saginaw. In 1941-1942 there were 422 enrolled in course work other than the summer session. The same year a "Labor School," open to union and non-union workers, was first offered in Grand Rapids, Muskegon, and Manistee.

From the beginning of Catholic Junior College, there were priests on the faculty. Monsignor Anthony Volkert, chancellor of the diocese, continued as a lecturer in philosophy and religion, a role he had in Sacred Heart College at its opening at Marywood in 1922. As the college developed, Father Bukowski and the Board arranged for priest faculty for the summer sessions. Father Edwin C. Garvey, CSB, PhD, of Assumption College in Windsor, taught philosophy of education courses beginning in 1939 and subsequent summer sessions throughout the 1940's. In 1940, Father Joseph A. Luther, a former Jesuit from the University of Detroit and chaplain at Marywood, became regularly associated with the college as an instructor in religion and speech. He was particularly conversant with the social teachings of the Church and was a popular speaker at the college's Catholic Evidence Guild, social science forums, and the labor courses. His versatility extended to prowess as a basketball coach of the "Tommies" in 1941-1942 and as coach of the debate team. In January 1945 Father Henry Nauer (1894-1950), a native of Germany who had worked in Trinidad for nearly thirty years, joined the religion and philosophy faculty.

Concurrent with the naming of the college after St. Thomas Aquinas, a Thomistic influence became evident in the institution. It can be traced to John A. Oesterle, a native of Grand Rapids, who began a brief but influential career at Aquinas in 1940, and to the 30-year tenure of Sister Gonzaga Udell. A graduate of the University of Detroit in 1937, and of Laval University in 1940, Oesterle had also had a year's postgraduate studies with Mortimer Adler of the University of Chicago. While there he became a member of the Third Order of St. Dominic and continued as an active member of the chapter in Grand Rapids. Under Dr. Oesterle's direction there was soon a Summa club to complement the Missal clubs at the college. The Dominican fathers built on that interest and transformed the "religion" courses into a theological and philosophical track which remained largely Thomistic until 1970, the year in which the college implemented the findings of its institutional self-study (1968-1970).

In the summer of 1942 Mother Euphrasia negotiated both for a permanent Dominican chaplain at Marywood and a Dominican faculty for the college. Father Leo Arnoult, OP, of the University of Notre Dame and St. Mary's College, taught a course on "The Architect of the Universe" using Walter Farrell's *Companion to the Summa,* and Father Vincent Donovan, OP, gave two courses on Gregorian chant. Father Arnoult continued the Thomistic coursework in summer sessions until 1949, and returned often as student retreat master or Academic Day speaker. In 1942, the college had the services of another outstanding Thomist, Dr. Herbert T. Schwartz, professor at the Dominican House of Studies, Washington, who taught a course on "Science and Wisdom." Father Charles Wilson, OP, began college level religion courses for members of the novitiate in the fall of 1942. Father Philip P. Reilly, OP, was the first Dominican priest to be appointed to the full-time faculty. He taught religion and social science and served as Dean of Men for the 1943-1944 academic year. On September 19, 1946, Father B. Urban Fay, OP, who had previously taught in summer sessions, was appointed to the regular faculty to teach philosophy and religion. In the fall of 1947 Father Martin E. Garry, OP, joined Father Fay on the regular faculty. A third Dominican, William B. Tarrier, joined the faculty in the fall of 1948.

The Dominican fathers taught primarily in the theology and philosophy departments, though in the 1950's Fathers Bernard Hart, Thomas H. Kaufmann, and Adrian T. English strengthened the history and sociology faculty. In addition to their teaching duties, the fathers frequently served as college chaplains, deans of men, moderators of student programs, advisors and mentors to the entire college community. The Dominican fathers provided a major pastoral dimension in the life of the college for over forty years. With the exception of Father Wilson, the Dominican fathers resided first at the downtown campus, sometimes at Marywood, and later at Aquin Hall, a residence built by the congregation for the Dominican priest faculty. Father Bukowski first lived at 53 Ransom Street, but with the expansion of the college moved to the Robinson Road campus.

In addition to the regular faculty, there was an ambitious program of monthly guest lecturers and artists, as well as faculty-student programs in conjunction with the weekly meeting of the students' Catholic Life Conference. In the fashion of medieval learners, the students moved about the city from one auditorium to another for assemblies. The Knights of Columbus Auditorium, the Ladies Literary Club, St. Cecilia Auditorium, and later the Wealthy Theater were frequent venues.

The college, often in collaboration with Marywood Academy, presented an array of social theorists and practitioners: Peter Maurin, Baroness Catherine de Hueck, Dorothy Day, Luigi Ligutti; of theologians and philosophers: Walter Farrell, OP, and Mortimer Adler; of humanists and writers: Frank O'Malley, Robert Maynard Hutchins, Theodore Maynard, Frank Sheed and Maisie Ward; of poets and dramatists: Alfred Noyes, Urban Nagle, OP, Gilbert Hartke, OP, Seamus MacManus; of journalists and people in the news: Max Jordan, Louis Budenz, Sister Rose Matthew, Maryknoll prisoner of the Japanese. On December 1, 1944, Baron and Baroness von Trapp, their seven daughters and chaplain Father Franz Wassner visited the college. In 1941 the college began its Aquinas College Lecture Series, which continued for more than forty years as a college and civic service.

It was a varied fare: philosophical and religious investigations, professional perspectives, international events, environmental issues, musical and theater performances. There was also a range of college-based groups, among them the Catholic Evidence Guild, Pax Romana, an International Relations club, the Book-a-Month club, and *Le Cercle Français*. There were numerous Catholic Action opportunities, some of them projects of Father Bukowski. On November 2, 1938, he began a "Center for Negro Instruction" which later came to be known as the Martin de Porres Center. Every Wednesday evening the St. Vincent de Paul store on 75 Grandville Avenue was opened for the informal meeting. The first evening Father Bukowski gave a lantern-slide presentation on the Life of Christ for four visitors. The following week a visiting missionary gave a talk on the "Beauties of the Faith" for 27 blacks and two Indians. R.J. Farrell, director of the St. Vincent De Paul Store, and Jerome Roach, instructor in sociology at the college, helped Father Bukowski in the first years. College and community volunteers helped the project expand to a full program of instruction and entertainment presented every Wednesday of the academic year. By its second year, 1940, a Vacation School for Children was a part of the activities. In May 1942 a second center, Augustine House, was opened at 646 Logan Street in the southeast section of the city. The programs of instruction, recreation, and hospitality gradually expanded to six nights weekly. In September 1947 Lewis Clingman, instructor of history and political science, and his wife Dorothy moved to Augustine House as resident directors.

The president's annual report for 1943 included a section on "Wartime Activity." Carl Absmeier, '43, was the first Aquinas man to leave for the Army Air Corps after the war broke out, and Dorothy Joseffy was the first Aquinas woman to "sign up" for the WACS. The *Aquinas Herald* regularly reported student and faculty enlistments, news from training camps, and, in May, 1943, the death of freshman Vete Bartnick, who had joined the Polish Squadron of the Royal Air Force. Faculty as well as students began to be affected by the war: Thomas Murphy enlisted in the Navy and served in the Guadalcanal and Solomon campaign; John Oesterle was drafted in the fall of 1943, leaving his wife to finish teaching his classes. The college physician, Dr. John Whalen, had joined the Army soon after the declaration of war and Dr. Stanley Moleski was hired in his place.

On November 5, 1942, Mother Euphrasia attended the solemn raising of a "Service Flag" honoring the 116 Aquinas students in the armed forces. By the end of the war four gold stars had been added to the flag. Beginning in December 1945 the students began working for the erection of a shrine honoring the Aquinas war dead. On May 6, 1950, at the third annual Marian Congress, Bishop Haas dedicated the World War II Memorial Shrine in honor of Our Lady of Fatima. The campus shrine was funded by projects of the Student Guild and constructed solely by the students.[4]

The war brought curricular changes as well. As early as January 1942 an aviation course was offered. Thomas Murphy, instructor in economics and secretarial science and a licensed pilot, gave the course work and Edward Engemann, Jr., college senior and director of the Belding City Airport, arranged flight instruction. The college's war measures included a First Aid course, summer courses in bacteriology and chemistry for nurses, and a physics course for naval reserves. In 1944-1945 a Polish Seminar was offered in conjunction with the Bishops' Committee for Polish Relief. Dr. Florence Hornback, social service director of St. John's Home, who subsequently taught sociology on a part-time basis, Monsignor Noa, Dr. Francis Richardson, and others presented the 40-week seminar to train relief workers for Poland.

The January 1942 semester was shortened by omitting the patronal feast day and Easter vacation to allow students to "join up." The college participated in the area colleges' war chest drive each November. Sister Noella Byrnes, instructor in history and a keen student of current affairs, sold United States defense stamps at the college's main desk, a project later taken over by the Women's League. Recruiters for the armed forces and cadet nurses were given hospitality in the college parlor. The college was approved for the Army Reserve Program and for Navy V-1 Program. In February-March 1943 the army reserves were called into active duty. Gas rationing and travel restrictions caused the interruption of the college's extension programs "for the duration."

In 1941 a tuition rate of $3 per semester hour was charged each of the more than two hundred sisters attending the summer sessions. The lay part-time rate in 1941 was $5 per semester hour, or $50 per semester for ten or more semester hours. The next year tuition was increased to $5 per semester hour for the sisters. For the lay students a special tuition refund was initiated "owing to the draft law."

On May 26, 1942, the college graduated its first lay senior class, five men and three women: Charles Beckmann, Edward D. Engemann, Jr., Roma Jesiek, James McKnight, Margaret Milanowski, Edward Razmus, Audrey Snyder, and Joseph Yelle. A baccalaureate Mass was held at Marywood on Sunday, May 24, and commencement ceremonies took place at St. Cecilia Auditorium on Tuesday evening. Dr. Jerome Kerwin of the University of Chicago gave the commencement address. Academic hoods of maroon and silver, the college colors, were first worn for this occasion. The first class to have spent four years at the college as a four-year institution graduated in May 1944.

On September 27, 1944, representatives of Michigan colleges and universities met to consider the implications of the GI Bill of Rights. Aquinas College was subsequently approved for funding of veterans in most of its programs. In its October 1944 meeting the Board began planning for the expansion[5] necessary with the return to peace. In April 1945 an extraordinary opportunity presented itself to the congregation. The Lowe Estate, 1607 Robinson Road, built in 1908 by Edward and Susan Blodgett Lowe at an estimated cost of $1,000,000, came on the market. The heirs, faced with heavy encumbrances after the death of Edward Lowe in 1938, sought buyers. By February 17, 1939, it became public knowledge that Bishop Pinten was seeking the property, less than a half-mile from the congregational motherhouse, for a relocated St. John's Orphanage.[6] James Rowland Lowe, heir and executor, petitioned

*OPPOSITE*
*Holmene, the former m[*
*house of Edward and S[*
*Blodgett Lowe*

*The Carriage House o[*
*Lowe Estate*

ADMINISTRATION BUILDING, AQUINAS COLLEGE, GRAND RAPIDS, MICHIGAN

ALBERTUS HALL, SCIENCE BUILDING, AQUINAS COLLEGE, GRAND RAPIDS, MICHIGAN

Grand Rapids township officials for a change in zoning regulations to allow the orphanage within the township. Within a short time, however, Grand Rapids business educator M. E. Davenport secured the property for the University of Grand Rapids.[7]

Mother Euphrasia first heard of the property's availability on April 17, 1945, the day of her return from the Mothers General Conference in Newburgh, New York. On April 20, Mother Euphrasia and Sister Joachim had an appointment with Bishop Haas. The following day Bishop Haas, Monsignor Malone, and Father Anthony Arszulowicz visited the property. The bishop gave Mother permission to pursue the sale but, if possible, for less than the quoted $150,000. On April 22, Mother and the council met and approved the purchase. Sister Felix prepared a comprehensive statement of congregational assets and liabilities which she and Mother presented to the bishop on April 24. The bishop recommended that the sisters contact Edward Frey and Michael Leonard, officials of the Union Bank of Michigan and members of the Aquinas College Advisory Board, to press Davenport for a reduced price.[8] Local financing was arranged while a hurried petition was made to the Holy See through the apostolic delegate in Washington to permit the congregation to undertake further debt.

The headlines for the April 27, 1945, *Grand Rapids Herald* announced "Aquinas College Buys University of G.R. Site" and then "IL DUCE IN BAG; HITLER FACES TRAP." For $115,000 the Aquinas College corporation had acquired 67 acres of prime real estate with four substantial buildings: Holmdene, the manor house; the carriage house; stables; and a small brick winery. There were professionally planted gardens within a landscaped park, a creek, and a small artificial pond. It was intended that the downtown campus be used for evening school, for science laboratories and music, and for the sisters' residence and women's dormitory; the new buildings would be used for humanities, physical education, and administration.

With the acquisition of the Lowe property, the value of the college plant grew to $386,336.56. Both the Aquinas College corporation and the Sisters of the Order of St. Dominic corporation were responsible for the mortgage. At the very outset, there was some consideration of a major construction of an administration-classroom building on the new site, a project of at least $400,000.

That phase of development was not begun until 1954, during the first term of Mother Victor Flannery.

The first major project was the renovation of the stable for the physical education and recreation programs. Harry Mead of Grand Rapids was engaged as architect. The work, begun in July 1946, was completed the following year at a cost of approximately $43,000. "Holmdene," the chief building on the estate, continued as the administration and classroom building. There, too, modifications were made. On the basement level, a tunnel was built for approximately $10,000 to provide internal access to a large ground floor room to be used as a Men's Union. In the summer of 1946 the third-floor ballroom was prepared as the chapel. The Blessed Sacrament was reserved there and Mass was offered daily. During the summer of 1946 three of the sister faculty took up permanent residence on the third floor of the manor house-administration building.

The terms of sale allowed for possession on May 1, 1945. The sisters agreed to let the university complete its current term, which ended on June 18. On June 25, five sisters took up residence at the main building. Others joined them during the summer. On July 9, Father Bukowski blessed the rooms in use, and on July 12, offered Mass there for the first time. Mothers Euphrasia and Eveline joined the sisters and the janitor, Mr. McDonald and his little daughter Rose, for the event. Throughout the summer the sisters from Marywood spent every moment that could be spared from the official horary, summer school studies, and harvesting the gardens, in "bees" at the new campus to prepare for the opening of classes on September 20.

At the beginning of the second semester, January 1946, a North Central Association visitation was under way. On March 27, 1946, the college was fully accredited as a four-year liberal arts institution. The Robinson Road purchase provided for the projected growth: by the fall of 1947 the enrollment reached 564, of whom 266 were freshmen, and 183 veterans on the GI Bill. There was a contingent of foreign students, from Guam, Saipan, China, Nigeria, the Philippines, and Canada.

As the college was expanding, the congregation continued to meet needs in the Michigan dioceses. In 1940 Bishop Pinten appointed

Father Linus Schrembs to St. Mary parish, New Salem, and shortly thereafter directed Mother Euphrasia by phone to send sisters to reopen the school. After a midsummer 1940 visit, Mother Euphrasia insisted on restoration of the almost derelict wood frame building before the sisters returned. A year passed and a new pastor, Father Francis Schultz, was appointed before the readying of the school. In September 1941 Sisters Olivia Robach, Juliana Barilla, and Felicitas Gerhart reopened the school, helped by the stalwart community supervisors, Sisters Estelle Hackett and Paula Murphy, who brought books and school materials. The pastor arrived with groceries and later the parish women came with a shower of household goods. It was the way of all beginnings. From 1946 to 1949 the school was classified as a public school without modification of curriculum or role of the sisters. In 1967 the school was consolidated with Visitation school, North Dorr, and Saint Sebastian school, Byron Center, as Holy Family school. The congregation continued to serve that school until 1970. In 1971 the area came under the jurisdiction of the Diocese of Kalamazoo.

In 1940 a new parish school, Sacred Heart, was begun in Muskegon Heights. It was the last school dedicated by Bishop Pinten. Sisters Veta Marie Gase, Ildephonse Ryan, Felicitas Gerhart, Rose Miriam Visner, Rose Vincent Blake, Bede Frahm, and Constance Nizol were the first assigned there. The new school was opened on September 10, 1940, for 284 pupils in grades one through seven. For two years the sisters lived in the school building, their living space decreasing as grades eight and nine were added and enrollment increased to over 400. In 1943 ten sisters moved to a residence near the school.

In June 1948 Father Joseph Henige, pastor of St. Joseph parish, Pewamo, Michigan, asked Mother Euphrasia for sisters. The six-grade school had once been staffed by the Sisters of St. Joseph, Kalamazoo, and until that year by the Sisters of Christian Charity of Wilmette, Illinois. The first Dominicans assigned there were Sisters Ignatia Parisey, Cyrilla Hallahan, Denise Suprenant, and Fidelia Zepnick. The congregation continues to serve in the school to the present.

During the summer of 1946 Mother Euphrasia promised Father Eugene Paddock assistance for St. Alfred parish at Taylor Center (Inkster). The parish, founded as a mission of St. Mary Magdalen parish, Melvindale, in 1943, had grown out of the wartime employment boom. The parish plant on busy Telegraph Road was then a complex of three barracks recently used for prisoners of war at the Willow Run military air base. A house a block distant was purchased for a temporary convent for Sisters Vincent Ferrer Rasch, Emmerica Ziegler, Francis Clare Alvesteffer, and Michaela Schrems. The four sisters and a lay teacher opened the five-grade school for 175 students. In 1948 ground was broken for a new eight-grade elementary school, and sisters continued to be added to the faculty. Congregational service continues in the parish to the present.

Our Lady of Grace parish, Dearborn Heights, was founded in 1924 and was under the care of the Marianhill Mission congregation. With the post-war expansion surrounding Detroit, the parish opened an elementary school for which Mother Euphrasia promised sisters. In late August, 1948, Sisters Columbkille (Catherine) Swift, Ann Catherine Harrand, Martin Porres (Ann) Kostrzewa, and Euphrosine (Mary) Sullivan arrived to organize the six-grade school. Grades seven and eight were added the following years.

In 1947 Mother Euphrasia promised Father C.A. Murphy congregational staffing in another subdivision of the Melvindale parish. St. Francis Cabrini school in Allen Park was to be opened in September 1949.

In addition to the regular service offered in parochial settings, the congregation took on new forms of catechetical instruction in several locales. On September 8, 1944, after the annual appointments were made and sisters settled in their missions, an urgent plea came to Mother Euphrasia for more sisters. Father R. E. Fitzpatrick, Superintendent of Schools for the Diocese of Saginaw and pastor of St. John the Baptist parish, Carrollton, and of St. Matthew, Zilwaukee, asked for staff for a school of religious instruction for parish children attending public schools. While there were no sisters available, the prospect moved Mother. She asked Sisters Estelle Hackett and Paula Murphy if they would be willing to do double duty as school supervisors and program directors-teachers. A house next to the rectory in Carrollton was remodelled to provide a classroom, library, kitchen, and bathroom. It was blessed on September 24 as *Schola Maria*. The sisters commuted from Mount Carmel convent in downtown Saginaw. There were 304 children enrolled on the first day. Children attending the Carrollton, Merschon, and Liberty public schools came daily, either immediately after Mass or during the noon hour. Twice a week children from Zilwaukee came by bus.

In September 1946 a second Mary School was opened in Zilwaukee in the newly-erected St. Matthew church. On September 14, 1949, children from Kochville first came by chartered bus. In May 1952 there were close to 200 coming twice weekly for instruction. In 1953 the parish, under the direction of Father Thomas Horton, opened a grade school and, in 1954, the catechetical program was transferred to the Mission Sisters of the Holy Spirit.

On June 26, 1947, Mother Euphrasia received Bishop Haas, Fathers Anthony Arszulowicz and Edmund Falicki, and their guest, Father Daly, CSsR, of Regina, Saskatchewan. They sought to convince her of the worth of catechetical correspondence schools such as Father Daly and the Sisters of Service were conducting in Saskatchewan. It was an outreach which Mother Eveline had admired in 1931 during a visit with the Sisters of Service in Edmonton. On March 2, 1948, the Religion Correspondence Course was formally launched. Bishop Haas appointed Father Raymond Sweeney as diocesan director. After a preliminary survey, 35 children in the missions in Grayling, Indian River, and Roscommon, Michigan, were enrolled. It was uncharted territory for the congregation and the work of planning was given to Sisters Estelle Hackett and Olga Mizzi in August 1947. Sister Joachim, secretary general and talented artist, took over Sister Estelle's role in March 1948.

Mother Benedicta's vocation goal, "50 in the 50th year," had been reached only in 1929. Vocation efforts throughout Mother Eveline's administration had been extraordinary and far-reaching: the European and Canadian ventures, and the establishment of the aspirancy. Throughout the war years young women seeking admission were few. A vocation booklet, *Come and See*, was published in October 1946 and sent to senior girls in all the high schools taught by the sisters. In September 1942 there were six postulants; in the September 1947 there were 21. Mother Euphrasia reported each fall to the sisters the numbers of postulants, "only five," "just six," and urged the sisters to prayer and greater encouragement of young women. Though the numbers were small, there was a stability among the applicants during Mother Euphrasia's administration. Between the Chapters of 1942 and 1948, of the 95 young women entering the congregation 85 received the habit. As of July 1948, there were 606 professed sisters,[9] 49 of these with temporary vows, and 21 novices. Since the 1942 Chapter, 68 novices had been professed; 24 sisters had died, fifteen had left the congregation.

Upon the completion of her second term, Mother Euphrasia had but one expressed wish, "not to be a superior." Nevertheless, she was appointed to the office several times in her remaining twenty-two years: at Catholic Central, Grand Rapids, Marywood priory, and St. John's, Essexville, Michigan. She was elected by the thirteenth General Chapter to serve as vicaress-first councillor to Mother Victor from 1954 to 1960. The assignment to Essexville in September 1962 was a particularly sensitive task as the congregation and local community were recovering from the accidental death of five sisters missioned there. Mother Euphrasia died on May 17, 1970, in her eighty-second year, after having received the farewells and expressions of gratitude from hundreds of her sisters.

On August 4, 1947, at the last jubilee ceremony over which Mother Euphrasia presided as mother general and the twenty-fifth celebrated at Marywood, a verse choir presented a *Benedicite for Jubilarians*.

> *All ye smiles and all ye tears*
> *Molded into silver years,*
> *Praise God!*
>
> *Praise God, each little C-a-9*
> *With A and B and C in line.*
> *Degrees for which we've had to work,*
> *Papers that we did not shirk*
> *Give praise to God.*
>
> *Lemon pie for Sunday treat*
> *Monday's washing clean and sweet*
> *Praise ye the Lord.*
>
> *Praise God! mosquitoes in the dorm;*
> *Bright summer sun that keeps us warm*
> *Give praise to God.*
>
> *Inspectors well upon their way*
> *And each successful P.T.A.*
> *Pastor's feast day well devised,*
> *Classroom quotas realized*
> *Praise God!*
>
> *Praise God, each credit that we lacked,*
> *And every trunk we've quickly packed.*
> *Praise God, ye little tickets dear*
> *That seal our fates for one more year.*

*Hours of joy and hours of pain*
*That we can never live again;*
*Hours of peace that we have spent*
*Before the Blessed Sacrament,*
*Praise God! Praise God!*

*All ye smiles and all ye tears*
*Molded into silver years*
*Give praise to God![10]*

These were the works which Mother Euphrasia understood best: praying, keeping school, receiving "tickets" without question, graciously blending joy and pain. She had faithfully looked well to the ways of her house in the midst of tumultuous times.

# 16

# UNLESS THE LORD BUILD THE HOUSE
# MOTHER VICTOR FLANNERY

*M*other Euphrasia's last work as prioress general was to prepare for General Chapter. During April 1948, elections took place to secure the delegates for the twelfth General Chapter. Seventy-four delegates, 6 ex officio and 34 sister superiors and 34 non-superiors, gathered at St. John's Home on Saturday, July 3, 1948. It was the last Chapter to be held there. The following day, July 4, 1948, in the presence of Bishop Haas and Monsignor Robert W. Bogg, chancellor, they elected Sister Victor Flannery, a member of the outgoing council, as sixth prioress general of the congregation.

Mother Victor was elected on the first balloting with 38 of the 75 ballots cast. Her council was Sisters Aline Needham, Marie Celeste Stang, Jerome Smithers, and Thomas Margaret Curran. Sister Joachim Visner was reappointed secretary general and Sister Felix Brand treasurer of the congregation. Mother and her council selected Sister Gerald Grace as mistress of novices.

Jennie Ursula Flannery, born on April 5, 1895, in Saginaw, Michigan, was the fourth of twelve children of James and Jane McLaughlin Flannery. James Flannery was a native of Ireland, Jane McLaughlin came from Canada. The family was conspicuous for its contribution to the Church: three daughters to the Dominican sisters, Sisters Victor, Mary Jane, and Jane Frances, and two sons to the priesthood serving the Diocese of Grand Rapids, Fathers James and William Flannery. Jennie was confirmed in the Catholic Faith by Bishop Richter in 1907.

Her schooling was with the Dominican sisters at St. Joseph parish school. During the summers of her high school years she worked as cashier and filer in a department store. On September 29, 1911, after her graduation from high school, she entered the congregation

*Mother Victor Flannery, sixth Mother General, (fl. 1948-1966)*

*Five Flannery vocations to apostolic life: Sisters Mary Jane, Jane Francis, Mother Victor, Fathers William and James Flannery*

at St. John's Home. She was the 274th sister to receive the habit from Mother Aquinata and eventually the last mother general who had known Mother Aquinata. On April 9, 1912, she became Sister Mary Victor of St. Joseph. The following Monday, she related in later years, she was teaching in Holy Trinity school, Alpine. The seventeen-year old diminutive Dominican asked a high school lad of the same age and much greater stature what it was he found so interesting in a newspaper, only to hear from him of the clothing ceremony of Jennie Flannery the previous week.

The proximity of the Alpine mission to Grand Rapids allowed her to complete the course work she had begun in the Novitiate Normal.[1] She was among the first sisters of the congregation to attend summer sessions at state universities. In 1919 she attended Central State Teachers College in Mount Pleasant, and subsequent summers she studied at Western State Teachers College in Kalamazoo. She received the Bachelor of Arts degree from Central State Teachers College in August 1926. She took advanced degree work at Marquette, Western State, and De Paul universities in English literature. She was certified to teach English, history, science, and Latin. The sisters' customary program--teaching from September to mid-June, then a six-to eight-weeks summer school and a week-long retreat during the long vacation--was the pattern she followed for close to forty years.

Sister Victor taught for thirty-seven years in grade and high schools staffed by the congregation. After Alpine, she spent a year at Sacred Heart Academy. Then, from 1917 to 1921, she taught the entire junior high program in St. Mary parish, St. Charles, Michigan. In 1922 she went north to Suttons Bay, where she taught grades nine and ten. The next three years she spent at Our Lady of Perpetual Help, Chesaning, on the high school staff. In 1925 she opened St. Stephen mission in Grand Rapids as superior and junior high school teacher. In 1931 she returned to Our Lady of Perpetual Help, Chesaning, as superior, principal, and high school teacher. She taught at Saints Peter and Paul high school in Saginaw from 1937 to 1941. From 1942 to 1948 she was superior of the convent and principal of St. Joseph grade and high school in Muskegon, Michigan, and served at the same time on the general council of Mother Euphrasia.

Mother Victor's mission history gave her a thorough knowledge of the missions and of the sisters in the congregation as well as a strong sense of the need for flexibility and availability for mission needs. Each summer, from mid-July to August 15, the mother general and her council spent long days making up the "mission list" for the academic year. For the individual sister the annual assignment was the single most important exercise of her vow of obedience. Assignment was to a particular parish or congregational school, to a grade level, sometimes even to specific course work, and to the company of other sisters so assigned. For the congregational officials it was a deployment of staff to meet a vast network of commitments made with bishops and pastors. The overwhelming number of sisters was assigned to schools; a much smaller number to housekeeping and food service in the convents associated with these schools; an even smaller number, to nursing and administrative tasks.

Mother Victor had a comprehensive knowledge of mission needs: the number of sisters required, the academic and physical strength of each of the sisters, the layout of convent, school, and church, and an understanding as well of the personality of the sisters she sent to the task. There is a tradition that she approached problem solving in a unique way, particularly in personnel assignments. Stories are told of sisters being selected for service on a mission by reason of a chance meeting with Mother in the halls or by a "sighting" in chapel. Nevertheless, she approached major tasks with thorough planning and consideration of alternatives. Once apprised of available information, she was decisive and firm. Though she adjusted decisions where necessary, she remained at ease with decisions made. The "care of souls," a charge dictated by canon law and the traditional role assigned the mother superior, was of real concern in her relations with the sisters.

The official means of communication between the mother general and the membership continued to be the "circular letters," the correspondence sent from the motherhouse to all the houses of the order. Mother Victor, like Mother Eveline, used the opportunity to report on congregational programs, among them building projects authorized by General Chapters; to call attention to points of observance; to explain financial procedures; to give an account of the most recently deceased sister's last days. In this way the sisters learned the general business of the congregation and received instruction and direction intended for all.

Formal visitation of each house of the congregation was also a part of the mother general's annual tasks. Observing the constitutional regulation for a traveling companion, she was sometimes accompanied by the treasurer, the supervisor of schools, sometimes by a sister in transit to another mission, or, in the case of the Michigan missions, by a sister driver. At the formal visitation of each convent, Mother personally and directly conferred with each sister.

The mothers general also wrote personal letters to the sisters-- letters of condolence, encouragement, permissions sought and answers given, feast day greetings shared. Mother Victor had a wide range of communication skills. She appeared at great ease in addressing both large and small groups and in her contacts with professional and business persons. She was a rapid and accurate typist and she used the telephone for much business with a remarkable recall of numbers and addresses. Senior sisters spoke of Mother Aquinata's attentiveness to detail; Mother Victor was equally gifted. She held in mind numerous details, large and small, from knowledge of a sister's family and academic record, to the addresses and phone numbers of over eighty missions. Hers was a direct and comprehensive management of the business and ministry of the congregation.

In her report to the 1948 Chapter on the state of the congregation, Mother Euphrasia summarized the work of the previous six years and suggested an agenda for the future:

> Our present great material need is for more space at Marywood and I feel that we are financially able to undertake a building project now. I did not want to do this during the last year of my term since it will be better for a new administration to start it and carry it to completion. We also need an administration building at Aquinas.

Mother Euphrasia also noted that a congregational customary, requested by the 1942 Chapter as a complement to the Constitution of 1941, was near completion. The 1948 Chapter approved a draft for congregational use until the next General Chapter. A manual of etiquette originating with the Sisters of Charity of Mount Saint Vincent on the Hudson also came into use, primarily in the novitiate. "Cared for in the Customary" became a formula for addressing petitions directed to Chapters as well as for referring to directives on observance.

These endeavors suggest a pattern of practice and codification which applied both within the congregation and in the larger Church. In many respects, the writing and promulgation of regulations lagged behind practice. The outcome was the use of norms which reflected a concern for traditional ways at a time when there were indications of newer approaches and worldwide influences that could not be overlooked. Mother Victor was singularly adroit at reconciling these influences.

The 1948 Chapter resolved that steps be taken toward the building of accommodations for infirmary, novitiate, and administrative offices. After the work of assignments was completed, Mother and her council laid out a program for building. In a single weekend in November 1948, they went, two by two, to colleges and motherhouses in Dubuque and Duluth, Cincinnati, Detroit, Monroe, Plymouth, and Adrian. They approached loan and mortgage companies; they sought the advice of old friends at Notre Dame and Marquette; they appraised architectural firms. Bishop Haas, attending the bishops' meeting in Washington, DC, made inquiries on behalf of the congregation. In November 1948 two committees of sisters were named, one for a motherhouse building, the other for a college administration building. In January 1949 Father J. A. Foley, OP, from Louisville, Kentucky, an authority on Dominican traditions in architecture, served as consultant to the council and building committees. Initially, a major building southeast of the present motherhouse was planned for a chapel, administrative offices, infirmary, and novitiate.[2] Plans included the eventual completion of the current motherhouse with an east auditorium wing. On January 26, 1949, the sisters met with Harry L. Mead[3] and Charles M. Norton of Grand Rapids to draw up architectural plans.

The original plans for a separate building called for an outlay of almost treble what the congregation could afford. A second and a third revision, still for an independent building, were double the financing available.[4] By April 1952 bids were taken, the lowest for $1,200,000. Financing previously arranged was withdrawn. Further revisions brought the cost projections down to $750,000 for a freestanding building no larger than the west wing of the present motherhouse.

It was decided, therefore, to complete the motherhouse with an east wing. Messrs. Mead and Norton revised the plans once again and new financing was arranged with McMahon and Hoban of Chicago for a loan of $650,000. The additional $100,000 was to come from current funds and donations. As part of the financing, Mother Victor successfully sought from the bishops a reversal of the 1942 regulation which took from the congregation the income from music lessons and stipends as organists for parish Masses. The contract was awarded to DeYoung and Bagin of Grand Rapids, general contractors, and ground was broken on June 9, 1953.[5] On December 8, 1954, the Marywood community gathered for the first time in its new community room on the first floor of the five-story wing completing the original motherhouse building.

Meanwhile, the fabric of the motherhouse and smaller buildings, both interior and exterior, required constant outlays of funds. A small farmhouse to the east of the main building, part of the original Doty property used for a lay employee's residence, was removed in 1950, while the "cottage" at the entrance to the property was converted into a dormitory for aspirants at a cost of approximately $1600. In 1950, the Holy Year, a grotto of field stone and masonry was built with monies raised by Marywood Academy. The outdoor altar and statue of the Blessed Mother became a focal point for outdoor processions and celebrations.

Financing of building projects involved the assessment of current expenses and commitments. Several pieces of congregational property were sold: Holy Angels, Traverse City, to the Diocese of Grand Rapids,[6] land in Chesaning,[7] the convent in Melville, Saskatchewan,[8] portions of the downtown college campus and of the Robinson Road campus,[9] and part of the Finn estate.[10] The Merrill Home in Saginaw was transferred to the Diocese of Saginaw, and the convent in Peñasco, New Mexico, was transferred to the Archdiocese of New Mexico. The congregation added to the Marywood property a small tract on the western boundary next to the garage, and in May 1960 purchased the small bungalow and lot at 247 Lakeside, NE, contiguous to the motherhouse property. In the early 1950's a summer festival and ox roast were added to the roster of fund-raising events. In 1953-1954 donations from the sisters and income from projects, among them used stamp collecting and rag sales, brought in over $70,000 for the building program.[11]

The completion of the motherhouse was a major achievement but one tempered by the sisters' realization that it would suit the present more than the future:

> Nearly five years had elapsed since the architects had begun work on the plans--plans that at the outset had embodied all that went to make up the dream of the Sisters for an ideal motherhouse--one that envisioned future needs for years to come, including a convent chapel that would do honor to their Eucharistic King, as well as ample sleeping space and convenience to care for anticipated growth of the community.[12]

*FACING PAGE Mother Victor Flannery at eastwing entrance, Marywood, November 1954*

While the façade and setting of congregational buildings presented a certain grandeur, they were basically institutional with an economy and frugality in appointments and personal space. Norms of poverty and the ideal of the common life as well as a cautious business sense of the mothers general and councilors dictated a basic conservatism with respect to property and lifestyle.

Within a short time the increasing number of candidates and a policy of more extensive formation created the need for additional dormitory space. In October 1958 Lourdes Hall, created from the enclosure of the northwest roof garden of the academy wing of the motherhouse, was opened as a dormitory for forty young sisters. The project, designed by Mead and Norton and built by Owen-Ames-Kimball, cost $100,000.

*Ground breaking for the Aquinas College Administration Building: Monsignors Bukowski and Anthony Arszulowicz, Sister Marie Celeste Stang, Messrs. Dwight Owen and Gerald McShane (with shovel), Mother Victor Flannery and Sister Aline Needham, November 19, 1953*

During the months of revision of the motherhouse plans, Mother and her council decided to build a residence for the Dominican fathers serving Aquinas College.[13] A two-story brick building of 100 feet frontage at 143 Lakeside Drive on the eastern edge of the motherhouse property provided six suites of rooms, as well as a reception room, parlors, dining room, recreation area and three-car garage. Mead and Norton were hired as architects and Strohm Construction as general contractors. Ground was broken in November 1952, and Aquin Hall opened at Christmas 1953. Subsequently a larger kitchen and utility area were added at a cost of $33,000.

The second major building task enjoined on the administration by the 1948 Chapter was provision of an administrative facility for the college. While a committee had been named in 1948, full scale

*Theological ground breaking: Sisters at Aquinas College's Theological Institute, summer 1952, first classes in St. Andrew cathedral basement*

*First Theological Institute Commencement, Marywood, summer 1955*

*FACING PAGE*
*Jubilees: Diamond Jubilee in Michigan, 1877-1953, a festive meal at Marywood*

*Silver Jubilee of Nazareth Sanatorium, New Mexico, 1955*

attention was not given to the project until 1951. In September 1951, the Grand Rapids Fire Department called attention to serious hazards in the downtown buildings. It was decided to sell the property rather than undertake extensive repairs, and a buyer was ready at hand. In January 1953 the 69 Ransom Avenue property was sold to the YMCA for $210,000. Terms of sale allowed for the college to maintain occupancy for a further 18 months. The need of replacement facilities--science laboratories, music studios, convent for the sisters, residence for the priests, dormitory, and classrooms--was pressing.

In January 1953, D. A. Bohlen and Son, an architectural firm from Indianapolis, was hired. Simultaneously a fund-raising firm was contracted to conduct a capital campaign. Lawson Associates of Rockville Center, New York, had conducted a successful campaign in the diocese for Catholic Central. The drive was an endeavor supported and encouraged by Bishop Haas, who wrote to all clergy on August 12, 1953:

*I am appealing to you today for help in raising funds for Aquinas College, Grand Rapids. Although Aquinas is not under the direct control of the Diocese, it is doing the work of the Diocese in a very direct way.*

*No one can deny that the Christian education of youth is a primary duty of our sacred ministry. Yet when all is said and done, the Dominican Sisters of Marywood, together with the other splendid religious communities of teaching nuns laboring in the Diocese, are carrying this burden almost alone and singlehanded.*

*Actually our teaching Sisters furnish the teaching power in our schools by training themselves out of the meager salaries which the faithful provide for them. It is our plain duty to come to their assistance.*

*It may be asked, "In what way does Aquinas College contribute to our grade and high schools?" The answer is that it contributes most directly by helping to staff them with properly accredited teachers. In a word Aquinas trains Sisters and Sisters train our primary and high school children. The relation is no less direct than that. Our duty is plain.*

*In addition Aquinas trains not only Sisters. It trains our young men and young women for four years after their four years of high school. It lays before them not only the secular sciences, but also it teaches them God's law and how to walk in it.*

*...The success of the campaign is essential to the growth of religion for generations to come....*

Bishop Haas was the first contributor; within a week of the campaign's opening he sent Mother Victor a check for $5,000. On

August 29, however, the bishop died suddenly and a halt was called to many projects in the diocese, including the campaign and the construction at the college.

On March 23, 1954, Pope Pius XII named Bishop Allen J. Babcock, auxiliary bishop of Detroit, to succeed Bishop Haas. Bishop Babcock was born in Bad Axe, Michigan, on June 17, 1898, and was educated at the University of Detroit high school, Assumption College, and the North American College in Rome. He was ordained in Rome on March 7, 1925. Early appointments included pastoral curacies, six years as student chaplain at the University of Michigan. In the late 1930's he was vice rector of the North American College in Rome. Since 1942 he was rector of the Cathedral of the Most Blessed Sacrament, Detroit, and, since 1942, auxiliary bishop of the archdiocese.

On Wednesday, May 19, 1954, Bishop Babcock was welcomed to the diocese in the customary manner by the priest consultors who met him as he crossed the boundary of the diocese near Portland, Michigan. The four-car cavalcade proceeded to Grand Rapids, where the first stop was at Aquinas College. At the entrance to Holmdene, Mother Victor and her council, Monsignor Bukowski and the faculty, along with 200 students in academic attire, greeted the bishop with *Multos Annos Vivat*, a traditional welcoming hymn for bishops. From there Monsignor Bukowski and scores of priests accompanied the new bishop to The cathedral where more than 2,000 grade and high school children cheered his arrival. He was installed as the seventh Bishop of Grand Rapids on Thursday, May 20, 1954, by Edward Cardinal Mooney.

Within a month of his installation, the bishop presided at the college and academy graduations, and at investiture and profession ceremonies at Marywood. On July 4, 1954, he presided over the election of congregational officers. Financing the expansion on the college campus also required close interaction between Bishop Babcock and Mother Victor during the ensuing years.[14] In April 1959 he sent $5,000 "as a contribution of the Bishop" for the college's expansion fund.

In 1954 the congregation renegotiated its mortgage with McMahon and Hoban of Chicago to allow for a $1,500,000 loan from the Northwestern Mutual Life Insurance Company. Construction was begun with the monies from the sale of the 69 Ransom properties. The Owen-Ames-Kimball firm successfully outbid five other general contractors. Ground was broken on November 19, 1953.[15] An academic procession brought the participants from Holmdene, the chief building on the property, to the site on a wooded hillside. Monsignor Bukowski broke the soil with a pick. A shovel, presented by D. A. Bohlen, architect, was given to Mother Victor, who removed the soil. All of the members of the general council, Sister Mildred Hawkins, dean of the college, Mothers Eveline and Euphrasia, and T. Gerald McShane, president of the college's Advisory Board, participated in the ground-breaking. Monsignor A.P. Arszulowicz, chancellor of the diocese, spoke on behalf of the diocese and Church. Ground-breaking ceremonies became familiar activities for Mother Victor and her councilors.

The original plans showed an E-shaped, four-story structure with towers capping the central, south, and north wings.[16] "Unit A," the main and center wings, was to be completed in the first phase of building (the south and north wings, intended for subsequent years, were never added). The cornerstone was laid on September 29, 1954, and the new building was blessed on October 11, 1955, by Bishop Babcock. The effects of expansion were immediate: enrollment increased 26% from September 1954 to September 1955, from 598 students to 754. In September 1955, extension branches, which had ceased due to wartime gas rationing, were resumed in Muskegon and Saginaw.

The original manor house, "Holmdene," became Aquinas College priory, although some sister faculty continued to live at Marywood. Monsignor Bukowski lived in a small wing of the house from 1940 to 1958, when the congregation purchased a home on Briarwood Street for the president for $17,500. Holmdene remained the chief residence of the college sister faculty until 1981 when the building was restored to its original features and used for administrative and faculty offices.

By 1958 enrollment at Aquinas College neared 900. Expansion was imperative. In April 1958, Mother Victor sought permission from Bishop Babcock to embark on a fund-raising campaign. During July 1958, the Community Counselling Service of New York City did a feasibility study on financing the expansion. The study indicated that while college expansion would receive some support, all the works and missions of the congregation should be targeted in every diocese where the sisters served. The college expansion was to extend over a twelve-year period. A contract was signed on August

11, 1958, for the firm to conduct a campaign to raise between $1,750,000 and $2,000,000; the fee was set at $90,000. Subsequently, the goal was scaled down to $1,200,000. Funds raised were designated for a science building, a house of studies for student sisters, a women's dormitory, and a gymnasium-activities building, to provide for faculty expansion and increase the college's student aid program. The consultation provided a long-range plan both for the college and for the congregation.

The campaign was directed by three representatives of the Community Counselling Services, Patrick McNeely, George Babich, and John Riley, and was aided by a distinguished committee from the western Michigan business community, headed by Peter M. Wege. The sisters themselves did much of the work of solicitation. The goal of $1,200,000 was exceeded by $100,000 by October 1959. In September 1959 the college hired its first director of development, Eugene Kennedy, formerly of Loyola University. A long-range college development program of $8,000,000 was set in motion.

While ownership and policy direction remained with the congregational officers in their capacity as the college's Board of Trustees, the college's fiscal supervision was regularized. The Advisory Board, formed in 1942, was expanded to a Lay Board of Trustees under the direction of C. Arthur Woodhouse and vice chairman Joseph M. Walsh.[17] The college became increasingly more responsible for its operational budget. The boards, congregational and lay advisory, devised a long-range and orderly expansion plan for the college. Well-conceived and executed fund-raising programs were undertaken for the building. The congregation continued its financial underwriting of the college through payment of principal on the mortgages related to earlier expansion and through the contributed services of sister faculty and staff. There were, however, into the late 1960's emergency transfers of funds from congregation to college to meet payroll deadlines, tuition deficits, and sundry cost overruns.

On September 18, 1959, ground was broken for the new science building. The 212 foot long building, facing Robinson Road at its south entrance, provided in its three stories laboratories, offices and storage, a lecture hall, and small greenhouse. The building, named after Saint Albert the Great, medieval Dominican scientist and saint, opened for classes in the fall 1960 semester. The former Albertus

Hall, initially the Lowe family's carriage house, was renamed Jarrett Hall. It continued to be used for classrooms until its renovation as an experimental theater. In 1951 an addition had been made to Jordan Hall, originally the estate winery, to allow for the relocation of the education department hitherto housed at Marywood. For almost three decades, Sister Bernetta Zeitz directed the college's elementary education certification program, a ministry of professional preparation and vocational and personal counseling that reached throughout the state.

On Sunday, March 1, 1960, ground was broken for the House of Studies, on the northeast corner of the campus at 1760 Fulton Street. The facility was a scholasticate, that is, a house of intellectual and spiritual formation for the newly professed members of the congregation. In his inauguration of the International Union of Superiors General in 1952, Pope Pius XII had emphasized the need for extensive and ongoing formation of religious. Professional preparation became the central emphasis of the Sister Formation movement, a remarkable collaborative effort of American women religious begun in 1953. Beginning in the late 1950's through the mid-1960's there was throughout the United States a surge in applications to the religious life. More living space and program development were imperative.

The scholasticate building, designed by Roger Allen and Associates, provided a three-story dormitory wing with 28 private rooms on each floor, joining a two-story main wing with kitchen and dining areas, reception rooms, recreational areas, guest rooms, and chapel. C.D. Barnes and Associates of Grand Rapids constructed the building. During the year of its construction over fifty scholastics were housed at Marywood in recreation rooms and halls commandeered "for the duration," and on the third floor of St. Andrew convent and in "the annex," a nearby house on Sheldon Street.

The House of Studies was dedicated on June 18, 1961, by Bishop Babcock. On November 23, 1962, the eve of Thanksgiving, the sisters moved to their new residence, where Sister Rose Miriam Visner was the first superior. It was maintained as a congregational residence, located on the college campus, with the congregation paying maintenance and a share of utilities and related services to the college. In 1972, when reorganization of the Board of Trustees transferred ownership of the college from exclusively congregational control, an agreement was made for the congregation to retain the House of Studies. As the number of candidates declined in the 1970's, the facility became a residence for senior sisters and in 1985, a part of Aquinas College.[18]

In September 1961 the college acquired for $50,000 the "Gate House," a two-story house at the Robinson Road entrance to the campus originally part of the Lowe estate, for a women's residence. It, along with several houses along Lake Drive[19] comprised the college dormitories. There were also privately owned houses in the vicinity approved by the college for student housing. This housing was subject to occasional visitation by the dean of students. Eventual lack of adequate housing and the desire for more coordinated supervision soon made on-campus housing a priority. On October 27, 1961, the cornerstone was laid for a new residence hall for women. Regina Hall, constructed at an estimated $550,000, was located on the eastern boundary of the campus, near the convent. It was dedicated on September 28, 1962. Sister Thomas Kyran (Elizabeth) Eardley was appointed directress of the 160-bed facility.

Additional women's dormitory space was required by the following year. On June 19, 1963, the college purchased Willowbrook, the stately home of Augie Busk at 1901 Robinson Road, for $72,500, for a senior women's dormitory. The house later was used for Emeritus Center, an innovative continuing education program for senior citizens, and with further expansion of the college in the late 1980's, as the president's home. In 1966 a wing was added to Regina Hall to accommodate an additional 144 women. The $626,000 construction was financed by a self-liquidating loan from the Housing and Home Finance Agency and the sale of securities purchased by a 1956 grant of the Ford Foundation.

On October 9, 1964, St. Joseph the Worker Hall was dedicated by Bishop Stephen Woznicki. The three-story residence hall for 156 men was situated on the west boundary of the campus adjoining St. Thomas the Apostle parish properties. Financing was through a self-liquidating loan of $500,000 secured through the United States Housing and Home Finance Agency and a private gift of $100,000.

On September 24, 1965, the cornerstone was laid for Wege Center, which became operational at the opening of the January 1966 semester. The three-story student center was built at a cost of

$750,000 with a self-liquidating loan[20] and a gift of $150,000 from the Wege Foundation of Grand Rapids. It was the final building of the Aquinas expansion program undertaken by Mother Victor as chairman of the Board of Trustees. The physical education-assembly building remained for her successor to complete.[21]

Under Mother Victor's leadership, the college also developed academically. Since the summer of 1952 the Dominican fathers of St. Joseph Province had conducted a theological institute for sisters. The curriculum, based on a study of the *Summa Theologica* of St. Thomas Aquinas, extended over four, then six summers, and led to a Master of Arts degree. The school was first conducted in the basement of St. Andrew cathedral and in classrooms of Catholic Central, then it moved to St. Paul Seminary in Saginaw. In 1969, to broaden its student clientele, the program returned to the Aquinas College campus as the Aquinas Institute of Religious Studies (AIRS). In 1971 the institute became a component of the year-round curriculum. Sister Jane Marie Murray was especially influential in broadening the curriculum to include scriptural, liturgical and religious education.

Until its closing in 1983 AIRS was a major source of continuing education within the congregation, both for updating degree work and for the theological formation of the sisters. Like the liturgical revival of the 1930's, the theological program became a central and invigorating experience in congregational life. It readied the congregation for the renewal and adaptation of its own structures and attitudes which had been called for, first by Pope Pius XII, and then by Pope John XXIII. It further prepared sisters to assist in the transformation of parish life and worship which Vatican Council II mandated.

In the spring of 1960, in conjunction with the periodic review of the college by the North Central Association, the first steps were taken to inaugurate a graduate program. Sister Gonzaga Udell was appointed chairman of the graduate division. Course work leading to the Master of Arts in English and in history was begun during the 1960 summer session and continued during the academic year. At the May 27, 1962, commencement the college conferred the degree of Master of Arts upon its first three graduates. The program was discontinued in 1967 due to the presence of university extension programs in the city.

Beginning with the fall semester 1962 the number of full-time Dominican priests on the faculty increased to six; the total faculty numbered 85. With the rapid growth of the campus plant and programs, reorganization of administration was in order. In September 1963 Sister Aline Needham replaced Sister Mildred Hawkins as dean of the college and assumed the duties of vice president of the college. Sister Aline, a graduate of Western Michigan University and Marquette University, had extensive experience in academic administration and, as a councilor to Mother Victor since 1948, she was well acquainted with the college operation.

Expansion of facilities and programs was undertaken in the Southwest as well as in Michigan. In 1947 Mother Euphrasia and her council had agreed to the transformation of Nazareth Sanatorium into a psychiatric care facility. Initially Nazareth was linked with Sandia Ranch Sanatorium, a facility conducted by John W. Myers, MD. A brochure describing services offered by the two sanatoria indicated that:

*Either Sanatorium operates much the same as a general hospital so far as finances are concerned. The basic board and room rate is $8.00 per day. Patients receiving shock therapy usually require extra nursing and there is a charge of $5.00 per day for shared nursing. ... Separate statements are rendered for physicians's services. Laboratory fees, medications, laundry, etc., are extra. Board, room, and nursing care are payable two weeks in advance.*[22]

Care was not limited to the mentally ill. Alcoholic patients were admitted by special arrangements for a minimum period of one week at a flat rate of $110 per week for board, room, and nursing care. Patients with drug addiction were also admitted by special arrangement and were expected to remain for a minimum of twenty-eight days at a cost of $275. There was as well a limited number of beds available for "domiciliary or custodial care" patients.

With its transformation into a psychiatric care facility in 1947 Nazareth Sanatorium began a new phase of operation. The training of sister-nurses began to reflect that emphasis.[23] In 1948 the hospital became an affiliated school for the psychiatric training of registered nurses. Students from St. Joseph Hospital, Albuquerque, St. Joseph Hospital, Phoenix, and St. Joseph Hospital, Denver, were enrolled at Nazareth under the direction of Sister Patricia Jane Dorfler. The program continued until 1958, when crowded conditions caused the Phoenix and Denver affiliates to relocate until new facilities were opened at Nazareth in 1961. Sister staff grew to 26 in 1965 but was gradually reduced to two by 1976.

Since its beginning in 1930, building construction and maintenance at Nazareth had been piecemeal. In January 1949 Mother Victor sought authorization from the bishop to complete construction. From 1948 to 1955 over $100,000 was spent on remodeling and construction, which was funded in part by a congregational loan of $50,000 to the Nazareth Hospital Corporation. George Babich of the Community Counseling Services conducted an eight-week campaign to raise the additional monies for the hospital expansion. Aided by a Friends of Nazareth Committee, the sisters in New Mexico solicited pledges of more than $121,000.[24]

By 1958 the 40-bed facility proved to be inadequate for the increasing patient census and the new methods of treatment. Robert G. Biddle of Albuquerque was engaged as architect to draw up plans for a separate building with accommodation for over seventy patients. At the same time an Advisory Board was formed. The president of the University of New Mexico made an offer for relocating the hospital on property adjoining the university. The offer, attractive to the sisters and lay board, was subsequently withdrawn. Meanwhile regulations governing psychiatric care required separate housing for nurses. Madonna Hall, a residence for approximately 25 nurses, was begun in January 1960. With Hill-Burton funding, a 92-bed brick facility was constructed in 1961 by La Mesa Builders for approximately $60,000. The building, approximately 450 feet southeast of the original two-story adobe, was dedicated by Archbishop Edwin V. Byrne of Sante Fe on May 7, 1961, as Villa Siena. Approximately $100,000 of the $650,000 expansion had come from Hill-Burton funds, the remainder from donations solicited by the sisters in the funds drive and a mortgage of 500 acres on the mesa. A wing added to the hospital in 1964 completed the building program.

On the feast of St. Rose of Lima, August 30, 1955, Mothers Victor and Eveline, Sisters Blanche, Ernestine, and Felix joined the sisters in New Mexico for the silver jubilee of Nazareth Sanatorium. Archbishop Byrne of Sante Fe celebrated a Solemn Pontifical Mass in the garden of the sanatorium.[25]

On March 6, 1952, Mother Victor announced to the sisters a "Community secret": the congregation was to assume the administration of a hospital in California. There were apostolic, professional, and practical reasons for the decision:

*For the past twenty years our Sister nurses have been praying that the Community would accept a hospital. Every Sister, I am sure, recognizes the fact that each of us wishes to work in the field for which she is prepared and our Sister nurses share that desire.*

*...Since each Sister assigned is to receive a salary the Community has nothing to lose and much to gain that will be added to our rapidly depleting coffers. ...we are undertaking this new work for the honor and glory of God. Brawley which is 90% Protestant has been begging for Catholic Sisters to run the hospital. Of course, it is a recognized fact that Sisters can always run a hospital more economically and more efficiently--and may I add more religiously--than lay people. May the personnel assigned to Brawley be God's chosen instruments to draw the residents of the Imperial Valley closer to His Sacred Heart. ...*

*...I think you will agree that a California mission is an asset for any Community and the uniqueness of our position in this instance warranted a favorable decision.*

In December 1951 Bishop Charles F. Buddy had written to Mother Victor for sisters to staff a newly-constructed district hospital in Imperial County in Lower California. Pioneers Memorial Hospital, Brawley, was an 80-bed facility with quarters for 30 nurses. Mother Victor and Sister Giles Chartier visited the site in January 1952 and by March 1 the congregation had agreed to assume the administration of the hospital for three years. The contract stipulated that not less than four nor more than eight sisters would be furnished during the contract period. On August 15, 1952, Sisters Rose Therese Kundermann, Mary Brendan Donovan, Patricia Ann Howe and Justyn Krieg were appointed to Brawley; Sister Francis Marie LaPorte arrived in November as superior of the group. The following year the quota of eight sisters was met. Contracts were subsequently renewed until 1972 with the number of sister personnel varying from four to ten. The first sisters at Pioneers Memorial Hospital found their services warmly received. Their insistence on the introduction of the Catholic Code of Ethics, however, proved highly contentious. Eventually controversies on ethical issues led to the sisters' withdrawal.

The administration of a second health care facility was added in 1955. Mother Victor and her council agreed to staff Guadalupe General Hospital in Santa Rosa, New Mexico. The ministry, under consideration since 1951, was at first declined due to the limited size of the hospital. On July 1, 1955, the congregation began its first three-year contract with the 24-bed, county-owned facility. Sisters Giles Chartier, John Dominic Krausmann, Francis Borgia Goyette, and Marie Arthur Fleming first served there. By 1964 the sister staff grew to its full complement of nine. While the hospital remained small, it became a center for emergency care for over four thousand persons in several counties. In 1966 the congregation received special commendation for ten years of accident-free operation of the hospital. On June 1, 1970, due to the changing requirements of hospital administration and a decline in the number of sister nurses in the congregation, the congregation ceased its role at the hospital. Operation of the hospital was taken over by the Presbyterian Medical Services of the Southwest. The sisters left a record not only of professional and compassionate health care but of missionary and exemplary presence in the county.

On June 1, 1963, the congregation assumed the administration of a third health care facility in El Centro, California. Oasis Valley Convalescent Home was an 82-bed facility for patients needing long-term postoperative care or nursing care only. The city of El Centro, twelve miles from the Mexican border, is in the desert where temperatures range from 115 degrees to near freezing. Unlike other health care facilities staffed by the congregation, Oasis Valley was a for-profit institution. It had, however, been built under a Federal Housing Administration program which restricted profits to 6%. Assured that the sisters would not be used for excessive private gain and wishing to have a mission in the locality of Brawley, some fifteen miles north, Mother Victor signed a three-year contract.

Sisters Rosemary Homrich, Bridget McGarry, Francis Louise Savage, Grace Licavoli, Reginald Strahl and Francetta McCann were first assigned there. Contracts stipulating the services of not less than four nor more than eight sisters were signed until 1969. Beginning that year, because of the declining numbers of nurses and the personnel needs at the congregation's new infirmary in Grand Rapids, contracts provided for no less than two nor more than three sisters, one of whom would serve as administrator. A 29-bed addition was constructed in 1973. Two sisters of the congregation remained at Oasis Valley Home until May 1974.

Mother Victor's final building project grew out of her first. With the curtailment of plans for a separate chapel and novitiate building on the motherhouse property, projections for infirmary space had been affected. In August 1964 the Grand Rapids Fire Department ordered the congregation to cease using the fourth floor in the main wing for living quarters. Internal partitions and a wood frame kitchen area had been added over the years to accommodate the increasing numbers of infirm sisters. The sisters were immediately alerted to the need for a building fund. Construction was begun in 1966 and completed in 1967 on the three-story structure some 200 feet west of Lakeside Drive and 60 feet north of the Pine Drive. The million dollar project was funded through congregational outlays[26] and the donations of benefactors. The 43,000-square-foot structure, designed by Roger Allen and Associates of Grand Rapids, provided rooms for 78 sisters. Though linked to the motherhouse by an underground tunnel, the infirmary is a full service facility providing chapel, kitchen and dining areas, recreation and reception rooms, nursing stations, and related health care areas.

The building was completed in 1967 and dedicated by Bishop Allen J. Babcock as Aquinata Hall in memory of Mother Aquinata Fiegler. The stained glass windows of its Chapel of St. Catherine of Siena represent the beatitudes. They were designed by Sister Blanche Steves and executed by the Grand Rapids Art Glass Company. Father Thomas H. Kaufmann, OP, was appointed chaplain and served in that position for twenty years.

In 1953 the congregation, with its sister congregations derived from Ratisbon, celebrated the hundredth anniversary of the nuns coming to the United States. It was also the seventy-fifth anniversary of the sisters' presence in Michigan. On June 2, 1953, Mother Victor wrote to the sisters:

*On the eve of our Diamond Anniversary would it not be well to pause and ponder a bit. Seventy-five years! Three-quarters of a century! Three generations! Have we not grown from a group of five members to over seven hundred Dominican Sisters, Novices, and Postulants! Sisters, we are the heirs of that valiant and self-sacrificing woman--Mother Aquinata and her co-workers--and for a time, at least, we are basking in the warmth and light and joy of Christ purchased for us by their many and noble conquests. Are we cognizant of the great debt owed to them and to our older Sisters still shouldering many of the Community's burdens? Do we realize the privileges and comforts that we are enjoying today are ours because of the innumerable hardships endured by our predecessors? Do we appreciate the fact that slowly but surely we are becoming more Dominican? If we do, let us strive ever more vigorously to become perfect religious and loyal daughters of our Congregation of Our Lady of the Sacred Heart....As a sublime expression of our profound gratitude to Almighty God may the personal Deo Gratias of each Sister blend in rich harmony with the Te Deum of our Daily Office.*

The chief public event was a pageant given in the Grand Rapids Civic Auditorium on Sunday, May 3. *Aloft His Torch*, written by Sisters Evangelista Rohrl, Robina Zoellner, Francis Ann Tatreau, and Jean Milhaupt, was presented by students of Aquinas College, Marywood Academy, Catholic Central high school, and St. Joseph Seminary, under the direction of Anthony J. Brink of the Aquinas College faculty. Tickets were distributed throughout the state to pastors, parish representatives, civic leaders, and especially to young women who might become candidates. Ticket sales yielded $3,757.16 for the building fund. Over 5,000 attended.

On August 4, St. Dominic's Day and the traditional jubilee day, a Solemn High Mass of Thanksgiving was celebrated by Monsignor Raymond Baker, vicar general. Bishops Albers, Woznicki, and Rancans, a score of monsignors, 100 priests, and representatives of Dominican congregations from throughout the United States joined the congregation. Bishop Woznicki read a special greeting from Monsignor Giovanni Baptista Montini, prosecretary of the Vatican. Immediately after the Mass, Bishop Haas appeared to greet the guests and congratulate the sisters. He had just been released from St. Mary Hospital. It was his first public appearance after his heart attack on May 27. He would be seen again publicly only for the national liturgical conference held later that month.[27]

A brief history of the congregation also entitled *Aloft His Torch* was written by Sister Eloise Mosier for the jubilee. It was the first occasion the congregational coat of arms was used.[28] A mural of the coat of arms was painted above the east wing entrance of Marywood.

From July 4 to July 9, 1954, the thirteenth General Chapter and the last of the "Fourth of July Chapters," was held at St. Joseph Seminary. By a nearly unanimous vote, 78 of the 82 votes cast, Mother Victor was reelected to a second term of six years. Mother Euphrasia Sullivan, Sisters Marie Celeste Stang,[29] Aline Needham, and Annette Kain were elected as her council. Only Sister Annette, chair of the Aquinas College music department, was new to the work of the general council.

# 17

# RIPE FOR THE HARVEST

*D*uring Mother Victor's administration there was a great deal of activity in the mission field: beginnings and endings, expansion and decline, signs of things to come, signs of passings. The beloved Canadian mission was evaluated and closed; the health care apostolate was expanded; a new and demanding Latin American mission was begun. Population growth in metropolitan Detroit and Grand Rapids called for new and enlarged congregational commitment. Smaller communities were now able to provide a parish school while some older parish schools could no longer be served. These developments were, in some respects, the maturation of the diocesan system with its emphasis on parochial schooling and the results as well of the post-war economy and the "baby boom."

Immediately after her election in July 1948, Mother Victor was faced with two issues with direct bearing on congregational ministries and finances, and ultimately on the definition and scope of mission. What came to be known in the congregation as the "Dixon Case" and the "Lay Teacher Problem" were symptomatic of national trends.

Mother Euphrasia had first learned of impending trouble in New Mexico in September 1947. Sister Claire Marie Duffy, superior of Holy Cross convent in Santa Cruz, wrote Mother of a visit to San Juan Pueblo. There the sisters learned of a petition being circulated "by some men from Dixon" to have the sisters removed from San Juan. A parishioner from Santa Cruz, posing as a member of the press, gained more information in Dixon. The sisters made an appointment to see the archbishop and found a delegation from the State Department of Education there on the same business. The Archbishop thought, reported the sisters, "the uprising...not merely local but that influence is coming from without."[1]

The immediate cause of contention was provided by some dissatisfied citizens in Dixon, a community of some 1200 in Rio Arriba County, 45 miles north of Santa Fe. In 1946-1947 a five-room school building was built through private subscription by donors, some of whom intended a school entirely free of religious influence. The County School Superintendent gave the contracts to two Franciscan sisters, one as principal, the other as teacher. For the past six years the Sisters of St. Francis of Paste, Colombia, had taught school in Dixon in the public school, in a building formerly a parochial school which they now owned. The sisters were, in the opinion of the local School Superintendent, qualified public school teachers and tenured for the district. They were, in the opinion of the contentious, however, teachers forcing Roman Catholicism upon children of other denominations. Many parents would not allow their children to attend the new school.

On September 16, 1947, State School Superintendent Charles L. Rose and members of the State Board of Education heard the representations of the parties, including that of Father William T. Bradley, Superintendent of Catholic Schools in the archdiocese, and ordered that any imposition of religion, if it existed, cease. The department requested that only lay teachers be hired for the first six grades in the newly-erected school at Dixon, that the Catholic sisters teach only the seventh through the twelfth grades, that busses arrive at and leave the school on schedule, and that no religious instruction be given during school hours.

Archbishop Byrnes promised compliance on behalf of the archdiocese and of the 132 religious of several congregrations teaching in the public schools. The protagonists, however, wanted complete laicization of faculty. In a press interview on January 20, 1948, Harry L. Bigbee, former judge and Santa Fe attorney representing 28 plaintiffs--the Dixon committee, the American Civil Liberties Union, and the Protestant Committee for the Separation of Church and State--stated their aim: "to fight for the separation of church and state, to insure free public schools and to eliminate all denominational religious training in all schools supported by taxes in New Mexico and elsewhere." The controversy was widely covered by state and national press, and other New Mexico communities in a ten-county area were drawn into the controversy on "religious encroachment."

In March 1948 over 300 persons--the members of the State Board of Education, Governor Mabry, government officials, 145 religious teaching in public schools--received subpoenas in the legal action. Brother Benildus, a Christian Brother, was designated "liaison man" and William J. Barker of Santa Fe, a retired judge, was chosen as attorney for the Archdiocese of Sante Fe for the court hearings. A defense fund was created, with the religious congregations to contribute $150 for each of their members named as a defendant in the case. The congregation sent a check for $3,900 for its 26 sisters teaching in New Mexico. The case, opening in Albuquerque on April 30, 1948, was continued until September 27, 1948. District Judge E. T. Hensley, Jr. of Clovis, New Mexico, presided over the ten-day hearing.

The record in the case consisted of 140 "Interrogatories" fourteen-pages long, sent by the plaintiffs' counsel to the priests and religious. The latter were asked, among other things:

> *When did you become affiliated with the Order to which you belong? (no. 6)*
>
> *What proportion of your time do your vows and obligations to your Order and Church require that you devote to your Order and its objectives? (no. 10)*
>
> *How much of your salary do you retain for your own use and what disposition do you make of the remainder? (no. 13)*
>
> *On what occasions are all or any portion of the children in your classes conducted to church in a group? (no. 33)*
>
> *Was High Mass celebrated in connection with graduation exercises in your school? (no. 34)*
>
> *Describe all pictures that have been displayed on the walls of your classroom during the current school year. (no. 46)*
>
> *How often does the priest in your community visit the school? (no. 55)*
>
> *When were the last crucifixes removed from the walls of your classrooms? (no. 66)*
>
> *Do you teach the children in your classes how they should prepare for a good confession? (no. 71)*

Sister Maura McDonald, principal of the Peñasco high school and superintendent of the Peñasco Independent School District, Sisters Loretto Omlor, Seraphine Wendling, and Carmella Conway were called to the witness stand during the ten-day trial. It was indeed a trial for the sisters. Congregational mission policy, the signification of the habit, the sisters' daily routine, teaching aides, and personal exchanges were challenged.[2] On October 25, 1948, Mother Victor wrote to the sisters in New Mexico:

*I am writing this letter to all in New Mexico to assure you that although so many miles separate us, the Sisters here and I are with you in spirit and in prayer. We are keeping close tab on happenings in the Southwest through your letters and newspaper clippings. Sister Maura's detailed circular letter was interesting reading but we all know that the events themselves were agonizing. I hope you won't have to go through any more of it.*

*We know that God is with us. Our presence in the schools of New Mexico or any other school is for only one purpose--to bring God into the lives of the children. If that purpose is thwarted in the public schools it will be accomplished in some other way. God knows why all this is, and we are in His hands.*

*I hope you don't have to go through any more torture. My heart aches to think of your being before the public eye in such a way...*

On Saturday, March 12, 1949, Judge Hensley filed his decision on Public School Case No. 22178.[3] He held that there were breaches of separation of church and state in the 25 schools involved in the Dixon case. The general effect of the ruling was that 143 religious named in the decision were barred from teaching positions in 25 schools. All state school boards were prohibited the use of buildings not under the absolute control of the state, of free bus transportation by the state for students in parochial schools, of the purchase of "Catholic school only" books by the state, of the furnishing of free textbooks to parochial schools, of the teaching of any sectarian doctrine in tax-supported schools, of holding of school in rooms where religious or sectarian symbols were displayed, and of paying persons teaching sectarian doctrines.

Archbishop Byrne wrote to major superiors of the involved congregations seeking support for an appeal of the decision and for replacements for those barred from teaching. Mother Victor and her council decided that they could neither replace the twenty-one Dominican sisters barred from teaching in New Mexico nor support the appeal. Mother and Sister Aline traveled to New Mexico in Holy Week of 1949 to explain their position to Archbishop Byrne.

The congregation had made a quarter-century investment of sister personnel, of special training to meet certification and cultural requirements, and financial outlay[4] in New Mexico. It could not continue to do so at the same rate. Congregational service in public schools would cease and service in parochial schools would be considered on a case by case basis. The sisters were told of this policy change both by visitation and letter:

*June 13, 1949*

*Dear Sisters [in New Mexico],*

*The contents of this letter may come as a surprise to you, but with an over-all picture of the Community in mind, I feel it is my duty to say a few words to you covering the establishment of parochial schools in New Mexico.*

*Sisters, do not urge your pastors to write me for reduced salary rates nor for extra Sisters. I cannot comply with their wishes. As I explained to most of you during my visit, the Community is not in a position to handle a $30,000 deficit without the public school money. Some of the lay teachers in the North must be replaced from Sisters from New Mexico or we shall be obliged to borrow money to pay our current salaries. I am sure none of you would expect **your** Community to do that.*

*All through the years your Community has been doing a tremendous amount of charity, hence we have no SINKING FUND from which we may draw. Now that we build in order to have at least sleeping quarters, we must depend on your co-operation to have **nth** degree to meet the interest demands. This will not be possible on less than a $500 a year salary.*

*As much as I would dislike to see any school closed I feel in conscience bound to tell you that God may have His own reason for such a drastic measure if it should come to pass. It may be that you are to work elsewhere to earn your heaven...*

*Make no improvements on any convent; buy no furniture, etc.; make no arrangements whatever with the Pastor; let all be done directly between the Pastor and the Motherhouse. In the initial stage of parochial development it behooves us to step cautiously. What we do this year will be taken as a criterion.*

*God bless you all!*

In her customary letter accompanying the annual assignments, Mother Victor told all of the sisters on August 12, 1949, about the two "community problems": closing the mission in Peñasco and paying lay teachers. The mission would be closed temporarily. It was, in Mother's view, a matter of justice that some of the sisters remain in New Mexico:

> *Since the New Mexico missions kept the wolf from the door in the 30's when many northern missions were receiving only sufficient salary for survival, we have an obligation to the Spanish people and dare not close their schools if they are willing to support them.*

On August 1, 1949, Mother informed Monsignor Schoeppner of the Archdiocese of Santa Fe of her decision to close the Peñasco mission, clarifying the connection between lay salaries and New Mexico missions:

*As explained to His Excellency, we have been able to keep the schools in New Mexico only by hiring lay teachers in Michigan and paying their salaries from the New Mexico public school money. Now that this pecuniary aid will not be forthcoming you can readily see how, with the best will in the world, we cannot increase the number of Sisters teaching in Peñasco.*

The Peñasco mission, established in 1926, functioned as an independent school district of which Sister Maura McDonald was the current superintendent. In the 1948-1949 school year ten sisters and twelve lay teachers were employed at the school. The convent was owned by the congregation, the school buildings belonged to St. Anthony parish. The school was now to function without sisters. Additional lay teachers were hired, four of the lay women allowed by the congregation to live rent-free in the convent in return for maintenance and care of any emergencies. The following summer sisters returned to the convent in Peñasco for catechetical programs. In September 1950 a six-grade parochial school was opened by Sisters Ruth Wolfe and Lily Zahm. Sisters remained in ministry in Peñasco until 1989, although the convent property had been deeded to the parish in 1951. The parishes in Belen, Santa Cruz, San Juan, and Ranchos de Taos opened parochial schools in September 1949. The sisters' temporary departure from Peñasco had enabled Mother Victor to accept two parish schools in Albuquerque.

San Ignacio parish first convened in 1916 in the second story of a neighborhood store on Highland Street in old Martinez Town, a settlement in north Albuquerque almost as old as the "Duke City." A church was built in 1926 with the help of Father Ferdinand Troy and other Jesuit fathers. In September 1949 Mother Victor, keeping a promise made by Mother Euphrasia, sent Sisters Emmerica Ziegler and Consuelo Chavez to begin a school. They lived in a small three-room adobe house with a tin roof, their first days there with candlelight. School for 69 pupils in pre-school and grades one and two was held in the former American Legion Hall. School opening was brightened by the arrival of the school supervisors, Mother Eveline and Sister Paula Murphy, who brought along with them textbooks and school supplies from the sisters in Michigan schools. Neighboring parishes gave desks and blackboards. School and convent needs were financed by inventive means--raffles, bake sales, and mysterious gifts from St. Joseph. Within a year of opening, the number of pupils had more than doubled, and the church sacristies were taken over as classrooms. A new convent and school were dedicated in January 1956. The school grew to a full eight-grade elementary program, staffed by three and sometimes five sisters, and lay teachers. The congregation withdrew sisters from the mission in 1969.

The congregation also began a long-term service in northeast Albuquerque at the new parish of Our Lady of Fatima. Father Joseph Charewicz was so eager to provide schooling for the burgeoning Catholic population that the school was the first of the parish buildings. The school drew from many neighborhoods in the Heights area and was for a time known as Heights Catholic. Sisters Ignatia Parisey, Euphrosine (Mary) Sullivan, and Lily Zahm were the first assigned there. Within five years, the school population numbered over 300 with six sisters and two lay faculty members, and gradually it grew to require eleven sisters. After the demolition of the old "San" in 1973, Fatima became a gathering place for sisters in the Southwest. Dominican sisters continued to serve school and parish needs until 1989.

In 1961 another New Mexico mission was accepted. On September 5, 1961, classes were begun at the Nativity of the Blessed Virgin school, Alameda, a suburb of Albuquerque. Sisters Eleanore VanDyke, Emmerica Ziegler, Grace Ellen Martin, and two lay teachers began the school with 140 pupils in four grades. Opening the school, with so many aged and ill in the congregation and with young sisters in longer training programs, was a hardship. It was, however, the keeping of a thirty-year-old promise. On October 12, 1960, Father Edward Rutowski, pastor of Nativity parish, wrote to Mother Victor reminding her of the promise Mother Eveline had made in 1928 to Father Troy, pastor of Nativity parish, when she accepted the land used for building Nazareth Sanatorium. Mother Eveline apparently had agreed that the congregation, when it could, would staff a school in the parish. Mother Victor responded at once:

*First of all, Father, let me say that if a promise was made to Father Troy that our Congregation would supply Sisters to staff a school in Alameda, then that promise would most assuredly be fulfilled.*

*...As a religious community, Father, we have reached the point in our existence where it is physically impossible to take on new schools. What we give to one we have to take from another. I hope the time is not far distant when the*

*Archbishops and Bishops of the country will make a ruling that will equalize the quota of lay teachers and establish a basis for apportioning the available Sisters among old schools and new. In the present situation it takes practically all of the young Sisters who are coming from the novitiates of the various communities to make replacements, leaving none for the opening of new schools.*

*In spite of what seem insurmountable obstacles, our community will do what it can for you next fall...*

The parish grew rapidly and each year pressure to add to the sister faculty increased but the congregation was able to send no more than five sisters, and usually just four. In 1970 the congregation, in conjunction with other religious congregations in Michigan, formulated a compensation scale for the services of the sisters in parishes. Resultant compensation issues and personnel difficulties at Alameda caused an impasse resolved by withdrawal of the sisters in May 1971.

The commitment to new parishes in New Mexico grew out of a sense of justice to the Catholic people of the state. In Michigan there was also considerable development of the mission field. Some new missions were accepted at the urging of bishops, while others were taken on, partly for increased recruiting opportunities.

In August 1950 sisters of the congregation began regular ministry to St. Basil parish in South Haven. During Mother Eveline's administration the congregation had conducted a summer school of religion there. The small city was a popular Lake Michigan resort center sixty miles south of Grand Rapids. There had been a Catholic community in the area since 1857, served first by priests of the Detroit diocese, and after 1937, by priests of the Lansing diocese. Father George P. Horkan, pastor from 1947 to 1958, had seen the parish through the building of its school and had arranged for Dominican sisters as teachers.

On September 5, 1950, Sisters Samuel (Margaret) Shaffer, Margaret Ann Kaiser, Jane Francis Flannery, Rose Thomas MacIntyre, and Cabrini (Dorothy) Giglio and a lay teacher enrolled 127 pupils in six grades in the new school building. An addition to the school was made in 1961. In 1962 Father Frank J. Burger offered Mother Victor the use of the parish's stately old convent home with its Lake Michigan frontage as a summer vacation center at no cost to the sisters. Mother's response was a measure of the pace of religious life at the time. She wrote on May 24, 1962:

*Father, so very few of the Sisters, aside from those who are actually ill, are free this summer that we shall not be able to avail ourselves of the vacation possibilities at South Haven during the month of July. I shall be very glad to send some there during August. It seems strange that I find myself almost as hard pressed for Sisters to vacation as for Sisters to teach school. So be it! Father, let us pray--and maybe someday... .*

Subsequently many sisters of the congregation benefitted from the generous offer of the parish.[5] Two Dominican sisters continue to serve this parish now in the diocese of Kalamazoo.

A second school in the area was opened in September 1951 at Douglas, Michigan. St. Peter parish, Douglas, in the diocese of Grand Rapids, had been under the pastoral care of Father Charles Nugent since 1940. In September 1951 the parish opened a six-grade school for 90 pupils in a former venetian blind factory. Sisters Magdala Host and Leah Dorian took up residence in the second story of the building. Seventh and eighth grades were subsequently added and the staff increased to three sisters and one lay teacher. Enrollment was at its highest in the 1961-1962 school year. A gradual decline led to the closing of grades seven and eight in 1965. At the end of the 1972 school year, projected enrollment for grades one through six was only 55. Consequently Sister Aquinas Weber, Mother Victor's successor, informed parish officials of the need to end the congregation's commitment to staff the school. The congregation was willing, however, to make personnel available for new forms of catechesis and service. In August 1972 two sisters returned to develop a program of religious education and Christian service for the Douglas-Fennville-Bravo-Pullman area. The appointment of the two sisters who were bilingual was an acknowledgement of the needs of the growing Hispanic community.[6] A sister continues to serve in the area to the present day.

In 1950 the congregation assumed the direction of St. Mary school in Alma, Michigan. Sisters Vincent DePaul Roberts, Francella Bovin, and Marie Eugene Charbonneau were the first assigned to the six-grade school with its 107 children. The sixth grade was discontinued in 1969 when a new middle school was opened in the city. The sisters left when the parish school closed in 1971.

Since 1903 the Dominican sisters at St. Joseph's, Weare, a country parish set amidst farms, were the only women religious in Oceana County. From that mission, the sisters had gone to neighboring Hart and the mission church at Elbridge, an old Indian settlement,

# The Mission Field
## 1877 - 1966

Melville
Saskatchewan, Canada
1929

Ranchos de Taos 1935

Penasco 1926

Dixon 1925

Santa Cruz 1928

Alameda 1961

Santa Rosa 1955

Fatima 1949
San Ignacio 1949
Nazareth 1930

Belen 1933

Austin 1960

Brawley 1952

El Centro 1963

Beaver Island 1899

Onaway 1911

Charlevoix 1906

Boyne Falls 1914

Peshawbestown 1887
East Jordan 1909
Gaylord 1909
Alpena 1911

Suttons Bay 1900
Mancelona 1911

Lake Leelenau 1888

Traverse City 1877

Hannah 1907
Grayling 1962

Marinette 1923

Peshtigo 1920

East Tawas 1916
Tawas City 1957

Prudenville 1954

West branch 1917

Port Austin 1879

Weare 1903
Vernon 1915

Hart 1950
Beal City 1901
Fisherville 1914
Essexville 1889
Ruth 1888

Auburn 1915
Bay City 1881
Gagetown 1888

Mt. Pleasant 1889
Munger 1925

Carrollton 1913

Merrill 1907
Saginaw 1885

Alma 1950
St Charles 1909

Muskegon 1879
Ravenna 1959
Carson City 1907
Chesaning 1906

Muskegon Heights 1940
Wright 1893
Maple Grove 1902

Alpine 1901

Grand Rapids 1889
Pewano 1948

Lowell 1960

New Salem 1918
Byron Center 1908

Douglas 1951
North Dorr 1918
Detroit 1966

Dearborn Heights 1948
Melvindale 1929

South Haven 1950
Battle Creek 1880
Allen Park 1950
Taylor 1946

Adrian 1879

South Bend 1921

Chimbote, Peru 1963

for weekend catechism classes and sacramental preparation. Summer schools of religion, along with sisters returning to their homes for visits, had augmented sister presence in the area. In 1950 Father Charles Popell secured from Mother Victor a promise to staff St. Gregory parish's new elementary school in Hart. Off a central hall there were convent rooms on one side and three class rooms on the other. The first year Sister Wilmetta Murphy taught grades one through four and Sister Josita Wilson, grades five through eight. A lay woman gave music instruction in the third room. Sister Coletta Baumeister provided housekeeping services for the sisters. In 1953 a third sister was added to the faculty. In the 1966-1967 school year grades seven and eight were discontinued. In 1967 a lay woman joined the two sisters on the faculty. At the end of the 1967-1968 school year a total religious education program, conducted by lay staff, replaced the grade school. A Dominican sister was later employed as director of the program.

Suburban development required another parish school on the southeast side of Grand Rapids. Immaculate Heart of Mary parish came under the care of the Oblates of Mary Immaculate. In September 1952 Dominican sisters opened the eight-grade facility. Sisters Samuel Schaffer, Ann Kathleen Mooney, and Theresa Bray were assigned to the new school with 141 pupils. At the end of Mother Victor's administration in 1966 there were five sister faculty and twelve lay teachers. Several sisters continue on the predominantly lay faculty to the present.

In 1949 Father John Collins, first pastor of Blessed Sacrament parish in northwest Grand Rapids, arranged with Mother Victor for sisters to staff the parish's elementary school upon its completion. When the school opened in September 1950 Monsignor Anthony Arszulowicz was pastor. Sisters Theodine Andres, Alan (Margaret) Thomas, Charlotte Schaub, Herman Marie Maez, Barbara Ann Seymour, and Thea La Marre were first assigned there. For several years the sisters boarded at St. John's Home, where Sister Borgia Hawkins was superior and resident director. Eventually two houses on Eleanor Street were converted into a convent. From the first to the second year, enrollment increased from 267 to 389, and a seventh sister and two lay women were added to the faculty. In 1958 two grades commuted to St. John's Home and an eighth sister was added to the faculty. From 1972 to 1980 a Dominican sister developed a many-faceted religious education program for the parish. A lay principal was hired for the school in 1976. Gradually the number of sisters on the school faculty declined, a single sister remaining until June 1982. Sister presence in the parish continued through parish membership and residence in parish-owned housing throughout the 1980's.

In 1954 sisters began to serve in the parish of Our Lady of the Lake, Prudenville, Michigan. Sisters Valeria Tomkowiak, Martha Obermeier, Christine Jozwiak, and Eileen Marie Preuter opened the six-grade school of 64 pupils. Sisters remained there until the school closing in 1981. Since 1987 a member of the congregation has been principal of the reopened elementary program, joining another sister of the congregation who has served the parish as pastoral minister since 1985.

In the fall of 1957 Mother Victor was able to send two sisters to Tawas City. The parish of Immaculate Heart of Mary had been formed just five years before. Father Joseph A. Castanier, pastor since 1953, had secured the old St. Joseph school, East Tawas, for the parish school. In 1957 there were some ninety pupils in the eight-grade school. Sisters Thea La Marre and Maria Tardani were assigned to care for grades one to five; a layman taught the remaining three grades. The two sisters lived with the sisters in East Tawas, four miles east. Dominican sisters in the area provided weekend and summer catechetical programs in Standish and Alger. In 1967 the Tawas City and East Tawas Catholic schools were consolidated in a single six-grade program taught by four sisters and two lay women. Dominicans remained at Tawas City until 1981.

The Sisters of Charity of Cincinnati had staffed St. Catherine school, Ravenna, Michigan, since its opening in September 1955. It was the first Catholic grade school in the county beyond the city of Muskegon. In 1955 a lay woman was added to the faculty. At the close of the 1957-1958 school year, due to the universal shortage of sisters, the Ohio-based congregation withdrew its sisters from the small rural community east of Muskegon. The pastor, Father S.L. Betka, had been pastor for 25 of the 50 years of the parish's existence. Responding to Bishop Babcock's plea, Mother Victor sent Sisters Rose Francis Greiner, Evangela Ronning, Thomas Estelle Bryan, and Sharon Marie Duperon to take over the grade school of 270 pupils. A sister of the congregation serves as principal and teacher in the school to the present.

In 1960 Mother Victor agreed to the temporary staffing of St. Mary school, Lowell, Michigan. Dominican sisters from Ireland had conducted the school from 1953 to June 1960. Father Speer Strahan, pastor of the parish and lecturer in literature at Aquinas College, secured from Mother Victor a promise to staff temporarily the small school, some fifteen miles east of Grand Rapids. His plea to Mother Victor on July 27, 1960, was one of the more historical and plaintive of the many she received:

*You once mentioned to me, why should you send Sisters to places that have produced no vocations? Your own Sister Paula prides herself on being from Lowell, as she will tell you if you ask her. Furthermore, Father Flanagan and Father Howard counted themselves as natives of Lowell. And as for coming from a place where there were no Catholic schools, you will recall that Mother Evelyn was born in Mancelona; that Monsignor Bolton was raised in Frankfort; that Father Horton of Saginaw was born in Manton; and that until I was 17 years old, I lived in Fife Lake where there was Mass once a month....*

*I know that you are not looking for large parishes and large schools and if they were offered to you, you would find difficulty in staffing them. I know you realize one does not need numbers to do good work, or even one's best work. ...Today is St. Anne's day and I have asked the grandmother of Our Lord, who thought so much of little children, to have pity on St. Mary's parish in its distress.*

Over the next ten years first three, then two sisters were sent to the school, commuting from Marywood each day. The lay faculty grew to three in 1967. In 1970, as a result of a study commissioned by the 1969 Chapter of Affairs, the congregation concluded its operation of the school.

St. Paul the Apostle parish, first known as "St. Stephen's Annex," was opened in 1962 in the southeast section of Grand Rapids to accommodate the rapid suburban development in the east Grand Rapids area. In 1965 two sisters and three lay faculty staffed the first temporary school rooms. The sister faculty lived first at Marywood, then at Immaculate Heart, and later on Alexander Street. Sisters of the congregation served the parish until June 1976.

During the 1948-1949 school year sisters from Gaylord taught religion on a weekly basis for over 100 area children. Urged by Bishop Haas, the St. Mary, Grayling parish began a building program for a combination church-school building. Upon its opening, Sisters of St. Joseph staffed the school. In September 1965, at Bishop Babcock's urging, Dominican sisters replaced them. Sisters Cecilia Faber, Janet Brown, and Anne Monica Shalda were first assigned there. With two lay women they conducted a full eight-grade program for 130 students. The school was one of several the congregation ceased to staff upon the conclusion of the 1969-1970 school year. In that year the parish came within the newly created Diocese of Gaylord. In August 1974 the convent was reopened as the home for two sisters from Grand Rapids and a sister from Racine, Wisconsin, who were employed by the Office of Christian Education and Pastoral Ministry of the diocese. They were later joined by a Sister of Mercy. Intercongregational teams, hired by a diocese and serving a large district, came to be one of many new ways sisters served parishes and dioceses.

In 1950 Alpena parishes reorganized their schools to provide a consolidated high school. Alpena Catholic Central was staffed by Felicians from Livonia, and Dominicans from Adrian and Grand Rapids. The original parish grade schools continued with the Felicians at St. Mary's, the Adrian Dominicans at St. Bernard's, and the Grand Rapids Dominicans at St. Anne's. In 1958 the congregation took over the staffing of the high school with thirteen sisters on the faculty and Sister Richard Kinnally as their superior. Sisters continued there until the school closed in June 1971.

In 1953 Muskegon parishes also developed a consolidated high school program. The new Catholic Central, on a 69-acre campus at Barclay and Laketon Avenues, was staffed by four Sisters of Mercy from Detroit, two Bernadine sisters, twelve Dominican sisters from Grand Rapids, diocesan priests and lay faculty, headed by Father Louis B. LaPres. The Bernadine sisters left in 1959 and, in 1960, Sisters of St. Joseph of Kalamazoo and Felician sisters were added to the faculty. The twelve Dominican sisters,[7] assigned to the high school resided in convents throughout the city until, in 1957, a home was purchased at 1240 Fourth Street. On November 13, 1966, thirty new classrooms, a chapel and auditorium, chaplain's quarters, and two convents were dedicated. The convents were to accommodate the four congregations of religious women[8] and the Christian Brothers who had joined the faculty in 1962.

From 1966 to 1970 there were seven sisters from Grand Rapids assigned to Muskegon Catholic Central, by 1976 three sisters. In the 1970's it became increasingly difficult to match available personnel with curricular assignments from the superintendent. The congregational placement policy inaugurated in the 1970's allowing for application by individual sisters for open positions enabled continuance of Dominican presence, though in greatly reduced numbers, on the Catholic Central faculty through 1990. From 1978 to 1984 a member of the congregation was superintendent of the Greater Muskegon Catholic Schools, the chief administrative position for the schools in the Muskegon deanery.

The congregation could not accept the offer made in May 1961 to staff a new Catholic Central high school in Manistee, Michigan. It would have required, as Mother Victor said, taking from one to give to another.

One of Mother Victor's first visitations after her election was to Canada. In late October 1948 she brought her views to the council. St. Henry grade school was staffed by one sister and three lay teachers; the high school of only thirty-eight students by three sisters who needed, nevertheless, to present the full program of studies required by the provincial government. The difficulty of the state examinations and the government regulation allowing only teachers who were Canadian citizens to recommend students for advanced work contributed to the decline. The council advised withdrawal of the congregation from the Melville school in favor of a congregation of Canadian sisters.

Efforts to secure replacements were made the next year and a half. On April 30, 1950, Archbishop O'Neill informed Mother that the Sisters of Charity of St. Louis were willing to take over the school in September 1950. In May, Sisters Joachim and Felix travelled to Melville to arrange for the transfer of property. The six sisters assigned there returned to Grand Rapids at the conclusion of the 1949-1950 school year. Our Lady of Sorrows school, Grand Rapids, was also given over to the care of another congregation. In 1953, the Consolata sisters from Italy took over the direction of the school to meet the changing language needs of the parishioners.

In late summer 1950 several missions were begun throughout the state. Father Clare A. Murphy had laid the groundwork with Mother Euphrasia for sisters to teach in the new parochial school in Allen Park near Detroit.[9] In August 1950 Mother Victor assigned Sisters Paschal Barth, Michaela Schrems, and Delores Wendling to St. Francis Cabrini school. Three lay teachers completed the faculty for the 325 pupils. A sister was added in 1951 and another in 1952. By May 1953 there were 350 children in the school and over 1,000 on its waiting list. The congregation could not provide sufficient sisters for the rapidly growing school. Moreover diocesan policy required that congregations be responsible for the compensation of lay teachers. In order to stabilize the school faculty, the archdiocese contacted several communities for replacement of the Dominican sisters, while at the same time requesting the services of the departing Dominican sisters in other archdiocesan schools. A congregation of Franciscan sisters from Pittsburgh was able to provide eight sisters for the 1953-1954 school year with promise of yearly increases in staff. Consequently, the Dominican sisters regretfully left St. Francis Cabrini parish in June 1953.

The "Faith by Mail" program begun in March 1948 was first located at Marywood and directed by Sister Joachim Visner. Mother Victor heartily supported the project with sister staff, space, and minimal financial remuneration. By 1951 the project was carried on by four sisters working full-time, a lay secretary, a part-time worker from the college, and a host of sister volunteers, including a day a week from Mother Victor and Sister Joachim during the first semester of 1951. In August 1951 the program was relocated in the fourth floor of St. John's Home. There the sisters composed lessons, saw to the printing and mailing of materials, and then read and annotated the lessons and encouraged the correspondents, who by 1957 numbered more than 2,000. These were mostly children in Michigan, Wisconsin, and Texas, but there were also adults in prisons and mental institutions among their clients.

Sisters Joachim Visner and Rosalia Genovese illustrated the materials which complemented the Baltimore Catechism and other books chosen for the course. After three years of operation, the sisters realized the need for a core text reflective of current theology and liturgical spirituality and specifically designed for the school's clientele. Mother Victor assigned Sisters Marie Dominica Viesnoraitis and Ligouri (Mary) DeHaus to write, and Sister Rosalia to illustrate, the course materials.

The achievement was not unlike the work of the Collegeville Summer; the three sisters spent the summer of 1951 and countless hours surrounding their full-time teaching assignments throughout 1951-1952 in the production of the lessons which comprised the course and book called *Christ in the Family*. In 1955 Sisters Ligouri and Marie Dominica wrote *We Learn about God* which, in 1966, was translated into Spanish for use in Mexico. The materials received a welcome reception by catechists in the United States, Canada, and Mexico. The congregation undertook the printing and distribution of the course materials and the two books. Pricing was an indicator of the times: each of the books complete with worksheets cost under a dollar, and for multiple copies a 25% discount was given. Nevertheless, for many inquirers this was "too dear." The decision to market the materials privately proved time-consuming and financially unrewarding. Above all, it limited the distribution of well reviewed catechetical works.

The Diocesan Fund for the Faith, initiated by Bishop Haas in 1949, paid for office and materials costs, and a dollar a day for board at St. John's Home for each of the sisters involved in the correspondence ministry. Mother Victor pledged the services of the sisters as a measure of the congregation's commitment to the work of evangelization and for the blessing of vocations. Several factors led to the closing of the school in June 1960. Bishop Babcock did not care to sponsor the project to the same extent as had Bishop Haas. Confraternities of Christian Doctrine were well-established within the Diocese of Grand Rapids and new forms of catechesis were developing. Moreover, the seventy-five year old setting for orphanage, temporary motherhouse, and correspondence school was about to be razed.[10] Renting alternate space was not feasible.

Nevertheless the staff who had seen the correspondence school work through its last years was itself transported to a new location. One of the school's most appreciative clients, Father Joseph Pawlicki, CSC, a pastor in the Diocese of Austin, Texas, arranged for Sisters Francella Bovin, Lorraine Gibson, and Guadalin Lopez to relocate in Austin where they continued until 1967.

In addition to the ordinary works of administration of the corporation and congregation--correspondence, finances, buildings management, record keeping, continuing education, placement services, counseling--the central office, virtually Mother Victor and Sisters Joachim and Felix continued and expanded its publishing services. There was a monthly circular letter from the mother general, an occasional retreat conference or sermon, *Contacts* from the Supervisors Office, Christmas cards designed and lettered by the sisters, and materials for the correspondence program. In October 1947 *Come and See*, an illustrated vocation pamphlet, first appeared. In April 1950 the *Marywood Messenger* was first published. The quarterly newsletter featured correspondence between Judy, later Sister Moyra, and Polly. From 1950-1957 the

*Dear Polly* vocation letters were sent to girls throughout the midwest and New Mexico. In subsequent years there were revivals of the vocation letter.

On September 8, 1953, Pope Pius XII proclaimed in the encyclical *Fulgens Corona* the opening of the Marian Year. As part of the worldwide observance, Marywood Academy formed Marian Publications. To meet the needs of classroom teachers and the widening catechetical ministry, and to promote the liturgical apostolate of the congregation, Sister Servatia Respondek developed a range of posters and banners for classroom and individual use. Her first project was *Our Lady's Datebook*, a portfolio of posters celebrating the feasts of Mary, Mother of God. Under Sister Servatia's direction, students prepared line drawings for lithographing. There were liturgical, biblical, and seasonal series as well as art education, citizenship, and courtesy sets. Students and neighborhood children packed print materials for sending out by train and truck. In the same year the congregational offices assumed the direction of Marian Publications and Sister Servatia formed Apostolate Publications to continue the development and distribution of posters and banners. Publication begun in 1953 was discontinued in 1985. Millions of student art pieces had been sent throughout the United States, Canada, South America, and Africa.

The congregational publications offered a range of items: Christ in Our Family for catechetical programs; *Mary's Joys in Drama* by Sister Rosalina Gregoraitis; *Sue's Letters to Sally*, a series of 12 vocation aids; and Holyday-Holiday Posters, illustrated by Sister Rosalia Genovese, a booklet of *Fatima Meditations*, and "sympathy folders." These materials were reviewed by diocesan officials and given the imprimatur of Bishop Babcock. *The Rosary and the Living Word*, a book of visual meditations on the rosary by Sister Rosalia Genovese, was published by Helicon Press of Baltimore in August 1964. The following year Sister Rosalia prepared a set of fifty-six educational charts as teacher aids in word building, the "new" mathematics, and art for publication by Oddo Publishing of Mankato, Minnesota.

Since 1942, by decree of the bishops of the Saginaw and Grand Rapids dioceses, the congregation had been paying the salaries of lay teachers in the parochial schools when it was not able to provide the desired number of sisters. In the Grand Rapids diocese the regulation was not always strictly kept. In a four-month period in 1948 the congregation had, nevertheless, paid out over $3,000 in the Grand Rapids diocese. In the Saginaw diocese the regulation was strictly enforced and in the 1948-1949 school year over $30,000 was paid in lay salaries. At Saints Peter and Paul school, the congregation was paying some $3,000 annually for lay teachers even though there was no room in the convent for additional sisters. Mother Euphrasia had brought the matter to Bishop Murphy's attention but business was delayed during his lengthy illness.

Mother Victor resumed the negotiations. She placed before Monsignor Sonefeld, vicar general of the Saginaw diocese, the untenable situation. The congregation was, in some instances, supplying the staff for parish schools at no cost to the parish. There had been, as well, a gradual encroachment on music moneys earned in after-school hours and on Saturdays. She informed the pastor of St. Joseph school, Bay City, that the congregational contract would be terminated at the end of the 1949 school year unless the parish would take over the payment of lay salaries and resume payment of sister salaries. It was a confrontation, albeit conducted with exquisite courtesy, which would be repeated on several occasions in several parishes.

The changes in the status of the sisters in the New Mexico missions had an obvious effect on congregational income. Income which had "kept the wolf from the door" during the Depression and which had greatly contributed to offsetting paying for mortgages and to continued education ceased. The legal action in New Mexico had not only signalled a change in attitude toward the role of religious in a changing world but had also demonstrated the precarious basis of religious economy throughout the nation. In August 1949, when Mother Victor told the sisters about the temporary closing of the Peñasco, New Mexico, mission she spoke also about the payment of lay teacher salaries:

*There is a community problem that I wish you to know first hand. It will be necessary to have lay teachers in many of our schools. Since the Community is not able financially to care for the salaries of these lay teachers, we have asked His Excellency Bishop Haas of this diocese and Monsignor Sonefeld of the Saginaw Diocese if that responsibility could be shouldered by the parishes. With that permission granted we have contacted the respective pastors, hence it will not be necessary for any principal to concern herself with lay-teacher salaries. Sisters, if a lay teacher has been assigned to your school, do all you can to make her a success and her work pleasant. We have no substitutes for these lay teachers.*

*...The acute teacher shortage this year is due to the fact that eleven Sisters who received teaching assignments last year will not be teaching this year. Some of these Sisters will be used in other types of work. ...*

In 1950-1951 the Archdiocese of Detroit issued revisions of its educational and financial policies, reinforcing the requirement of congregational assumption of lay compensation. Particularly in the rapidly growing Detroit area schools, this norm posed difficulties for the congregation. From the congregational standpoint it was better to close a school than to pay lay teachers in several schools.[11]

For two decades, from 1937 to 1957, the number of applicants to the congregation declined. There was, however, a certain stability to the membership. Departures from religious life were rare, a reflection both of contemporary theology of vocation and of societal patterns. Vocational choices were customarily made in the late teens and seldom reconsidered. Societal rejection of "former nuns" had not yet been fully eradicated. It was primarily ill health, advanced age, or death which reduced the number of sisters available.

At the same time, the postwar population boom created a national demand for more sisters in parochial schools and in hospital management and patient care. Mother Victor was confronted with a sea of petitions coming in for one more, two more sisters. The petitions came in formal letters, in Christmas greetings, by phone, telegram, in unscheduled visits of pastors in the parlor. Mother frequently wrote of having too few laborers for "fields ripe for the harvest," of an imbalance of "supply and demand," of being unable to provide sisters by either the "new" or "old" math.

In her letter to the sisters for Septuagesima Sunday, 1957, Mother urged the sisters to continue their vocation efforts:

*Vocation Month is just around the corner. I am enclosing a little resumé of the 1956 Notre Dame Vocation Institute. Peruse it carefully. It speaks for itself. We need vocations! Many, many vocations! Let us aim at 75--at least one from every mission.*

*May I ask that the Sisters do not urge their Reverend Pastors to see me to beg for Sisters. According to the wish of His Holiness the Community has initiated a program whereby all young religious will be better prepared than their predecessors. Who among us would wish it otherwise!!! The training of these young religious should not be interrupted to substitute for a Sister whom God has called or will call from the ranks. That there will be no additional teachers for September 1957 is obvious since our first group will have had only three years of college training by that time.*

*...Sisters, let us bear in mind since our Holy Father has recently requested that religious teachers be adequately prepared before beginning the work of the apostolate, souls will not be reaped and vocations will not be sown by shoddy performance in either the spiritual or the apostolic life. The Community dare not expect maximum blessings if it does not heed the voice of Christ's Vicar.*

*Principals and teachers should make an earnest effort to make their respective Pastors see the problem from the Community standpoint. The LAY teacher is now a permanent and important part of our school system and there will always be need for a number of them in our schools. Make plans immediately to retain LAY personnel (if satisfactory) or secure new LAY members for your 1957 faculty. Until such time as the Hierarchy of the United States will see fit to give the Sisterhoods a plan envisioning a radical redistribution of Sister-teachers in order to meet the almost overwhelming demands thrust upon them by the continuing growth of the Catholic school system, we shall try to carry on without closing any schools.*

There was no plan worked out for "radical redistribution." Mother and her council devised a working ratio of 80% sisters to 20% lay faculty, which was subsequently changed to 70% sisters to 30% lay. Congregational leaders, if not pastors and parishioners, saw a need for radical change in the parochial educational system at least a decade before Vatican Council II.

By the time the number of applicants increased, from about 1958 until 1970, new state regulations and formation philosophies required lengthened preparation. The congregation's largest class to date entered in the fall of 1959--53 postulants and 28 aspirants. There was a "full house" at Marywood; building was imperative. In 1958, the west wing roof garden was transformed into a dormitory and, in 1960, the House of Studies was begun on the college campus. It was a national phenomenon experienced by most "active" congregations: increased demand, increased supply, extensive building for intensive education and formation programs.

Building and education were, however, in "the real world" at current costs and specifications. The old quasi-monastic economy could no longer care for the increasingly aging population of congregations nor support the expansion.[12] The carefully regulated domestic economy by which congregations raised much of their own food, bought wholesale, made their own clothing and sometimes were fitted out in government surplus shoes; which relied on the charity of physicians and dentists and of sister congregations which owned hospitals; the economy which required festivals and fancywork and "collecting" to keep the system going could be stretched no further.

For fifty years the monthly salary ranged from $20 to $50 per sister in a parish role. Customarily half the salary was sent to the motherhouse for maintenance of the novitiate, care of the sick and elderly, continued education of all, and "seed money" for building programs. In December 1955 and again in June 1956 Mother Victor asked the bishops for a raise in salary to be paid over a twelve-month period and with some provision for hospitalization. On November 5, 1956, Bishop Babcock agreed to raise the salary to $75 per month for ten months, with the suggestion that

> the teaching sisters in the Diocese of Grand Rapids manifest an appreciation for the consideration given their community by being willing to aid pastors in supervising the care of the sanctuary and by aiding me in my attempt to look after the religious instruction of children in public schools by being willing to assist in this religious instruction when they are needed.

Mother Victor readily accepted. She wrote to Bishop Babcock on November 8, 1956:

> I am deeply grateful...the more so because I am well aware of the sacrifice it entails on the part of Pastors and people. ...To us it is a gift from Heaven that will lessen our worries in no small measure.

The sisters would give their cooperation "wherever and whenever it is possible." In the fall of 1962, Mother was again faced with the need to negotiate for a raise in the stipend. She wrote to Bishop Babcock on September 6, 1962, asking him to consider two facts:

> First: A picture of our present salary and our feeling that current expenses cannot be met from it. Last year the Community spent for Education alone $50,874 and for Medical Care over $40,000. Perhaps, a raise in the Diocesan salary scale plus some fringe benefits could be explored by you, Your Excellency, if you see fit.

> Second: Our present SUBSTITUTE lay-teacher problem. If a Sister becomes ill and is absent from her post for a time, the Community has been asked to pay whatever the substitute requests. At times, this has taken from our already depleted coffers the salary of four or more Sisters. I am wondering if some adjustment could be worked out regarding this.

The requests were repeated on August 6, 1963. That fall the Diocese of Grand Rapids developed a Handbook of Policies and Practices for Elementary and Secondary Schools. The salary was to be raised to $100 per month for each sister with an annual medical allotment of $75.[13] All congregations were to comply with fund raising regulations.

The lay-teacher dimension came to be viewed in a new perspective. Missions were no longer "ours," either in the sense that schools were "Dominican" or as fully-operated by members of the congregation with lay faculty there by a kind of temporary sufferance until more sisters could be found. The supply-demand imbalance, the need of congregations for larger stipends, the growing number of competent and certified lay faculty, and the expanded theology of lay participation--all changed the parochial system. What was once accepted by the sisters as extracurricular or unusual--catechism classes, "churchwork," adult programs, lay teachers--was soon to be transformed into the sisters' chief works and preferred way of collaboration.

# 18

# THE MIND OF THE CHURCH

*T*he first General Conference of the States of Perfection was held in Rome in 1950. The conference theme *De accomodata renovatione statuum perfectione*, "On Adapted Renewal of the States of Perfection," provided the agenda for the next two decades. In retrospect renewal and adaption within religious congregations touched four principal areas: the interior life and modifications in liturgical life; the manner of serving the neighbor; regular observance; the formation of young religious.[1]

The meeting itself has been linked to an extraordinary chain of developments, including the evolution of formal organizations of religious superiors. On the national level were the Conference of Major Superiors of Religious Congregations of Women (CMSW), forerunner of the Leadership Conference of Women Religious (LCWR), and the Conference of Major Superiors of Religious Congregations of Men (CMSM). On the international level was UISG, the International Union of Superiors General. These conferences, many institutes of spirituality, and the Sister Formation Conference, all contributed to the extraordinary transformation of religious women "from nuns to sisters."[2]

Mother Victor did not attend the first World Congress in 1950; she received, however, a summons in 1952. On September 7, 1952, in the customary letter to the sisters on the opening of the school year, Mother Victor informed them of a letter she had received from the apostolic delegate on August 30. There was to be a meeting of the General Superioresses of Institutes of Pontifical Approbation in Rome on September 11-13, 1952. It was imperative that all attend, and if that were impossible, a representative should be appointed. Mother Victor immediately contacted Mother Mary Dominic, mother general of the Dominican sisters in New Orleans and president of the Mothers General Conference, to represent the congregation. However, on September 4 she received a phone call from Father Timothy Sparks, OP, Socius to the Master General of the Dominican Order, telling her she must herself attend. There was, she wrote, "one very important matter to be discussed and Father Sparks worries about the result unless the American communities are there to present the AMERICAN side of the matter." Tickets and passport were secured for a September 9 departure with five other mothers general.

In her letter to the Sisters on Rosary Sunday, 1952, Mother gave an account of the journey:

*Yes, I am home! God bless you, one and all, for your prayers. The trip was most pleasurable. In addition to attendance at the meeting which our Holy Father [Pope Pius XII] called I was privileged to visit many shrines, etc., as you know from the snatches of letters assembled and sent to you before I returned. September 30 was my landing date, bringing me home in ample time to keep an October 1 appointment. Since you were kept abreast of my whereabouts up to September 22 I will give you a glimpse of the next few days.*

*Before leaving Florence we (the six mothers general) visited Prato where the body of St. Catherine di Ricci is preserved in a glass casket under the altar in the room in which she died. We were given a first-class relic of the saint. Our next stop was in Bologna where we assisted at Holy Mass at the tomb of St. Dominic. One of the Dominican Fathers who spoke English escorted us around the cloister, half of which the government has confiscated for a hospital. The entire building had been seized in 1810 and half of it returned in 1921.*

*From Bologna we went to Milan. We were very fortunate there as reservations had been made at the Berna Hotel which happens to be adjacent to the church of St. Camillus de Lellis. Holy Masses continue at one or more of the many altars from 6:00 a.m. until 12:00 p.m. A bus tour through the city with stopovers at many places brought us to the Milan Cathedral just as the Cardinal with a retinue of about twenty Bishops, fifty Monsignori, countless priests and a large group of the laity were proceeding to the High Altar for a Solemn Pontifical in honor of St. Thecla, one of the patronesses of the cathedral. Such an array of color! The festooning above the altar was out of this world.*

*Leaving Milan for Paris Thursday I had little hope of getting a reservation, but while the other Mothers were in the TWA office arranging for their Lourdes trip a message came from Rome that a cancellation had just come in and that I was to receive the place. I was both happy and sad--happy that I could keep the appointment that was going to mean money for the community [building program] but sad since it meant that I would not be able to see Lourdes, as the only return flight to Paris would have been September 29 and I was scheduled to leave the day before.*

*A little later, when I have had time to organize my notes, I will give you a resume of the analysis of the needs of the Church today as outlined for us by His Holiness....*

The mixture of elements--a pilgrimage to Dominican shrines, the panoply of ecclesiastical splendor, the imperatives of fund-raising at home and the longing for a visit to Lourdes--all against the need for "time to organize," to study "the needs of the Church today," and the need for consideration of "the American side of the matter" presaged what would become a major work, one of both dismantling and construction, that would engage sisters for decades to come.[3]

The value of a Roman component in the formation of women religious had been stressed in the September 1952 conference. In October 1954 the Roman Institute of Sacred Studies, *Regina Mundi*, was opened. The Cardinal Prefect of the Sacred Congregation of Religious asked the bishops of the world to promote the new institute.[4] Mother Victor responded, "We shall do our best, when circumstances permit, to avail ourselves of the opportunities offered."[5] A house in Rome had been one of the original and recurring emphases of the Dominican Mothers General Conference, though by 1955 it was under the broader description of "training of young sisters and novice mistresses." Dominican leaders, along with the leadership of the Sister Formation Conference, watched the development of Regina Mundi with interest.

With Mother Victor there appeared to be none of the caution that some congregations had for the Sister Formation Conference. She found it a major source of help for the task at hand. The conference had the full approval of the Vatican's Congregation for Religious and was jointly sponsored by the National Catholic Education Association and the Conference of Major Superiors of Women then under the leadership of Sister Mary Daniel Turner, SNDdeN. It was simply "the mind of the Church." Mother and Sister Cecile Byrne,[6] mistress of novices, attended the Sister Formation Conference in St. Louis, Missouri, in January 1955. The council approved modest donations toward the support of the conference secretariate.[7] The familiar blue *Sister Formation Bulletin* became part of early feminist literature in convents of the congregation.

The central emphasis of the Sister Formation Conference was the content of formation programs for young religious, thorough professional training and a sound theological grounding. There was widespread discussion on what made a "complete religious," with resultant model curricula, mental health workshops, and institutes of spirituality, especially throughout the Midwest.

Intercongregational collaboration became widespread. "Credentials" became a watchword. There were also appointments for advanced study for professed sisters, either as future faculty at the college or for educational and health care positions throughout the dioceses.[8] Summer study continued for all members of the congregation, now intensified with workshops, pre-service, in-service and mini-courses, and interim sessions. In the 1960's, with the increase of candidates and the new philosophy of professional preparation, there was extensive building in congregations of religious women to provide houses of formation.

The decision to keep the younger members "in" for extended training required fortitude. The expanding mission field and growing urban schools created a great demand, while the aging of congregational membership decreased the supply. September 1957 was set by the Chapter of 1954 as the target date for the beginning of a comprehensive formation program. In the meantime, novitiate classes would remain for a second, and if possible, a third year of college work. Implementing the new formation program was Mother Victor's most difficult task.[9] It was also one which contributed to a new conception of mission and religious life.[10]

The effects of the decision were influential in the work of the fourteenth General Chapter. On June 17, 1960, in the presence of Bishop Babcock and instructed by him in the requirements of postulation, the Chapter voted to send to the Holy See a postulation, a formal request to set aside the constitutional provision limiting the term of office to two six-year terms. A two-thirds vote was required by canon law; 53 of 79 votes cast were for postulation. It was virtually a vote to extend Mother Victor's administration to eighteen years. The petitioners, the general councilors, and secretary of the Chapter, cited Mother Victor's good health--she had celebrated her sixty-fifth birthday on April 5, 1960, with no physical problems--and gave five reasons for the extraordinary request:

*1. Our novitiate has more than doubled in the past twelve years, due in great measure to Mother Victor's efforts, encouragement, and approachability.*

*2. Retaining our young Sisters at the Motherhouse for more adequate spiritual and professional training has created a grave problem, which will extend over the next few years, or until a sufficient number has been prepared to again insure the normal flow of workers into the apostolate. Eminent prudence and tact are needed in this situation.*

*3. Due to the growth of the Congregation during the past six years and particularly in the past three years,[11] the launching of an extensive building program has been necessary, to provide room for our postulants and our temporarily professed Sister students. New hospital and college buildings are under construction or in the planning stage. Another six years would give time for completion of these works.*

*4. Aside from her knowledge of the existing situation and the extraordinary organizational ability which makes Mother Victor's guidance seem almost indispensable, the Sisters express themselves as feeling that her deep spirituality is needed to direct us at this particular time. She has ruled with firmness and kindness. Her motherliness makes her accessible to each and every one at all times. The sick and aging Sisters are her special care, and the time is at hand when more extensive provision must be made for them. Another building will be needed.*

*5. Above all, Mother's prayer life and dependence on Divine Providence are a source of inspiration.*

The postulation was confirmed by the Holy See on July 28, 1960, and received on August 9, 1960.[12] The Chapter resumed on August 17, 1960, for the election of the general council and the business at hand. Sisters Aline Needham, Leonard Lynch, Norbert (Marjorie) Vangsness, and Agnes Leo Hauser[13] were elected as councilors. It was Sister Aline's third term as councilor to Mother Victor. Sisters Joachim Visner and Felix Brand were reelected as secretary general and treasurer.

The five-point petition to the Holy See had set forth the congregational agenda as the capitulars saw it for the next six years. In the Chapter there were, however, intimations of things to come: discussions on the use of the Divine Office and other prayers in English, the abolition of order of precedence in receiving communion, limitation of the wearing of mantles, slight modifications of the habit, and the development of a project similar to the religious correspondence school. The Chapter was conducted in the traditional manner: ordinances of the previous Chapter were reviewed and new propositions relating to discipline, clothing,[14] rubrics, education, methods of election of delegates, and the works of the sisters were considered. Precedent remained a common resolution. There were, however, new authorities being cited, among them the *Sister Formation Bulletin*, which was quoted in a discussion on the preparation of sisters for administrative positions. Chapter was not yet the agent for major change that it would come to be within the decade.

Mother Victor's final six years in office largely coincided with the chronology of Vatican Council II. On January 25, 1959, at the close of the Church Unity Octave, Pope John XXIII announced to the world his intention of summoning a general council. The last general or ecumenical council, Vatican Council I, had closed in 1870, almost a century before. On December 25, 1961, Vatican Council II was solemnly convoked. The first session ran from October 11, 1962, to December 8, 1962. On June 3, 1963, Pope John XXIII died and within a month he was succeeded by Giovanni Baptista Montini, Pope Paul VI. From September 29, 1963, to December 4, 1963, the council met in its second session. The following year, from September 14, 1964, to November 21, 1964, the council held its third session. A fourth and final session was opened on September 14, 1965. On December 8, 1965, Vatican Council II was solemnly closed.

The Council proved to be not only an extraordinary chapter in church history but an event of global proportions. As church women the sisters eagerly welcomed news of the council in the secular and religious press. The conciliar documents served both as revelation and reformation for religious and lay alike. The 1960's proved to be a decade of extraordinary visual images: the panoply of council, of papal funerals, coronations, and visits abroad; of nations shaken by coups and by assassination.

While the 1960 General Chapter did not provide a legislative agenda for Mother Victor and her council, there were indicators for study and preparation for change. This was a mark of her final administration: a careful consideration of the signs of the times and a planned, controlled adjustment. In September 1960 she appointed a committee to translate into English the congregational prayers said in Latin. Fall 1964 brought the first major visible change. On September 27, English was first used in the refectory prayers at Marywood, and on Rosary Sunday, October 3, the Little Office of the Blessed Virgin in English was first recited in choir at Marywood. In Advent of that year, English was partially used in the celebration of Mass. On Passion Sunday, March 27, 1966, the first liturgy completely in English was celebrated at Marywood. Immediately after Easter Sunday, 1966, renovation of the Marywood chapel was begun so that, reported the congregational annalist, "the celebration of the Sacred liturgical rites may take place in an appropriate and artistic setting."[15]

In February 1965 Mother Victor invited sisters professed between fifteen and twenty-five years to participate in a "renovation program" for the month of July at Holy Rosary Academy, Bay City. Father Vincent M. Reilly, OP, of the St. Joseph Province directed the "tertianship" for forty-five sisters in July 1965 and again in 1966.

There were also renovations under way on a congregational level. On May 31, 1966, the Sacred Congregation of Religious granted to superiors of religious congregations powers formerly reserved to the Sacred Congregation or to the apostolic delegate. In the case of alienation of property and the contraction of debts, formerly reserved to Rome, norms were to be set by national or regional conferences of bishops. Dispensations from temporary vows, allowances of leave of absence for study, health, or the apostolate, among other matters, were now the prerogative of congregational officials. Dispensation, which had been a valued feature of Dominican governance since the Middle Ages, was extended throughout the polity of the Church. In some respects, the campaign Mother Eveline had waged on a diocesan level had been resolved for the universal Church.

In April 1966 the Postconciliar Commission on Religious sent directives to all congregations explicating the conciliar document *Perfectae Caritatis* and its principles for the "appropriate renewal of religious life." A new vocabulary was added to the lexicon of religious policy-making and values: "collegiality," "subsidiarity," "dialogue," "theologizing," "experimentation," "mandate." The documentary groundwork was laid, the first steps of re-formation of the ethos and work of the congregation taken in Mother Victor's final years. It was, nevertheless, a process fully monitored by Mother Victor.

For many the changes were experiences of joy, for others, of loss-- aesthetic and ascetic--of the familiar and the universal. Marble altars, gold-leaf embellishment and familiar statues were replaced with wood paneling, handmade banners and a table altar facing the congregation. The otherworldliness of Gregorian chant gave way to a sometimes prosaic English psalmody. Rank and precedence, which had once provided a sense of order and stability, were shaken if not gone; new patterns were yet to emerge. Sister formation, received in the novitiate and reinforced by annual retreats and by the mothers general from Mother Aquinata to Mother Victor in letters, visitation, and admonition, had been built on the premise that religious had left the world and were essentially different from the laity. Long after the grilles were removed from the parlors of Holy Angels convent, "cloister" remained a feature of religious outlook. The motherhouse provided a sylvan retreat from "the world."

In a practical way sisters had been the "teaching Church" for generations of American Catholics. In parochial schools and outreach programs, sisters presented the truths of the Faith, they showed the way through an otherwise mysterious liturgy, they encouraged a range of piety and social action. "Sister says" had been for many the local manifestation of the universal authority of the Church. Nevertheless, forging congregational and individual outlooks on the challenges posed by the times was difficult for the sisters. For women whose Rule and formation had enjoined deference toward others and restrained discourse, dialogue was a hard-earned skill. The recreation periods which had been part of the daily horary had not generally led to sustained theological discourse, scriptural reflection, or what would come to be called values clarification.

In 1962 the sisters at Aquinas College priory began a weekly discussion of Cardinal Suenens' *The Nun in the Modern World*. They began also to pray the office in English on "an experimental basis," the formula provided by Vatican Council II for the first tentative modifications of horary, prayer forms, modes of government, and eventually of habit. New forms of asceticism were required. For sisters as well as lay persons the conciliar and post-conciliar years were times of major transformation.

Since the summons to Rome in 1952, the call to religious superiors to commit to foreign ministry had become increasingly strong. In April 1958 Pope Pius XII created the Pontifical Commission on Latin America. Cardinal Marcello Mimmi, the president, appealed to the Dominican Mothers General Conference for financial support, for the encouragement of study among its membership, and for missioners to Latin America. The Reverend Michael Browne, OP, Master General of the Order, wrote to all Dominican Mothers General on September 3, 1958:

*As in the time of our Saviour, so also today, the harvest is great but the laborers are so few. His Holiness is surely not unmindful of the great demands made upon our Daughters in St. Dominic for assistance in their own country, especially in the field of teaching personnel. But the need for help in Latin America is so urgent that He calls out to them to do whatever lies in their power to help save thousands of souls, already children of the Church through Baptism, who are in danger of losing, or who have already lost the priceless gift of Faith.*

*The apostolate in Latin America is in a special way, a truly Dominican work. Our Father, St. Dominic, labored among those who were in much the same sad situation as the peoples of Latin America are today. May his spiritual Daughters "mindful of the rock from which they have been hewn," be "champions of the faith and true lights" in the world of Latin America, so dear to the paternal heart of His Holiness, the Vicar of Christ.*

In March 1960 Mother Victor sent a donation to the Commission on Latin America towards the support of a Latin American priest's study in Rome. In August 1961 a representative of the Holy See, Monsignor Casaroli of the Secretariat of State, spoke to the Conferences of Major Superiors of Men and Women at the University of Notre Dame. It was, he said, the wish of Pope John XXIII that religious congregations send 10% of their personnel to Latin America. To the many congregations present the much-publicized tithe spelled urgency and sacrifice, if not a literal possibility.

The commitment to a foreign mission was a venture equal to the ventures of Mother Eveline, full of risk and requiring endless consultation and planning. There is, however, no record of formal commitment to foreign ministry in the proceedings of the General Chapter of 1960 nor in the minutes of the general council. In her customary fall letter inaugurating the beginning of the 1961-1962 mission year, Mother Victor wrote:

*At the recent National Congress of Religious held at Notre Dame, August 16-19, the Most Reverend Egidio Vagnozzi, apostolic delegate to the United States, the Most Reverend Antonio Samore, Archbishop of Tirnovo, Secretary of the Pontifical Commission for Latin America, and the Reverend John Considine, MM, Director of the Latin American Bureau, NCWC, emphasized the pressing needs of the Church in the Latin American countries. Each in turn tried to analyze for the assembled Major Superiors the **Appeal** of the **Holy See** which has been directed not to **Superiors** but to **Institutes**. All exhorted us to give personnel--not merely what could be spared but to sacrifice the best. Each Congregation was urged to assume a definite responsibility over a ten-year period.*

*Our council has not yet had ample opportunity or time for discussion as to what our plan will be; however, know that the Community will do its share. With this in mind I am asking for volunteers for this new mission work with the following qualifications:*

> *Good health, professed between ten and twenty years, and a truly apostolic mission-minded religious.*

*There must be a period of study before undertaking the arduous task and those selected for the work will receive definite information within the next three years. God's blessing will be with us if we try--in spite of our very grave needs at home-to serve in a small way the exploding population of Latin America.[16]*

The call for volunteers echoed Mother Eveline's *Klosterberufe Gesunde, brave Madchen...nach Amerika* of thirty-five years before. It marked as well a new chapter in the relation of Church and congregation to the changing world.

In the spring of 1962 the Dominican Fathers of St. Joseph Province were invited to direct the prelature of Chimbote, Perú. Father Richard Vahey, OP, the province's director of foreign missions, advised the provincial, Father William Marrin, to accept. By December the province had officially accepted, and transferred Father James C. Burke[17] from Concepción, Chile, to Chimbote. The decision of the Dominican Fathers, with whom the congregation had collaborated closely, appears to have been influential in the choice of site for the mission of the congregation in the third world.[18]

On October 29, 1962, the congregation extended its blessing to Sisters Marie Dominica Viesnoraitis and Herman Marie Maez, the volunteers chosen for the Latin American mission. They were enroute to Cuernavaca, Mexico, for linguistic and cultural preparation at the Center for Intercultural Formation. The four-month program, under the direction of Monsignor Ivan D. Illich, was a rich blend of theology, Scripture, cultural enrichment and social analysis of the Latin world. There were, as well, practical pastoral assignments in the *barriadas* of Mexico City. Informally the sisters were incorporated in a network of missioners, religious and lay, single and families, working in Mexico, Central and South America, who provided mutual assistance and support.[19]

The sisters wrote home each month, their long letters a form of missionary *relationes* and a consciousness-raising source for the entire congregation. On December 29, 1962, midway in their course in Mexico, they wrote:

*[In early December] Father Illich met the eight American sisters at 4:00 in our recreation room. He is leaving for Brazil this coming week and wanted to have a little visit with us before departing. He won't be back until January. He runs a school there similar to this one. He told us how, in a way, all of us who would be the first ones in our new missions, would be the foundresses not of an Order or Congregation but of the* **spirit** *of our Order.*

From December 28, 1962, to January 11, 1963, Mother Victor and Sister Aline were in Perú to further the groundwork for the part the Dominican sisters of Grand Rapids would take in the mission field of Perú. They were welcomed in Lima by Romolo Carboni, apostolic nuncio, with whom Mother Victor had corresponded throughout the latter months of 1962. There was a round of visits, sight-seeing, and consultation, and then the arduous trip on to Chimbote, some 250 miles north of Lima in the province of Santa. Within a ten-year period Chimbote had grown from a fishing village of 5,000 to an industrial center of some 120,000. Many of the Indian-Spanish people had recently come from the surrounding mountains to the arid seacoast village to take advantage of the expanding fish-processing and steel industries. The population grew to a quarter million within the first decade after the sisters' arrival.

Upon her return, Mother wrote Cardinal Cushing, Archbishop of Boston and chairman of the Bishops' Committee for Latin America, in what she called her "first begging letter":

*In planning to send personnel to Latin America we are finding the financial responsibility involved in building a convent beyond our means. Chimbote--the challenge of the Andes--where the population explosion has left much to be desired by way of living conditions, is our choice. The poverty of the people, the sudden population growth without adequate religious instruction, and the Peruvian law which requires at least one hour of such instruction a week for all children, have been some of the determining factors in this choice.*

*The St. James Fathers whom we met at Chimbote and the Dominican Fathers at the Language School feel that the answer for this decade is catechetical work in the public schools....*

*Two of our Sisters presently studying at Cuernavaca will be leaving for Chimbote February 15 and temporary accommodations have been provided for them. Their work for this school year will be to assist the Sisters of St. Joseph from St. Louis who are staffing one of the few already erected schools. By 1964 our Community wishes to have eight Sisters there doing catechetical work.* [20]

The motivation reflects Mother Victor's fundamental orientation to the Church and the apostolic nature of its mission. It was for her a matter of "salvation of souls." There was as well a spirit of adaptability and availability. The work "for this decade" was to be catechetical.

*18*  309  *The Mind of the Church*

Mother also wrote to all the sisters on February 2, 1963. In the thirteen-page letter, the longest in her eighteen-year administration, she told of her first impressions of Chimbote,

*Leaving sunny Perú with temperatures around 80 daily and arriving here twelve hours later to be welcomed by a six below temperature placed me in a horizontal position with a severe cold for more hours than I would care to disclose....*

*Wednesday, January 2...we left the hotel [Chimu Hotel, Chimbote] to locate the St. James Fathers to find out **when** and **where** Holy Mass would be offered the next day.*

*Looking a bit lost as we walked along the only paved sidewalk in town, a lady came to our assistance and offered to have her husband who was manager of a local gas station drive us to the place where she thought the Fathers lived. After driving a short distance we learned the Fathers had moved.... By this time darkness had fallen, and with very few lights to show us the way plus MUD roads to hinder our progress, we finally reached the place--a two-apartment building. By Chimbote standards it was a palace! Fathers Moore, Mitchell, Murphy and Clarke urged us to come in and SIT on their new furniture, which had been acquired just two weeks prior to our coming....Their comments were not discouraging; neither were they encouraging. They stressed the necessity of doing catechetical work in the public schools. Then Father Moore offered to drive us back to the hotel and promised to call for us at 7:15 a.m. for Mass in the little chapel at 7:30. Our dear Lord loved poverty, but I am wondering if the Manger Crib was not in better condition to house the God of Heaven!*

*...Sisters, the population has mushroomed with such rapidity that the poor have absolutely NO comforts. By comparison the slum areas of the U.S. are palatial. Since all Peruvians are Catholics, at least nominally, you can see how they look to anyone who may be of help to them, although they appear very happy and would probably continue their existence in poverty without much ado. It is very easy to influence the poor who have nothing to lose--or so they think. The mentality of the Peruvian seems such that even the better class see no wrong in being a Communist. The Chinese Communists are now stronger in Perú than the Russian Communists. Many study in China. Eleven Chinese cells came to Perú in 1962. In Lima students are refused admission at San Marco University and are given scholarships to Havana. They are transported in Cuban ships.*

*If ever the fields were ripe and ready for harvesting, Chimbote is! The race is on--Communism or Catholicism! Which will eventually carry the laurels of victory may depend entirely on an all-out effort on the part of the missionaries. We can't all **go** but we can all **pray** that those working there, under the most primitive conditions, be not too discouraged when they labor so hard and that there seems to be no visible sign of success. Without a doubt Chimbote is the challenge of the Andes!*

Fear of Communism was part of the perspective of the times, part of the ethos of cold war and of Roman Catholicism's condemnation of "atheistic materialism." The transformation of Cuba was in its early stages; the missile crisis in the Caribbean but a few months past. Communism would prove to be less a menace than the overwhelming economic and social burdens left by colonialism and maintained by self-serving native regimes and, since 1980, the terrorist movements which have disrupted the country.

On February 16, 1963, Sisters Marie Dominica and Herman Marie landed on Peruvian soil. For several days they stayed with the Maryknoll sisters and later with the Sisters of St. Joseph at the Military Hospital in Lima. These sisters served as a kind of apostolic port of entry, giving hospitality and assistance to sisters of thirty-six congregations as they moved in and out of the country. Early in 1962 the Dominican sisters of Adrian began their work in La Perla Callau near Lima. The Dominican sisters of New Orleans established a mission in Perú in 1964, and the Dominicans from St. Mary of the Springs, Ohio, settled in Chimbote in 1965.

On Tuesday, March 12, 1963, a *colectivo*, the public taxi service, brought the two Grand Rapids sisters over the Andean foothills to the Pacific seaport of Chimbote. Sisters Martina, David Marie and Kathleen, three Sisters of St. Joseph of Carondolet, St. Louis, shared their small home with them for over a year. They had come to Chimbote the previous month and taken over a school for the children of the employees of the Santa Steel Corporation. The Dominican sisters of Grand Rapids and the St. Joseph sisters shared a fruitful ministry of education and health care in the area. Mother Victor had prepared the way for that collaboration with Mother Eucharista, superior general of the Sisters of St. Joseph. In the months the sisters were settling in Chimbote a community of Dominican fathers was also being formed. Monsignor James C. Burke, OP, and his Dominican confreres became familiar helpers and colleagues of more than twenty American women religious laboring there in 1963.

In May 1964 *Convento San Martín* was ready. The four-room cement block building was constructed with funds from Bishop Burke and the St. James fathers. It was located along the Pan American highway in San Martín parish, Miraflores, since 1962 in the care of priests of the Missionary Society of St. James the Apostle, the group of American diocesan priests founded by Cardinal Cushing for missionary work in Latin America.[21] The congregation provided furnishings, dispatching at one time ten trunks of household goods and sending sufficient monies for goods

Photograph of bearer

Jennie (Jane) Flannery
Mother Mary Victor

No. 726741

PASSPORT

United States
of America

U.S. DEPT. OF JUSTICE
ADMITTED
SEP 29 1952
NEW YORK
N.Y.
IMMIG. & NAT'Z SERVICE

LLEGADA
LIMA - CALLAO
DIC 29 1962
Permanencia Autorizada
NOVENTA (90) DIAS
DIC

Visas
ROMA
(AEROP. CIAMPINO)
10. SET. 1952
3 ENTRATA 3

SALIDA
LIMA - CALLAO
ENE 11 1963

SÛRETÉ NATIONALE - PARIS
28 SEP 1952
SORTIE

REPUBLICA DEL PERU
LIMA - CALLAO
SET 22 1965
SALIDA

DEL PERU
SET 11 1965

*Traveling beyond the thirty-mile limit. Mother Victor travels to Italy and Perú.*

*Departure blessing, October 30, 1962, Sisters Marie Dominica Viesnoraitis and Herman Marie Maez with Mother Victor Flannery at Grand Rapids airport*

*Sister Marie Dominica and lay catechist in **chosa** school*

TOP
First Communion Day
December 1, 1963

BOTTOM
Visit to the **Asilo de San José**

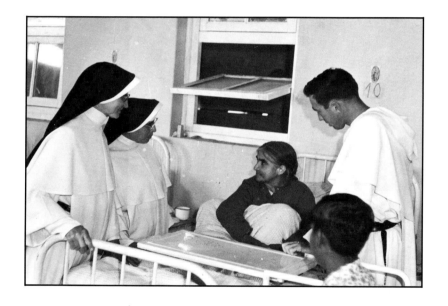

FACING PAGE

TOP
Honorary Degree reception, Aquinas College, May 30, 1965. Bishop Babcock, Mother Victor, Monsignor Bukowski. Congressman Gerald R. Ford in background.

BELOW
Funeral Mass for five Dominican Sisters, October 2, 1962. St. Thomas the Apostle church, Grand Rapids

to be purchased in Perú. The convent was included in the Cardinal's two-day visit to Chimbote in 1964. He found it pleasing, the sisters reported, because "it smacks of poverty." In May 1965 several rooms were added, a gift of Cardinal Cushing, to accommodate the growing community.

Initially the sisters joined the Sisters of St. Joseph as faculty in the privately funded school. While the school was neither public nor parochial, it was subject to the Ministry of Education. The faculty became acquainted with the intricacies of government regulation and bi-monthly examinations in the April-to-December school year. The children were mostly of middle class origins, and the program was a traditional elementary program. The sisters called upon their American colleagues for assistance with school supplies, teaching aids, and religious articles.

Situating their main work in an educational institution for the middle class represented a current mission perspective: the need to educate the leaders and managers of the next generation. As Mother Victor had anticipated, the overwhelming poverty of the Chimbotans soon took the sisters into the *barriadas*. In July 1963 they began catechetical work in the *Barriada Acero* in the poorest section of the city. The number of children grew each week, far surpassing those in the regular school. A Mission Fund was established to channel donations from the congregation to Chimbote.

On August 18, 1963, the congregation held a formal departure ceremony for Sisters Maria Teresita Garcia and Georgiana Kowalski, missioning them to Chimbote. Mother Victor selected the Institute of Intercultural Communications at the Catholic University of Puerto Rico for their training. They arrived in Perú on December 17, 1964, and shared the work of school teaching and catechesis. Eventually only Sister Herman Marie taught in the grammar school, the other three working in the *barriada*. Sister Herman Marie was, the sisters wrote, on May 18, 1964:

*...our breadwinner. The three of us are earning no salary for our catechetical work. We are depending on her salary and your sacrifices for our livelihood....One lady said that our community had provided the best for us as a good father sacrifices to provide the best for a daughter who is leaving his home to begin her own.*

*...Schools are multiplying rapidly and preparing teachers is the only answer to the need. This year there are over 2,000 children of school age in Chimbote who are not in school due to lack of educational facilities or, in some cases, extremely poor economic conditions in families. ...By Tuesday evening we are footsore from walking through the soft brown sand from one school to another all day, mentally exhausted from thinking and teaching in Spanish, and "heart-sore" at seeing so much poverty and misery, but we are happy and satisfied that we've reached so many souls and brought them some of the truth of God.*

From year to year the designated "breadwinner" changed. To the work of formal education and catechesis was added care of the elderly in the *Asilo de San José*, a home for the aged near the convent, and a commitment to conduct a maternity clinic. The congregation's next missioners reflected the changing emphases: Sisters Rosemary Homrich, Innocence Andres and Margaret Mary Birchmeier were registered nurse-midwives. Sister Rosemary arrived in Perú on June 22, 1965. In their July 25, 1965, letter to the congregation the sisters remarked:

*On August 1st Sister [Rosemary] will take over the **Asilo** completely. Please pray for her as our Community has undertaken a truly tremendous responsibility--those beginning life (at the Maternity Hospital) and those at the eve of life (in the Old Age Home). We catechists come in between. This is interesting as well as advantageous as now our work is such that it has an appeal for everyone.*

Sisters Innocence and Margaret Mary were the last sisters Mother Victor assigned to Chimbote.[22] In preparation they attended the intercultural training program at the Catholic University of Puerto Rico and an eight-month midwifery course in Santa Fe. Mother accompanied them to Perú, arriving in Chimbote on September 12, 1965, and remaining until September 19, 1965. She brought news that the community need no longer have a resident breadwinner. The congregation and its network of Chimbote supporters would underwrite the mission to allow all the sisters to serve in the most direct way possible.[23]

During the fall of 1965 a maternity hospital of thirteen beds was built in the parish, constructed and equipped with funds from the United States. A small outpatient clinic, the *Posta Médica de San Martín*, begun in 1963 with a Peace Corps nurse volunteer and a local aide, grew into a flourishing clinic. Medical supplies, often solicited by the sisters in Michigan, sometimes came with visitors or in trunks with catechetical materials. In 1971, under the direction of Sister John Cassian Logue, SSJ, from Kalamazoo, Michigan, a laboratory was developed to provide diagnostic services to the maternity hospital and the outpatient clinic.[24]

The ministry of the sisters encompassed the range of the spiritual and corporal works of mercy: instructing the ignorant, clothing the naked, healing the sick, comforting the bereaved, and burying the dead. It was as well a work of advocacy, bringing the needs of the people to the attention of national and international agencies, and to churches and communities throughout the United States. *Convento San Martín*, Chimbote, remains to the present one of the most vital manifestations of congregational commitment to evangelization and to healing presence.[25]

In the exchange of letters between Mother Victor and Father Vahey, OP, which ultimately led to her selection of Chimbote, Father Vahey referred to a recent congregational publication, *Salve Regina, Mater Misericordiae*. It was a memorial booklet for a tragic event in the congregational history. On Friday evening, September 28, 1962, seven sisters from St. John's, Essexville, were travelling north to Lake Leelanau. Their station wagon was struck by an oncoming car near Mesick, Michigan. Four of the sisters died immediately: Sisters Ferdinand Bauer, Rose Imelde DeHaus, Joseph Ann Popp, and Jeanne Anne Brunett. Three others were critically injured: Sister Phyllis Schoenborn, Wenceslaus Szosinski, and Olga Mizzi. A physician from Jackson, Michigan, was an eyewitness and gave immediate aid. A priest, state policemen and doctors from Cadillac came immediately. Sister Phyllis was taken to the hospital in Reed City where she died on Sunday, September 30, just as the four caskets reached Marywood. Sisters Wenceslaus and Olga were taken by ambulance to Mercy Hospital, Cadillac, and later to St. Mary Hospital, Grand Rapids, to begin months of convalescence. The driver of the speeding car and his passenger, a 44 year-old man and his mother from nearby Beulah, were killed in the crash.

At the time of the accident Mother Victor was in Columbia, Missouri, enroute to the Southwest for the annual visitation of the missions. She immediately returned to Grand Rapids to comfort the injured, make funeral arrangements, and plan for the educational needs of the Essexville community. There were messages of condolence from throughout the state and nation. Some sent stipends for Masses, donations toward the funeral expenses, offers to assist in the school hard pressed with the loss of seven sisters, promises of convalescent care for the injured. There were letters from former students, one who as a child had seen old Holy Rosary

Academy in Essexville burn in 1904; from graduates of Grand Rapids' Catholic Central studying at Marquette University; from leaders of hundreds of religious congregations; from hospital aides in Cadillac and Reed City; from priests throughout the country; and from bishops gathering in Rome for the first session of Vatican Council II. The letters were pages in the story of the congregation's ministry for almost a century. "Yes," wrote one woman, "the whole church mourns."

On 10 a.m., Tuesday, October 2, the funeral was held at the parish church of St. Thomas the Apostle in Grand Rapids. Dominican Fathers Charles P. Wilson, Adrian T. English,[26] and John Hart said the Solemn Mass of Burial in the Dominican rite. Thirty high school boys from Essexville ushered in the five caskets, four to the front, one at center aisle. Sisters of the congregation, grieving families, representatives of Church and state, and Essexville and Bay City students filled the church, the church basement, and the church yard to say farewell. Congregational hospitality included a meal for the many hundreds who attended the funeral. On October 8, the nearly 1,000 pupils returned to St. John school, Essexville, staffed the week previously by twelve Dominican sisters and twelve lay faculty.

While there had been congregational growth in so many areas--new buildings, new works, new members--the suddenness and magnitude of loss shocked the congregation. It was, as well, the personal loss of five beloved colleagues, three of whom had blood sisters in the congregation. In Mother Victor and the congregation's name a notice of gratitude was sent to the Catholic papers of the state:

*It is with hearts full of gratitude that we, the Dominican Sisters of Marywood, express our deepest appreciation to our countless friends and benefactors for their many spiritual and material manifestations of sympathy in our recent bereavement. Such expression of faith and Christian charity helped greatly to lessen the sorrow which Divine Providence willed to send us when He called to Himself five of our beloved Sisters.*

What Mother Victor called "the night of our greatest sorrow" became woven into the congregational fabric:  a final departure ceremony for five at month's beginning, a departure ceremony for two to mission in Latin America at month's end. Her capacity to carry on in the midst of such sorrow was a further measure of Mother Victor's leadership and spirituality.

On September 22, 1964, in a letter inaugurating the school year, Mother included a list of particulars under the title "Family Bulletin." The range of topics was an indication of both the continuities and changes the sisters were experiencing. There were the dates of coming festivals at Marywood, Holy Rosary, and Aquinas College; reminders on prayers for the session of the General Council, on having the weekly chapter of faults, and on the necessity of reading all decrees from the Holy See; directions on how to order rosary materials, and on the tone to be used for chanting of refectory prayers. There was also a list of Suggested Books for Spiritual Reading and Meditation, a list which included both old classics and works by contemporary authors, such as Adrian Van Kaam, Karl Rahner, and Barnabas Ahern. The sisters were at the same time reminded of a protocol from the Sacred Congregation for Religious restricting the use of television and radio. There were to be no private sets, and "except for NEWS programs and instructive and religious programs, superiors MUST or at least may consider all other programs to be contrary to the religious spirit, especially if they are watched merely for recreational purposes."[27]

Less than a month later, on the Feast of Saints Simon and Jude, 1964, Mother wrote a reflective letter on the challenges of the times and of the "new face of poverty":

*The rapid changes and continued progress of our times will take extreme **poverty of spirit** not to **cling too much** to the past. The present is our challenge and we must meet it as Dominic would were he here today! In short, Sisters, what you and I must do today to be witnesses to Christ in the world is: **Find** Dominic's **tune** for this nuclear space age; **find** what our **witness** be and then **adapt** Dominic's tune to these needs.*

*...Let us take up the challenge set before us and as good Dominicans throughout the centuries have always done, co-operate in every possible way with the clergy that the NEW LOOK the Vatican Council wishes may materialize according to the inspiration of the Holy Spirit.*

In preparation for the fifteenth General Chapter in June 1966, Mother reminded the sisters of the decision of the 1960 Chapter to delay a thorough revision of the Constitution until after the changes which were "inevitable in the wake of the Vatican Council." On September 22, 1964, she asked each sister to study the Constitution and to submit on index cards suggestions article by article. Constitutional revision would be a persistent work for the next twenty-five years.[28]

On June 3, 1966, Mother wrote her last letter to the congregation, a blend of the customary reflection on the closing of the school year, on endings and beginnings, on committing the past to God, and on the central themes of Dominican spirituality: "our patrimony from our Holy Father...based on work, study, and prayer." She concluded with a valedictory to the congregation:[29]

*No other Prioress General of the Grand Rapids Dominican Sisters has ever been so deeply indebted to this Community as I am. Your spirit of cooperation at every turn, your many sacrifices to further each and every project initiated by the General Council, your long hours spent on the study of the Constitutions that the delegates may be presented with the thinking of the Community as a whole, your many prayers when the acceptance of God's plan involved dangerous and difficult demands, your encouragement when the future, unrolling a panorama of splendid but terrible scenes, provoked anxiety beyond endurance, and finally your desire to be true Dominican religious in this era of turmoil when religious life is not quite fashionable and is questioned by so many--ALL make me indebted eternally to you.*

*Know, too, that as I leave office I carry with me the memory of many great women in this Community--women who have given me a much clearer understanding of my own Community--women who have increased my desire and capacity to serve God's Church. For all I am deeply grateful.*

*And now, one last THANK YOU. May the Prince of Peace lavish His choicest blessings on you for your boundless generosity to me.*

The letter closed with her customary "Sincerely in Mary Immaculate, Mother."

On Monday, June 13, 1966, forty-six delegates to the fifteenth General Chapter convened at Marywood. Mother prefaced her official report of her administration with remarks on the nature of the tasks at hand:

*We are assembled here today to take the steps preliminary to the election of a Prioress General. This group of delegates is assuming a tremendous task in a time when the whole Church seems to be in a state of flux and turmoil--much of it caused by devotees of some particular statement taken out of context from one pronouncement or other. The matters to be treated as well as the time it is being held give great importance to this Chapter. We must proceed slowly. Not all the NEW is good nor is all the OLD--bad. It will take much prayer, prudence and working together for a common goal to have these days--when completed ratified in heaven.*

*...May I paraphrase from St. Augustine and say: "What I have been for you terrifies me: what I am with you consoles me. For you I have been your Major Superior; but with you I am just a fellow religious. The former was a duty; the latter a grace. The former was a great danger; the latter, salvation." Continue to pray for me.*

On the following day, in the presence of Bishop Babcock, the delegates elected Sister Mary Aquinas Weber as immediate successor to Mother Victor and the seventh in the line from Mother Aquinata Fiegler. Sisters Letitia Van Agtmael, James Rau, Euphrosine (Mary) Sullivan, and Norbert (Marjorie) Vangsness were elected to her council. Sister Thomas Ann (Helen) Miller became secretary general, Sister Faith Mahoney, treasurer.

The business of the Chapter was so extensive that a second session was planned for the following summer, a notion suggested by Mother Victor in her opening remarks. The old categories of business no longer held, new agenda were under way. Apart from the elections, the traditional secrecy surrounding Chapter deliberations was replaced by the first of "Chapter Briefs,"[30] daily communiques to the sisters on the topics and tone of the discussions. By her own preference the sisters soon came to call Mother Aquinas "Sister;" by Chapter action the sisters came to call their leader "Prioress General," a return to earlier Dominican traditions and an indication of new emphases. A new period had begun.

After completing eighteen years of congregational leadership, Mother Victor received, along with all the other sisters, her annual assignment. She was to be superior of St. Francis (the former Holy Angels) convent in Traverse City. After three years there, she returned to Grand Rapids in an administrative position at Aquinata Hall. From 1972 to 1982 she enjoyed a quieter life "in the Valley," first at Holy Family convent in Saginaw and then at Sacred Heart convent, Merrill. On March 17, 1982, she went to Aquinata Hall and died there on September 19, 1983.

Father Martin J. Toolis, homilist at Mother's funeral, told of a midsummer visit at Aquinata Hall. On leaving her room, he said, "If in a sermon to the sisters in the Marywood chapel, I told them I had a message to all the sisters from you, what would that message be?" She glanced downward with a very serious look, repeated the question "What would that message be?" then was silent for several moments. Finally, she said,

> Tell them to remember that when they came to the convent, they came to save their souls. [Pause] The sisters have to do all kinds of work. I did many kinds of work myself. We have to work to meet the needs of the Church as they occur. [Another pause] But we cannot neglect the first and most important work that brought us to the convent in the first place: to save our souls.[31]

# AFTERWORD
# A PREFERRED FUTURE

$S$ince July 1966, four sisters have served as prioress of the congregation, Sisters Aquinas Weber (1966-1972), Norbert (Marjorie) Vangsness (1972-1980), Teresa Houlihan (1980-1988), and Carmelita Murphy (1988- ). The office of mother general, once both an administrative and maternal role, has evolved into a position of corporate and pastoral leadership shared with full-time councillors.

For seventy-five years mothers general had governed and administered the congregation according to the Rule and Constitution and their own style. Apart from an Extraordinary General Chapter in October 1926, convened to study a constitutional draft, the General Chapter was primarily the context for election. In 1966, with the encouragement of Mother Victor for a second session of the General Chapter, there began a fifteen-year period of institutional self-study, largely through Chapters of Election and of Affairs.

Agenda took on a new meaning, not simply as items to be reacted to, but as significant areas for study and action "in the light of Vatican II." Chapters, held almost biennially for two decades, were at once invigorating and energy-consuming. In 1985 an area structure and general assembly were added to the congregation's government. These features enable more frequent consultation with the sisters on congregational matters and provide opportunities for strengthening the family bonds of the now geographically dispersed congregation.

From the beginning of the sisters' work in the United States there has been evidence of adaptation: new schools opened; care of orphans and aged undertaken; health care facilities staffed; and diocesan, state, and international boundaries crossed. The institutional growth described in the previous chapters included decisions to depart from as well as to begin works in particular places.

The general ferment of the times and the Church's counterpart, Vatican Council II, gave rise to a quarter-century of far ranging change in secular and religious life. Population changes affecting parishes, the increase of lay workers, altered perceptions of religious vocation and mission, financial demands on congregations and parishes, the need for increased professionalism, the gradual enculturation of Catholics within North American society, and the challenge of the third world and of the poor--all of these affected how sisters live and work.

Gradually the well defined territory of "our" places disappeared. There were, however, often in the same communities once served by the congregation's teachers, new needs for a single religious educator, a pastoral assistant, or, more recently, a parish administrator, or a liturgy coordinator; for a social worker, or a food service manager in county-wide programs. There are as well many new places where the sisters serve. The fixed mission field has become a complex of entries in an ever-changing data base. Nevertheless, it is still the Dominican work--"to praise, to bless, to preach"--that the sisters undertake.

Since 1965 there has been a dramatic decline in the number of sisters. Societal influences, among them, new patterns of delayed vocational choices and of life commitment, and values to which the vowed life of poverty, celibacy, and obedience are opposite, have affected entry and departure patterns. Congregational policy now requires greater maturity and experience in its candidates. Congregational membership, like the surrounding American population, grows older. By 1994, the centennial of the establishment as an independent congregation, membership is likely to be near 350 sisters.

Since the early 1950's, and greatly accelerated by Vatican Council II, newly discovered principles--collegiality and subsidiarity in matters of governance, and adaptation in matters of ministry, custom and costume, and interaction with society--have brought the sisters, the congregation and individual sisters, back "into the world." The next volume of *Period Pieces* must take into account the developments in institutional structure, in the spirit and practice of mission and presence in "the world," and in the flowering of personal creativity and generosity of all the sisters.

The congregation sees itself, not unlike the original Ratisbon community, faced with the challenge of taking on new works, of going new places, of living more simply, with fewer members and diminished resources. Called once to serve an immigrant Church, the sisters serve now in a post-immigrant, yet newly immigrant Church. The challenge is not solely an imposition from external forces but, in the thematic emphases of the congregational leadership of the 1980's, "a preferred future."

# Notes

## Foreword

**1** Sandra L. Myers. *Westering Women and the Frontier Experience* 1800 - 1915. Albuquerque: University of New Mexico Press, 1982.

**2** *Journey Continued. An Autobiography.* NY: Charles Scribners, 1988. p. 293.

## 1                 Ratisbon Roots

**1**   Ratisbon is the place name derived from the medieval Latin *Ratisbona*. Regensburg is the modern German name of the city, located in the state of Bavaria, West Germany, where the Danube, Naab and Regen rivers meet. The pioneer sisters were inclined to use Ratisbon in speaking of their European origin. The congregations originating from the 1853 mission of the Holy Cross convent, Regensburg, identify themselves as Ratisbon congregations.

The Order of Friars Preachers, i.e., the Dominican fathers, established a United States province in 1805. Through their influence an indigenous American Dominican sisterhood developed, i.e., the congregations of St. Catharine, Kentucky (1822), St. Mary of the Springs, Columbus, Ohio (1830), Holy Name, San Rafael, California (1850), Most Holy Rosary, Sinsinawa, Wisconsin (1850). These and later Dominican foundations identify themselves by their American origins.

**2**   In 1896 the motherhouse was transferred to Newburgh, New York. The motherhouse of the original foundation of the Ratisbon sisters was first in Williamsburg (Brooklyn), New York, and later transferred to Amityville, New York.

**3**   Mary Philip Ryan, OP, *Amid the Alien Corn.* The Early Years of the Sisters of Saint Dominic, Adrian, Michigan. St. Charles, Illinois: Jones Woods, 1967. pp. 325-326, n.14.

**4**   This summary of M. Benedicta's administration is based on Mary Hortense Kohler, OP, *Life and Work of Mother Benedicta Bauer*, Milwaukee: Bruce, 1937, Chapter 5.

**5**   *Ibid.*, p.77.

**6**   The *Ludwig-missionsverein* was one of several societies founded in the nineteenth century to aid Catholic missions in Asia and America. This society, founded in 1838 in Munich, was especially helpful to the Ratisbon mission. Kohler cites it as a major factor in the missionary spirit and endeavors of the age. It contributed almost $900,000 to several American missions between 1844 and 1916 (*op.cit.*, p.90, n.339).

**7**   Ryan, *op. cit.*, p. 29, following Mary Thomasine Blum, OP, *History of the Sisters of the Third Order of Saint Dominic of the Congregation of the Most Holy Rosary, Newburgh, New York.* Washington, DC, 1938, p. 10. The letter appeared in a collection of German letters sent to Sister Jane Marie Murray, Grand Rapids, by Mother Ignatia, Prioress of Holy Cross Convent, in 1928.

# 2             Cross Bearers

1  Sister Mary Philip Ryan writes, "the only recorded comment about the four nuns during their first few days in New York is that they spent the feast of St. Rose of Lima, August 30, in Holy Redeemer church in tears." *op. cit.* p.35.

2  Eugene J. Crawford, MA, *The Daughters of St. Dominic on Long Island.* The History of the American Congregation of the Holy Cross, Sisters of the Third Order of St. Dominic of the Diocese of Brooklyn. NY: Benziger, 1938. p.72. Ryan, *op. cit.*, pp. 36-39; Crawford, *op. cit.*, pp. 53-58., Kohler, *op. cit.* pp. 100-105, with facsimile of the original German text.

3  Crawford, op. cit. p.72.

4  See Mary Ewens, *The Role of the Nun in Nineteenth Century America.* New York: Arno Press, 1978.

5  The Second Street motherhouse (later Newburgh), is the origin of the "Ratisbon congregations" of Caldwell, New Jersey; Blauvelt, New York; Adrian, Michigan; Everett (Edmonds), Washington; Tacoma, Washington; Akron, Ohio; and Grand Rapids, Michigan. Crawford, *Op. cit.*, p.80. The interpretation implies some pain in the development. See Crawford, pp. 114-116, for financial arrangements in establishing the new house.

6  Blum, *op. cit.*, p. 40.

7  Ryan, *op. cit.* p.44. The tradition is kept in all the Second Street foundations. The Adrian, Michigan, version related by Sister Mary Philip includes the daisy field simile. The Grand Rapids tradition focuses on "a peninsula dotted white."

# 3             God's Acres

1  Of the six, two would have leadership roles in other Ratisbon congregations, Mother Camilla Madden (1854-1924) as provincial and first mother general of the Adrian, Michigan, congregation, Mother Angela Phelan as first novice mistress in Adrian, and later provincial of the Aberdeen (later Everett, then Edmonds), Washington, Dominicans.

2  Sister Cherubina Seymour (1866-1938) entered the congregation on July 21, 1881. In 1934 Mother Eveline asked her to gather data on the earliest sisters, those from New York and those who had entered in Michigan. From those notes, Sister Joachim Visner, secretary general of the congregation from 1936 to 1966, wrote *The Memoirs of the Sisters of St. Dominic,* a major source for this section of the narrative.

3  Wilhelmina Hartleb, a first cousin of Mother Aquinata, entered the postulancy at Second Street on June 19, 1872, the day of her arrival in New York from Germany. She remained at Traverse City until May 1879 when she was recalled to New York. On August 28, 1879, she returned to Michigan to begin the mission at St. Mary's, Adrian. She was among those who moved into the new Holy Angels convent, Traverse City, in 1883. Her name alone is entered on the mortgages and property arrangements made with the Hannah Lay Company for the land upon which the Academy was built. She became a member of the Board of Trustees of the Academy in 1884. In 1922 she took up permanent residence at Marywood, the new motherhouse in Grand Rapids, where she celebrated her

Golden Jubilee, the first to do so in the congregation after her own cousin, Mother Aquinata, in 1914. She died in 1930 at age seventy-five, then the oldest member of the congregation.

**4** It was then the custom to bury sisters in the place of their death. A few sisters have been buried in family plots. There are twelve burials in Bay City (1885-1935), seven in Traverse City (1881-1915), two in Gaylord (1918, 1930), two in Saginaw (1884, 1923), one in Suttons Bay (1918), one in Muskegon (1885), one in Maple Grove (1909), one in Mount Pleasant (1969), one in Midland (1979), one in Ionia (1926), and five in Albuquerque, New Mexico (1931-1973). There are two burials in Saskatchewan, Canada (1935,1971). In Grand Rapids, the main places of burial are St. Andrew Cemetery (111 burials from 1891 to 1952) and Resurrection Cemetery (355 burials from 1950 through 1989). There is one burial in Calvary Cemetery, St. Mary parish, Grand Rapids (1913).

**5** *The Grand Traverse Herald*, July 10, 1884, p.5.

**6** The McCarron sisters, Sisters Ligouri and Cyprian, were pioneers in several missions in Michigan. Sister Ligouri was appointed novice mistress when the missions were grouped into a province in August 1885. After the separation of the province from New York in 1894, the two sisters remained with the Grand Rapids congregation to assist in the transition. They returned to New York in July 1896. Sister Cyprian is pictured among the guests at Mother Aquinata's Golden Jubilee in August 1914.

**7** In July 1886 Father Charles Coppens, SJ, preached the "Big Retreat" for thirty Sisters at Holy Angels, Traverse City. The first clothing ceremony had been held there in May for Sister Henrietta Gagnier. Receptions and professions were held there until 1894, thereafter in Grand Rapids, first at St. John's Home, for large groups at St. Alphonsus church, and after 1922, at Marywood, the new motherhouse. The novitiate was moved from Traverse City in 1911.

**8** In 1920, perhaps as part of the financing of the new motherhouse in Grand Rapids, appraisals were sought on the Holy Angels convent-academy and two valuations presented, one for $82,375, the other for $54,688. As early as 1884 a portion of the land was deeded over to Henry J. Richter for the use of St. Francis parish, the bishop being the legal owner of parish properties within his diocese. In 1925, an additional strip, 12 feet wide, was given to the parish in return for the promise of the erection and upkeep of a fence. In 1951 the convent-academy was sold by the congregation to the diocese in exchange for a financial consideration and the use of a specified number of cemetery plots in the new Resurrection Cemetery near Grand Rapids. The house subsequently became known as St. Francis convent. The 1883 portion was demolished in 1971; the annex served as a sisters' residence through the 1980's.

**9** Jane Marie Murray, OP, *History of the Sisters of St. Dominic, Grand Rapids, Michigan*, 1927, pp. 26-27. Unpublished manuscript written for the fiftieth anniversary of the sisters' arrival in Michigan.

**10** The institution was listed in Albert Baxter, *History of Grand Rapids* (New York and Grand Rapids: Munsell, 1891), p. 35. and a reference was made to "ten sisters of the Order of St. Dominick...under Mother Angela as superior...."

**11** As late as the mid-1960's a statue of St. Joseph was a customary furnishing in the congregational treasurer's office. Throughout the congregation the feast of St. Joseph, March 19, was kept as a recreation day even though it fell during the Lenten season.

**12** *The Minutes of the General Council,* I, 1892-1935, record proceedings of a special meeting in February 1916, with the community officers and Bishop Richter, in which, "the advisability of erecting an elevator for the use of the institution was also considered. Eventually a contract was made with the Otis Co. of Cleveland, Ohio, for the sum of two thousand four hundred dollars to be taken from the funds of the Community and to be replaced by the Asylum as occasion offered." In 1929 the financial arrangements between the congregation and St. John's Home were part of difficult negotiations between Bishop Joseph Pinten and Mother Eveline Mackey.

**13** Father Frencken to pastors of St. Joseph parish, 1930 to 1936, published for the St. Joseph parish centennial, July 1989.

**14** *The Michigan Catholic,* Grand Rapids, April 28, 1990, reports on the 125th anniversary of St. Joseph school. In 1900, Father Ege recorded, "During the year 1899, I expected to complete a sisters house (solid brick), but on account of the poor crops, I was not able. I expended about $1,800. This does not include gratuitous labor on the part of the parishioners. It will cost 7-800 dollars more when completed." A decade later a "solidly constructed" school was built for $7,000. Three Dominican sisters continue on the school staff of six. Some of the 105 pupils come from families having five generations taught by sisters.

# 4            Preparing the Way of the Lord

**1** The Diocese of Detroit, created in 1833, encompassed the entire lower peninsula of Michigan. The upper peninsula was included in the Diocese of Sault Ste. Marie, later called Marquette, formed in 1853. The new Diocese of Grand Rapids comprised the 39 counties of the lower peninsula, north of the southern line of Ottawa, Kent, Montcalm, Gratiot, and Saginaw counties, and west of the eastern line of the counties of Saginaw and Bay counties, a total of 22,561 square miles. There was an estimated population of 50,000 Catholics, thirty-six priests, thirty-seven churches with resident pastors, and seventeen parochial schools with 2,867 pupils.

**2** Joseph Henry Richter was born April 9, 1838, at Neuen Kirchen, Oldenburg, Germany. In November 1854, at the age of sixteen, he came to the United States and settled in Cincinnati where he completed his secondary education at St. Paul day school. There was, his contemporaries said, no evidence of his German origins in his speech. His seminary training was at the Jesuit College of St. Francis Xavier, St. Thomas Seminary, Bardstown, Kentucky, and at St. Mary's of the West, Cincinnati. In fall 1860, at the request of Archbishop John Purcell, he began his theological studies at the new North American College in Rome. He received the degree of Doctor of Divinity in 1864, and was ordained on June 10, 1865, by Cardinal Patrizi, vicar general of Rome. He returned to Cincinnati accompanied by his widowed mother, his sister and brother, and his friend Augustine Meyer, later a priest of the archdiocese of Cincinnati. His first assignment was as vice president of Mt. St. Mary's of the West. In 1869 he became pastor of St. Lawrence's, a new German parish. He also served as chaplain of Mount St. Vincent Academy, Cedar Grove, motherhouse of the Sisters of Charity. During his tenure at St. Lawrence's, he completed a church-school building, secured land for the parish, and brought the parishioners through a difficult language controversy. See Dennis Morrow, "Bishop Henry Joseph Richter and the Diocese of Grand Rapids, 1882-1916," unpublished manuscript, 1972; and John W. McGee, *The Church in the Grand River Valley, 1833-1950. Grand Rapids, Michigan, 1950.*

3 *The Michigan Catholic,* Feb. 3, 1883.

4 Mary Philomena Kildee, OP, *Memoirs of Mother Mary Aquinata Fiegler, OP.* Grand Rapids, Michigan: James Bayne Company, 1928. pp. 7, 11. Some obituaries (May 1915) of Mother Aquinata referred to "one surviving brother Arnold."

5 It was the custom of Second Order congregations to address as "Mother" superiors of houses and the members of the general council in their role as "Mothers of Counsel." Third Order Dominican congregations retained the title for the major superior, the mother general. Prior to 1921, several of the pioneer sisters, among them, Sisters Assisium, Clementina, Boniface, Villana, were addressed as "Mother."

6 Kildee, *op.cit.,* pp. 32-33.

7 Ryan, *op. cit.,* pp. 97-113.

8 *Ibid.* pp. 139-142. Under the direction of Mother Angela Phelan the missions in the far west developed into a province of the New York motherhouse. Both the Adrian, Michigan and Everett (Edmonds), Washington provinces became independent congregations in 1923.

9 This summary of membership occurs in several accounts. It is, however, difficult to reconstruct an exact membership list. The congregational register has seventy-five entries prior to August 30, 1894, (including those who had already died; but excluding New York sisters who had labored and died in Michigan). See "Grand Rapids Dominican Sisters," below. Numbers 3,4,7,11,17, and 18 are New York sisters who labored and died in Michigan before 1894.

10 Letter of Dominic M. Scheer, OP, Socius to Andrew Frühwirth, OP, Master General, Dec. 26, 1894, states these requirements. A diploma of affiliation was promised. One of the last efforts of Mother Aquinata relates to this promised diploma, which finally came to the congregation in 1918. This correspondence is part of the canonical case brought both to the diocese and to the Sacred Congregation of Religious during the administration of Mother Eveline Mackey (1927-1936). Mother Aquinata included "Nov.*[sic]* 26, 1894, the date our Congregation was affiliated with the Order in Rome...." in her very brief chronology.

11 Ryan, *op. cit.* pp. 156-164, again provides the most thorough account of this event. See also Kildee, *op. cit.,* p.63, and Blum, *op. cit.,* p. 64.

**12** Blum, *op. cit.*, p. 64, gives the 1894 declaration of separation as the basis. Kildee quotes Bishop Richter, "Mother Aquinata has made her vows to me. She has also arranged with me for a reception and profession this month." *op. cit.*, p.64.

# 5             There, The First Novice

**1** Corporation minutes record the activities of the legal entity begun in 1892. In 1897, with the canonical election of congregational officers, entries were made in the *Minutes of the General Council*. The early years, ca. 1892-1927, primarily record elections, land transactions, and mission openings. From 1927-1966 minutes included congregational and corporate business of the Sisters of St. Dominic, and some matters relating to Nazareth Sanatorium and Aquinas College.

**2** In 1932 Mother Eveline asked the congregation to pray for Sister Bernard, the recent victim of a tragic fire in New York. She had been a stalwart pioneer and companion of Mother Aquinata in the Michigan missions for sixteen years.

**3** Mary Alvesteffer, OP, currently serving on Beaver Island, has written a lively account of the Dominican sisters on Beaver Island. See "Times of Their Lives," *The Journal of Beaver Island History*. Volume III, 1988. pp. 177-201.

**4** A letter, dated July 18, 1899, from Francis A. Stace shows he examined the abstracts of lots 1 and 2, block 23, Campau addition. The property, once that of Elias Matter, had been held by the Grand Rapids Savings Bank since 1893 with mortgages amounting to $16,000. A tax receipt dated December 23, 1899, shows the assessed valuation at $9,000. A treasurer's day book (no longer extant) showed the sisters paid $11,500 for the property. Two brick buildings, the Matter residence and a barn, were on the property. The sisters spent $1,823.30 in remodeling the home. They took up residence in the summer of 1900 and in the meantime collected $15 a month rent for the house and $22 for the barn rental for the whole year. A five-story addition was begun in the spring of 1901. The addition, remodelling, and land costs totalled $34,273.10. The east half of lot 3 (33 feet frontage on Fountain Street adjoining lot 2) land was secured from Albert Bremgartner on September 16, 1902, for $3,500. This lot included a two-family brick residence. In 1911, the sisters bought lot 12 (66 feet frontage on Ransom Avenue and adjoining lots 1 and 2 on the south) with a frame house from John and Georgiana Platte for $7,400.

**5** "Mother Benedicta O'Rourke," *Memoirs of the Sisters of Saint Dominic,* II, 1935-1948, pp. 114-116.

**6** In 1941 Edna McGarry Woods wrote for *Veritas*, the Marywood Academy yearbook, "I remember it all as yesterday. Sister Benedicta had been my teacher in all subjects. On examination day she put me up to a public school examiner and she would have nothing to do with my questions and would not correct them, either....I nearly passed out and told Sister I just could not write the exam. She gave her head dress a jerk and said, 'Edna, you answer *every* question; you know them.'....I was delighted with the likeness on the leaflet of Mother Benedicta. I will put it in my prayerbook, and feel now like praying to her rather than for her. When there are few pupils and one is alone as I, one has a great love for her teacher. Mother's wonderful teaching has been a great influence on my life."

**7** Bertha Brand, later Sister Mary Felix, completed the commercial program in June 1909. Within days she was hired by the business office of Herpolsheimer's, Grand Rapids, where she worked until entering the congregation on September 12, 1914. In her autobiography of 1929 she reflects on the tutelage of the sisters at the Academy, of the business sense she gained there, and of Sister Eveline Mackey's keen appraisal of the girls. Sister Felix was the first registrar-librarian at Catholic Junior College and, in 1936, was elected treasurer of the congregation, a position she held for 30 years.

**8** *Rapport*, January 1974.

**9** The transcript of Jennie Flannery (Mother Victor), who entered the congregation on September 29, 1911, shows the following courses were offered in the 1911-1912 Novitiate Normal program: Rhetoric 100A, Elements of Music 101, Music 104, Agriculture, Advanced Botany, Elementary Latin, Public Speaking, Physical Education, and Penmanship. In *Rapport* 1974 Sister Gonzaga Udell told about Sisters Benedicta O'Rourke, Borromeo Donley, and Monica Kress leaving Sacred Heart Academy for daily Latin and Greek lessons at Bishop Richter's residence. In 1911 and thereafter young sisters (Sister Gonzaga included) were stationed in Grand Rapids to take advantage of the bishops's lessons given each day at four o'clock at Sacred Heart Academy. Sister Gonzaga wrote, "Our Latin text for study was Caesar's Gallic Wars. None of us in the class, of course, had the time that real activity would demand, but by the copious use of the 'pony' we made a rather favorable impression on his Lordship." In the summer of 1912 Sister Gonzaga took Sister Benedicta's course in physics, "with the newly adopted practice of laboratory experiments."

**10** McGee, *op. cit.*, pp. 199-205, 306-310. See also Marie Heyda, OP, *Catholic Central and West Catholic Central High Schools*, Grand Rapids, Michigan: Spartan Printing, 1981.

**11** The twelve-page pamphlet speaks of Mother Aquinata as "for thirty-five years...the guiding spirit of our community," a perspective which suggests that during the years prior to and through the provincialate Mother was in fact the major superior, and there was relatively little connection with New York; or that as early as 1914 the sisters did not know the full extent of the link between the province and the New York congregation. The author of the booklet also gives 1887 as the date of the independence of the congregation.

## 6          Simple and Good

**1** In spite of the official positions she held, there is relatively little recorded of her life and influence. Senior sisters referred to her insistence on the "letter of the law" when she was novice mistress or had novices within her household. Minutes of the General Council do not always mention her in the meetings of council, perhaps due to the distance of her mission, perhaps due to the leadership style of Mother Aquinata. Sister Eucharia Doris (1891-1990) recalled that at the time of her entrance in 1914 senior sisters said that Mother Villana was reluctant to come to Grand Rapids for business due to the predominance of "the Germans" on the council.

**2** This is the only information available on the Chapter of 1915. A change had, however, been made in term of office. For in 1918 another election was held. *The Minutes of Council*, I, p.25, record a special meeting held with Bishop Gallagher on August 3, 1918, setting the election date for officers of the community for August 11, 1918. A later entry records the election results. It is not clear whether this was a General Chapter or a meeting of the corporation officers. There is no official record in the archives of a Chapter held in 1918. It is possible that in 1915 it was understood that Mother Gonzalva was elected to complete the third term of Mother Aquinata (i.e., until August 1918). This does not appear likely inasmuch as a new council was also elected in 1915. From her letter of resignation in 1919, it appears that Mother had been re-elected by a Chapter.

**3** There are several connections between Bishop Schrembs and the congregation. He was born in Regensburg on March 12, 1866, and came to America in 1888 to begin his priestly studies at St Vincent's, Latrobe, Pennsylvania, where his brother had entered the Benedictines some years earlier. This was the abbey Dom Boniface Wimmer directed. It is likely that this is the Benedictine connection referred to in vocation stories of several of the German sisters at the turn of the century. Bishop Schrembs was influential in directing Marie Gautier, Sister Reparata, to enter the congregation in 1913. An interview with *The Grand Rapids Herald*, at the time of his consecration as auxiliary bishop in February 1911, related:

> *The chance that brought Msgr. Schrembs to Grand Rapids was nothing short of providential. About a year after Bishop Richter was consecrated, Msgr. Schrembs was teaching school in a seminary at Louisville, Kentucky. He had finished his classical course in Pittsburgh at the age of 14 and, being too young to continue his theological studies, was compelled to follow some other line of work.*
>
> *While thus engaged he took the examination for a public school teacher and was offered a $3000 [sic, more likely $300] position, but his heart was in theology, and he hit upon a plan of writing to twelve different bishops asking them to adopt him as a student... . The first acceptance was from Henry Joseph Richter, of the new diocese of Grand Rapids. This was the turning point in his life. He decided to come to Grand Rapids....It was surely providence that prompted him to open that letter from Bishop Richter and to cast his lot with this struggling diocese of 30 priests in an almost new section of the country. One of the offers was from Archbishop Gibbons of the Archdiocese of Baltimore... .*

He was Auxiliary Bishop of Grand Rapids from February to August, 1911, when he was consecrated as first Bishop of Toledo. He became Bishop of Cleveland in 1921, and in 1939 archbishop. At his invitation, in 1922, 40 Dominicans from the Caldwell, New Jersey, congregation formed an autonomous congregation in Akron, Ohio. He died on November 2, 1945.

**4** The property was in the Fulton Heights area, a wooded hill district east of the city limits. It was served by Rural Free Delivery postal service, route no. 3 and reached by "trunk phone." The area was annexed to the City of Grand Rapids in 1960.

**5** *Isabella County Herald*, January 17, 1990, on the school's 75th anniversary.

**6** Each summer the number of sisters attending Notre Dame increased. Officials and faculty of the University were often guests at Marywood, some serving as mentors in the development of the collegiate programs. Sisters encouraged young men to attend the University and some Dominican alumni entered the Holy Cross congregation. It was customary to appoint a superior for the "Notre Dame crowd" in the summer and during her tenure Mother Euphrasia occasionally visited them in South Bend.

# 7                Joy Days

**1** On November 19, 1919, Bishop Kelly wrote that paragraphs 276 and 277 of the constitutions were not applicable. The council was to elect a new councilor to take Mother Benedicta's place and, "As I have intimated to you in a former communication I desire you to propose Sister Mary Eveline for the position of Vicar to the Mother General." In 1916 a Rule and Constitution was distributed throughout the congregation but almost immediately there seem to have been modifications made either by the Ordinary of the Diocese or through the influence of the Code of Canon Law promulgated in 1917.

**2** Sacred Heart church in Grand Rapids, completed at about the same time, was also designed by Brielmeier. The two buildings were among those featured in the Buildings Section of *The Grand Rapids Herald*, Sunday, March 4, 1923.

**3** During the construction period two loans were secured from Massachusetts Life Insurance Company, in 1921 for $250,000 and, in 1922, an additional $60,000. Community properties in Grand Rapids, Traverse City and Bay City were put up as collateral. The Diocese of Grand Rapids loaned the congregation $35,000; St. John's Home loaned $30,000. Smaller loans were offered by priests, friends, and the architectural firm. Most of these required 6% interest payments. In 1929 a mortgage for $370,000 was negotiated with the Lincoln National Life Insurance Company and, in 1939, another mortgage for $280,000 was arranged with the Connecticut Mutual Life Insurance Company. The sisters were fully apprised of the indebtedness of the congregation.

**4** The ministry was discontinued in August 1949 by Mother Victor Flannery. In her letter to the resident women, Mother pointed out that the building did not, nor ever would, belong to the congregation, and the ministry had been sustained "over a long period of time and under many pecuniary difficulties." The estate had, in fact, been willed to the Diocese of Grand Rapids in which Saginaw was then located. After 1949 the property was transferred to the Diocese of Saginaw and in particular for the use of SS. Peter and Paul parish.

**5** For example, Sisters Genevieve Gauthier (1876-1944), Agnes Senecal (1876-1943), and Bertrand Lalonde (1877-1987) who entered in 1891 at the age of 14. They had a two-year postulancy at St. John's Home during which they attended

St. Alphonsus school. Mother Aquinata required that they be sixteen for the reception of the habit. In 1900 Matilda Rohrl and Christina Ropp, both age 13, arrived from Bavaria "to convert the Indians." They were placed at Holy Rosary Academy, Essexville, until their reception as Sisters Evangelista and Emmanuel three years later.

**6** At that Chapter the method of election was discussed. In a letter dated May 16, 1921, Mother Benedicta indicated that there had been some dissatisfaction in the 1919 election. For the ensuing election the old method would be used, i.e., all sisters twelve years professed should be permitted to have an active voice in the General Chapter. She judged that the sisters were "not quite ready" for the representative method set forth in the 1916 Constitution and in conformity to the new Code of Canon Law.

**7** Numerous references to music money in letters between succeeding prioresses and pastors indicate opposition to the policy and occasional reversion to the previous arrangement. An anecdote dating from the 1920's tells of correspondence between Sisters Celestine McCue and Adelaide McCue, blood sisters. Sister Celestine reported to her sister, then on the general council, that after several contacts the pastor on her local mission still would not comply with the 1921 directive to return the music money. Finally, it was said, Sister Adelaide wrote to Sister and told her to overlook the matter. A postcard came by return mail with the message, "Millions for Defense, Not One Cent for Tribute!"

**8** *Contacts*, The Official Organ of the General Council of Schools, Vol. 2, no.1, (February 1931).

**9** Sister Blanche Steves, August 4, 1947, at the 1947 jubilee celebration, the Silver Jubilee of the class which had moved to Marywood in October 1922.

**10** Congregational mission lists were not common until the 1940's. Several sources indicate the following were assigned to Marywood in 1922: M. Benedicta O'Rourke (both Mother General and prioress of the house), Sister Seraphica Brandstetter (bursar), Sister Loyola Finn, novice mistress. School faculty: Sisters Estelle Hackett (principal to 1924 and high school-college teacher), Evangelista Rohrl (music), Hortense Belanger (high school), Jane Marie Murray (high school-college), Aquin Gallagher (high school-college), David Steele (high school), Joachim Visner (art), Clarence Hansen (high school commercial department and private secretary to Mother Benedicta), Aline Needham (grade school), Gerald Grace (grade school), Rose Catherine McDonnell (grade school), and house staff, Mother Clementina Coyle, Sisters Sebastian Claeys, Ernestine Kokx, Benevenuta Carroll, Rose Anthony Bedard (bakery), Ann Denise Hogan (bakery), Jane DeChantal Host (Mistress of Junior Girls and laundry), Mellita Tague (Mistress of Senior Girls). There were 25 novices and 12 postulants.

**11** Mother signed both her circular and personal letters "Sister." Sometimes she used her title "Mother General." Until 1927 it was customary for members of the Second and Third Orders of the Dominican Order to use "OSD" for Order of St. Dominic. In 1927, by decree of the Master General of the Order, the sisters were permitted to use "OP" for Order of Preachers.

**12** On January 10, 1926, the Board held a special meeting on "the question of taxation." Sister Seraphica was assigned to gather data on congregational properties in Traverse City, Bay City, and Grand Rapids. Council minutes for July 18, 1926, mention having all the sisters register at Marywood for voting, "for future protection." In a letter to the sisters on October 23, 1926, Mother asked that the sisters send in ballots, with full family name, duly notarized, to the Township Clerk, Precinct 3. "Vote 'No'," she instructed, "regarding annexation to the city. Marywood doesn't wish to go in yet." An entry in the minutes for October 5, 1926, may reflect the fear of coming taxation or simply good business sense. At that meeting the sisters discussed the "advisability of getting a Board of Directors for Marywood to consist of about fifteen or eighteen men." The decision was to work out this plan. There is no subsequent reference. Bishop Pinten, installed in the same month and known for his business acumen, seems to have assumed that role. A lay advisory board for Catholic Junior College was begun ca. 1936.

**13** Sant Ilona is the Hungarian form of St. Helen.

# 8             Upbuilding the Church

**1** On August 24, 1920, Mother Benedicta wrote to Bishop Kelly about the low enrollment in the Boyne Falls school and asked permission to withdraw the sisters from that parish. The bishop wrote on the bottom of her letter, "Dear Mother Benedicta, The above petition is granted. Kindly inform the Father in charge. Sincerely, E.D. Kelly, Bp. of G.R." The letter suggests an easy working relationship in which good sense and courtesy prevailed.

**2** The archives has a single-page typewritten document in an envelope in Mother Eveline's handwriting entitled "Green Bay Diocese Sisters' Contract." By 1927, the salary for a sister-teacher "where Sisters own their home, paying for the heating, lighting, water, and its general upkeep" was $400 per annum; $300 for each sister-teacher "where sisters live in a house provided and kept up by the parish." A candidate having full charge of a class was to receive $250 per annum; a candidate acting as assistant teacher, $200. A sister conducting a church choir was to receive $100; a sister organist $1 for each function; a sister serving as sacristan $50. Washing of church linens for one priest per annum was $50, and $20 for every additional priest.

**3** In her 1928 Easter letter Mother Eveline added a postcript to her letter, "We need Sisters to teach religion in some of our Vacation Schools in Michigan and Wisconsin. It is not an easy job. Just the zealous need apply. You may volunteer." During her adminstration vacation schools were added in Canada.

**4** In the letter of convocation dated April 1, 1924, Mother announced, "On account of the present conditions of the Community, it has been deemed advisable that the former method of voting be employed, viz., all Sisters twelve years professed shall have an active voice in the Chapter."

**5** Such a formal convocation was quite unusual until the "Chapter of Affairs" and "Renewal Chapters" following upon Vatican Council II.

**6** See below, Chapter 17.

**1**   Joseph Gabriel Pinten was born in Rockland, Ontonagon County, in Michigan's upper peninsula on October 3, 1867. Within a year the family moved to Calumet and there he spent his youth. He attended St. Francis Seminary in St. Francis, Wisconsin, from 1881 to 1885 for classical education, and then the College of the Propaganda in Rome for theology and philosophy. He was ordained in Rome on November 1, 1890.

In 1891 he returned to the Diocese of Marquette where he first served in the parish of Detour in Chippewa County. Many times he hiked the forty miles from Detour to the Sault and back, often on snowshoes when drifts were impassable. One winter he was called to minister to an Indian on one of Les Cheneaux Islands. He spent all his savings, $11, to get a dogsled and dogs to take him there. Returning in a blinding snowstorm the dogs broke away, upset the sled and left the young priest to walk miles to his home. Later he was sent to Iron Mountain where he was especially suited to minister to the Italian-speaking community still there from the mining era. He was subsequently assigned to L'Anse on the Keewanaw Bay where Bishop Baraga established the church. He also served in Marquette as chancellor and later vicar general of that diocese. In 1912 Pope Pius X honored him with the title of domestic prelate.

**2**   Father McGee reported that Bishop Pinten insisted on calling the ceremony "enthronization," an indication of his precision and sense of authority, *op. cit.*, p. 354. An elegant invitation to the enthronization and a copy of the banquet program are kept in the congregational archives but there is no record of who attended.

**3**   Father Robert W. Bogg, who had served as pastor of St. Mary parish, Lowell, St. Joseph parish, Grand Rapids, and St. Thomas the Apostle parish, Grand Rapids, became the bishop's secretary during the early years of his episcopacy, and later the vice-chancellor. Father Raymond H. Baker was chancellor in 1936 at the time of the ecclesiastical decision. It appears the two priests had only indirect roles in the confrontation between Mother Eveline and Bishop Pinten and Monsignor Volkert.

**4**   There is one reference in the council minutes to the relocation of a sister "in accordance with the bishop's request." Other items, considered of consequence at the time, e.g., the advisability of taking over a sanatorium in Santa Fe, opening a school in Chicago, allowing a sister to visit her mother in California, sending the Constitution to the sisters for study, seem to have been decided upon by Mother and her council.

**5**   In 1929 Mother requested that every member in the congregation write an autobiography. It is from her own lengthy notes that this biographical sketch is written. Mother also wrote an extensive interpretation of the conflict between the congregation and the diocese as well as annotated pieces of correspondence. She laid the foundation for archives through directives on annals, autobiographies, and school record-keeping.

**6**   Mother Eveline told of the preparations at Sacred Heart to accommodate the Girls Catholic Central. Every able-bodied person was solicited to move furniture, including Dr. Hyland, a distinguished Grand Rapids physician, and Father John

A. Schmitt, rector of the Cathedral, who brought down the beds from the fourth floor dormitories and replaced them with desks.

**7** Her master's thesis was titled *The Syntax of St. Augustine's Confessions, Book V*. Her mastery of Latin served her well as teacher, promoter of the liturgy, and translator of the Constitution.

**8** This is the first Chapter for which a membership list and minutes are available. The membership list has 216 names, perhaps a list of those eligible by reason of twelve years' profession. There is no information on the number with passive voice. Business matters were discussed under two headings, committee reports (four committees, Conventual Reports, Educational Problems, Finance Problems, and Music, had been appointed the previous day) and consideration of the points in the General Chapter Decrees of 1921, the modest little leaflet used in the two preceding General Chapters. Apart from the canonical requirements, the conduct of this Chapter seems to have set a pattern for those to follow until 1966, the first which reflected the themes of renewal enjoined by Vatican Council II.

**9** When Mother reviewed her autobiographical notes, she appended the following list of accomplishments.

### First Term - Three Years
1. 15 Sisters study Liturgy summer at St. John's
2. Religion Text Books Christ Life Series Srs. Estelle and Jane Marie Fr. Virgil
3. Summer lectures on Liturgy
4. Use of Missal
5. European trip for Postulants
6. House Opened in Canada for postulants and help on Missions
7. Sanatorium Nazareth
8. Santa Cruz, San Juan opened
9. Mission List

### Second Term
#### July 1930-August 1936
1. Houses opened: St. Mary Magdalen Belen
2. Father Nolan's Visit
3. Dominican Conference
4. Sisters Mildred and Bertrand to Europe
5. Sr. Edith permission
6. Catholic Junior College 1930 Dr. Conway [sic] Fr. Bukowsky [sic] 1932
7. Papal Status

**10** The description is taken from Monsignor William J. Murphy's eulogy at Mother Eveline's funeral, September 24, 1958.

**11** There is no reference in the minutes of the 1936 Chapter. Perhaps the bursar's report detailing the extent of the congregation's indebtedness discouraged any consideration of a vacation house. Another factor may have been the prospect of a donation of land with cabin on Beaver Island from Thomas Gallagher, uncle of Sisters Alexandra and Leonora Gallagher.

**12** Certificates of Dedication Number 278 indicates 26¼ acres were designated in 1935-1940; Number 507 indicates 28 acres designated from 1940-1945.

**13** In December 1927 a folio-sized letter to be sent to friends, benefactors, and former pupils was professionally printed. The work and sacrifices of the sisters since their arrival in Michigan on October 22, 1877, were summarized. The particular needs of liquidating the extensive debt on the motherhouse and the building of an infirmary were laid out. Benefactors would be remembered in daily Mass, First Sunday Communion, evening devotions, public novenas, and a memento in the Office of the Dead, "richer dividends than most investments would earn." The only extant copy of the letter is in the Archives of the Diocese of Grand Rapids.

**14** Sister Sienna's case was among the testimonials included in the petition sent to Rome in 1929 as a first step in the beatification of Sister Reparata. After serving in New Mexico for over 48 years, Sister Sienna died in Michigan on June 4, 1986, at age 97.

**15** The shrine was not completed until the administration of Mother Euphrasia Sullivan (1936-1948). In the late 1980's the shrine became a focal point in a newly created parish of St. Therese.

**16** Sisters Clarence Hansen (1891-1934) and Marie Therese Harp (1909-1931), both diagnosed as tubercular, were missioned to New Mexico to benefit from the climate. They taught in the missions there until the sanatorium was opened and their conditions were too advanced to be healed. They were buried in Albuquerque.

**17** A financial statement for the period December 29, 1929, to July 1, 1931, shows receipts from Infirmary Fund $28,592.97, community savings $12,169.58, interest $2,535.60, sisters' patrimony (borrowed) $13,052.62, donations $1,575, and discounts $316.03, a total of $58,141.80, was used for the Nazareth construction.

**18** In 1936 a tile roof replaced the temporary roofing put on in September 1930. The cost was approximately $3,500. In fall 1937 Mother Euphrasia and her council considered either selling the sanatorium or completing sufficient rooms to make it self-supporting. $5,000 was borrowed from an Albuquerque bank to pay for architectural consultation and the building of an annex with four sleeping rooms. Council minutes show an annual outlay of moneys for the sanatorium-- pumps, furnaces, chapel extension, finishing of dining room, transportation, in addition to regular maintenance. Extensive work was done on Nazareth property during Mother Victor's administrations.

**19** The officers were Mother Eveline Mackey, Sisters Blanche Steves, Coletta Baumeister, Ernestine Kokx, Crescentia Wucherpfenning, Clarence Hansen, and Mark Scanlon. The term of existence was for fifty years; there was no capital stock. Sister Coletta Baumeister of Albuquerque was named the statutory agent.

**20** See Mary J. Oates, "Catholic Laywomen in the Labor Force, 1850-1950," in *American Catholic Women. A Historical Exploration.* Karen Kenneally, CSJ. NY: Macmillan, 1989, p. 99.

**21** It appears that in cases where sisters served in a parish managed by members of a religious order or outside the diocese of Grand Rapids a contract was negotiated, viz., with the Redemptorists for St. Alphonsus, Grand Rapids, the Servites in Belen, and the Diocese of Green Bay (see chapter 8, note 2). The contract with the Servites, made for three years, contains customary agreements on provision of faculty to meet school needs (as well as possible), provision of a comfortable home, with utilities and "other necessary conveniences," allowance for music tuition to go to the sisters; and more unusual provisions: sharing of a garden in lieu of a salary for a sister housekeeper, provision of spiritual benefits (daily Mass, when possible, confession, monthly spiritual conferences). The salary provision is of interest: "...that the salary received by the Sisters from the Public School Board be given to the Servite Fathers, except three hundred and fifty dollars ($350.00) per year for each Sister. At the end of three years all the salary received shall remain with the Sisters unless the Servite Fathers and the Sisters enter into a new contract, for a period not exceeding two years, with such new adaptations as may be then warranted by prevailing conditions."

**22** This amount was often contested by local school boards and there was a good deal of negotiating between the archbishop, mothers general, and county superintendents until 1949, when the practice of using religious as teachers in the public schools ceased.

**23** The property was lots 1-16 in block 46 of the Montevista addition, between Los Lumas Road, Dartmouth, Roma, and Girard Avenues. The Monte Vista property was taxable. In July 1940 Sister Marie Catherine Clayton, prioress at Nazareth Sanatorium, was authorized to sell the property as well as ten acres of orchard and cleared land west of the Fourth Street highway, pieces which would subsequently become prime real estate, to raise funds for a chapel at Nazareth.

# 10                                                           Crusades

**1** At the time Sister Seraphica was a council member and bursar general, Sister Philomena a member of the council and principal of Girls Catholic Central. In 1937 Sister Edith (1894-1989) formally transferred to Holy Name Monastery, Cincinnati, Ohio, a Second Order cloistered convent of the Dominican Order to which Sister Reparata Gautier (1892-1927) had transferred in 1924. Sister Edith was given the name "Mother Aquinata" at her profession.

**2** *General Council Minutes*, I, p. 69. The plan was formally voted upon, three in favor, one in opposition. This is one of the earliest evidences of Mother Eveline's intent to secure constitutional approval. The mention of Father Louis Nolan, OP, along with Father Sauvage, CSC, suggests even more serious constitutional issues inasmuch as Father Nolan was a member of the Sacred Congregation of Religious.

**3** "Call to the cloister. Healthy, courageous [or decent] girls between 14 and 26 who have religious vocations to America are asked to consider the Order of St. Dominic. For further information please write to the Dominican Sisters, 29 Bergmannstrasse, Munich." The rather direct prose was probably Sister Coletta's.

**4** Father Edward Cantwell, CSsR, Provincial Superior in St. Louis, in his letter to Redemptorists in Ireland, remarked:

> ...a most fervent and zealous body of Religious women. Their Community is very dear and close to the St. Louis Redemptorists. For forty years we have worked side by side in Michigan, the Mother-house & Novitiate of the Dominicans being next door to our Grand Rapids convent and church. In fact, it was the Redemptorists of New York who met the pioneer Sisters of this community on their arrival in America from Germany, and hence gave them their start in the New World. 'And now,' writes their Mother General, 'it is but in keeping with our history that your Fathers meet the spiritual daughters of these pioneers on the other side of the sea again.'

**5** In 1929 the rate of exchange was $4.80.

**6** On June 18, 1928, Sister Coletta wrote to Mother Eveline, "We think your little plan, of having a convent here and in Ireland would be just fine and better for the girls also. By the time they come from Ireland over here, or from here to Ireland they get half way across and it will be the same with language." They had also been advised that if they wanted German girls they needed a house in Germany, Irish girls a house in Ireland, Dutch girls, a house in Holland and so forth.

**7** A translation from the German original by German-speaking sisters at Marywood for Mother Eveline's use.

**8** Roermond was a small province of Holland between Germany and Belgium. The Bishop of Roermond was approached by Father Frencken and the sisters and he gave permission for them to settle there. A copy of the 1927 Catholic Central yearbook, *The White and Blue*, was given to the bishop to acquaint him with the sisters' work. Father Frencken asked Mother Eveline to send the bishop copies of *Veritas*, the Marywood Academy yearbook, and of the Constitution.

**9** There is a small piece of evidence that Mother considered a European trip before it was discussed in council. In a letter dated November 1, 1928, Mr. Grace told Mother Eveline that he did not, as she must have thought, have a permanent suite on the *Leviathan*. In the letter he enclosed a check "to help towards the trip which you are contemplating...."

**10** In the "European Project" archives, there is a single-page statistical report on foreign vocations:

**IRELAND:**
16 came from Ireland directly
7 went back to the world
6 returned to Ireland directly from here; 1 has work in Grand Rapids.
Of those seven, one was in poor health and six were not fitted for the life.
This means that 44% did not remain and 56% did remain.

**GERMANY:**

10 came directly from Germany

4 went back to the world

2 returned to Germany directly from here; 2 went to their uncle in Montana. Of the four who returned to the world, one was in poor health and three were not fitted for the Religious Life.

This means that 40% did not remain and 60% did remain.

**CANADA:**

25 came directly from Canada

2 went back to the world

1 left because of poor health, at our request and has since entered the Ursuline community in Toledo, and the other returned to her home in Canada, at our request, because of family difficulties.

This means that 8% returned to the world and 92% remained.

AUTHOR'S NOTE: Of the four German candidates who were prepared at Einsieldeln, Switzerland, all received the habit. Two left shortly thereafter, while the two remaining celebrated their 60th year in Dominican life.

**11** The congregational archives has a heavily annotated address book of Mother Eveline's in which she entered addresses, financial notations, book titles on selected subjects (e.g. India, Latin helps), health care formulae, an overview of the European contacts, building plans, etc. An entry on the "Route to Canada" reads:

> *Leave G.R. at midnight, arrive in Chicago 7:10 A.M., leave on Northwestern at 10:20 A.M., Reach St. Paul 9:00 P.M., leave St. Paul 8:30 A.M. on North Pacific, reach Winnipeg 11:20 P.M., leave Winnipeg (except Sat.) 2:30 P.M. or 10 P.M., reach Melville (11 hours).*

Railroad passes were sent around the congregation for those traveling, often determining travel schedules and occasionally stopovers when the passes had not caught up with the travelers. During vacations and school breaks sister artists were sometimes asked to produce ceramic pieces or paintings for gratuities for the "railroad men" in exchange for the railway passes. In the case of Canadian travel, sisters traveling from Winnipeg used a Northern Pacific pass for the Winnipeg to St. Paul, Minnesota, portion. When they arrived in St. Paul, they were to go to St. Joseph hospital to pick up the Northwestern pass. If there wasn't time, Grace Mackey, Mother Eveline's sister, or a Mr. Bowler would bring it to the station. If there were overnight delays or an unaccompanied candidate, Grace Mackey would provide hospitality at her apartment in St. Paul. In Chicago, the sisters were to buy half-fare tickets to Grand Rapids. Explicit directions for travel were issued by the mother general or the treasurer well into the 1960's.

**12** Two, Sisters Winifred Fieber and Loretta Wanner, were professed in the congregation; one left during the postulancy, the other returned to her home from Melville. They kept a charming and childlike journal of the year in Melville, which accompanied the convent annals for the congregational archives.

**13** A June 1929 report to the diocese indicated current membership at 505; of these, 447 were professed, 38 novices, and 20 postulants. A 1934 report to the Master General's office in Rome showed membership at 575; of these 528 were professed, 28 novices, and 19 postulants. In unofficial reports aspirants were included "in the novitiate."

# 11                Crusades of the Spirit

**1** Sister Jane Marie's papers and two taped lectures in 1975 give a clear account of the congregation's involvement in the liturgical movement. In addition to correspondence from the period and Mother Eveline's circular letters, *Contacts*, an in-house journal, is a valuable source of information on the application of the liturgical renewal. See also Mary Kathryn Oosdyke, OP, *The Christ Life Series in Religion* (1934-1935): *Liturgy and Experience as Formative Influences in Religious Education*. Doctoral dissertation, Boston College, 1987.

**2** Paul B. Marx, OSB, *Virgil Michel and the Liturgical Movement*. St. Paul: Liturgical Press, 1957. Marx writes "...it would be difficult to overrate Busch's role in the founding and guidance of the American liturgical apostolate," p.117. Virgil Michel told Father Busch, "In my notion you always had the position of chief worker and consultory," *Ibid*.

**3** A pre-primer, primer, and readers for grades 1, 2, and 3 were published by the Macmillan Company in May 1930. Sister Mary Estelle of the Sisters of the Order of Saint Dominic, Grand Rapids, Michigan, is credited as author. In her report to the ninth General Chapter in August 1930 Mother Eveline noted the favorable response to the books with their "natural, easy presentation of truths which have direct bearing on the lives of children...the charming character of the home life...attractive illustrations." "The Macmillan Company," she continued, "considers it worthy of note that the London office, traditionally slow to express approbation, has voiced its appreciation of these books, and is ordering a thousand copies of each reader." Corinne Pauli Waterall illustrated the pre-primer and primer, Charlotte Becker the other six books in the series. The books were given ecclesiastical approbation by Cardinal Hayes, Archbishop of New York.

**4** The Sisters of the Order of St. Dominic, Marywood, Grand Rapids, Michigan, were credited as authors. The books were published by the Liturgical Press, Collegeville, Minnesota, and were part of the Popular Liturgical Library (Series III, No. 5). Ecclesiastical permissions were given by Alcuin Deutsch and Virgil Michel, the imprimatur by Joseph F. Busch, Bishop of St. Cloud. There is no record of consultation with Bishop Pinten on the sisters' involvement. The speed with which the books were prepared (the imprimaturs were dated between July 31 and August 10, 1939) suggests that Bishop Pinten was not consulted.

**5** The series of eight books, one for each of the elementary grades, was credited to Dom Virgil Michel, OSB, PhD, and Dom Basil Stegmann, OSB, STD, of St. John's Abbey, Collegeville, Minnesota, and The Sisters of the Order of St. Dominic of Marywood, Grand Rapids, Michigan. The work was essentially that of Sisters Estelle and Jane Marie. Cardinal Hayes of New York gave his imprimatur to each of the volumes. The series received widespread critical acclaim throughout the Catholic press. Mother Eveline personally addressed unfavorable reviewers. Such was the case with *The Michigan Catholic*, the Detroit diocesan newspaper, where she addressed each point of a critical review. She was eager for approval and book sales, though none of the well-bound cloth volumes sold for more than 80 cents each.

**6** Sister Jane Marie's work and influence is summarized in the *New Catholic Encylopedia,* Volume XVIII, Supplement, 1978-1988, p. 310.

**7** Most of the sisters receiving advanced music education attended the American Conservatory in Chicago, the Chicago Musical College, or the School of Music of the University of Michigan, Ann Arbor.

**8** In compliance with Mother Eveline's directive of 1929 that all sisters write an autobiography, Sister Jane Marie wrote on August 14, 1929:

*This summer I had the privilege of attending the Liturgical Summer School held at St. John's Abbey, Collegeville, Minnesota. I think I can never sufficiently appreciate what this has meant for me. With a better understanding of the liturgy has come a clearer realization of what it means to be a member of Christ's Mystical Body, and of participation in the holy Sacrifice of the Mass. What seemed in the past to be the rather scattered objectives of the religious life, are now combined in the one aim--that set up by Pope Pius X--'to re-establish all things in Christ.' The liturgy has given me new courage to work for the glory of God and the sanctification of souls, for I know better than ever before, that I am not working alone,--that through participation in the holy Sacrifice I am sustained by the divine energies of Christ, and 'I can do all things in Him who strengtheneth me.'*

**9** A Franciscan gave the May retreat in Santa Cruz, New Mexico. The Michigan retreats, scheduled for August 16-25, were conducted by a Redemptorist in Traverse City, a Benedictine at Marywood, and a Dominican at Holy Rosary, Bay City. These arrangements suggest the somewhat eclectic spirituality of the congregation.

**10** In her remarks to the ninth General Chapter, August 1930, Mother Eveline paid special attention to the congregational involvement in the liturgical movement. She cited book reviews and letters from the United States, Europe, and New Zealand, and remarked about the widespread distribution, "It is interesting to know that the distribution of these books has carried beyond the United States. About a week ago a request...came from Honolulu, and last year the Bishop of New Zealand ordered fifty sets for distribution among various convents. Sample sets have been sent to England, Ireland, and to Marianhill, South Africa. During the International Liturgical Conference held in Louvain this summer, all of the publications of the Liturgical Press have been on exhibit, and our books *With Mother Church* were among these. Moreover, an account of our contribution to the Liturgical Movement in America was included in the official report on the Growth of the Liturgical Movement in the United States...read at this Congress."

**11** Mother Eveline continued to plan. In her multi-purpose address book she sketched out a comprehensive "Marywood Ground Plan." In addition to the already existing academy-convent, she foresaw grade school buildings to the west of the academy, novitiate and infirmary buildings where Aquinata Hall now stands. Along the east side of the road from the entrance on Fulton Street she sketched a library-auditorium, a gym-pool building, several residence halls, a liberal arts building, and a hall of science.

**12** There was also to be a downtown branch of Marywood Academy's school of music. *The Michigan Catholic* of September 1, 1932, announced, "as an accommodation to its downtown pupils" a school of music at 222 Fulton Street, East "in the heart of the shopping area." The sisters offered private and class instruction in piano, voice, harmony, counterpoint, composition, and history of music as well as special classes for children of pre-school and early school age.

**13** Sister Martin Fehan served as the first administrator and, after the appointment of Dr. Confrey, as Assistant to the Dean and superior of the household. During the summer of 1931 she and a laywoman virtually "set up school" in the old Sant Ilona Hall, hauling furniture from attics to restore classrooms and sleeping quarters for the eleven sisters who were to serve with Dr. Confrey as administration and faculty. Sister Felix Brand was registrar and first librarian of record. In 1932 Sylvia Laithwaite, later Sister Malachi Laithwaite, a certified librarian, took on the work of building a collegiate library and continued as director until her retirement in 1971. She was assisted by college women who were paid as WPA workers. Sister Agnes Marie Flohe served as treasurer and instructor in Latin and German. The first sister faculty were Sisters Bertrand LaLonde, French; Gonzaga Udell, philosophy; Thomas McNamara, music; Emeline Hessman, mathematics; Marcelline Horton, biology and botany; Noella Byrne, history; Aquin Gallagher, English; Mark Scanlon, chemistry and physics; Sylvester Maus, business courses. In 1933 Sister Kyran Moran succeeded Sister Martin as Director of Studies and occasionally taught religion courses. Mother Eveline was president and, with her council, the Board of Trustees. In 1937 Mother Euphrasia transferred the college presidency to Father Bukowski due to accrediting policies requiring separation of controlling board and administration. The transfer of responsibility was likely her personal choice as well.

**14** In an August 1931 circular letter to the sisters, Mother Eveline explained, "Catholic Junior College, you know, is taken care of by our Congregation the same as Marywood College but I asked the Bishop to make it very plain that the diocese is back of the institution on account of its being co-educational."

**15** In *Orate Fratres* (1930-1933), *The Junior College Journal* (1933-1934), *Education* (Fall, 1933), *Grail*, *The Catholic Apostolate*, and *Sentinel of the Blessed Sacrament*. In January 1934 Benziger published the text Dr. Confrey developed for the seniors at Catholic Central as *Social Science for Catholic High Schools*. The *Teachers' Digest* for the text was dedicated to "Mother M. Eveline Mackey, OP, Teachers' teacher, whose first concern is children's souls." Dr. Confrey sent copies of *Travel Light* (1933), a collection of his fiction, to all the high schools of the diocese as a recruiting device.

**16** Sister guests boarded at Marywood. A 1936 Chapter regulation set the fee for sister guests at $100 per semester for tuition, room and board, and transportation. From February to June 1936 four Dominican sisters from Speyer,

Germany, lived at Marywood. Destined for The Lady of the Valley Convent in Meyers Fall, Washington, these sisters stayed with the congregation to learn English. Two of these sisters taught in congregational missions, Lake Leelanau and Carson City, during the 1937-1938 school year. In May 1942 one of the original visitors, Sister M. Alacoque, returned with a companion for a three week stay at Marywood, "getting help in music and observing the work in our schools...these Sisters have a sweet love and reverence for Marywood as their first home in America." (*Annals*, 1942, May 13.)

**17**  The many points of the pronouncement follow those raised by Mother Eveline in her five-page letter of July 22, 1932, to the Apostolic Delegate Pietro Fumasoni-Biondi and with Bishop Pinten.  There were two grievances prior to that in 1932, namely:

*1. With eccelesiatical approbation we established, in 1899, an academy in Grand Rapids which the Most Reverend Henry Joseph Richter assured us would be the only Catholic academy in the city.  Some years later the Sisters of Mercy opened an academy at Mt. Mercy, which of necessity, in a city of this size, cut our territory in two and our enrollment showed the result immediately.*

*2. We opened our college at Marywood in the year 1922. Our Ecclesiastical Superiors planned for this and encouraged us to open a college as soon as we were prepared.*

Almost immediately the Sisters of Mercy planned to open a similar institution of learning at Mt. Mercy. [In 1924] The most Reverend Edward Dioynsius Kelly, DD, protected us by denying the Sisters of Mercy the right to open a college, because he saw it was not opportune to have two Catholic colleges in a city the size of Grand Rapids.

**18**  *Aquinas College Magazine*, Spring 1969, pp.4-5.

**19**  On the reverse of correspondence dealing with this and other college matters over which Monsignor Volkert and Mother Eveline disagreed, Mother wrote:

*To the members of our Community of the Future who may read this letter; In defence of our Administration I must append this: a full explanation with which Monsignor was very statisfied was given him on October 5, 1934, concerning the three young men mentioned in No. 6 of this letter. We were not aware that the Diocese looked upon our Catholic Junior College as "their diocesan college" and had hired these young men ourselves.  One had been in the college the previous year (Dennis Mohler) and the second was hired six months before Rev. A. Bukowski (whom the Bishop appointed dean) was put in the college (Mr. J. Duffy) and the third was a young man whom Rev. A. Bukowski had asked to come to help with only his expenses paid.*

*This letter and, in fact, most of the other letters in this file, were written by Rt. Rev. Monsignor Volkert after the misunderstanding came (Nov. 11, 1934) concerning our Papal Status over which we had little control. Rev. Louis Nolan came to this country as a Visitator, questioned our status, said he believed we were always papal and went back to Rome and proved it.*

# 12                                              Victory!

**1** The group first met on January 2-3, 1931, with Mother Eveline an ex officio member. The sisters adopted as a slogan "Strive for Perfection" and as aims: "To realize the Christ-Life in our Pupils through participation in the Life of Christ's Mystical Spouse--the Church; the formation in the Sisters of the highest religious and cultural development; the mastery of the technique of teaching." On November 16, 1932, Bishop Pinten established a diocesan School Board comprised of Fathers Thomas L. Noa, Raymond Baker, James Flannery, and Raymond Sweeney to "examine and propose matters relating to the school calendar, classroom programs, curricula, textbooks, and other activities that may require attention." There was no sister member but the Board was to "co-operate with pastors and Sister Superiors and Supervisors."

**2** At the time Mother Eveline was negotiating with the bishop for permission to build a convent in Melville, Saskatchewan. The bishop would permit no loans nor interest payments. On April 25, 1929, she wrote a "public version" for the sisters to share but enclosed for Sisters Mercedes and Ursula a more personal appraisal:

*...The Bishop insists just at present--one never knows when he may suddenly change--that the Sisters cannot take upon themselves to pay any interest. He would, of course, not give you the interest if he were up in Canada. In fact, he has just compelled us to pay the interest on the Infirm Priests' Fund loan, and not only interest, but compound interest computed semi-annually. I felt very much like telling him when he insisted that a stranger charge no interest that it was queer after fifty years we had to pay compound interest in the Diocese of Grand Rapids, but that would never do. There is where I must quietly submit without a word, and that is one of the reasons why I say a diocesan comunity is in a bad way sometimes.*

*...Sometimes I think Bishop's holding us back is for the best, but it is very hard to work under such strain.*

*The priests of this diocese seem to be more dissatisfied from day to day with everything the Bishop is doing. He is looking poorly himself, and maybe sometime in the near future he might leave us, but it is just as positive that he might be here for the next twenty years, so don't plan too much on this.*

The note was repaid as ordered; there is no evidence that any payment was made to the congregation for the services at St. John's Home. In the congregational annals for January 25, 1939, Sister Joachim Wisner, secretary general, wrote:

*In conversation last week with Sister M. Felix, Syndica General, the Most Reverend Bishop Pinten mentioned a debt of $60,000 (not including interest) which was contracted with the Diocese of Grand Rapids by Reverend Mother M. Benedicta during the administration of the Most Reverend Bishop Kelly, and which we were under the impression was cancelled while Mother M. Eveline was in office by a counter claim in consideration of the services of our Sisters at St. John's Home. Mother M. Euphrasia called on His Excellency today accompanied by Sister M. Alphonsine. Bishop told Mother that he had no intention of being hard in the matter--was very indefinite as to what he considers our obligation.*

**3** In February 1930 Father Joseph Vogl, chaplain at Marywood, presided at the canonical erection of four Dominican confraterities in Sacred Heart Chapel: the Rosary Confraternity, the Holy Name Confraternity, the Angelic Warfare, and the Blessed Sacrament Confraternity.

**4** Sister Albertina had secured materials from the archives of the Archdiocese of New York, the Newburgh Dominicans, and the Society of the Propagation of the Faith in Rome. The case was built on three propositions:

*1. That we became a separate Congregation, based on the evidence:*

*a) an entry in Mother Aquinata's notebook in her own handwriting.*

*b) note from Archbishop Corrigan of New York to Bishop Richter, dated July 18, 1894, making reference to this separation.*

*c) Bishop Richter's letter to Archbishop Corrigan, dated July 25, 1896, in which he makes several references to the separation.*

*2. That we are known in Rome as the Congregation of Our Lady of the Sacred Heart, based on the evidence:*

*a) A diploma of affiliation with the Order of Preachers of our Community as the Congregation of our Lady of the Sacred Heart, November 26, 1894. (reference to in Mother's Notebook)*

*b) A communication from the Sacred Congregation of the Propagation of the Faith, dated March 31, 1896, relative to our transfer from the Second to the Third Order.*

*c) Bishop Richter's letter to Archbishop Corrigan, dated July 25, 1896, stating why Mother Aquinata remain in Michigan after having been separated from the East.*

*d) The letter from the Sacred Propaganda dated September 30, 1896, ratifying the change from the Second to the Third Order.*

*e) Letters from the Sacred Congregation of the Propaganda of the Faith, dated August 27, 1897; September 17, 1903, confirming the elections of Mother Mary Aquinata as the Mother General on two successive elections.*

*3. Living Witnesses who heard Bishop Richter announce to an assembly of the Community on August 30, 1894, that the separation had taken place.*

**5** The sisters, ranging in ages 55 to 63, were asked where they were when the separation took place, their memories of the event, and what changes took place as a result. Mother Benedicta remarked, "The establishment pleased most but was displeasing to one or the other who were from the East." This view was reinforced by Sister Cyrilla who testified, "The Bishop announced in the chapel; I was in the chapel at the time; the New York Sisters felt it very keenly." Sister Augustine was more specific. "I remember," she testified, "Sister Cyprian expressed displeasure." And as a change remembered, she said, "Some of the Sisters left and returned to New York." When asked about her memories of Bishop Richter's statement about the establishment, she said, " I remember Bishop Richter told us we would have access to authority more readily, or something to that effect. It caused some consternation on the part of those from the East."

**6** On June 19, 1935, she saw things differently. She wrote to Father Louis Nolan, OP, that "the Diocese of Grand Rapids had no documents to prove that our Congregation was reduced by the Holy See to a Diocesan Institute. In the absence of any document, the Most Reverend Ordinary of the Diocese instituted an action before the Diocesan Court of Grand Rapids to prove by decree of said Court that the erection was legally made. Of course, before this was done, we were told to send in a petition for the same; this we did in good faith on December 28, 1930. ...We see now that the material on which the Court based its decision only went to prove that we were legally separated from New York and, as you recogized when you were here, some of it might be used to prove that we are Pontifical."

**7** Monsignor Volkert had lectured twice weekly at Marywood Academy since its opening in 1922. He instructed the novices in philosophy and theology and was a frequent guest at congregational celebrations. Mother Eveline occasionally sent him a check of $80, interest payment on a loan of $2,000. In January 1937 he asked Mother Euphrasia for full payment of $2,075.

On the occasion of his appointment as vicar general in 1934, Father Patrick Carroll, CSC, Vice President of Notre Dame and friend of the congregation, wrote a poetic tribute "To Our Friend" which served as the text for the Sisters' congratulatory card. Later Mother Eveline annotated the text, "When this was given to him, **he** was a real **friend**. He did not remain very true to us afterwards, be it noted. Mother Eveline." There must have been some reconciliation because a letter of June 20, 1945, from Monsignor Volkert, then living in Muskegon, to Mother Eveline reflects appreciation for a letter, interest in Mother's activities, and anticipation of a visit. He concluded, "For the summer I wish you a happy season, fruitful in good works and divine blessings. After we arrive at our age and condition we desire nothing else but that God be good to us."

**8** Dominican Archives, Sinsinawa, Wisconsin, serve as the official repository for the fifty years of Conference activities. Dominican archives throughout the United States contain interesting pieces on the implications, real and imagined, of the implementation of the five-fold program outlined by Father Nolan. The Sinsinawa archives contain a letter from a member to Mother Samuel Coughlin, Sinsinawa mother general from 1909-1949, reporting the Dominican fathers' "rage" over the plans, in particular that of a House of Studies for Sisters in Rome. It was feared to be, the sister reported, a Roman scheme to unload Dominican properties recently returned to the Order by Mussolini's government. (There was some truth in the proposition. Properties historically associated with the Order had recently returned to Dominican ownership. A restoration drive had reached to the United States and, in spite of the Depression and great building debts, Mother Eveline among other mothers general had contributed to the restoration of buildings.) In 1936 it was rumored that the Angelicum, badly in need of repairs, was offered to the Conference for a million lira.

Some Dominican fathers in the United States appear to have opposed the concept of the Conference, perhaps fearing too great uniformity and "Romanization." In the late nineteenth century, the Dominican fathers had suffered from foreign vistators' criticisms. Father Clement Thuente, OP, a well-known orator and retreat master of St. Joseph Province, was cautious about the project. He was a good friend of Monsignor Volkert and may have communicated his reservations. In the spring of 1935 Monsignor Volkert substituted Father Thuente for young Father Allen J. Babcock as the retreat master at Marywood.

There were Dominican advocates of the plan as well. As early as 1906 Bishop John T. McNicholas, OP, had written to the mothers general about Master General Cormier's interest in the Dominican sisters. There was great similarity in the language of his suggestions and the invitation of Father Nolan. The notion resurfaced in 1925 with Archbishop McNicholas encouraging such an association. He recommended a "round table" discussion and retreat as part of the meetings, all of which became standard features of the Conference for decades.

**9** On her return she designed a letterhead and had stationery printed on the Marywood press. Mother Samuel, Conference president, objected to formal stationery, thinking the absent congregations would deem it "presumptuous."

**10** Within a month of the Conference's first meeting a minor tempest developed over the issue of the adoption of the Divine Office. Joseph Wagner, Inc., publishers of the Dominican Sisters Office Book, a version of the Little Office of the Blessed Virgin Mary, wrote to all Dominican houses throughout the United States. The implication was that the Divine Office was not quite suitable for Dominican use, that there were not editions readily available. There was speculation that Father C.J. Callan, OP, one of the editors of the Office Book, was behind the publisher's campaign. Father Nolan indicated that Father Callan had been reprimanded for his role in the matter, which situation added to the reservations some of the American Dominican fathers had towards the Conference.

**11** Mother responded that she thought it advisable to put the question of the acceptance of an entire community to the 1936 Chapter. If the congregation was pontifical she could receive Mother Catherine. On March 13, 1936, Sister Marie Catherine Clayton, native of Ireland, transferred to the congregation. Father Nolan arranged the transfer from the congregation of her first profession, a Portuguese Dominican Congregation, through a Portuguese bishop so Bishop Pinten would not be involved. Sister Marie Catherine's early training in Portugal had been interrupted by the revolution of 1910. For several years she was among the exiled sisters who went from England, to Ireland, and then to the United States, some ending in Kenosha, Wisconsin. A licensed nurse, she spent many years in the administration of Nazareth Sanatorium in Albuquerque.

**12** The Document N. 2306/35, dated April 23, 1936, was addressed to Bishop Pinten. It read:

Most Excellent and Reverend Lord,

A doubt was submitted to the mature consideration of this Sacred Congregation of Religious as to whether the Sisters of the Third Order of St. Dominic in your diocese are to be considered of Pontifical right or only diocesan, and all the facts of the case having been considered and especially the vote both of His Eminence Cardinal Laurenti, an expert in this matter, and of the Sacred Congregation of Propaganda, it has decided to reply as follows:

THE INSTITUTE IN QUESTION MUST BE CONSIDERED OF PONTIFICAL RIGHT.

Will your Excellency please communicate this reply to those interested, and with my greeting,

I remain, Your Excellency's devoted servant,
Fr. L. H. Pasetto, Secy.

**13** The bishop did not wholly leave the matter. On August 5, 1936, he wrote to Monsignor Egidio Vagnozzi, Auditor in the Apostolic Delegation, telling him that a "prominent priest of this diocese ...said that he was much alarmed as to the existing conditions at Marywood." The bishop enclosed an anonymous letter dated August 3, 1936, allegedly written by "A Sister of Saint Dominic" on behalf of some four hundred sisters. The effect of the letter was that many were displeased with the change in canonical status and above all the loss of "the privilege of choosing our Superiors as we have done in the many years past." The Apostolic Delegate reminded the bishop of the areas of jurisdiction remaining to him: quinquennial visitation and some supervision of finances. He asked the bishop about his perceptions of the election on August 9, to which Bishop Pinten replied that he had sent a delegate, Father Robert Bogg. The bishop further commented:

*In my letter of July 24, addressed to the Apostolic Delegation, it was stated that in my judgment it would be 'deplorable should Mother Eveline be reelected to the office.' I am afraid some of the Sisters would have left the Community. There are others who concur in this opinion. A pronounced ill-will existed against her. The newly-elected Mother Euphrasia has, I am happy to say, the respect, confidence and good-will of the Community. This augurs well for the Dominican nuns of this diocese.*

**14** Circular letter, September 3, 1929.

**1**  Sibbie Sullivan, remembered by the sisters for her stately presence, quiet grace, and "picture hats," died in 1979. Linens with handmade lace from Margaret O'Grady Sullivan's dowry were given to the congregation in 1989 by the Frank Sullivan family.

**2**  In 1936 Sister Joachim Visner began congregational annals, a practice which continued until 1976. The first years, from 1936 to 1942, were in chronicle style and provide interesting detail and commentary.

**3**  Papal status did not immediately open channels of "counsel or relief." The congregational archives keeps a single-page document, written in French and dated January 23, 1940, announcing that the Pontifical Year Book now lists religious institutes of women of pontifical right. The form notice was presented in an inner envelope addressed to "Madame la Superieure des Soeurs du Tiers Ordere de. St. Dominique di N. Dame du S. Coeur, Grand Rapids, U.S.A." On the outer envelope, postmarked February 9, 1940, addressed "A Son Excellence Rev.me. Mgr. Joseph Pinten, Eveque de Grand Rapids, 165, Sheldon Ave., Michigan. U.S.A.," there is a note reading, "This is preserved not for its value, but because it is the only mail received from the Vatican during the years 1936-1940, after we were declared "Papal" although we have reason to believe that other letters and documents were sent to us. These envelopes show the manner of addressing mail to our Congregation. Sr. M. Joachim, Sec'y."

**4**  On one occasion Bishop Haas brought the sisters a gift of a small wood ashtray with a note on its provenance.

*From Msgr. M. Vassallo, V.G. San Juan, Puerto Rico, September 17, 1941. Asubo Wood, a hard-wood, now extinct. This ash tray was made with asubo wood taken from a beam supporting the floor in the old Santo Domingo Convent, built in 1521 by OP's in San Juan, P.R. I received the above ashtray from Msgr. Vassallo, Sept. 17, 1941. Francis J. Haas.*

**5**  *Minutes of General Council*, April 23, 1937. One of the laymen to be retained was Richard O'Brien who had served as chauffeur and chief engineer. A kind of folklore lingers in the congregation about the lay employees, "The Men" and women, who served at Marywood. They are remembered with appreciation and affection.

**6**  The slender red cloth volume was almost a year in coming and was, in fact, a duplicate of the one intended for Mother Euphrasia. Cardinal Pasetto, Secretary for the Sacred Congregation of Religious with whom Father Nolan had negotiated during the spring of 1936, had signed and sealed the text on February 2, 1937. The papers were then sent to a bindery in Rome. On March 10, 1937, the bound volume was sent to Bishop Pinten by Dr. Giulio Biondi, *spedizionere per Affari Ecclesiastici*, along with charges for 1,188 *lira* for printing, tax, and postage. The text  was sent to Bishop Pinten as Ordinary of the diocese in which the congregation's motherhouse was situated. It was expected that he would communicate to the sisters the reception of the approved document. He did not do so. Again Father Nolan was asked to intervene. A second text was sent directly to the sisters and received on January 25, 1938. In 1940 Bishop Pinten resigned and retired to his home in Marquette, Michigan, where he died on

November 6, 1945. In May 1946 Father Robert Bogg, chancellor of the diocese, found the original constitution book in its brown paper wrapping at Bishop Pinten's home and personally delivered it to Mother Euphrasia.

**7** Mother Euphrasia hesitated to present the text to Bishop Pinten for his imprimatur. Finally, in October 1940, she asked Mother Eveline, then in Saginaw, to sound out Bishop Murphy on whether he would give the imprimatur. He agreed but after Bishop Pinten's resignation on November 1 advised that the text be given to Bishop Albers, the ecclesiastical administrator. He, in turn, agreed to give the permission but with the naming of the new bishop, printing was delayed again.

Bishop Plagens received the draft on March 24, 1941, and within a week commented on its excellence. The press of his new ministry, however, kept him from the final approval. On June 12, he had a heart attack and was hospitalized. Nevertheless on the following day a package came to Marywood at 5:00 p.m. In his room at St.Mary Hospital, the bishop had written "Imprimatur + Joseph C. Plagens Eppis. Grandormensis die 13-Junii, 1941" on the typescript. The draft was at the printers by 6:15 that evening.

# 14            For the Duration

**1** Sister Jane Marie continued her liturgical studies, especially under the direction of Father Vincent Kennedy. From 1945 to 1950 she prepared a church history, published by the Bruce Company. Due to intervening teaching and writing assignments, she did not complete the three-year program until June 1, 1950. Her licentiate degree in theology, *magna cum laude*, was the first awarded by the Institute to a woman.

**2** Monthly announcements and directives from the school supervisors took the place of *Contacts* from September 1936 to 1940. In February 1940 monthly publication was resumed although the quality of paper and printing deteriorated. In December 1942 it became a quarterly publication. Contributors were not always named, but many articles are in Mother Eveline's style. It does not appear that Mother Euphrasia contributed to the paper nor did she exercise much direct control over the General Council of Schools or the supervisors' office.

**3** See David S. Bovee, "Catholic Rural Life Leader: Luigi G. Ligutti," *US Catholic Historian*, 8,3. Fall 1989, pp. 143-161.

**4** The midwest Province of St. Albert the Great, centered in River Forest, Illinois, had been created in 1939. The congregation continued its earlier connection with the Province of St. Joseph, applying to its provincial for faculty, chaplains, and retreat masters, until ca. 1976. Dominicans from the central province were, however, frequent visitors and often concelebrants at jubilee and college functions.

**5** Father Wilson was born in Boston on November 29, 1905. He received a Bachelor of Arts degree from Boston College in 1927 and entered the Dominican Novitiate, St. Rose, Kentucky, in 1931. He studied philosophy at the House of Studies, River Forest, Illinois, and theology at Somerset, Ohio, and Washington, DC. He was ordained in 1938 by Archbishop M. J. Curley and served St.

Vincent Ferrer parish in New York City until his appointment to Grand Rapids in 1942.

**6** With the house annals for 1940-1941, St. Mary convent, Muskegon, submitted a list of materials read in the refectory, including:

*How to Read a Book - Adler*
*Building Character from Within - MacMahon*
*The Psychology of Asceticism - Landwirtz*
*The Mass and The Life of Prayer - Thorold*
*When the Sorghum was High - Considine*
*Of His Fullness - Vann*
*The Church and The Catholic - Guardini*
*Orthodoxy - Chesterton*
*The Road to Rome - Belloc*
*The Son of God - Adam*
*Survival Until Seventeen - Feeney*
*Confirmation in the Modern World - no author stated*
*Conversation with God - Thorold*
*Murder in a Nunnery - Shepherd*
*Student Teaching - Schorling*
*Dominican Saints*
*Says Mrs. Crowley, Says She - Hurley*
*A Map of Life - Sheed*
*Periodicals: The Torch, The Catholic School Journal,*
*Orate Fratres, America, and Ecclesiastical Review.*

The list, including Dominican and contemporary Catholic authors as well as others, demonstrates both the professional and religious character of the group of fourteen sisters. It was probably a list replicated in many convents of the congregation.

**7** Master General Cormier had come in 1930, his *Socius* Father Louis Nolan in 1934. In January 1942 Father Norbert Georges, OP, promoter of the cause of canonization for Blessed Martin de Porres, spoke to the sisters and students on "Blessed Martin's Broom." In March 1942 Walter Farrell, OP, author of *The Companion to The Summa,* was engaged by Aquinas College to give a lecture at the Civic Auditorium. Fathers Clement Thuente, Albert Drexelius, and Vincent Urban Nagle were among the many Dominican retreat masters. The sisters at Marywood and Aquinas College welcomed Fathers Francis Wendell, Gerald Vann, and other distinguished Dominicans.

**8** In 1944 William Bonniwell, OP, published *A History of the Dominican Liturgy* (NY: Wagner, Inc.). That same year copies were purchased for the novitiate and community libraries and the sections on the Dominican calendars, the Mass, Office, and Compline and the *Salve* processions were carefully annotated. The Dominican rite was used at Marywood and the novitiate choir was schooled in the nuances of Gregorian chant according to that rite. In 1948 Father Bonniwell conducted the August retreat at Marywood. It was a "splendid retreat," the annalist recorded, although he was a very reluctant and outspoken guest.

**9** In particular, the sisters witnessing the cure worked toward the spread of the devotion. Within the congregation there is a tradition of stories, some with charm and humor, related to the efficacy of the prayer. This devotion, like that to Sister Reparata, is attested to in the personal belongings of the older sisters who keep prayer cards, badges, and mementos of the cure.

**10** The congregational archives contain dozens of letters, prayer cards, and several personal items of Sister Reparata--serge scapular, a face veil, prayer books, as well as the responses to the 1937 questionnaires. There are evidences of her lingering influence also among the personal items kept by senior sisters-- copies of her letters, prayer cards, and *The Grain of Mustard.* On March 21, 1937, Sister Edith Welzel entered the Cincinnati cloister where Sister Reparata had died. Sister Edith had entered the congregation on April 9, 1912, and may well have been influenced by Sister Reparata who entered the following year. For many years Sister Edith expressed a longing for cloistered life. Her letters contain some aspects of the devotion expressed in Sister Reparata's writings.

**11** The data available for statistical summary are scant and widely divergent. An undated sheet filed with items on relations with the Diocese of Grand Rapids for January 1945 suggests the aging population of the congregation.

*Of 249 teaching sisters who entered during the first fifty years--from 1864\* to 1914:*

| | |
|---|---|
| *141* | *are still actively engaged in school work* |
| *2* | *for more than 60 years* |
| *6* | *for more than 50 years* |
| *27* | *for more than 40 years* |
| *44* | *for more than 35 years* |
| *62* | *for more than 30 years* |
| *108* | *deceased - average age **32 years** (not clear whether this is number of years in profession or age).* |

*In addition to the above 249, 29 left soon after receiving the habit.*

\* The year of Mother Aquinata's first profession. Author's note.

**12** Sister Genevieve died on September 24, 1944. She was replaced on the council by Sister Joachim Visner, who also continued as secretary general.

**13** One of the effects of a delegate system may have been to shift representation to the "elders" of the congregation. In virtually every subsequent Chapter there has been discussion of the manner in which representation is achieved.

**14** In August 1943 the congregation celebrated a second Diamond Jubilee, this time for Sisters Adelaide McCue (1859-1945) and Matthia Selhuber (1865-1953). Only Mother Clementina Coyle (1858-1950) outranked them. Seven of the year's ten golden jubilarians were alive, among them Sister Genevieve Gauthier, a member of the council, and Sisters Bertrand LaLonde (1877-1977) and Catherine Van Anhold (1875-1972), whose life dates testify to the increasing longevity of the sisters.

**15** The address was published in 1945 as *The Catholic School and Citizenship* by Central Bureau Press, St. Louis, MO.

**1** On April 22, 1948, Father Bukowski was among eleven priests of the diocese raised to the rank of monsignor. With Fathers Arszulowicz and Shaw, Father Bukowski was designated a Papal Chamberlain with the title of "Very Reverend." While Monsignor Bukowski was of such a nature as to discourage familiarity, students affectionately referred to him as "Mon Buk."

**2** On March 23, 1946, the Board amended its constitution and by-laws to provide for continuity of membership. The board was to consist of not less than six nor more than nine members of the congregation. "They shall be the Prioress General who is ex officio president of the board; her four Councilors (one of whom may be at the same time the secretary general); the syndica general, who is ex officio treasurer of the board; and the Secretary-General who is ex officio secretary of the board. Should it happen that in any election, held ordinarily at the end of the six-year term of the Prioress General or extraordinarily at her death or resignation, an entire new General Council is elected, the incoming members shall elect, in addition to themselves, two members from among their predecessors. Should it happen that by such an election there is a change of all but one member, then one member shall be elected from the preceding Council."

In July 1946 the position of Sister Jerome Smithers was questioned by a board of examiners of the North Central Accrediting Association. Sister Jerome replaced Sister Mildred Hawkins as dean of the college in 1942. She was elected as a member of the council in July 1942, and so served a triple role: member of the Sisters of St. Dominic Corporation, member of the Aquinas College Corporation, and Academic Dean. The difficulty was resolved by her resignation from the Aquinas College Board.

**3** In 1931 Sister Bertrand finished a two-year course leading to the *Diplome de Professeur la langue Français* at the Sorbonne. She and Sister Mildred went on to the University of Fribourg in Switzerland, Sister Bertrand to continue her studies in French and Spanish, Sister Mildred in classical languages. Sister Mildred later transferred to the University of Munich, from which she received the PhD in 1938, in Greek, with Latin and history minors. From her rooms at 101 Turkenstrasse, Munich, she wrote letters to the sisters about trips to Greece, Italy, the British Isles, and Dominican shrines. As an eyewitness to the tumultuous politics transferring the Weimar Republic into the Third Reich in the 1930's, she became a popular speaker in college classes on the subject.

Sister Bertrand remained at Aquinas College until 1965; Sister Mildred was dean of the college from 1939 to 1942 and again from 1949 to 1963, the year of her retirement. Sister Mildred was the first member of the congregation to celebrate her 100th birthday; Sister Bertrand died in 1977 in her 99th year.

**4** On May 31, 1989, the shrine was rededicated to honor veterans of World War II, the Korean and Vietnam Wars. Joseph and Mary Beth Hansknecht, class of 1950 and sponsors of the original fund drive for the shrine, donated $10,000 toward the maintenance of the shrine statue. The donation honors their late son, Stephen Paul, class of 1983.

**5** There are two detailed eyewitness accounts of the steps leading to the purchase of the new campus, by Sister Felix Brand, treasurer general, "because this purchase is bound to be an important one in the history of our community," and by Sister Joachim Visner, secretary general and congregational annalist.

**6** *The Grand Rapids Press*, February 17, 1939.

**7** Davenport founded the University of Grand Rapids in 1936. Dr. Paul F. Voelker, state superintendent of instruction from 1933-1935 and a former president of Olivet College and of Battle Creek College, was the president. Davenport was also president of the Davenport-McLachlan Institute which offered commercial and business education. Day classes for the institute were given in connection with the university at Holmdene. With the sale of the Robinson Road property, the institute program was transferred to the Lucid Private Secretarial School at 129 Fulton Street, another Institute holding. These programs were part of the evolution of Davenport College. The university invited Aquinas College to take over the School of Pharmacy. The council declined the offer and the program was subsequently incorporated into the professional schools at Ferris State College, Big Rapids, Michigan.

**8** During the negotiations Sister Jerome Smithers, a member of council and dean of the college, acted as liaison with Messrs. Frey and Leonard who were conferring with Mr. Davenport, and with Mother Euphrasia and Sister Felix at the bishop's residence. The quotation was not lowered; an option of $5,000 was to be paid immediately. Permission from the Holy See was required as the congregational debt would exceed $100,000. This permission could be secured only through the apostolic delegate in Washington, DC, the normal channel for business since the confirmation of the congregation's papal status. Mother and Sister Felix went to the chancery office to secure the necessary papers, then called at the train station for information on express trains to Washington. Rather than mail the papers, it was thought that two sisters could take them to the apostolic delegate more swiftly. The bishop telephoned Washington for an appointment with Archbishop Cicognani. Father Carroll, the archbishop's secretary, promised to relay the case to the delegate and to return the call the next morning.

By 8:30 a.m, April 26, Mother and Sister Felix were at the bishop's residence. At 8:45 a.m., the call came from Washington. Permission was granted. There were then hurried conferences with Leon. W. Harrington, attorney, and Messrs. Frey and Leonard, and visits to various safe deposit boxes. A $115,000 loan at 2½% was negotiated and signed and a check for $5,000 delivered to Mr. Davenport. Mother Euphrasia returned to Marywood in time for Little Hours at 11:30 a.m. Subsequently Mother Euphrasia sent the apostolic delegate a letter of thanks, the necessary papers, a check for $115 for the tax placed on the transaction, and a check for $100 for some work of charity which appealed to the delegate.

**9** Of these, 570 were on active duty: 445 in teaching, 78 in domestic work, 18 in administrative or office work; 8 prefects, 1 librarian, 1 in writing, 4 in nursing, 15 of the newly professed in studying. There were 16 who were infirm and assigned light duties, and 20 who were infirm and off duty. There were approximately 12,000 students in grade schools, 4,400 in high school and 500 in college taught by the sisters in 1948.

**10**  With permission of the author, Mary DeHaus, OP.

## 16          Unless the Lord Build the House...

**1**  See Chapter 6, note 9.

**2**  *Minutes of General Council*, 1948-1951, p. 95a. January 22, 1950.

*The plans...call for placement of the building with the main entrance at the crest of the hill, bringing the south wall about even with the north border of the [old]tennis court. The building provides 150 sleeping rooms for Sisters, 8 [feet] X 12 [feet]. First floor--reception rooms, community room, guest dining-rooms, classrooms for young Sisters, refectory, kitchen, and laundry, sewing room. Second floor--chapel, general offices, supervisors' offices, postulate, sleeping rooms for guests, about 25 sleeping rooms for Sisters. Third floor--novitiate and infirmary. Infirmary includes treatment-room, doctors' room, nurses' station, refectory and kitchen. Fourth floor--entirely devoted to sleeping rooms.*

**3**  *The Michigan Catholic*, March 31, 1949, features "Harry L. Mead--Church Architect." Mead began his architectural career in 1902 with the Grand Rapids firm of W.G. and F.S. Robinson, who had done much work for Bishop Richter, including St. John's Home.

**4**  On April 24, 1949, the congregation petitioned the Holy See to borrow $1,000,000. Permission was relayed through the apostolic delegate, with a tax of $500 for the service. The initial financing, reviewed by Bishop Haas and Leon Harrington, congregational lawyer, was arranged with the Ziegler Company of West Bend, Wisconsin, for $1,000,000 at 3½% and on a bond issue at approximately 3%.

**5**  *The Grand Rapids Herald*, November 22, 1953, and April 11, 1954, and *The Western Michigan Catholic*, September 30, 1954, report on construction progress.

**6**  Father Kohler initially offered $25,000 for the buildings and property. The property was appraised at approximately $80,000 by a Traverse City realtor; $40,000 by another "though by no means...the present reconstruction value." (*Minutes of General Council*, Volume 7. 1948-1951, p. 60, entry for June 29, 1949). On January 3, 1950, Mother reported to the council Bishop Haas' offer to the congregation of 2,000 cemetery lots in the new Resurrection Cemetery in exchange for the Traverse City property. The council declined that offer while acknowledging the need to purchase some cemetery lots (*Ibid.* p.94). Initially the council sought $50,000, later $30,000. (*Ibid.*, p. 104 entry for April 18, 1950). A formal petition was directed to the Holy See to sell the property for $32,000. (*Ibid.*, p. 119, entry for July 3, 1950). The final agreement included free use of the convent for housing extra sisters during the summer or "anytime in perpetuity" and for the diocese to give the congregation 500 cemetery plots, with the congregation having responsibility for upkeep.

**7**  Our Lady of Perpetual Help parish offered $1,000 for a "grove" the congregation owned in that village.

**8** The Sisters of Charity of St. Louis agreed to take over the congregational work at St. Henry school, Melville, beginning in September 1950. The convent and its furnishings were offered to them for $5,500, "book value--$8,000 less depreciation."

**9** In the summer of 1954 the congregation sold to St. Thomas the Apostle parish a strip of land 628.35 feet long and 60 feet wide for $5,500. The land, with 60 feet frontage on Fulton Street, was intended as a parking lot and driveway for the parish. Since 1948 the parish had sought the land but the congregation declined until college expansion was well charted. The sale included an agreement for an eight-foot right of way across the south portion. The original plans for St. Joseph the Worker Hall included a parking lot and two-way drive at the corner of Youell and Wilcox Park streets. Some members of the church committee and local parishioners, fearing increased traffic in the area, expressed their objections in May 1963. As a consequence, the design was altered to a small parking lot and a single lane access road to the dormitory. The 1954 right of way was, however, inadequate. The matter was put before Bishop Babcock, who pointed out that the property was, as is all property commonly considered diocesan or parish, in the name of the bishop in trust for the parish of St. Thomas. It was his wish that the college be allowed whatever property was needed to meet government regulations. A portion of the property sold to the parish was later given for Mercy Respite Center.

**10** Sister Loyola Finn, daughter of a pioneer family in northwest Grand Rapids and of St. Alphonsus parish, inherited several pieces of property and cash. The monies were occasionally referred to in discussion of building a congregational chapel. In 1951 a small tract was sold on Schafer Road for approximately $500; another on Twenty-eighth Street was sold in 1966 for $195,000.

**11** The 1953 Fall Festival netted $17,478, the largest source being the raffle of a "two-tone green, four-door Buick" which was displayed on the Marywood circle for weeks prior to the November festival. Building fund income for June 1953-June 1954 included $5,000 from Bishop Haas and $1,000 from Bishop Woznicki of Saginaw.

**12** *Annals*, III, 1948-1960, p.3.

**13** At the council meeting on November 11, 1950, Mother called attention to an outlay of $790.19 "for meals at hotel, etc., since there is no Sister housekeeper...since the beginning of the school year." This "pointed to the necessity of some other arrangement at Aquinas concerning care of the priests." *Minutes of the General Council*, 1948-1951, p. 142.

On September 19, 1959, Mother Victor reported to the council on a meeting she had had with Father W.D. Marrin, OP, provincial of the Province of St. Joseph, and with Father Ferrer Smith, regent of studies, in New York City on July 23, 1959. The meeting grew out of a seemingly chance remark by one of the Dominican priests on the Aquinas faculty that the Dominican fathers had "no status in the diocese of Grand Rapids." The fathers hoped for inclusion in the funds drive for the erection of a priory in Grand Rapids, in its first stages for 14 to 16 men, on its own grounds, i.e. neither on Aquinas nor motherhouse property. The land and building would subsequently be ceded to the province.

There would need to be, Fathers Marrin and Smith pointed out, salary increments to compensate for the maintenance and housekeeping services now rendered by the sisters. Mother inquired whether an enlargement of Aquin Hall would suffice, or perhaps the adaptation of an old mansion, such as the Franciscan friars had in the former Wurzburg mansion on Lake Drive. The fathers' "dream" was, however, on a larger scale. Mother, "while being very courteous and apparently unsurprised, made it very definite that while she would take the matter up with her council there could be no thought of including this project in the plans of the immediate future." Mother inferred, continues the General Council Minutes, that the time might come when the bishop would permit the Dominican fathers to put on a drive for such a building.

On October 6, 1959, Mother Victor wrote a consummately diplomatic letter to Father Marrin. She cited the scope of the permission given by the Holy See, terms of the contract with Commmunity Counselling Services, the solicitation of funds already in progress, and a general historical argument. "The Sisters have waited eighty years, Father, for this permission [to conduct a fund-raising campaign in the diocese], but the Sisters were pioneers in Michigan." (Bishop Pinten had withdrawn permission for a drive in 1927-1928 to coincide with the golden anniversary of the congregation in Michigan). *Minutes of the General Council*, September 19, 1959. pp.133-136.

**14** On January 6, 1955, Mother Victor sent a formal request to Bishop Babcock for his approval of a request to the Holy See that the congregation borrow $650,000 to complete the administration building. Canon law required this procedure of congregations of religious women seeking loans of this magnitude. During the period of the college expansion, regulations allowed the ordinary of a diocese to give permission for loans to $22,000. The amount was modified in subsequent years. In April 1949 the apostolic delegate to the United States gave permission for the congregation to borrow $1,000,000 to build the motherhouse. Only $650,000 was borrowed at that time. In December 1953 permission was obtained from the Holy See to transfer the permission to apply on the construction at Aquinas College. The additional $650,00 sought was to apply to college expansion. A tax of $205 was to accompany the petition. Ordinary business with the Holy See, for example, approval of changes in sisters' wills, constitutional rescripts, dispensations, had taxes from $6 to $13 per request in the 1950's.

**15** The *Western Michigan Catholic*, November 19, 1953.

**16** In 1962 the tower became the center for ABS, the Aquinas Broadcasting Society, headed by Father Hugh Michael Beahan, priest of the Diocese of Grand Rapids. WXTO, an FM radio station licensed by the Federal Communications Commission, broadcast a full program of classical music, news, and lectures, and offered broadcasting internships to students of speech and drama.

**17** At the February 1966 meeting of the Lay Board of Trustees, Joseph D. Cavera, Peter M. Wege, and August G. Gutmueller were inducted as members. Michael Leonard, T. Gerald McShane, and Monroe B. Sullivan were given honorary life memberships in recognition of twenty-five years of service to the board.

**18** In July 1985 Richard E. Riebel, president of Foremost Insurance of Grand Rapids and Aquinas College trustee, bought the building and approximately two acres of land from the congregation for $500,000. He subsequently deeded the property to Aquinas College. The building was renamed Hruby Hall in honor of Norbert J. Hruby, president of the college from 1969 to 1986, and is used for academic services and dormitory.

**19** The Lake Drive houses were subsequently sold. Two houses, at 1601 and 1603 Robinson Road, were acquired in the early 1960's and used first for lay faculty residences, later for sister faculty. These were sold in 1981 when housing was no longer part of the compensation agreement between sister employees and the college.

**20** The congregation petitioned the Holy See to borrow $600,000. A series of six hundred $1,000 bonds maturing periodically over a period of 38 years would be held by the US Housing & Home Finance Agency and interest on the obligation derived from current revenue at the Student Center. In August 1965 the Sacred Congregation of Religious conferred upon the apostolic delegate the faculty, among others, to permit loans, alienation of property, etc. to the sum of $500,000.

**21** In March 1967 the college announced the beginning of "Forward 70," a fund drive to raise $2,150,000 for a physical education-assembly building, library, and art center. The first was dedicated in January 1969, the fine arts center in 1983. In 1977 renovation costing over $500,000 expanded the college library area to the entire second floor of the administration building. A new library was the main objective of a funds drive begun in 1990.

**22** "Sanatorium Facilities in New Mexico for the Treatment of Patients with Nervous or Mental Disorders," undated, ca. 1950.

**23** In June 1960 nursing personnel included 25 registered nurses, ten licensed practical nurses, five sisters with bachelor of science degrees in nursing, one sister with a bachelor of science degree in nursing education, one with a master of science degree in nursing education, one with a master of science, and two sisters with bachelor of arts degrees. *Report of the Administration of Mother Mary Victor*, July 4, 1954 - June 16, 1960. Papers of the fourteenth General Chapter.

**24** Building and maintenance costs, training and commitment of sister personnel were major outlays associated with the Nazareth property. About 1960 it became evident that there were valuable mineral deposits on portions of the land. Mining of the gravel provided a major portion of congregational income in the 1970's and 1980's.

**25** The rambling adobe building remained as convent and congregational center in the Southwest until its demolition in 1973. On February 1, 1976, the hospital was sold to the Vista Hill Foundation of San Diego, California, and subsequently operated as Vista Sandia Hospital, a non-profit organization. The surrounding land was deeded to the corporation of the Sisters of St. Dominic of Grand Rapids. Sister Patrice Konwinski, OP, administrator of Nazareth Hospital at the time of the sale, remained in that position at Vista Sandia until 1980, when the sale and transfer of the hospital was completed. On December 15, 1987, Vista Sandia Hospital closed and the facility remains vacant. In 1988 a separate corporation comprised of congregationally-owned lands in New Mexico was formed.

**26** In March 1966 approximately 27 acres at 2100 Twenty-eighth Street, SE, part of the Finn inheritance, was sold for $195,000. A loan of $475,000 was negotiated with Union Bank and Trust Company.

**27** Mother Victor asked Sister Wendell Lennon (1892-1985), a registered nurse, to be on standby for the bishop. In the early hours of August 29, 1953, he called out to Sisters Robertina and Agnes Dominic, in service at the episcopal residence since August 1944. One sister remained with the bishop, the other called Sister Wendell, Dr. Arthur Tesseine, his physician, and nearby priests. Monsignor Bryant and Father Hugh Beahan administered the Sacrament of Anointing just before he died.

**28** In 1950 Sister Blanche Steves, an avid student of Dominican history, consulted with Father Hugh G. Quinn, chancellor of the Diocese of El Paso, Texas. He subsequently designed and executed the shield, which features Dominican and pious traditions of the congregation, and the geographic location of the motherhouse, and is circumscribed by the title of "Congregation of Our Lady of the Sacred Heart." Mother Aquinata may have requested that title for the new congregation in 1894 because it was a favorite devotion of Mother Hyacinth Scheininger, her superior and companion at Second Street. In January 1951 Mother Victor arranged for a novena to Our Lady of the Sacred Heart to be sent to all the sisters. The emphases on the Dominican and pious aspects of the congregational history may reflect Mother's visit to Dominican sites in Europe, the building projects, the Diamond Jubilee, and her active participation in the Dominican Mothers General Conference. From 1953 to 1955 she was president of the Conference and hosted its eleventh biennial meeting in the new wing at Marywood, April 14-17, 1955.

**29** Sister Marie Celeste, much beloved member of the Aquinas College science faculty, died on October 30, 1955, as the result of an automobile accident. Sister Joachim Wisner was appointed as fourth councilor until the general chapter in June 1960.

**17**                                                     **Ripe for the Harvest**

**1** *Annals*. Volume III. 1948-1960, Part One, p. 85.

**2** Sister Seraphine was asked about a rosary given to a Protestant child. It was, she explained, a gift given to the valedictorian of a graduating class who asked for a souvenir of her years with the sisters. Testimony as reported in the daily newspapers often lacked distinctions and was not always to the benefit of the church, for example:

*Two other developments highlighted the afternoon hearings. Sister Lucille, principal of the Peñasco grade school, testified that up until March, 1948, the parish priest customarily heard confessions in the public school library once a month between 1:30 and 3:00 in the afternoon. The practice was discontinued in March because of the publicity attending the Dixon suit, she said.*

*Sister Maura, superintendent of schools in the independent school district of Peñasco, said "sociology" is the term used to designate a catechism class for high school seniors and credit is given for the course. She also said the graduation exercises have been held in the church since classes became so large that no other building in Peñasco would hold them.*

From an unidentified newspaper clipping in congregational holdings on the "Dixon School Case" 1947-1949.

**3** *Santa Fe New Mexican,* March 12, 1949.

**4** Income from sisters' compensation in the public schools in New Mexico (ranging from $2,000 to $3,500 per full-time teacher) was used to support the sisters in the mission, to contribute to motherhouse upkeep, to maintain the local house, to pay for the salaries of lay teachers in that mission, and also to pay for the support of the priests in the mission. There were some few instances when the priest(s) had managed the sisters' salary and had failed to provide sufficient living funds for the sisters. Intervention by the mothers general and the archbishop had corrected these abuses but the issue of remuneration in New Mexico was complex. By 1949 the congregation was paying over $30,000 for lay teacher salaries in all its missions (not exclusively in New Mexico). This fact was a point raised in the consultation with Archbishop Byrne.

**5** In 1989 the parish offered to sell the superbly situated convent at 456 Monroe Boulevard to the congregation as a vacation home for approximately $250,000. The offer was declined in view of the cost and need for barrier free accommodations. The building was sold in 1990, the sisters vacating the premises on March 1, 1990.

**6** Parishes both in Allegan and Oceana counties began to be influenced by the increasing number of Hispanics employed as migrant labor. During World War II area farmland was worked by German prisoners of war and, upon their repatriation, by Spanish-speaking migrant laborers.

**7** On July 8, 1955, Bishop Babcock wrote in his own hand a letter to Mother Victor asking her to review her fall appointments and specifically not to reduce the number of sisters at Catholic Central, Muskegon.

*I hate to do this. ...the School simply cannot stand losing two Sisters of St. Dominic. Catholic Central, Grand Rapids, has a lower percentage of lay teachers, and is in a more solid financial condition than Muskegon. You will know best what to do, but I must ask you not to reduce the number of Sisters for Muskegon CC.*

*You know, Mother, that I hesitate to interfere with your work. And I will not be insistent except in a case of emergency. However I consider the situation in Muskegon an emergency for the time being.*

Within a week, Mother repled:

*I am most happy to abide by Your Excellency's judgment and wish and will assign the regular number of Sisters to Muskegon Catholic Central. While I am not quite certain, it seems to me that your letter implies that I may make up for the deficiency by taking one or two more Sisters from Catholic Central, Grand*

*Rapids. If I am mistaken on this point, Your Excellency, will you please let me know.*

It was a rare example of episcopal intervention, cautiously requested and graciously accepted.

**8** The convent was designed for 28 sisters, a wing for each of the four congregations with some central facilities. It was intended that each order would provide seven sisters for the faculty. On August 28, 1966, the four major superiors met to formulate policies on the chapel, office, devotions, renewal, silence in the house, meal etiquette, recreation, horarium, transportation, shared services. Some matters were left to the superiors assigned to each congregation at the high school. One was to serve as "coordinator and supervisor of services."

**9** In January 1950 Father William Murphy offered a 16-acre plot to the congregation for purchase as "a site for a Downriver Central High School for Boys or Girls or both," estimating a "potential of at least 2,500 students." Mother Victor quickly declined the offer, citing lack of funds for the building project and the burden of staffing the school. A congregationally-owned high school in a large urban area was a long-held hope among some of the sisters. Having one was considered a major reason that other congregations were getting many candidates. The predominantly rural and small town pattern of congregational missions did, no doubt, have a bearing on the number and outlook of candidates. See Joannes Flumerfelt, OP, *The Social Background of Vocations to the Dominican Sisters of the Congregation of Our Lady of the Sacred Heart, Grand Rapids, Michigan.* Master of Arts dissertation, Catholic University of America, Washington, DC, 1957.

**10** Monsignor Joseph C. Walen, superintendent of the Home from 1946 to 1967 and editor of the diocesan paper, *The Western Michigan Catholic,* wrote for the July 21, 1960, issue an account of the demolition and the new building to come. Sisters continued working in the new structure until 1976.

**11** Mother Victor to Father Antonin Kirschner, CMM, pastor of Our Lady of Grace parish, Dearborn, February 24, 1951; to Father Clare Murphy, pastor of St. Francis Cabrini parish, Allen Park, February 24, 1951, and June 22, 1951; and to Monsignor Carroll F. Deady, Superintendent of Schools, Archdiocese of Detroit, June 30, 1951. The policy contributed to the withdrawal of sisters from Allen Park.

**12** In June 1960 there were 827 members in the congregation; in June 1966 there were 875, distributed according to age in this manner:

| Age/Yr | 20's | 30's | 40's | 50's | 60's | 70's | 80's | 90's |
|--------|------|------|------|------|------|------|------|------|
| 1960 | 211 | 115 | 107 | 106 | 171 | 70 | 19 | 28 |
| 1966 | 240 | 159 | 82 | 115 | 116 | 137 | 26 | 0 |

**13** The stipend for sisters serving in parishes in Michigan was customarily the same in all the dioceses. During the depression there had been instances of parishes not being able to pay the sisters, some being five and six years in arrears. There was never a strict accounting for these years. Sisters serving in health care other than Nazareth were paid a considerably larger stipend, although not at lay parity. Sisters serving at Aquinas College did not receive a stipend as high as the diocesan rate. As late as 1968, the annual stipend per sister at the college was $900, regardless of academic preparation or responsibility. Thereafter, the stipend approximated diocesan standards. Lay parity remains under discussion at present.

# 18                                             The Mind of the Church

**1**  Paul Philippe, OP, Secretary of the Sacred Congregation of Religious, "Renewal and Adaptation of Religious Congregations," address to Major Superiors, distributed to congregation on May 20, 1965.

**2**  Marie Augusta Neal, SNDdeN, traces the beginning of the development of United States women religious "from nuns to sisters" to Pope Pius XII's convening of the World Congress on States of Perfection in 1950 in *From Nuns to Sisters*, Twenty-Third Publications, 1989, p. 29. "These groups [among them CMSW, CMSM, UISG] began the more systematic examination of the whole question of prayer and good works. They did so in the context of the new conditions of a modern post-war world, highly technologized and individually oriented in the West, with a new consciousness of the developing cultures of mission lands, now called the Third World nations." pp. 29-30.

**3**  In the next-to-final scene of the Diamond Jubilee pageant, "Aloft His Torch," the verse choir related:

> *And latest, Mother Victor hears the call*
> *To go to Rome - San Sisto, Dominic's cell -*
> *To feel the spirit of our origin*
> *The throbbing force of seven centuries,*
> *To bring back from the Father of Christendom*
> *A challenge: 'Make that ageless spirit*
> *The answer to this century's need.'*

**4**  The prospectus announced that the institute, running from mid-October to June for three years, was to *give to chosen members of every Order and Congregation of religious women, of Societies without vows and secular Institutes, and in general to women and girls dedicated to the pursuit of perfection and to apostolic work, a thorough and complete training in sacred studies, to prepare them either for the work of government and the guidance of others within their religious Institute or for apostolic labors outside, especially for direction and teaching in women's colleges and institutions of higher learning.*

Its location in Rome *not only guarantees its perfect conformity to the directives of the Holy See ... contributes to the spiritual development of the Religious by the increased sense of Catholicity that comes from contact with the center of the Church and with fellow-students from every part of the world; it also gives most valuable opportunities for studies historical and archaeological, artistic and humanistic.*

In its first year of operation there were 132 students, representing 58 congregations from 22 nations. Instruction was offered in four language sections, Italian, French, English, Spanish. German was to be added in subsequent years.

**5** Letter of Mother Victor to Monsignor A. P. Arszulowicz, September 23, 1955.

**6** Sister Cecile Byrne (1908-1965) was appointed novice mistress in 1954, the year she completed the graduate theological studies program at Providence College, Rhode Island. She brought to the novitiate a blend of theological, scriptural, and pastoral emphasis that complemented the congregation's participation in the nationwide sister formation philosophy. She died on April 1, 1965, mourned by young and old. Hers was the first English liturgy funeral celebrated at Marywood.

**7** *Minutes of General Council*, December 15, 1957, shows approval of a $30 contribution.

**8** In the 1955-1956 academic year two sisters were sent to Florence for advanced study, Sister Lois Schaffer in art and Sister Marie Raymond Baker in music. Sister Marie Raymond returned to the United States on the Italian liner *Andrea Doria* and was among those rescued when the ship collided with the *Stockholm* off Nantucket Island on July 25, 1956. She and a sister from London, Ontario, comforted terrified passengers during their transfer to the lifeboats of the *Isle de France*.

**9** Mother Victor in a public interview at the occasion of the congregation's centennial in Michigan, August 8, 1977. There are numerous letters in the congregrational archives from pastors pleading for more sisters and fewer lay teachers. Requests were sometimes linked with mention of the congregational fund drive for expansion of the motherhouse and college, a difficulty anticipated by Mother and others in the chapter of 1954. It was a time which required diplomacy and firmness.

**10** Congregations trained new members in the spirituality of the group and to meet the certification requirements of state boards of education. There was also, however, a fairly widespread notion that the performance of a task done under the vow of obedience would make up for any deficiences due to lack of preparation or talent. The Sister Formation Movement contributed much to the transformation of American religious women, establishing that they are in charge of their own destinies, that the call to serve is utmost, and that education is the key to service.

**11** See Chapter 17, note 12.

**12** Rescript, Protocol No. 2771/60. The business was transacted by Bishop Babcock. On August 17, 1960, Monsignor A.P. Arszulowicz read the decree and proclaimed Mother Mary Victor Flannery the lawful prioress general of the Sisters of the Congregation of Our Lady of the Sacred Heart.

**13** Sister Agnes Leo Hauser, a serene and gracious character, served as supervisor of schools during her term as councilor. She died suddenly on October 14, 1963, and was replaced on the council by Sister Joachim Visner.

**14** In the thirteenth General Chapter, July 1954, there was discussion of changing the style of veil. From October 1954 to Spring 1956, there was communitywide discussion, presentation of several models, and balloting. On June 11, 1956, the change in headdress--the elimination of the coif and inner starched lining of the veil--was implemented throughout the congregation.

On February 26, 1957, a formal petition was sent to the Holy See authorizing the change. The petition was placed "in fidelity to your Holiness' wish and need for simplification of the religious habit." The congregation justified its presumption to use the new veil before permission was granted because of an automobile accident in October 1955 which resulted in the death of Sister Marie Celeste Stang and the critical injury of Sisters Mildred Hawkins and Gonzaga Udell. Newspaper accounts alleged "the Sisters could not see." The petition cited better visibility, comfort and ease of movement, economy, and saving of labor as reasons for change.

The process for the change suggested the significance the issue of habit would have as well as the need for universal participation. The vote was secret. Of the 616 sisters voting in 1956, 365 voted for the model chosen, 118 for a second, and 133 for 17 other models. There arose some question as to whether the traditional veil could be kept. As a result, a second vote was taken, with some 115 voting for the traditional veil, and 462 for a change, and of them, 361 for the model chosen on the first ballot. It was an exercise in subsidiarity and democracy at its widest.

**15** Sister Joachim Visner, *Annals*, 1961 to 1966, p. 130.

**16** *Mother Victor Flannery, Circular Letters*, September 11, 1961, pp. 5-6, and Jan. 9, 1961, Oct. 20, 1961. The only mention in council meetings is recorded for Jan. 21, 1962, when "miscellaneous consultative business" was considered. "Letter from the Holy See and rescripts to the Constitutions requested by the General Chapter were read and discussed, also three letters regarding various missions in Latin America."

**17** A native of Wilkes-Barre, Pennsylvania, Father Burke had, before his entrance into the Dominican Order, served as a medical corpsman. He had been a missionary in Chile for three years before his installation on February 10, 1963, as prelate of Chimbote. The *prelatura nullius* was an ecclesiastical division into which the church in Perú was divided to accommodate a law that no foreigner could be ordinary of a diocese. By 1967 that law had been changed. The prelate had all the powers of a bishop, excluding the power to ordain. In 1967 Monsignor Burke was consecrated by Cardinal Cushing as bishop of the newly-created Diocese of Chimbote. He remained in Chimbote until 1978 when he was appointed co-adjutor of the Diocese of Wilmington, Delaware. A native Peruvian, Bishop Luis Bambaren, was installed as Bishop of Chimbote on July 25, 1978.

**18** On February 10, 1962, at the first of the Long-Range Community Planning Committee meetings, Mother Victor raised the question of financing the Latin American venture. About $1,000 a year per sister would be needed, as well as training and flight costs. "If we were to go to Bolivia, there would be an income equivalent to about $20 a month per Sister, since anyone may be hired to teach the compulsory religion courses in the public schools. Over and above this, the financial problem is our own to solve. Also in Bolivia the Dominican Fathers would be near to give spiritual help." *Minutes*, February 10, 1962, p. 5. In October 1960 the Sinsinawa Dominicans had begun a mission in Santa Cruz, Bolivia.

**19** There were also old friends and acquaintances who facilitated the enculturation. James Hough, son of Pearl Mackey Hough, Mother Eveline's sister, had a home in Cuernavaca. The Houghs eased the sisters' passage through customs on their arrival and provided occasional hospitality. Upon her arrival in Lima, Sister Herman Marie met Ethel Knecht, a papal volunteer in Perú whom she had known in Albuquerque as a public health nurse.

**20** Letter of January 15, 1963.

**21** Richard Cushing, *The Missionary Society of St. James the Apostle*, Daughters of St. Paul: Boston, 1962, a brief account of the society founded in 1959.

**22** The full roster of Chimbote missioners includes Sisters Marie Dominica Viesnoraitis (March 1963-1981), Marie Maez (March 1963-1969), Maria Teresita Garcia (December 1963-1989), Georgiana Kowalski (December 1963-1968), Rosemary Homrich (1965-1967), Innocence Andres (1965-1971), Margaret Mary Birchmeier (1965 to the present), Aurora Valerio (1967-1984), Lillian Bockheim (1967 to the present), Jeannine Kalisz (1969-1975; 1978-1982).

**23** Sister Aquinas Weber, prioress from 1966 to 1972, reported to the 1972 Chapter that from 1966 to 1970 the congregation sent approximately $11,000 each year to the Chimbote mission. This did not include extraordinary building costs or post earthquake emergencies. The Society for the Propagation of the Faith, through its Missionary Cooperation Plan, included the Chimbote mission in its cycle of appeals in designated parishes of the Grand Rapids and Saginaw dioceses. The Dominican fathers on the faculty of Aquinas College customarily made the appeal for funds and sisters took up the collection. From 1965 to 1970 these collections brought in approximately $4,000.

The St. James fathers in the parish were originally from the Diocese of Pittsburgh. Since 1964 that diocese has held a Founders Day dinner to assist the pastoral, medical and social programs the priests and sisters conduct in Chimbote. The center, licensed by the state in 1990, raises approximately 60% of its funds through very modest fees (for example, newborn delivery is $1.65 and a physician's visit in clinic 25 cents.) Donations, many of which come from the Diocese of Pittsburgh, make up the additional 40% for operational costs. The center works toward full funding and operation by Peruvians.

**24** On Sunday, May 31, 1970, an earthquake struck northern Perú. Some 200 Chimbotans died and 75% of the city's native dwellings were destroyed. The convent, the Asilo, and maternity hospital were so badly damaged that they were subsequently leveled. The Grand Rapids Dominican sisters, scattered about the city at one task or another, were unharmed. The two sisters who lived with them, along with a colleague from another mission, were at the convent of the Columbus, Ohio, Dominican sisters. In a single movement the convent collapsed, killing Sister Edith Marie, OSF, and Sister Gabriel Joseph, SSJ. Sister John Cassian Logue, SSJ, was completely buried save for one hand; she was rescued quickly and suffered only a head wound and chipped vertebrae. The congregation organized a Chimbote Fund to which the sisters, their families, benefactors, and school children donated. By July 22, 1970, almost $24,000 was given for Chimbotan relief. A new temporary maternity hospital was dedicated on March

25, 1971, on the site of the former Asilo. In 1981 the facility was expanded. Programs include deliveries, prenatal, well-baby, post-partum clinics, and, since 1985, a malnutrition clinic. The hospital also is used for medical consultations and emergency hospitalization.

**25** Service to Latin America broadened in the following decade. From 1971 to 1975 Sister Jean Reimer, registered nurse, served in Chimaltenango, Guatemala, as a member of the Latin American Mission Program (LAMP), a collaborative ministry in association with an established program. In April 1975 she was joined by Sister Jeanine Kalisz, missioner from Chimbote. From their base in the parish of San Andres Itzapa, they had a widespread ministry in the interior of the province. It was the area served on several occasions by Monsignor Bukowski after his retirement as president of Aquinas College. On February 4, 1976, Guatemala was severely damaged by earthquake, with over 2,000 dead and entire villages destroyed. During the month of March Sister Rosemary Homrich joined the sisters to assist in relief. Through Project Reach Out, a standing committee of the congregation for emergencies, a gift of $3,000 was sent, along with countless donations given on behalf of the suffering Guatemalans. After several months' relocation in Michigan, Sister Jean Reimer returned in 1977 to Guatemala as a pastoral minister in Acatenango, in the Diocese of Solala. She was assigned by the bishop to rebuild the parish church which had been devastated by the earthquake. She raised funds, organized volunteers and supervised workers for the construction. During her stay she assisted in the development of eight "base communities" within the parish. In 1979-1981 Sisters Helen LaValley and Ann Elizabeth Porter joined her in the work of faith and church building. As political conditions worsened within the region, the safety of foreigners, particularly missioners, was precarious. In November 1981 Sisters Jean Reimer and Helen LaValley and others were kidnapped and held for five days by Guatemalan military forces. International pressure from the U. S. State Department and church groups brought about the sisters' release. They returned to Grand Rapids on November 26, 1981.

**26** Adrian "Ted" English, OP, (1899-1964), was an esteemed member of the Aquinas College faculty since 1952 and a strong, resolute character whose teaching and counsel contributed greatly to the formation of the sisters. A master of European history, he also taught moral theology in the institute of theology during the summers it was conducted at St. Paul Seminary in Saginaw. He taught the novices a comprehensive course in Dominican history and served as an informal mentor to Mother Victor. He died in the Marywood chapel while saying Mass on Saturday, February 29, 1964. Following his funeral from St. Andrew cathedral, Grand Rapids, he was buried, according to the custom of the Order, in the nearest Dominican cemetery, in Somerset, Ohio.

**27** Prot. N. 01742/53, "Family Bulletin," September 22, 1964.

**28** In 1961 the Rule and Constitution were reprinted. It was the approved text of 1941 with the several rescripts authorized by the Holy See. It was not until May 31, 1990, that the new Constitution was approved by the Congregation for Religious and Secular Institutes.

**29** There were numerous private acknowledgements of Mother's service. On January 25, 1965, Mother was publicly honored by Central Michigan University, her alma mater, with an honorary doctor of laws degree. On May 30, 1965, Aquinas College conferred honorary doctorates upon Mother Victor, U.S. Senator Philip A. Hart and Representative Gerald R. Ford, for distinguished service to Michigan and to the nation.

**30** The *Acts and Ordinances* of the thirteenth General Chapter were distributed on October 18, 1954, but not read, as decreed by Chapter, in the refectory at Marywood "due to the presence of the novices and postulants." A copy was therefore given to each sister at Marywood. By 1966 Chapter business was reported in the "Chapter Briefs," and by 1969 non-chapter delegates were welcomed as observers and lay persons as consultants.

**31** Funeral homily, September 22, 1983.

# SELECT BIBILOGRAPHY

**Dominican Archives, Marywood, Grand Rapids, Michigan.**

*Minutes of the General Council, 1892 to 1980.*
Circular Letters (Letters of mothers general to all sisters)
*Rule and Constitution.* Holy Cross Convent, Regensburg, 1853.
Sinsinawa Mound, Wisconsin, 1896. Grand Rapids, Michigan,
versions: 1916, 1938, 1941, 1960, 1969, 1990.
Customaries
Correspondence of mothers general
      with the Holy See
      with bishops
      with pastors
      with Dominican fathers
      with individual sisters
      and others
Papers and memorabilia of mothers general
*Annals of the Congregation,* 1936-1966
Papers of General Chapters, 1897-1988
*Memoirs of the Sisters of St. Dominic*
Files of deceased sisters
Mission Lists
Local Missions
      annals; printed histories; correspondence
Minutes of Nazareth Corporation
Minutes of Aquinas College Corporation
Marywood Publications: *Contacts, Rapport,*
      *Aloft His Torch* (1953), *Response* (1977)
Selected tapes from oral history collection
Special collections:
      Dominican Mothers General Conference
      Dixon, New Mexico Trial
      Reparata Gautier, OP
      Maura MacDonald, OP
      Jane Marie Murray, OP

## BOOKS AND ARTICLES

---------, 1853 *Golden Jubilee,* 1903. Holy Cross Convent, Brooklyn, NY. Farmingdale, NY: Nazareth Trade School, 1903. 65 pages.

Alvesteffer, Mary, OP. "Times of Their Lives. Dominican Sisters on Beaver Island." *The Journal of Beaver Island History.* Vol. III, 1988, pp. 177-201.

Bauch, Patricia A. "Legacy of the 'Sisters' Schools," *Momentum,* September 1990, pp. 23-27.

Blum, Marie Thomasine, OP. *History of the Sisters of the Third Order of St. Dominic of the Congregation of the Most Holy Rosary, Mount St. Mary-On-The-Hudson, Newburgh, New York.* Master of Arts dissertation, Catholic University of America, Washington, DC, 1938.

Crawford, Eugene J., MA. *The Daughters of Dominic on Long Island.* The History of the American Congregation of the Holy Cross, Sisters of the Third Order of St. Dominic of the Diocese of Brooklyn. New York: Benziger, 1938.

Curry, Lois, OP. *Women after His Own Heart.* The Sisters of Saint Dominic of the American Congregation of the Sacred Heart of Jesus, Caldwell, New Jersey, 1881-1981. New York: New City Press, 1981.

Ewens, Mary. *The Role of the Nun in Nineteenth Century America.* New York: Arno Press, 1978.

Flumerfelt, Joannes, OP. *The Social Background of Vocations to the Dominican Sisters of the Congregation of Our Lady of the Sacred Heart, Grand Rapids, Michigan.* Master of Arts dissertation, Catholic University of America, Washington, DC, 1957.

Heyda, Marie, OP. *Catholic Central and West Catholic High Schools.* A History of a Diocesan Venture, 1906-1981. Grand Rapids, Michigan: Spartan Press, 1981.

Kildee, Mary Philomena, OP. *Memoirs of Mother Aquinata Fiegler, OP.* Grand Rapids, Michigan: James Bayne, 1928.

Kohler, Hortense, OP. *The Life and Works of Mother Benedicta Bauer.* Milwaukee: Bruce, 1937.

McGee, John W. *The Catholic Church in the Grand River Valley,* 1833-1950. Grand Rapids, Michigan, 1950.

O'Rourke, Mary Alice, OP. *Sown on Good Ground.* Centennial History of St. Mary Cathedral Parish, Gaylord. Gaylord, 1984.

Ryan, Mary Philip, OP. *Amid the Alien Corn.* The Early Years of the Sisters of Saint Dominic, Adrian, Michigan. St. Charles, Illinois: Jones Wood Press, 1967.

Sisters of St. Dominic. *Life of Mother M. Camilla Madden, OSD.* Adrian, Michigan: Sisters of St. Dominic, no date.

Sister Mary St. Peter, OP. *Sister Mary Rose of the Sacred Heart, OP. Features of Sanctification.* NY, 1972. Copyright José Morales, PhD. Printed in Italy.

Walz, Maximilian, CPPS. *Life of Sister Mary Reparata Rose of the Sacred Heart, OP. The Child of my Sacrament of Love.* NY, 1972. Copyright, José Morales, PhD. Printed in Italy.

White, Joseph M., editor, *The American Catholic Religious Life.* Selected Essays. NY: Garland Publishing, Inc., 1988.

# SISTERS OF SAINT DOMINIC
# GRAND RAPIDS, MICHIGAN

1 Aquinata Fiegler (1848-1915)
2 Boniface Hartleb (1855-1930)
3 Celestine Ostendorp (1861-1885)*
4 Martha Mueglich** (1848-1893)*
5 Clementina Coyle (1858-1950)
6 Antoninus Jellig (1859-1935)
7 Borromeo Ahlmeyer (1861-1881)*
8 Xavier Flynn (1859-1885)*
9 Gonsalva Bankstahl (1860-1921)*
10 Alexia Flynn** (1847-1904)*
11 Bernadetta Lawless (1856-1884)*
12 Chrysostoma Schmittner (1862-1935)*
13 Villana Carmody (1854-1916)*
14 Assisium Finnegan (1854-1915)*
15 Bartholomew Junemann (1859-1930)*
16 James Walsh (1861-1932)*
17 Isabel Ferris (1858-1885)*
18 Justina Daly (1861-1894)*
19 DeSales Desmond (1843-1898)*
20 Adelaide McCue* (1859-1945)**
21 Cherubina Seymour (1866-1938)
22 Mary Andrew Kernan* (1863-1935)***
23 Eleanore Heinl (1862-1930)*
24 Matthia Selhuber (1865-1953)*
25 Marcolina Zengel (1856-1926)*
26 Seraphica Brandstetter (1863-1930)*
27 Paschal Farnen (1864-1924)*
28 Albina Pirk (1869-1907)*
29 Adalberta Wagner (1869-1937)*
30 Huberta Burghardt (1863-1900)*
31 Henrietta Gagnier (1868-1893)
32 Albertina Selhuber (1871-1964)*
33 Aloysius Miller (1870-1942)
34 Ignatius Deegan (1864-1916)
35 Berchmans Deegan (1868-1943)
36 Vincentia Cunningham (1857-1934)*
37 Francis Doyle (1860-1899)
38 Clare Brophy (1869-1961)
39 Benedicta O'Rourke (1871-1935)
40 Marcella Farnen (1870-1949)
41 Ceslaus Pentenrieder (1867-1962)*
42 Louise Perron (1871-1924)

43 Mercedes Dargis (1871-1953)
44 Alphonsus O'Rourke (1873-1937)
45 Scholastica Burghart (1873-1945)*
46 Fidelis Reicha (1871-1949)
47 Alacoque Wingen (1870-1935)
48 DeChantal Burns (1865-1915)
49 Cyrilla Hallahan (1873-1951)
50 Cecilia Giles (1866-1948)
51 Isabella Ryan (1873-1891)
52 Xavier Connelly (1861-1931)
53 Beatrice Cottrell (1866-1944)
54 Sylvester Maus (1874-1949)
55 Celestine McCue (1872-1929)
56 Innocence Yaklin (1874-1955)
57 Letitia Smith (1870-1924)
58 Eveline Mackey (1875-1958)
59 Borromeo Donley (1875-1909)
60 Philomena Kildee (1875-1941)
61 Benvenuta Carroll (1862-1942)
62 Imelda Delor (1872-1947)
63 Lewis Carmody (1868-1921)
64 Anastasia Hebert (1876-1961)
65 Martina Drohan (1859-1898)*
66 Bonaventure Burns (1874-1963)
67 Augustine LaFleur (1868-1951)
68 Margaret Mary McGee (1871-1946)
69 Raymond Hudzinski (1873-1959)
70 Agnes Senecal (1876-1943)
71 Genevieve Gauthier (1876-1944)
72 Bertrand Lalonde (1877-1977)
73 Hildegarde Miller (1876-1966)
74 Catherine VanAnhold (1875-1972)
75 Gertrude Jaster (1873-1958)
76 Lawrence Cuddihy (1867-1961)
77 Loyola Finn (1872-1941)
78 Terencia Finn (1873-1912)
79 Josephine Schultz (1860-1893)
80 Henrietta McAllister (1874-1955)
81 Gabriel O'Malley (1874-1955)
82 Dominica Walsh (1877-1963)
83 Matilda Miesen (1876-1912)
84 Thomas McNamara (1876-1945)

Based on the congregational register and necrologies. * designates entrance in New York;
** designates lay sister status; *** designates tranfers from other congregations.

| | |
|---|---|
| 85 Leo McDonald (1873-1931) | 134 Thomasine St. Laurent (1883-1950) |
| 86 Hyacinth Hines (1868-1942) | 135 Angelica Lanciaux (1887-1920) |
| 87 Emmanuel Wall (1878-1899) | 136 Ambrose Dupuis (1886-1935) |
| 88 Annunciata Dwyer (not known-1950) | 137 Dorothea Morio (1887-1968) |
| 89 Ursula Lanciaux (1875-1934) | 138 Stanislaus Zukowski (1887-1913) |
| 90 Baptista Krupp (1873-1939) | 139 Bernadine Martineau (1882-1964) |
| 91 Amanda McConnell (1879-1939) | 140 Geraldine Kenny (1884-1939) |
| 92 Rose Callahan (1880-1927) | 141 Cornelia Chesney (1886-1978) |
| 93 Aquinas Byrne (1874-1936) | 142 Julia Chesney (1886-1920) |
| 94 Angelica Selesky (1876-1902) | 143 Pius Flohe (1886-1941) |
| 95 Apollonia Cornelissens (1872-1951) | 144 Edwardine Sands (1886-1975) |
| 96 Teresa St. Laurent (1881-1954) | 145 Leona Malloy (1884-1923) |
| 97 Immaculata Senecal (1881-1942) | 146 Regina Andres (1888-1978) |
| 98 Reginald Reynolds (1877-1952) | 147 Alphonsine Reynolds (1883-1945) |
| 99 Borgia Hawkins (1875-1955) | 148 Alexia Früchtl (1886-1965) |
| 100 Monica Kress (1875-1943) | 149 Martina Ertl (1888-1968) |
| 101 Raphael O'Rourke (1878-1942) | 150 Lucia Brunner (1890-1964) |
| 102 Magdalen Impens (1880-1972) | 151 Pauline Keeler (1883-1973) |
| 103 Seraphine Wendling (1879-1966) | 152 Hilda Belkofer (1886-1937) |
| 104 Bernadette Dietrich (1883-1949) | 153 Patricia Doyle (1887-1962) |
| 105 Anna Marie Sommerdyke (1877-1953) | 154 Eulalia Auré (1886-1953) |
| 106 Henrica Frans (1877-1974) | 155 Winifred McCanney (1882-1926) |
| 107 Helena Morio (1883-1976) | 156 Clarissa Mazurek (1887-1959) |
| 108 Veronica Podleski (1882-1959) | 157 Antonia Stallmann (1883-1954) |
| 109 Angela Lalonde (1873-1957) | 158 Clotilda Gauthier (1888-1977) |
| 110 Rose Marie McAllister (1882-1957) | 159 Sebastian Claeys (1888-1961) |
| 111 DeSales Rose (1879-1947) | 160 Francis Dennert (1887-1957) |
| 112 Constance Martel (1880-1932) | 161 Christina Quaderer (1889-1972) |
| 113 Dominic LeRoux (1882-1962) | 162 Barbara Zuker (1886-1946) |
| 114 Martha Obermeier (1877-1976) | 163 Stella Chesney (1883-1931) |
| 115 Caroline Hart (1879-1966) | 164 Norberta Boerakker (1887-1969) |
| 116 Josephine Erbisch (1878-1956) | 165 Bertha Gutknecht (1880-1971) |
| 117 Loretto Omlor (1877-1972) | 166 Jordan Ruhl (1882-1940) |
| 118 Antoinette Knauf (1878-1909) | 167 Isidore Studer (1883-1955) |
| 119 Carmelita Dutmer (1883-1958) | 168 Marcelline Horton (1883-1961) |
| 120 Bernard Callahan (1882-1960) | 169 Amata Baader (1884-1937) |
| 121 Coletta Baumeister (1884-1955) | 170 Gerard Simmel (1886-1971) |
| 122 Gonzaga Udell (1887-1983) | 171 Josepha Monterman (1886-1968) |
| 123 Camilla Bowkus (1885-1919) | 172 Casimir Zukowski (1888-1985) |
| 124 Emmanuel Kopp (1888-1964) | 173 Agnes Marie Flohe (1889-1973) |
| 125 Evangelista Rohrl (1888-1976) | 174 Pelagia Douglas (1889-1928) |
| 126 Alexandra Gallagher (1885-1974) | 175 Felicitas Gerhart (1888-1958) |
| 127 Eugenia Bruton (1885-1908) | 176 Theodora Jasinska (1888-1981) |
| 128 Richard Kannally (1885-1973) | 177 Zita Pantus (1886-1958) |
| 129 Ildephonse Ryan (1880-1974) | 178 Irene Hekker (1889-1975) |
| 130 Agatha Battle (1884-1920) | 179 Isabel Foley (1885-1955) |
| 131 Rosalie Kropf (1885-1926) | 180 Carola Jones (1889-1960) |
| 132 Petronilla Tureck (1886-1961) | 181 Alban Fredette (1885-1982) |
| 133 Mildred Hawkins (1886-1988) | 182 Roberta Nickle (1891-1976) |

| | |
|---|---|
| 183 Avelina Ward (1889-1927) | 232 Florian Kaiser (1891-1984) |
| 184 Rita Burghart (1881-1946) | 233 Electa Miller (1890-1977) |
| 185 Crescentia Wucherpfennig (1888-1968) | 234 Ursuline Pilon (1893-) |
| 186 Edmund Flohe (1888-1966) | 235 Humilitas DeCourval (1894-1965) |
| 187 Helen Marie Callahan (1888-1948) | 236 Aurelia Fedewa (1892-1983) |
| 188 Henry Dalke (1890-1939) | 237 Theodosia Foster (1894-1983) |
| 189 Joseph Mahoney (1889-1986) | 238 Emmerica Ziegler (1895-1973) |
| 190 George Little (1876-1965) | 239 Leocadia Kocinska (1893-1961) |
| 191 Adele Hebert (1890-1969) | 240 John Scally (1888-1961) |
| 192 Jerome Smithers (1888-1968) | 241 Rosina Bleise (1888-1953) |
| 193 Euphrasia Sullivan (1888-1970) | 242 Laurentia Monahan (1891-1969) |
| 194 Hedwig Knauf (1888-1979) | 243 Albina Homminga (1891-1989) |
| 195 Ferdinand Bauer (1886-1962) | 244 Paul Schaub (1895-1968) |
| 196 Germaine Carey (1885-1970) | 245 Rose Mary Plamondon (1896-1983) |
| 197 Gregory Host (1885-1974) | 246 Kathleen Bannon (1892-1984) |
| 198 Lucille Hawkins (1889-1921) | 247 Sienna Wendling (1889-1986) |
| 199 Francis Regis Saucier (1891-1974) | 248 Marion Yaklin (1892-1957) |
| 200 Alice (Valley) Gauthier (1893-1959) | 249 Antoinette Yaklin (1896-1990) |
| 201 Callista Foye (1889-1923) | 250 Ida Walters (1893-1979) |
| 202 Eugenia Conley (1893-1977) | 251 Philippa Schmitt (1892-1979) |
| 203 Elvera Vaneses (1887-1967) | 252 Flavian Murphy (1894-1975) |
| 204 Ottilia Schaub (1891-1928) | 253 Nicholas Forcht (1895-1982) |
| 205 Eustasia Boundy (1892-1980) | 254 Cunegunda Zukowski (1893-1987) |
| 206 Michael Jones (1885-1963) | 255 Madeleine Mier (1893-1988) |
| 207 Edward Szturmowski (1888-1935) | 256 Lucina Dennert (1888-1962) |
| 208 Vincent Kropf (1890-1959) | 257 Francis Marie LaPorte (1888-1975) |
| 209 Honora McGarry (1891-1950) | 258 Victor Flannery (1895-1983) |
| 210 Stephen Lovay (1884-1935) | 259 Petra Burns (1889-1976) |
| 211 Mary Hogan (1893-1975) | 260 Maurice Mavelle (1889-1990) |
| 212 Teresita Doyle (1889-1932) | 261 Irma Gamache (1894-1960) |
| 213 Evarista Walters (1890-1975) | 262 Evangela Ronning (1891-1982) |
| 214 Bernarda Murray (1892-1956) | 263 Anita Tilmann (1892-1954) |
| 215 Florence Roberts (1892-1966) | 264 Joseph Marie Kuhn (1891-1986) |
| 216 Euphrosine Gross (1890-1929) | 265 Leonissa Housten (1894-1973) |
| 217 Ernestine Kokx (1892-1984) | 266 Annette Kain (1895-1970) |
| 218 Borromeo Clark (1891-1967) | 267 Kyran Moran (1890-1938) |
| 219 Edith LeBrecque (1885-1911) | 268 Lucy Marie Young (1891-1982) |
| 220 Georgiana Paterson (1893-1951) | 269 Alma Schweikert (1891-1976) |
| 221 Hortense Belanger (1886-1952) | 270 Esther Juskaitis (1894-1979) |
| 222 Marguerite Zuker (1889-1951) | 271 Rosalina Gregaitis (1895-1969) |
| 223 Eileen Ritzenhein (1891-1937) | 272 Martin Feyan (1891-1983) |
| 224 Evangeline O'Brien (1892-1977) | 273 Claudia Bedard (1890-1962) |
| 225 Francesca Gietzen (1889-1970) | 274 Mary Ellen Ryder (1897-1972) |
| 226 Florentine Shell (1894-1974) | 275 Beata LaMore (1893-1926) |
| 227 Estelle Hackett (1888-1948) | 276 Justina Schwind (1892-1932) |
| 228 Emeline Hessman (1892-1982) | 277 Jeannette Bonem (1892-1941) |
| 229 Grace Fraser (1890-1966) | 278 Athanasius Chartier (1894-1956) |
| 230 Anthony Johnson (1889-1917) | 279 Gelasia Grochowalska (1894-1975) |
| 231 Lorraine Gibson (1892-1976) | 280 Patrick Connelly (1890-1965) |

281 Nolasco Connelly (1892-1964)
282 Corona Andres (1895-1977)
283 Valencia Schwind (1891-1986)
284 Huberta Charron (1893-1990)
285 Anna Marie Webster (1897-1971)
286 Eloise Mosier (1896-1977)
287 Denise Suprenant (1897-1960)
288 Agnes Patricia Pashak (1887-1979)
289 Robert Donaghue (1888-1965)
290 Andrea Zahm (1894-1980)
291 Felicia Klein (1895-1914)
292 Blanche Steves (1891-1969)
293 Adrian Gallagher (1891-1935)
294 Gertrude Marie McCue (1892-1968)
295 Teresa Marie Steffens (1895-1989)
296 Margaret Marie Laux (1891-1958)
297 Natalia Ruczynska (1897-1974)
298 Leonarda Ruff (1897-)
299 Antonella Brooks 1895-1968)
300 Mechtildis Weigl (1887-1918)
301 Domitilla Mahony (1896-)
302 Daniel Mahony (1892-1973)
303 Matilda Henze (1891-1967)
304 Cleopha Kondratovicz (1895-1971)
305 Hilary Pulaski (1894-1967)
306 Stanislaus Souwlewski (1895-1973)
307 Sophia Latuszek (1897-1969)
308 Mellita Tague (1887-1976)
309 Pierre Gamache (1892-1948)
310 Valeria Tomkowiak (1894-1979)
311 Benita Gwisdala (1893-1983)
312 Perpetua Davis (1883-1970)
313 Felix Brand (1892-1983)
314 Caritas Maturen (1892-1926)
315 Eucharia Doris (1891-1990)
316 Lillian Kaminska (1892-1966)
317 Leo Marie DesJardins (1894-1979)
318 Augustina Gerschewski (1894-1967)
319 Romana Reamer (1894-1980)
320 Benigna Bollman (1896-1979)
321 Noella Byrne (1895-1958)
322 Jane Marie Murray (1896-1987)
323 Brigetta Bannon (1895-1966)
324 Agnella Droomers (1896-1988)
325 Jeanne LaFleche (1897-1987)
326 Felicia Bayer (1896-1986)
327 Mary Jane Flannery (1898-1981)
328 Veritas McCarthy (1894-1947)
329 Sylvia McLaughlin (1897-1927)

330 Wenceslaus Szocinski (1897-1984)
331 Rosaria Franckowiak (1897-1984)
332 Imeldina Franckowiak (1897-1951)
333 Luella Blanchard (1895-1982)
334 Rose Marie Willing (1896-1980)
335 Catherine Marie Roberts (1897-1967)
336 Adorine Grypma (1890-1982)
337 Alfreda Jasinska (1896-1981)
338 Illuminata Konwinski (1896-1976)
339 Ruth Wolfe (1897-1963)
340 Angela Marie Bellemore (1887-1986)
341 Dominic Marie Lynch (1889-1916)
342 Miriam Mulholland (1899-1984)
343 David Steele (1889-1975)
344 Aquin Gallagher (1898-1978)
345 Agnes Regina Moans (1895-1986)
346 Walburga Brust (1896-1919)
347 Hieronyma Donahue (1898-1981)
348 Annabel Bollman (1898-1985)
349 Alicia Andres (1896-1987)
350 Honorata Evans (1890-1938)
351 Generosa Walters (1895-1975)
352 Raymunda McConnell (1882-1918)
353 Stephana Garlick (1898-1954)
354 Delphina Pietrusinska (1897-1990)
355 Devota LeBlanc (1899-1977)
356 Rosella Poirier (1899-1953)
357 Leonora Gallagher (1893-1986)
358 Bertilla Doran (1898-1921)
359 Frances Clare Alvesteffer (1893-1987)
360 Mark Scanlon (1891-1990)
361 Concepta Lyons (1895-1955)
362 Wilfrida Perrault (1899-1987)
363 Urban Klees (1895-1972)
364 Edward Marie Mulvey (1887-1990)
365 Clarence Hanson (1891-1934)
366 Laura Garstecki (1899-1986)
367 Helen Moans (1899-)
368 Eugene Marie Forster (1897-)
369 Aquino Peterson (1898-1928)
370 Edwin Bozek (1895-1974)
371 Aloysius Marie Clearwood (1895-1984)
372 Leonilla Duggan (1891-1974)
373 Robertina McKenna (1893-1979)
374 Vincent Marie Callahan (1896-1947)
375 Caspar Henze (1894-1936)
376 Rose Dominic Oakes (1895-1977)
377 Fabian MacDonald (1897-1948)
378 Laurentina Neubecker (1893-1957)

379 Terencia Moran (1892-1979)
380 Damien Jacobs (1893-1970)
381 Rudolphine Wurn (1899-)
382 Dionysius Finn (1897-1983)
383 Emily Merkiel (1898-1984)
384 Anna Plamondon (1896-1989)
385 Vivian Keating (1897-)
386 Wendell Lennon (1892-1985)
387 Lamberta DePore (1893-1979)
388 Ernesta Hogan (1895-1928)
389 Clementia Hagens (1891-1989)
390 Andrew Sturmowski (1898-)
391 Gervase Miller (1897-1989)
392 Cyrinus Strauss (1898-)
393 Alexine LaCosse (1901-1956)
394 Constantia Davidson (1901-1962)
395 Ethelberta Moore (1901-1957)
396 Matthew Wacha (1897-1972)
397 Edwarda Yaklin (1893-1973)
398 Laurita Flohe (1898-1976)
399 Eustella Bellemore (1889-1978)
400 Marie Anthony Tomaski (1901-1971)
401 Angelique Bujold (1899-1987)
402 DeLellis Wagner (1901-1980)
403 Marie Celeste Stang (1892-1955)
404 Mechtilde Cordes (1896-1984)
405 Vincent Ferrer Rasch (1897-1983)
406 Olivia Robach (1895-1988)
407 Patrice Grace (1898-1967)
408 Maureen Hegarty (1892-1955)
409 Rose Francis Greiner (1894-1982)
410 Cletus Brow (1898-1988)
411 Timothy Wiesler (1899-1989)
412 Benedetta Bray (1897-1976)
413 Frances Agnes Loftus (1890-1990)
414 Joachim Visner (1891-1972)
415 Raymunda Clearwood (1893-1971)
416 Rose Anthony Bedard (1895-1984)
417 Thomas Marie McGee (1897-1990)
418 Clarice Quinlan (1900-1971)
419 Claire Marie Duffy (1901-1981)
420 Margaret Ann Kaiser (1902-1971)
421 Gerald Grace (1901-1970)
422 Aline Needham (1901-1986)
423 Benjamina Biess (1902-1982)
424 Robina Zoellner (1899-1983)
425 Dolorita Powers (1900-1946)
426 Luke Schulz (1898-1988)
427 Elizabeth Anne McCormick (1893-1984)

428 Agnes Therese Lynch (1900-1987)
429 Austin Gavit (1902-1960)
430 Isadora Madry (1901-)
431 Imogene Gallagher (1903-1969)
432 Frances Raphael Ryan (1893-1971)
433 Balbina Frankowiak (1903-1960)
434 Arthur Weltin (1894-1956)
435 Julia Link (1899-1979)
436 Elizabeth Rose Theisen (1902-1990)
437 Thomas Francis O'Rourke (1876-1956)
438 Jane DeChantal Host (1895-1978)
439 Rose Catherine McConnell (1895-1952)
440 Frederica Knieper (1903-)
441 Catherine Emmendorfer (1903-)
442 Camillus Vogel (1894-1987)
443 Dominic Marie Plamondon (1904-)
444 Rose Ann Johnson (1902-1990)
445 Ann Catherine Harrand (1904-)
446 Angelica St. Onge (1899-1988)
447 Agnes Leo Hauser (1900-1963)
448 Ann Denise Hogan (1898-1971)
449 Mary Basinski (1905-)
450 Ernest Dworschak (1883-1968)
451 Ignatia Parisey (1902-)
452 Francella Bovin (1897-1979)
453 Brendan Donovan (1905-)
454 Maura McDonald (1897-1986)
455 Redempta Karl (1901-1968)
456 Lily Zahm (1904-1985)
457 Norena Downes (1903-)
458 Kevin McLaughlin (1899-1971)
459 Celine Jacques (1899-1987)
460 Loretta Tacey (1906-1985)
461 Perpetua Maria Visner (1902-)
462 Juliette Belanger (1906-1986)
463 Vincent DePaul Roberts (1903-)
464 Leonard Lynch (1903-)
465 Frances DeSales Warren (1896-1975)
466 Wilmetta Murphy (1905-1985)
467 Thecla Nietling (1903-1982)
468 Josita Wilson (1900-1987)
469 Bryan Brady (1886-1988)
470 Mary LaNore (1894-1977)
471 Angus Black (1904-)
472 Magdala Host (1900-1980)
473 Paulette Korr (1907-1982)
474 Theodota Mercier (1899-)
475 Bernetta Zeitz (1900-1980)
476 Elizabeth Mary Visner (1900-1960)

477 Rose Miriam Visner (1903-)
478 Grace Ellen Martin (1908-1984)
479 Madeleine Sophie Schafer (1908-1989)
480 Cyprian Bohman (1903-1985)
481 Frances Anne Tatreau (1905-1985)
482 Leone Boucher (1905-)
483 Theophane Benkert (1905-1965)
484 Mary Margaret Kenny (1907-1967)
485 Zoe Lawrence (1899-1973)
486 Agatha Artman (1905-)
487 Annella Michalski (1904-1985)
488 Vera Schmeck (1905-)
489 John Berchmans Deegan (1901-1961)
490 Louis Samsa (1908-1978)
491 Servatia Respondeck (1909-)
492 Rose Ellen Wendling (1905-1989)
493 Henry Suso Lerczak (1908-)
494 Aquilina Prevost (1907-)
495 Cecile Byrne (1908-1965)
496 Bertille Tithof (1904-)
497 Clarabel Merkiel (1901-1967)
498 Francis Xavier Schmitt (1907-1984)
499 Blandina Stang (1900-1982)
500 Rose Imelde DeHaus (1905-1962)
501 Conrad Artman (1906-)
502 Euphemia Popell (1907-)
503 Grace Jean Davis (1904-1983)
504 Jane Frances Flannery (1904-)
505 Fidelia Zepnick (1908-1988)
506 Marie Terese Harp (1909-1931)
507 Anselma Weber (1911-)
508 Rosalita Prusevicz (1911-)
509 Louise Klees (1899-)
510 Frances Mary Adams (1907-)
511 Ann Perpetua Romero (1910-)
512 John Dominic Krausmann (1909-1989)
513 Rita Lucille Leirich (1900-)
514 Rose Dennis Demaray (1905-)
515 Thomas Bernard Richard (1910-1987)
516 Ann Therese Ruczynska (1903-1986)
517 Genevieve Clare Bedard (1906-1976)
518 Rose Gonzaga Szydlowski (1906-)
519 Ellen Therese Charron (1911-1988)
520 Marie Bernadette Jacques (1903-1972)
521 Agnes Thiel (1909-)
522 Thomas Aquin Piehl (1913-1929)
523 Thomas Margaret Curran (1898-)
524 Vita Marie Gase (1903-1977)
525 Ann Eugene Piasecki (1911-1982)

526 Rose Carlita Breitenstein (1908-1979)
527 Gertrude Ann Goyette (1905-)
528 Simeon Staudenmaier (1904-1985)
529 Dorothy Adams (1912-)
530 Letitia Van Agtmael (1912-)
531 Florence Agnes Klingler (1912-)
532 Josephita Griego (1911-)
533 Cyrena Hansen (1912-)
534 John Marie Bronersky (1909-)
535 Jean Durbin (1908-1935)
536 Anthony Claire Adomaitis (1911-1981)
537 Regina Marie Bedard (1907-)
538 Marie Dominica Viesnoraitis (1912-)
539 Joan LaFontaine (1908-1987)
540 Consuelo Chavez (1912-)
541 Paula Murphy (1893-1969)
542 Rose Alma Oliver (1910-)
543 Jean Catherine Bierscheid (1912-1979)
544 Anthony Marie Lotter (1886-1979)
545 Francis Borgia Goyette (1909-)
546 Columba Dillon (1907-)
547 Catherine Swift (1909-1980)
548 Joseph Ann Popp (1909-1962)
549 Marie Alexander Schafer (1911-)
550 Margaret Schafer (1911-1988)
551 John Baptist Schafer (1911-)
552 Helen LaValley (1910-)
553 Edna Weber (1907-1979)
554 Virgil Ghering (1910-)
555 Helen Louise Brogger (1910-1988)
556 Basil Fortenbacher (1910-1959)
557 Marie Colette Kosiara (1910-1930)
558 Thomas Edward Kennedy (1909-)
559 Bridget McGarry (1911-)
560 Margaret Spellman (1910-1986)
561 Jeanne d'Arc Ploof (1908-1989)
562 Giles Chartier (1902-1981)
563 Vincent Mary DeMatio (1911-)
564 Pancratia Klaus (1898-1985)
565 Rose Angela Leirich (1908-1989)
566 Marie Albertus Gray (1900-1986)
567 Ann Magdalen Reicha (1908-)
568 Theodore Mary Brzeczkiewicz (1912-)
569 Alice Clare Shine (1908-1985)
570 Rose Thomas McIntyre (1911-)
571 Albert Sagorski (1914-)
572 Dorothy Plamondon (1914)
573 Marie Vianney Giordano (1911-1988)
574 Ann Lucille McGowan (1913-)

575 Mildred Adams (1911-)
576 Rose Kathleen Carroll (1913-)
577 Marie Heyda (1910-)
578 Herman Joseph Schroeter (1905-1990)
579 Meinrad Ender (1913-)
580 Adriana Egloff (1911-)
581 Bride Ryan (1913-)
582 Ermina Thelen (1914-)
583 Theodine Andres (1914-)
584 Patricia Ann Howe (1907-1988)
585 Pelagia Litkowski (1911-)
586 Rose William St. Cyr (1906-)
587 Agnes Dominic Roberge (1909-)
588 Christopher Steinforth (1899-1977)
589 Marie Ida Obey (1912-)
590 Marie Elegia Timm (1913-)
591 Patricia Jane Dorfler (1910-1980)
592 Irene Therese Henze (1897-)
593 Katherine Power (1914-)
594 Marie Therese Rouse (1913-)
595 Marjorie Vangsness (1916-)
596 Malachi Laithwaite (1897-1980)
597 Jordan Marie Homulka (1916-)
598 Juliana Barilla (1911-)
599 Leah Dorion (1914-1989)
600 Peter Verona Kolenda (1914-1986)
601 Elizabeth Barilla (1915-)
602 Mary Alvesteffer (1915-)
603 Paschal Barth (1915-)
604 Leona Loyer (1916-)
605 Cecelia Popp (1911-)
606 Dolores Wendling (1914-)
607 Eleanore Van Dyke (1915-)
608 James Rau (1909-)
609 Loretta Marie Wanner (1912-1946)
610 Phyllis Crimmins (1912-1989)
611 Leo Mergener (1908-)
612 Kenneth Fitzgerald (1917-)
613 Aquino Boyce (1917-1974)
614 Rene Langlois (1916-1970)
615 Rose Callahan (1916-)
616 Helen Bolger (1915-)
617 Susanna Gilbert (1917-)
618 Marie Rosaire Longtin (1916-)
619 Lucille Leannah (1916-)
620 Marie Raymond Baker (1918-)
621 Patricia Clare Carroll (1914-1986)
622 Lucinda Lehmkuhle (1914-1980)
623 Bede Frahm (1915-)

624 Thomas More Connolly (1914-)
625 Rose Seraphine Sagorski (1917-)
626 Justyn Krieg (1912-)
627 Bridget Hall (1915-)
628 Rose Therese Kunderman (1902-1983)
629 Marie Catherine Clayton (1888-1962)***
630 Anna Kostrzewa (1916-)
631 Nathaniel Lenhardt (1915-)
632 Rose Aquin McGrath (1917-)
633 Genevieve Montreuil (1916-)
634 Winifred Fieber (1915-)
635 Ann Henry Keeler (1917-1984)
636 Kathleen Mooney (1915-)
637 Malvena Nadon (1917-)
638 Yvonne Richard (1917-)
639 Thea LaMarre (1918-)
640 Lois Schaffer (1919-)
641 Mary Alice MacDonald (1916-)
642 Audrey Kubian (1917-)
643 Constance Nizol (1917-)
644 Mary A. Morang (1915-)
645 Jovita Pekarchik (1918-1990)
646 Helen Meier (1919-1980)
647 Donata Judis (1917-)
648 Harriet Sanborn (1905-1991)
649 Mary DeHaus (1916-)
650 Aurora Valerio (1921-)
651 Emeliana Judis (1918-)
652 Elaine Mitchell (1920-)
653 Camilla Usakowski (1917-)
654 Karen Thoreson (1919-)
655 Eileen Popp (1920-)
656 Antonita Vigil (1922-)
657 Stephen Barilla (1919-1971)
658 Faith Mahoney (1917-)
659 Angele Richard (1919-)
660 Christine Jozwiak (1921-)
661 Jeanne Anne Brunett (1920-1962)
662 Lourdes Palazzolo (1918-)
663 Michaela Schrems (1920-)
664 Elizabeth Eardley (1921-)
665 Wilhelmina Knieper (1911-)
666 Sheila Wood (1922-)
667 Carmella Conway (1922-)
668 Eloysa Garcia (1920-1974)
669 Helen Jude (1921-)
670 Bernice Botwinski (1921-)
671 Jane Anthony Cherwinski (1921-)

381

| | |
|---|---|
| 672 Marie Andre St. Cyr (1910-) | 721 Louisa Mogdis (1928-) |
| 673 Beata Bugala (1922-) | 722 Thaddeus Kowalinski (1929-) |
| 674 Jeannine Kalisz (1923-) | 723 Eunice Cronin (1928-) |
| 675 Geraldine Fox (1923-) | 724 Rose Patrice O'Donnell (1930-1982) |
| 676 Edward Plamondon (1923-) | 725 Barbara Ann Seymour (1929-) |
| 677 Verona Wangler (1924-) | 726 Mary Courtade (1928-) |
| 678 Adrienne Adelman (1919-) | 727 Vita Licari (1928-) |
| 679 Angelina Abeyta (1923-) | 728 Edith Kahler (1930-) |
| 680 Villana Van Mullekom (1926-) | 729 Mary Catherine Brechting (1929-) |
| 681 Evelyn Schoenborn (1924-) | 730 Jean Paul Tilmann (1928-1984) |
| 682 Aquinas Weber (1923-) | 731 Marciana Danielski (1916-) |
| 683 Maurita Reynolds (1926-) | 732 Jean Marie Birkman (1930-) |
| 684 Mary Sullivan (1925-) | 733 Reparata Faubert (1930-) |
| 685 Mary Ann Otway (1926-) | 734 Marie Kathleen McCracken (1930-) |
| 686 Loyola Maestas (1926-) | 735 Marjorie Ann Kendall (1930-) |
| 687 Eileen Marie Prueter (1926-) | 736 Rose Mary Belanger (1930-) |
| 688 Marie Joseph Ryan (1925-) | 737 Charlotte Schaub (1930-) |
| 689 Lenora Carmody (1925-) | 738 Nancy Coyne (1929-) |
| 690 Phyllis Schoenborn (1925-1962) | 739 Lydia Korson (1929-) |
| 691 Marie Emile Rivard (1924-) | 740 Nancy Ann Flumerfelt (1925-) |
| 692 Diana Mlynarchek (1921-) | 741 Rosemary Homrich (1927-) |
| 693 Marie Bernarde Salazar (1927-) | 742 Ann Frederick Heiskell (1918-) |
| 694 Thomas Estelle Bryan (1927-) | 743 Marie Michael Jacobs (1930-) |
| 695 Michael Anne Nic (1927-) | 744 Ottilia Schaub (1925-) |
| 696 John Anne Paquette (1927-) | 745 Julia Mae Groulx (1926-) |
| 697 Viola Marie Henige (1927-1984) | 746 Maria Tardani (1931-) |
| 698 Marie Eugene Charbonneau (1926-) | 747 Marie Jude Wysocki (1931-) |
| 699 Anne Keating (1927-1988) | 748 Marie Eickholt (1924-1983) |
| 700 Mary Lee Pitre (1927-) | 749 Teresa Houlihan (1929-) |
| 701 Jean Milhaupt (1923-) | 750 Janet Mish (1931-) |
| 702 Olga Mizzi (1924-) | 751 Wilma Rajewski (1933-) |
| 703 Dorothy Giglio (1923-) | 752 Laurena Alflen (1932-) |
| 704 Phyllis Brown (1925-) | 753 Mary Martens (1925-) |
| 705 Monica Meyer (1928-) | 754 Maria Goretti Beckman (1933-) |
| 706 Jeannette Chiasson (1930-) | 755 Marlene Edwards (1933-) |
| 707 Theresa Bray (1927-) | 756 Teresita Garcia (1932-) |
| 708 Amata Fabbro (1928-) | 757 Geneva Marie Schaub (1932-) |
| 709 Margaret Thomas (1928-) | 758 Rose Elizabeth Powers (1928-) |
| 710 Marie Benedict O'Toole (1925-) | 759 Peter Mary Korson (1932-) |
| 711 Lupe Silva (1928-) | 760 Donna Brown (1932-) |
| 712 Margaret Schneider (1928-) | 761 David Therese Korson (1929-) |
| 713 Catherine Ann Winowiecki (1927-) | 762 Josine Schafer (1932-) |
| 714 Carol Ann Nowak (1923-) | 763 Beverly Pety (1934-) |
| 715 Emma Kulhanek (1929-) | 764 Phyllis Mrozinski (1930-) |
| 716 Helen Miller (1929-) | 765 Janice Mankowski (1933-) |
| 717 Rita Barreras (1928-) | 766 Bernadette Mooney (1933-) |
| 718 Audrey Sanchez (1929-) | 767 Michelle Wangler (1933-) |
| 719 John Therese Kusba (1928-) | 768 Joyce Kolasa (1933-) |
| 720 Stella Jozwiak (1928-) | 769 Dorena Gonzales (1932-) |

| | | | |
|---|---|---|---|
| 770 | Thomasine Bugala (1926-) | 819 | Marjorie Stein (1938-) |
| 771 | Simon Schulist (1928-) | 820 | Mary Catherine Fodrocy (1938-) |
| 772 | Magdalena Conway (1930-) | 821 | Susan Ridley (1938-) |
| 773 | William Mary Conway (1934-) | 822 | Lillian Bockheim (1938-) |
| 774 | Nancy Ribble (1934-) | 823 | Judith Kirt (1938-) |
| 775 | Jacqueline Hudson (1934-) | 824 | Katrina Hartman (1940-) |
| 776 | JoAnn Boucher (1936-) | 825 | Dolores Abeyta (1938-) |
| 777 | Michael Ellen Carling (1933-) | 826 | Joyce Ann Hertzig (1939-) |
| 778 | Jacqueline Bennett (1934-) | 827 | Margaret Mary Birchmeier (1939-) |
| 779 | Jeanne Marie Jones (1934-) | 828 | Nancy Malburg (1939-) |
| 780 | Donna Jean Thelen (1932-) | 829 | Marie Joy Yuhasz (1938-) |
| 781 | Margaret Kienstra (1927-) | 830 | Patrice Konwinski (1937-) |
| 782 | Geraldine Czolgosz (1926-) | 831 | Ann Hehl (1939-) |
| 783 | Mary Ann Ferguson (1936-) | 832 | Catherine Williams (1940-) |
| 784 | Jean Reimer (1929-) | 833 | Deborah Gallmeier (1939-) |
| 785 | Phyllis Lopez (1933-) | 834 | Mary Jo Beckett (1939-) |
| 786 | Robert Ann Erno (1936-) | 835 | Patricia Kennedy (1939-) |
| 787 | Elizabeth Bishop (1935-) | 836 | Yvonne Griener (1938-) |
| 788 | Rita Wenzlick (1935-) | 837 | Gail Ann Martin (1939-) |
| 789 | Lisa Marie Lazio (1935-) | 838 | Janet Brown (1939-) |
| 790 | Grace Licavoli (1934-) | 839 | Jean Kramer (1936-) |
| 791 | Catherine Anderson (1934-) | 840 | Alice Wittenbach (1937-) |
| 792 | Carletta Bockheim (1935-) | 841 | Diane Dehn (1937-) |
| 793 | Nathalie Meyers (1937-) | 842 | Joanne Davey (1937-) |
| 794 | Therese Rodriquez (1935-) | 843 | Mary Louise Stauder (1940-) |
| 795 | Emilia Atencio (1935-) | 844 | Joan Foley (1939-) |
| 796 | Ardeth Platte (1936-) | 845 | Rachel Guevara (1939-) |
| 797 | Mona Schwind (1936-) | 846 | Stephanie Heintz (1940-) |
| 798 | Mary Lucille Janowiak (1935-) | 847 | Mary Katherine Courtright (1933-) |
| 799 | Rena Ruddy (1931-) | 848 | Ann Mason (1936-) |
| 800 | Angelina Gonzales (1934-) | 849 | Irene Mary McDonnell (1940-) |
| 801 | Dolorita Martinez (1937-) | 850 | Janet Marie Heitz (1940-) |
| 802 | Roberta Hefferan (1927-) | 851 | June Martin (1937-) |
| 803 | Ellen Mary Lopez (1937-) | 852 | Agnes Mary Wojtkowiak (1941-) |
| 804 | Joanne Toohey (1937-) | 853 | Irene Chrusciel (1936-) |
| 805 | Bernice Garcia (1937-) | 854 | Joan Pichette (1939-) |
| 806 | Wanda Ezop (1937-1986) | 855 | Darlene Sikorski (1940-) |
| 807 | Joan Alflen (1937-) | 856 | Judith Ann Barber (1935-) |
| 808 | Doris Faber (1937-) | 857 | Kateri Schrems (1939-) |
| 809 | Ann Porter (1935-) | 858 | Sylvia Wozniak (1941-) |
| 810 | Madelyn Hronek (1936-1981) | 859 | Marita MacNall (1941-) |
| 811 | Lois Ann Sheaffer (1937-) | 860 | Joan Lehman (1941-) |
| 812 | Mary Ann Cudzanowski (1932-) | 861 | Ann Thielen (1934-) |
| 813 | Rosemary O'Donnell (1937-) | 862 | Tereska Wozniak (1938-) |
| 814 | Barbara Hansen (1938-) | 863 | Regina Mary Goeldel (1938-) |
| 815 | Cecilia Faber (1934-) | 864 | Jean Anita Williams (1941-) |
| 816 | Vera Ann Tilmann (1938-) | 865 | Joan Mary Williams (1941-) |
| 817 | Maureen Sheahan (1938-) | 866 | Joyce Mary Williams (1941-) |
| 818 | Joan Thomas (1938-) | 867 | Ann Norman (1941-) |

868 Margaret Hillary (1941-)
869 Susanne Tracy (1940-)
870 Marguerite Cool (1941-)
871 Suzanne Eichhorn (1930-)
872 Elaine LaBell (1942-)
873 Eileen Jaramillo (1942-)
874 Phyllis Ohren (1942-)
875 Jarrett DeWyse (1942-)
876 Mary Brigid Clingman (1942-)
877 Chris Herald (1942-)
878 Helen Bueche (1935-)
879 Mary Kay Oosdyke (1942-)
880 Rosanne Szocinski (1942-)
881 Carmelita Murphy (1942-)
882 Judith Drew (1941-)
883 Ann Walters (1942-)
884 Ann Michael Farnsworth (1943-)
885 Ann Terrence Wieber (1937-)
886 Anne Monica Shalda (1943-)
887 Linda Schoenborn (1943-)
888 Carmelita Switzer (1942-)
889 Marie Anne Goch (1934-)
890 Anne Jeffrey Selesky (1942-)
891 Edith Marie Schnell (1943-)
892 Josephine Mary Birchmeier (1943-)
893 Francetta McCann (1936-)
894 Mary Ellen McDonald (1941-)
895 Orlanda Leyba (1940-)
896 Mario Pavoni (1944-)
897 Mary Patricia Beatty (1944-)
898 Mary Ann Barrett (1944-)
899 Marie Carla Moeggenborg (1943-)
900 Anne Breitag (1944-)
901 Joellen Barkwell (1942-)
902 Jean Karen Wolosyk (1944-)
903 Marilyn Holmes (1945-)
904 Mary Navarre (1943-)
905 Maxine Plamondon (1944-)
906 Constance Fifelski (1945-)
907 Diane Hofman (1945-)
908 Dominica Nellett (1945-)
909 Julia Nellett (1945-)
910 Eva Silva (1945-)

911 Lucia Zapata (1945-)
912 Mary Ellen Novakoski (1946-)
913 Marie Celeste Miller (1945-)
914 Dorothy Jonaitis (1944-)
915 Carmen Rostar (1946-)
916 Susan Keller (1947-)
917 Carol Gilbert (1947-)
918 Dorothy Ederer (1943-)
919 Lynne Hansen (1943-)
920 Phyllis Klonowski (1948-)
921 Jude Bloch (1948-)
922 Gretchen Sills (1947-)
923 Lucianne Siers (1949-)
924 Roxane Dansereau (1949-)
925 Rose Marie Martin (1942-)
926 Maribeth Holst (1946-)
927 Diane Zerfas (1950-)
928 Jan Stobbart (1934-)
929 Ada Dominguez (1951-)
930 Lucia Zapata (1945-)
931 Alethaire Foster (1950-)
932 Elizabeth Amman (1952-)
933 Barbara Reid (1953-)
934 Charlotte Mondragon (1951-)
935 Nancy Brousseau (1947-)
936 Linda Thiel (1952-)
937 Sandra Delgado (1952-)
938 Mary Lou Houghton (1939-)
939 Mary Jane Fedder (1948-)
940 Genevieve Galka (1949-)
941 Judy Vahovick (1944-)
942 Rose Karasti (1955-)
943 Katheryn Sleziak (1952-)
944 Justine Kane (1957-)
945 Rene Johnson (1960-)
946 Theresa Binkowski (1961-)
947 Mary Donnelly (1955-)
948 Maureen Geary (1956-)
949 Joan Brown (1931-)***
950 Laurice DeRycke (1947-)***
951 Megan McElroy (1963-)
952 Kathleen Chick (1967-)

# Acknowledgements

*T*here are many to thank for the production of *Period Pieces*: Sisters Teresa Houlihan and Carmelita Murphy, prioresses who commissioned and saw the work to its completion; Grand Rapids Dominicans who read and advised on the text: Janet Mish and Jean Milhaupt, first readers and grammarians *par excellence*; the members of the general council, Barbara Hansen, Jarrett DeWyse, and Margaret Schneider, last readers and questioners; Brendan Donovan and Letitia Van Agtmael, advisors on special topics; Dorothy Adams and Ann Frederick Heiskell, proofreaders; Carol Ann Nowak who endlessly looked up this and that; Francetta McCann, photographer, who captured *The Recording Angel* at her most reflective moment; and Judith Ann Barber who prepared the illustration pages and took me to the lake when the task was too much.

I thank also sister Dominicans from the Adrian, Michigan, and Sinsinawa, Wisconsin, congregations: Mary Philip Ryan, author of *Amid the Alien Corn*, a splendid account of the Adrian Dominicans, and dear mentor, and her companion in the Adrian archives, Noreen McKeough, who reminded me of consistency and the "hooks and eyes" of style; Nona McGreal, Sinsinawa Dominican historian and associate of Francis J. Haas before his years as Bishop of Grand Rapids, who gave a final reading, great encouragement, and thoughtful words about proportion. There were wise readers from other walks of life as well: Anna and Katherine Lound of Shelby, Michigan--church women as much as any described in the foregoing pages; Tim and Christine Ziegler, friends, parents, active Christians, who read to see how it sounded to the "real Church," and Elizabeth Jennings, professor of literature at Aquinas College, who read for story and texture.

There is one person who must have a special line of thanks: Carmen Davis, computer specialist on the Marywood congregational staff, who gave form to the text, "word perfect" and spirit perfect.

There are also generous benefactors who have contributed to the printing of the book: Valerie Burhan, one of Sister Gervase Miller's Tuesday Scholars, and Peter M. Wege, longtime friend of the congregation and its works.

Lastly, I conclude this account which treats at length of mothers general, with thanks to a mother particular, Cornelia Schwind, of Merrill, Michigan, and to my family, Don and Margaret Schwind, Paul and Jean Schwind, and their dear families, who give me home and heart and local history.